Scarlet and Black

Volume 3

Making Black Lives Matter at Rutgers, 1945–2020

EDITED BY MIYA CAREY,
MARISA J. FUENTES, AND
DEBORAH GRAY WHITE

RUTGERS UNIVERSITY PRESS

NEW BRUNSWICK, CAMDEN, AND NEWARK, NEW JERSEY, AND LONDON

Library of Congress in Publication Control Number: 2016955389

ISBN 978-1-9788-2732-5 (cloth)
ISBN 978-1-9788-2731-8 (paper)
ISBN 978-1-9788-2733-2 (epub)

A British Cataloging-in-Publication record for this book is available from the British Library.

♾ The paper used in this publication meets the requirements of the American National Standard for Information Sciences—Permanence of Paper for Printed Library Materials, ANSI Z39.48-1992.

www.rutgersuniversitypress.org

Manufactured in the United States of America

In Memory of Our Colleague
Cheryl A. Wall
The Board of Governors Zora Neale Hurston Professor of English

CONTENTS

PART III
Making Black Lives Matter
beyond Rutgers, 1973–2007

Scarlet and Black

Introduction

DEBORAH GRAY WHITE

Chair of the Committee on the Enslaved
and Disenfranchised in Rutgers History

> In 1967 when I came to Rutgers, it was the year of the rebellion. When
> I came onto the campus, all the walls were white, all the faculty was
> white, all the students were white. And sometime during the "getaway"
> (they called it "freshman camp"), I ran into at least one other black
> person who was part of the kitchen staff, cooking at the camp. And
> then about two weeks in, I was walking across the campus and I saw a
> skinny brown man . . . It happened to be Richard Roper. And he was the
> first person that I had seen who was black. It was that stark. And . . .
> he told me that there was a meeting of the NAACP, and having come
> out of the civil rights movement and being newly black nationalist, of
> course I went to the meeting with the intent, "No, we're not going to
> do this, we're going to do something a little bit more militant . . ." That
> was the beginning.[1]

These words were spoken in 2019, by Vickie Donaldson, one of the "liberators"
who occupied Conklin Hall in 1969. The "skinny brown man" she spied, Richard Roper, was president of the campus chapter of the NAACP. Roper's recollection of "the beginning" corroborated Donaldson's. According to Roper, 1967
was when black students at Rutgers–Newark—"all 20 or 25 of them—decided
that the campus chapter of the NAACP was no longer relevant. It was not the
vehicle through which we could voice our dissatisfaction with the status quo.
We were ready to move and to make a big noise in the process."[2]

These remembrances of late 1960s Rutgers reveal a very different university than the one described by President Obama in his memorable 2016

1

commencement address. On that crisp, sunny spring day, Obama described Rutgers as an "intellectual melting pot, where ideas and cultures flow together among what might just be America's most diverse student body." He said that "America converges here, and in so many ways, the history of Rutgers mirrors the evolution of America—the course by which we became bigger, stronger, and richer and more dynamic, and a more inclusive nation."[3]

Obama's depiction of Rutgers as a multicultural, ethnically diverse power-house is the way Rutgers boosters like to think about their university. In fact, Rutgers's website uses the *U.S. News and World Report* and Best Value Colleges assessments of Rutgers–Newark as the "most diverse school in the nation" as a recruitment tool to attract students.[4] However, the sharply contrasting descriptions given by Donaldson and Obama should give us pause. They speak to the importance of change over time and force us to reflect on the process that brought about such a cataclysmic transformation. In this respect we do well to think about Obama's observation that Rutgers's history mirrors the evolution of America. Indeed, much had happened in the country and at Rutgers between the time Donaldson and Roper walked onto a mostly lily-white campus and the time when the first black president of the United States landed his *Marine One* helicopter on this once undiversified campus. This third volume, *Scarlet and Black: Making Black Lives Matter at Rutgers, 1945–2020,* explores this history. It places Rutgers University in the thick of the profound changes in higher education that came about as a result of the mid-to-late-twentieth-century black freedom struggle, and it examines the university both before and after that change. In doing so, it adds historical perspective to the meaning of Black Lives Matter and shows just how high the stakes have been at Rutgers.

Thanks to the changes covered in this volume, we now can document what one historian has called the "black revolution on campus" and what another has dubbed the "black campus movement."[5] Before the midcentury freedom struggle, what black people did—their epistemologies and ways of thinking, their contributions to world progress—seldom, if ever, made its way into classrooms or academic texts.[6] At Rutgers, as at other American universities, black lives *did not* matter. African Americans were the subject of study only when used as a counterpoint to demonstrate the superiority of Anglo-Saxon culture and physiology. As demonstrated in the first two volumes of *Scarlet and Black,* professors, students, and administrators demeaned and ridiculed black life. They provided the ideological foundation for enslavement, for debasement, and for Jim Crow laws—the legal separation of the races. Before the freedom struggle hit college campuses, black Americans merited consideration only as objects of humiliation; as demonstrated in volume 2, the very few who were allowed to attend Rutgers and other historically white colleges and universities (HWCUs) were forced to endure that humiliation while participating in campus activities meant to inculcate white Anglo-Saxon Protestant culture.[7]

But along with the sit-ins, picketing, boycotts, and marches that desegregated public spaces; the voter registration campaigns that opened ballot boxes; the court cases that expanded the workplace and housing; and the demonstrations of pride that undergirded their demand for power, both on and off America's campuses, young black Americans demanded a recognition of black lives. They insisted on an unbiased investigation of America's contemporary and historic oppression of black people and an objective examination of world history that included Africa as the beginning and center of world civilization. On campuses and off, young black people protested against discriminatory college admissions procedures and their exclusion from financial aid protocols and from campus cultural activities. And, as Roper proclaimed, they "made a big noise doing it."[8]

That noise reverberated at Rutgers and universities across the country. Part of the Black Power phase of the freedom movement, the black revolution on campus occurred when the civil rights movement shifted its locus out of the South to northern locales that had never been as open in their racism as the South but were nevertheless just as segregated and hostile to African Americans and other minorities. Black Power focused on the shortcomings of the nonviolent, direct-action movement that began in the immediate aftermath of World War II. By 1967, when Donaldson and Roper walked their isolated paths across Rutgers–Newark, public spaces in the South had been desegregated and blacks were allowed to vote in most southern states. However, across the nation police assaults were rife; redlining kept African Americans, even veterans, from obtaining government-secured loans and mortgages; blacks were still forced to take dead-end jobs; housing, especially in areas outside of the South, was substandard; and the schools in black neighborhoods reflected the black plight. African Americans shifted to Black Power because its strategy of self-help made blacks less dependent on white acceptance and participation, instilled race pride and self-respect, and emphasized black political power.

In essence, when teenagers and young adults like Donaldson and Roper arrived on predominantly white campuses in the mid-1960s, the first political move they made was to push the university to admit more students who looked like them. Across the United States this usually meant protesting for changes to admissions criteria and for financial aid. By insisting on the legitimacy of African American studies and on the intellectual capacity of a black professoriate, this desegregation generation disrupted the notion that only Europeans produced knowledge worth learning, and that only whites possessed the savoir faire to teach it.[9] As stated by historian Martha Biondi, in the late 1960s "black student activists asserted the right to attend college, especially public ones. Moreover, student protests stimulated demand for black faculty and sparked the desegregation of college curriculums with the creation of hundreds of African American studies departments and programs. More than the protests against the Vietnam War, black students' demands for inclusion in the late '60s produced the most lasting change in higher education."[10] According to historian Ibram X. Kendi, black student activists "forced the rewriting of the racial constitution of higher education."[11] In doing so, says Biondi, "the academic community would never be the same."[12]

The depth and extensiveness of the black student movement cannot be overstated. In the early 1960s, federal troops were needed to fend off white mobs and protect the few black students who were admitted to southern schools like the University of Georgia (1961), the University of Mississippi (1962), and the University of Alabama (1963). Rutgers was among the schools that responded to the mounting pressure from the civil rights movement by initiating a program in 1963 to recruit a small contingent of black students. Once Congress passed the Civil Rights Act of 1964 (which gave government agencies the right to withhold federal money from schools that discriminated), and then the Higher Education Act of 1965 (which provided federal funds to schools and financial assistance for students), colleges and universities started admitting more African Americans. Across the country, attendance by black students at HWCUs in 1965 shot up by 70 percent, or about 200,000 out of 4.5 million (4.5 percent). By 1967, black enrollment at HWCUs had increased to 5.15 percent.[13] Rutgers's black enrollment mirrored the national numbers. There were about one hundred undergraduates in 1965; by 1968, their numbers had grown to more than 400, or 3 percent of the undergraduate enrollment. Across the country, from 1970 to 1974, college enrollments for African Americans grew by 56 percent, compared to a 15 percent increase for whites. Rutgers enrollments again mirrored the change. According to historian and former Rutgers College dean Richard McCormick, by 1974, the university's full-time black undergraduate population numbered over 2,500, slightly more than 10 percent of the total student enrollment. Additionally, there were nearly 1,000 black men and women attending Rutgers graduate and professional schools, and 1,100 more were registered in the evening divisions of the university.[14]

Pressure brought by black students not only changed admissions policies but also the campus culture and curriculums. Before 1965 there was not a single African studies program in the country and almost no courses on African Americans.[15] When, in 1966, black students at San Francisco State created the first black student union and then created the first black studies department, they simultaneously disrupted the normalization of white college culture and the institutionalized idea that the only education that was valuable was that which began and ended with European paradigms. Black student unions legitimized African American arts and culture on white campuses, and black studies courses and departments legitimized scholarship by and about black Americans. In insisting that black people mattered—as subjects and as professors, in all areas of academic inquiry from the classics to the biological and physical sciences—campus activists demanded the broadening of the knowledge base that undergirded progress and protested the marginalization of all black scholars.

As at most schools, the founding of black student unions and black studies curriculums happened at Rutgers in the late 1960s and early 1970s. After attending a meeting on black empowerment at Columbia University, black men at Rutgers–New Brunswick created the Student Afro-American Society in late 1966.[16] True to Donaldson's and Roper's prediction, shortly after its first meeting in September 1967, the Rutgers–Newark NAACP chapter returned its charter to the national headquarters and created the Black Organization of Students (BOS). About the same time, black students at Rutgers–Camden launched the Black Student Unity Movement (BSUM). In March 1968, Douglass College women created the Black Students Committee. Other black organizations emerged, as did broadsheets like *Black Voice*.

These mouthpieces spurred change at Rutgers. In 1969, the Board of Governors initiated an Urban University Program (UUP) for so-called disadvantaged undergraduates. Preceding that program was the longer-lasting 1968 Educational Opportunity Fund (EOF) created by the New Jersey Department of Higher Education. The EOF provided financial aid as well as remedial courses, special counseling, social and cultural activities, and grievance mechanisms.[17] Not long after that, between 1968 and 1971, African American studies courses and programs were created on all Rutgers campuses. Along with course and curriculum changes, students lobbied for black faculty and staff, and very slowly the black population at Rutgers increased.

Although some white students allied with African Americans, Puerto Rican students were the staunchest supporters of diversification. In 1974, Puerto Ricans constituted 7 percent of New Jersey's population but only 2 percent of the college students of New Jersey.[18] Puerto Rican students not only supported black students in their crusade for change but they also created independent organizations to lobby for their own specific issues. The Puerto Rican Organization at Newark (1969), the United Puerto Rican Student Organization at Rutgers (UPRS, 1969), the Organization of Puerto Rican Students at Camden (1970), and the Douglass Puerto Rican Students (a chapter of the UPRS) all pressured the university to hire Puerto Rican faculty and staff. Puerto Rican students demonstrated and protested for bilingual staff to assist with academic counseling, recruitment, and retention, and they pressured the university to create a Puerto Rican studies department, which it did at Livingston College—first as a program in 1970 and then as a department in 1973.[19] And just like the African American students, they were relentless in their push to bring in and support more students, faculty, and staff who looked like them.

The explosion of black and Puerto Rican student protest on college campuses across the country in the late 1960s would suggest some coordinated movement with a centralized leadership, but nothing could be further from the truth. For sure, students were galvanized by the philosophy of Black Power, but each campus that saw black and other minority students take over buildings, occupy administrative offices, lead successful student strikes, and present governing boards with demands had their own indigenous leadership that grew from the local circumstances of oppression. In 1968 and 1969 alone there were nearly 200 organized black student protests across the country, and in each case, says Biondi, "students formed their own campus organizations and led their own struggles, even as they traveled to other campuses and learned from each other."[20]

In fact, students did not think in unison but learned from an assortment of black leaders and thinkers. In the late 1960s, James Farmer, Roy Innis, and Floyd McKissick of the Congress of Racial Equality (CORE) addressed students at Rutgers–New Brunswick, as did Andrew Young of the Student Nonviolent Coordinating Committee (SNCC), the Black Muslim minister Jeremiah Shabazz, the heavyweight boxer Muhammad Ali, and the first black congresswoman, Shirley Chisholm. Students were also addressed by noted authors Ralph Ellison and Louis Lomax and humorist and political activist Dick Gregory. Aside from Malcolm X's campus visit in November 1961, few black leaders of *any* political persuasion had been invited to Rutgers before the late '60s. Still, more than any uniform political philosophy, students were brought together by, as McCormick noted, "their sense that they were strangers in a white-controlled environment, that their numbers were too few, that there was too little in the social and academic spheres with which they could readily identify, and that changes had to be made."[21]

At Rutgers, as elsewhere, black and Puerto Rican students brought their neighborhoods to college with them; they did not want to have to divorce their community, culture, or race to get a college education. "There was a community that embraced us because we embraced it," said Vickie Donaldson. "We brought it with us every day when we came to the university; we didn't leave it at home and say, 'Oh, we're going to college today.'"[22] It was no coincidence that black students at Rutgers–Newark turned their NAACP chapter into the Black Organization of Students the semester following the five-day 1967 summer rebellion in Newark that left twenty-six people dead, more than 200 seriously injured, and property damage of more than $10 million.[23] Almost immediately after its founding, the BOS petitioned the Rutgers–Newark administration to tear down the fence that separated Newark's white campus from the black neighborhood that surrounded it. To black Rutgers students, the fence was tangible evidence that Rutgers–Newark wanted nothing to do with black people.[24] At Rutgers–Camden, the Black Student Unity Movement was a direct offshoot of the Black People's Unity Movement, a community activist group that lobbied for fair housing, education, employment, and law enforcement. The

BSUM wanted Rutgers–Camden to serve, not occupy, the surrounding community by creating a cultural center, a community foundation, and community access to campus facilities.[25]

This history and more is the subject of *Scarlet and Black: Making Black Lives Matter at Rutgers, 1945–2020.* Whereas the first volume showed us how Rutgers's founders grew rich from the profits of slavery, how they justified black debasement, and how New Brunswick African Americans resisted white control, and volume 2 showed us how the first black students navigated the exclusive white campus population and culture, volume 3 now demonstrates how African American students at Rutgers defied the status quo and made the university racially and culturally diverse. Unlike other studies of Rutgers University, this volume and the two preceding it look exclusively at Rutgers's institutional racism as it relates not only to African Americans but also to other groups affected by systemic exclusion.[26]

Largely because Rutgers experienced such tremendous expansion in the twentieth century—to five locations in the New Brunswick area, as well as north to Newark and south to Camden—this study of blacks at Rutgers from 1945 to the present is hardly comprehensive, but limited to what we, the editors, consider the highlights of Rutgers history with African Americans and other minorities during this period. It is divided into three parts. The articles in the first part explore Rutgers before the late 1960s. Really an extension of the second volume of *Scarlet and Black,* it continues the discussion of what life was like at Rutgers when only a handful of blacks and people of color attended. It also introduces the Newark and Camden campuses and communities, and discusses the way race as a subject of inquiry was handled on the New Brunswick campus. The articles in part 2 focus on the Conklin Hall takeover at Newark and the process by which multiculturalism was introduced at the New Brunswick, Newark, and Camden campuses. In part 3 we focus on incidents of racial tension that occurred toward the end of the twentieth and beginning of the twenty-first centuries—namely, demonstrations against South African apartheid, activist Assata Shakur's arrest and imprisonment, President Lawrence's "bell curve" remarks, and Don Imus's insulting comments about the Scarlet Knights women's basketball team. The epilogue speaks to Rutgers's embrace of cultural diversity and African American excellence by introducing the twenty-first president of the university, Dr. Jonathan Scott Holloway, an African American whose scholarly expertise is African American culture and history.

Although this volume marks the close of the written portion of the Scarlet and Black Project, we hope that this work inspires students' confidence in their ability to bring about change.[27] As we finish this project in the midst of the Covid-19 pandemic and worldwide protests over the murders of blacks by paramilitary police forces, we are enthused by the millions of young people who are demonstrating against inequality and who are once again declaring that black lives matter. Right now, monuments to the Confederacy are being dismantled and exposed as the symbols of hate that they are. This nation's history of inequality is being exposed for purposes of reconciliation and healing, and at least for now it seems that the logjams against police-reform legislation have been broken. We want to urge everyone, especially young Americans, to embrace this moment and this history, if only for what they say about students' abilities to effect change and truly make black lives matter. This project grew out of a 2015 student demand for inclusion, the same kind of demand that motivated students in the late 1960s. In 2015, students wanted to feel less alienated by Rutgers's environment and wanted this story of the institution's past to serve as the prologue to its future. It is in this spirit that we undertook this study and it is with great pride that we now hand it back to those who can use it to implement change. We want it to be inspirational. We expect Rutgers University to do more than advertise its diversity; we expect Rutgers to lead with it and be intentional about making diversity meaningful.

PART I

Prelude to Change

Circa 1944–1970

DEBORAH GRAY WHITE

"It was small, by today's standards," said historian and former School of Arts and Sciences dean Douglass Greenberg during his opening remarks at the 2015 Black on the Banks Conference. The symposium, held during the 250th-anniversary celebration of Rutgers's founding, was convened to remember the experiences of 1960s black Rutgers students. During his opening remarks, Greenberg drew a picture of the landscape traversed by the few blacks who braved the campuses of Rutgers and Douglass College. In contrast to the 21,000 undergraduates in the 2015 New Brunswick School of Arts and Sciences and the overall 45,000 students at Rutgers–New Brunswick, in 1968 there were only 10,000 undergraduates between Rutgers (6,500) and Douglass College (2,800). In the 1960s, Rutgers was segregated by gender (women went to Douglass and men to Rutgers College), but the university and the city of New Brunswick were also segregated by race, said Greenberg. Although the university did not begin to collect data on race until 1968—and then only because the federal government mandated it—all versions of the vague numbers "tell about the same story . . . of deep seeded [sic] and intransigent institutional racism." In 1968, Rutgers College, all four classes, was 1.4 percent African American. There were fewer than one hundred young black men out of 6,500 undergraduates, and almost half of them were freshmen. The graduating class of Rutgers College in 1968 had only eighteen black men; the class of 1969

9

had only fourteen. Douglass was 4 percent African American, but most were first- and second-year students. The graduating class of 1968 had only four African American women. In 1968 there were three African Americans on the faculty of Rutgers College and only one at Douglass. Greenberg concluded his remarks with this description: "Rutgers of fifty years ago was small, provincial, and very highly regarded for its academics both at Rutgers College and at Douglass. We were called a 'public ivy' and we were proud to say that." He added, "Rutgers wasn't for 'whites only' in the '60s, but it was surely for 'whites mostly.'"[1]

That first weekend of November 2015 was spent remembering, reflecting, evaluating, and analyzing what it meant to be a black student on Rutgers–New Brunswick's mostly white campuses in the 1960s. The consensus was aptly characterized in a *Rutgers Magazine* feature article a year later titled "Alone Together." In essence, almost all of the black students remembered Rutgers fondly–but not because Rutgers was welcoming or because they felt welcomed; it was because the few in attendance made their own community, and nurtured and mentored each other.

This was especially true for those who entered before 1968. Tom Ashley's (RC '64) remembrances were typical. The only black person on the basketball team for all four of his years at Rutgers, he felt especially isolated. When he saw another black person he would go up to them, introduce himself, and find out where they lived. "We were segregated from each other," he remembered. "Days would go by and you did not see an African American person at all. And you learned to adjust but at the same time you wanted more, and at the end of the day and by the time I graduated I realized that there was never any more." Juanita Wade Wilson (DC '66) spoke similarly of loneliness. She remembered being in the first class at Douglass that let black and white young women live together. As she recalled, her roommate could not understand why Wade was angry about race relations, and she had to educate her white roommate about the civil rights movement. Although she and her roommate subsequently became good friends, Wade said movingly, "I don't know how to express the loneliness." By the time he was a junior, Frank McClellan (RC '67) couldn't take it anymore. Describing his life at Rutgers as a "search for blackness," he recalled deciding that he was tired of the disregard Rutgers paid to the lives of black students. He gathered a few others and told them, "We got to fight . . . we can't just leave this university with a degree and leave this place the way it was when we came."[2] McClellan's resolution to do something about the isolation of Rutgers and Douglass students resulted in the formation of the Student Afro-American Society in late 1966–a Rutgers College organization that Douglass's black women participated in.[3]

If the experiences of these Rutgers–New Brunswick students sound much like those experienced by Vickie Donaldson and Richard Roper at Rutgers–Newark, it is because all campuses of the state university of New Jersey were similarly "mostly white."[4] Indeed, until the late 1960s, Rutgers was like most predominantly white schools in that it had only a handful of black and minority students and venerated an exclusionary culture that reproduced white Anglo-Saxon Protestant ideals.[5] And New Jersey was like most states that closed off opportunities to its black and brown communities by blocking them out of home and business loans, cordoning them off from the white-only suburbs, and locking them into dead-end jobs from which there was no escape. These students, politicized by their isolation and a new vision of the possible, would not tolerate the stasis at Rutgers or let its various campuses remain mostly white islands of opportunity.

This first part of *Scarlet and Black: Making Black Lives Matter at Rutgers, 1945-2020,* focuses on New Jersey and Rutgers *before* Rutgers admitted more than a handful of minority students. Though hardly comprehensive, it examines communities like Newark, Camden, and New Brunswick and suggests the kinds of concerns students brought with them. It also looks at the level of racial consciousness that existed at Rutgers College and Douglass before the late 1960s and explores whether these institutions had the capacity to change. The essay "Twenty-Twenty Vision: New Jersey and Rutgers on the Eve of Change" begins this section with a look at the general landscape of New Jersey and Rutgers in the 1950s and 1960s. It explains the impact of migration and the 1944 Servicemen's Readjustment Act (GI Bill), while also reminding us of the lack of racial and cultural diversity at Rutgers before the 1970s. The authors of "Rutgers and New Brunswick: A Consideration of Impact" move from the general to the local with a more targeted look at some of the changes that occurred in New Brunswick in the late 1960s. Although New Brunswick was largely segregated and, like many New Jersey towns, had right-wing tendencies, there were pockets of left-wing activity that drew in area activists, including students at Rutgers. This essay's analysis of the *All You Can Eat* alternative newspaper suggests the kinds of ideas that were a possible influence on a portion of students who matriculated at Rutgers in the late 1960s. Ultimately, this essay considers what impact, if any, Rutgers had on the black citizens of New Brunswick in the late 1960s.

The last two selections look closely at the Rutgers and Douglass campuses. "'Tell It Like It Is': The Rise of a Race-Conscious Professoriate at Rutgers in the 1960s" explores the thinking of Rutgers faculty and staff on racial matters. By examining the *Rutgers Faculty Newsletter* from 1958 through the takeover of Newark's Conklin Hall in 1969, it tracks the racial climate on the Rutgers–New Brunswick campus as expressed by its faculty and administrators. It analyzes not just the policies they endorsed and the intellectual work they undertook but also the language that reflected the feelings and thoughts of the white faculty and administrators about black people. It also notes student, faculty, and administrative work on racial matters prior to the cataclysmic changes that occurred in the late 1960s and analyzes the faculty response to the black student demand for inclusion, including their insistence on African American studies. "Black and Puerto Rican Student Experiences and Their Movements at Douglass College, 1945–1974" looks mostly at Douglass College before it changed its admittance policies. It examines the few black women who matriculated before the late 1960s and shows how they built community and managed the white campus culture. It examines their isolation and how things changed when more black students arrived. It also examines the few Puerto Rican women who matriculated at Douglass. Although there seems to have been only three of them, their experiences underscore how radically different Douglass was before the late '60s and early '70s.

In all, the articles in this part sketch the landscape of New Jersey and New Brunswick's Rutgers and Douglass Colleges. Although its chronology explores the reaction to the Conklin Hall takeover at Newark and the student protests that took place on all the Rutgers campuses, its predominant focus is on the period before the disruptures of the late 1960s.

1

Twenty-Twenty Vision

New Jersey and Rutgers on the Eve of Change

ROBERTO C. OROZCO, CARIE RAEL,
BROOKE A. THOMAS, AND DEBORAH GRAY WHITE

In her book on the black student movement, historian Martha Biondi notes that black student activism took observers by surprise.[1] Few seemed to know where the demand for the enrollment of more minority students or the hiring of minority faculty came from. Indeed, colleges and universities across the country were caught off guard by the demand for inclusion and diversity in the student body and faculty, and also in the types of courses that were taught and the kinds of social causes the university embraced. That it came as a surprise suggests that until the late 1960s, universities, even those located in predominantly black neighborhoods, were ivory towers in more ways than one.

Although the black student revolution that took place on college campuses in the late 1960s and 1970s was as national as racism, the shape it took on individual campuses grew organically from regional and local issues. With that in mind, this essay briefly reviews New Jersey and its state university on the eve of what historian and former dean of Rutgers College Richard McCormick called the "black student protest movement at Rutgers."[2] Although hindsight is, as they say, twenty-twenty vision, one could argue that, given state and local circumstances, it did not take a crystal ball or otherworldly visionary abilities to predict that change was inevitable at Rutgers.

Demographic Shifts

The demographic shifts of the post–World War II era helped set the stage for the transformation of Rutgers. Central to the changes that took place across the state was the influx of new people from Puerto Rico and the American

South. An examination of Latinx and black migration to New Jersey suggests the kinds of changes that would eventually take place at Rutgers.

The post–World War II period brought more Puerto Ricans to the New York and New Jersey area than ever before. The exact numbers are difficult to decipher because from 1950 to 1979 the census only recorded people of "Spanish origin." Not until 1980 did the census differentiate Latinx people. Still, a state agency reported a large influx of Puerto Ricans between 1950 and 1954; in 1954, 26,000 reportedly lived in New Jersey "on a yearly basis," and an additional 8,000 "seasonal farmworkers were brought in that year for the harvest season."[3] According to the Puerto Rican Congress of New Jersey, by 1970, the Puerto Rican population in Newark totaled about 27,000; in Camden, it totaled about 7,000; and in New Brunswick, Puerto Rican residents totaled 1,400. Statewide, by 1970, Puerto Ricans numbered 138,896.[4]

Part of the reason for Puerto Rican migration had to do with the reorientation of Puerto Rico's economic base from agriculture to manufacturing. Operation Bootstrap, a series of policies in the 1940s and 1950s that sought to modernize Puerto Rico by switching to an export-based economy, created job shortages on the island. This led to a mass migration to the United States, with a large number of migrants first settling in New York and then relocating to New Jersey and the surrounding areas.[5] Puerto Ricans were officially declared US citizens in 1917, and in 1952 the island was officially declared a commonwealth of the United States.[6] This unique relationship between the United States and Puerto Rico not only streamlined Puerto Rican migration but also made it easier to exploit Puerto Rican workers.[7] In the 1950s, Camden's Hispanic population grew from 125 to 6,000.[8] By 1954, for example, there were 8,298 Puerto Rican farm laborers in all of New Jersey.[9] Despite the protections that the Puerto Rican government tried to impose on New Jersey farm owners, workers complained that owners often refused to pay the stipulated wages, forced workers to work additional hours, and often provided inadequate food and housing.[10]

The many non-farmworkers who migrated to New Jersey also dealt with challenging circumstances. Although American citizens at birth, their Spanish language, rural background, poverty, and, for some, their dark complexion made life hard. Landlords overcharged for tiny apartments, police harassed them, and some bars refused to serve them. For example, when Ismael Acevedo bought a house in Dover, New Jersey, the seller advised that he not visit the house during the day, not tell anyone he was buying it, move in at night, and bring as few people with him as he could. When Acevedo asked why, the seller said, "Because that way they [referring to the neighbors] can't reject you."[11] Maria Agront, another migrant to Dover, expressed compassion for Puerto Rican men who, she said, were arrested for "any little thing." "They arrest them for walking or for standing. If they were in groups of three or more, they were arrested." From Agront's perspective, these men were "lonely, single men, with no place to go on their days off," who tired of their "furnished rooms, went out for fresh air and to talk to one another." But because rumor had it that Puerto Rican males were a dangerous lot who carried knives and picked fights at the slightest provocation, they were harassed and arrested.[12]

At the same time that Puerto Ricans were increasing their numbers in New Jersey, so too were African Americans. Black Americans had been present in the area since the arrival of European settlers in New Brunswick in the late eighteenth century. But between 1945 and 1970, the number of black Americans in the state consistently rose as blacks flowed in from Georgia, South Carolina, Virginia, and North Carolina. In 1940, African Americans were only 5.5 percent of New Jersey's population, but by 1970, that percentage had nearly doubled as blacks composed 10.7 percent of the population. Whereas in 1940 black Americans made up 6.3 percent of the New Brunswick population, by 1970, that number had more than tripled to 22.7 percent.[13] During the 1950s, Camden's black population grew by 58.6 percent, making blacks 25 percent of the city's population by 1960.[14] By 1970, Newark was a black-majority city.[15]

Opportunities were not as plentiful as blacks would have wanted. In 1943, Herbert Cartman became the first black police officer in New Brunswick and Herman Marrow established a dental office on George Street.[16] By 1945, the city had a chapter of the Urban League. But rapid growth in the years following the Second World War did not ameliorate racism in the city. Alice Archibald Jennings, the first black graduate of the Rutgers Graduate School of Education, was born and raised in New Brunswick and graduated from New Brunswick High School in 1923. She recalled experiences of racial segregation in New Brunswick movie theaters in the pre–World War II years.[17] And these experiences continued into the mid-1960s when, as she recalled, one could still find a pool on Livingston Avenue open only to the members of the all-white Sun and Splash club.[18]

Other parts of New Jersey were similarly racially segregated. As blacks moved beyond Atlantic City's segregated beach to enjoy the Jersey Shore, white bathers decamped for nearby all-white towns. In 1965, Newark's Olympic Park amusement center closed its doors as more blacks frequented the park, and throughout the state, blacks fought tooth and nail for educational equality. Despite the 1947 amendment to the state constitution that forbade segregation of schools on grounds of race, creed, or color, there remained overwhelmingly black and overwhelmingly white schools because housing patterns kept the races apart.[19] Two Newark reports issued in 1959 signaled the dismal state of things. One of them, *Economic Development of the Greater Newark Area: Recent Trends and Prospects,* noted the growth of population and employment in Newark's white suburbs to the detriment of its inner-city core, and the other, a report by the Mayor's Commission on Intergroup Relations, noted African

American complaints of overcrowded schools, of disproportionate numbers of inexperienced and substitute teachers in their schools, the deplorable short-age of textbooks, and the systematic rejection of black teacher applications.[20] Conditions like these were at the core of the urban rebellions that swept the nation in the 1960s; they were among the causes of the 1967 Newark revolts.

In sum, having migrated for greater opportunity, many blacks and Puerto Ricans found limited job and educational opportunities, subpar housing, and poor race relations.

New Jersey, Rutgers, and the GI Bill

Progress could have been made if the 1944 Servicemen's Readjustment Act, better known as the GI Bill, had been administered without prejudice. Passed by Congress in 1944, the GI Bill was designed to help returning veterans reen-ter American society as productive citizens. It allowed them to complete a college education at the government's expense, take out low-interest home loans, and collect unemployment compensation. The GI Bill transformed the nature of higher education for America's white citizens. Before the war, few working-class or even middle-class Americans attended college. As millions of returning veterans entered college classrooms, higher education ceased to be the preserve of the rich. The GI Bill also transformed the housing mar-ket, making home ownership more commonplace. As white veterans bought homes with government loans, they facilitated America's suburbanization and the rise of the white middle class.[21]

Black Americans experienced no such postwar boon. The bill itself did not discriminate, but because it was administered in accordance with local segregationist and discriminatory customs, it reproduced and exacerbated the same inequalities found in prewar America. The distribution of the GI Bill's educational benefits illustrates this. In both the pre- and postwar years, most of the country's predominantly white colleges held fast to segregation. Black access to them remained limited by de facto quotas, high selectivity, and the Veterans Administration's systematic refusal to pay the tuition of the few blacks who were accepted at white colleges. In the North and West, black enrollment in higher education never exceeded 5,000 during the late 1940s. Telling is the fact that out of the 9,000 students enrolled at the University of Pennsylvania in 1946, only forty-six were black.[22]

Segregation policies forced blacks to seek admission primarily to histori-cally black colleges and universities, which quickly became overcrowded. Like 95 percent of black veterans who utilized their higher education benefits, New Jersey's college-bound veterans went to HBCUs. But having lost funding during the Depression and the war, these schools had not the space, facilities, faculty, or state and federal support to educate all of the black students who applied.

As noted by historian Ira Katznelson, in 1947, some 20,000 eligible black veterans could not find places at HBCUs even under incredibly crowded conditions, and as many as 50,000 others might have sought admission had there been enough places.[23]

While national in scope, the impact and implementation of the GI Bill was felt in New Jersey in general and Rutgers in particular. Across the country, federal tuition grants helped colleges expand. Universities and colleges grew exponentially when states pitched in with grants and bond funds. Unable to accommodate the many eligible black veterans who applied, HBCUs, schools already underfunded by states, were unable to take advantage of this federal infusion of money. By contrast, flagship universities like the University of Wisconsin and the University of Michigan in the North and the University of Texas and the University of Alabama in the South were able to expand rapidly because of the GI Bill.[24]

Rutgers also benefited. For example, the total number of students swelled to the most it had seen in its 180-year history. As explained by historian Paul Clemens in his book *Rutgers since 1945*, the number of students attending the university swelled to nearly 15,000—9,000 of whom were veterans receiving tuition grants under the GI Bill. The massive influx of students posed a problem for the university because they had no place to house many of the new students. This meant that Rutgers had to build more dormitories and classrooms. Although state bonds would not fund most of this expansion until 1956, when Rutgers became *the* state university of New Jersey, federal money from tuition payments financed Rutgers's initial postwar growth.[25]

The influx of new students not only boosted the financial standing of Rutgers but also made for a more interesting student social life as students were given a plethora of old and new organizations to be a part of. Organizations such as the *Scarlet Letter* (the yearbook) and the *Daily Targum* (the newspaper) were reestablished after years in which they could not be sustained with the low number of students at Rutgers. Clubs such as debate and theater were created as well. By the end of the academic year of 1947, the university had more or less returned to the way things had been before the outbreak of World War II. Football games began to be played again, fraternity life returned, and the campus was alive with students going to class.[26]

The *Scarlet Letter* yearbook chronicled this vibrant life that the veterans and other new students found at Rutgers, but the lack of black students in its pages tells its own story. Although Rutgers did not keep records delineating the race of its student body at that time, researchers of *Scarlet and Black: Constructing Race and Gender at Rutgers, 1865–1945*, identified twenty-five black graduates who attended between 1888 and 1943. The *Scarlet Letter* shows little increase in that number. A brief glance through the 1947 book shows an entire section dedicated to Rutgers students and alumni who were lost during their service

FIGURE 1.1 White veterans in New Brunswick on Rutgers campus during the 1947 school year, *Scarlet Letter Yearbook*, 1947.

Courtesy of Special Collections & University Archives, Rutgers University

for their country. Furthermore, the yearbook dedicates space to talk about life when veterans returned to campus to finish off their collegiate careers and reveals who came to the school as incoming freshmen.[27] The absence of black students underscores what Shaun Illingworth, the director of the Oral History Archives at Rutgers University, said about Rutgers, African Americans, World War II, and the GI Bill—that from his own research and evidence from the oral histories of World War II veterans, "there were little to no black veterans affiliated with the university who used the GI Bill."[28] Illingworth's research is confirmed by that of historian Richard McCormick. He found that before 1967, most of the growth in the black student body did not come until 1965. Between 1965 and 1968, Rutgers, like other predominantly white schools, saw a fourfold increase in the number of black students (from 100 in 1965 to 400 by 1968). In the fifteen years prior to 1967, only about 200 blacks had received baccalaureate degrees out of the 24,000 that had been awarded.[29]

In sum, Rutgers benefited immensely from the GI Bill—but not New Jersey African Americans. Expecting overburdened and underfunded black colleges and universities to assume the burden of educating black veterans, Rutgers rejected black applications, keeping its student body almost lily white. Rutgers, it seems, was not that different from Princeton of 1942, where two out of three students opposed the admission of blacks and believed that those who were admitted should be banned from Prospect Street, the social hub of the college.[30] The sad fact is there were very few black students at any predominantly white schools until the late 1960s. Before the war, many blacks aspiring to go to college were not able to go because they lacked the financial ability. Tragically, after the war, when federal tuition grants made it possible for all veterans to go to college, African American veterans faced intractable discrimination—discrimination that their baby boomer children would not abide.

The Few and Far Between: African Americans at Rutgers

Rutgers University expanded exponentially in the years after World War II. With the assistance of state and federal funds, it increased its student body and expanded geographically. By the late 1960s, it had three locations—New Brunswick (Rutgers College, 1766; Douglass College, 1918; Livingston College, 1965), Newark (1946), and Camden (1950)—and each of these locations had also swelled in terms of numbers and space.

Minority students were few and far between, however. Before 1968, predominantly white campuses did not keep reliable records on the numbers of minority students it enrolled, but the numbers that do exist about Rutgers tell an unfortunate story. As noted earlier, in 1968, black undergraduates constituted only about 3 percent of undergraduate enrollment.[31] James Dickson Carr had graduated in 1892 and only about twenty-five more had graduated by 1943.[32] According to historian Richard McCormick, "It is doubtful that they [blacks] approximated one percent of the student body before 1965"—this when the overall undergraduate enrollment at Rutgers–New Brunswick was about 14,000. In 1968, there were ninety-five black students out of a total enrollment of 6,416; thirty-eight were freshmen. Of a faculty that numbered 558, there were three blacks. Douglass College was only a tad bit better, registering 115 black women in its 1968 class, which numbered 2,860 students. Most of the 115 black women had entered since 1965.[33]

Although located in cities that were rapidly becoming majority black, the campuses of Rutgers–Newark and Rutgers–Camden were as white as their sister campus in New Brunswick. In 1967, Rutgers–Newark had 2,500 undergraduates, of whom sixty-two were black. A few years earlier there had been no more than twenty. There were no blacks on the faculty. All the students commuted to campus because there were no residence halls; only a small minority came from Newark. The dismal statistics were repeated at Rutgers–Camden. The college enrolled nearly 1,200 undergraduates in 1968, but only seventeen were black. Three of the 150 law school students were black. The faculty numbered about 100, but there were only three academic professionals who were black.[34]

Although we have little personal information about the students who matriculated during the early postwar period, the few profiles that are available from Rutgers–Camden suggest the broad contours of life at Rutgers for blacks and other students of color.[35] Take, for example, Frederick Miller. "None but himself can be his parallel" reads the caption underneath Frederick Miller's senior photograph in the first *Mneme,* the Rutgers University College of South Jersey yearbook.[36] Of the forty-two graduating seniors, Miller stood out as the only black in his class and one of two black students at the institution in 1952.[37] Miller's story is one of the few within the decade of the 1950s that represented the role of black students in the long-standing history of what we know today as Rutgers University–Camden. Throughout the yearbook, Miller's involvement in student life is displayed in multiple student organizations and college sports. In 1954, he was secretary of the "R" club, served on the editorial team of the *Mneme,* played forward on the varsity basketball team, and was also a member of the baseball team.[38] His involvement in multiple student organizations throughout his senior year was similar to many of his peers whose involvement, as described under their senior photographs, spanned multiple organizations.

In 1953, Esther Mae Gee became the first black woman to graduate from Rutgers University College of South Jersey, and the only student of color out of the forty-one graduating seniors.[39] It would be five more years before another black woman would graduate from this institution.[40] Gee was described as "having the friendliest smile on campus . . . fun in and out of class . . . worries more than the whole class combined but always succeeds . . . and best trombonist at the Christmas party."[41] Her presence is seen throughout the first and second *Mneme* yearbooks. As part of the editorial staff of the *Mneme,* Esther Mae Gee helped in articulating the vision for the annual yearbook; in addition to serving on the Glee Club, German Club, Humanities Club, and Science Club, she was also a member of Delta Rho and part of the college's cheerleading team.[42] Her extensive cocurricular involvement coupled with her academic achievement positioned Gee as a student who helped to shape the narrative of student life at Rutgers University College of South Jersey.

Looking through the *Mneme,* at first glance the faces of students of color are not easily visible given the dearth of their presence within the institution. In the span of the decade of the 1950s, Rutgers University–Camden managed to successfully matriculate a total of nine black undergraduate students.[43] The class of 1954 included Isaiah M. Burrel, James A. Carrington, and Linwood H. Willis,[44] and the class of 1958 included Charlie B. Henderson, Richard E. Johnson, Yvonne Spell, and Elizabeth Valentine.[45] The absence of black students at Rutgers University College of South Jersey would become an issue as the 1950s closed and the 1960s progressed, particularly as white flight took hold and Camden became a predominantly black city.

FREDERICK MILLER
Box 21
Paulsboro, New Jersey
Social Sciences
Basketball , 1,2,3,4;   Baseball   3,4;
Mneme 4; Varsity Club 4.
"None but himself can be his parallel."

FIGURE 1.2 Frank Miller, senior portrait, *Mneme Yearbook,* 1952.

Courtesy of Special Collections & University Archives, Rutgers University

ESTHER MAE GEE
626 Kaighn Avenue
CAMDEN
Friendliest smile on campus . . . fun in and out of class . . .
worries more than the whole class combined but always
succeeds . . . best trombonist at the Christmas Party.
Mneme 3, 4; Glee Club 2, 3, 4; German Club 3; Humanities
Club 2, 3; Science Club 3, 4; Delta Rho 3, 4; Cheerleader 3.

FIGURE 1.3 Esther Mae Gee, senior portrait, *Mneme Yearbook*, 1953.
Courtesy of Special Collections & University Archives, Rutgers University

It was not until the mid-1960s that Latinx and Asian students made an appearance in the *Mneme*. In 1963, Anthony Alvarez became the first Latinx student to graduate from the institution. Similarly, Robert W. Hung graduated as the first Asian student at Rutgers University College of South Jersey. The name and photos of Christina Welch, the first Asian woman who appeared in the *Mneme,* were scattered throughout the yearbook in 1962, but no documentation exists of her graduating in the subsequent years. In 1965, Karen Luisa Aguilar, another Latinx student, graduated from the institution. With a more racially diverse student body, the institution managed to graduate twenty-four black students, five Latinx students, and two Asian students during the decade of the '60s.[46]

Black and Latinx involvement in student organizations became a crucial aspect of their integration to campus life. Their involvement at the institution varied each year but as the academic years went by, more student organizations were created that catered to their specific needs and social support. These included the local sororities Delta Rho, Sigma Epsilon Phi, and the Tau Epsilon fraternity.[47] In relation to national Greek organizations, the Omega Psi Phi fraternity, the first black Greek letter organization (BGLO) at the school and the fourth BGLO of the National Pan-Hellenic Council, chartered the Tau Beta chapter in 1971.[48] That same year, the Theta Chi chapter of the Delta Sigma Theta sorority was chartered on campus, but the chapter later merged to include Rowan University and Stockton University in South Jersey.[49] In 1973, black student organizations grew to six and included the Black Allied Students Association, the Black Cultural Festival, the Black Psychological Association, and the Urban Studies Committee. The Latin American Student Organization also reemerged in 1978 after years of inactivity, although its founding is not documented in the *Mneme.*[50]

Students of color were not the only group not visibly represented through-out the early decades of RU–Camden. For the first ten years of its founding, there existed only one faculty and administrator of color: William K. C. Chen was an assistant professor of psychology from 1956 to 1965.[51] It was not until 1962 that the college had its first Latinx faculty member, Eladio Cortes, who served as an instructor in Spanish. From 1963 to 1965, Chen, Cortes, and Juan Caballero were the only faculty of color within the entire college. Black faculty and other faculty of color increased in numbers at the end of the 1960s, especially in 1969, when eleven faculty of color were hired. This was the same year of the Conklin Hall liberation and also when black law students organized against the university administration.[52] At various points through the late 1960s, student activists demanded some form of advocacy and support as well as the hiring of more black staff and faculty across academic, administrative, and cocurricular programs. In 1970, the number of faculty and staff of color more than doubled, to twenty-four. This increase can be attributed to the increased enrollments of students of color and student demands for more expansive support.[53] Together, students, faculty, and staff pressured the university to remain accountable to the population and the surrounding community.

Prelude to Transformation

The late 1960s saw change come to Rutgers. However, it was not initiated by the university but came mostly from black students who were influenced by the national Black Power movement and the urban rebellions against employment and housing discrimination and police brutality. Rutgers's black students responded not only to national ideas of Black Power but to the persistent racism they encountered in their communities in New Jersey.

In mid-July 1967, the city of Newark experienced one of the worst instances of urban trauma in the history of the nation. Institutional poverty, state-sanctioned violence, and systemic racism toward the black and Puerto Rican communities led to violent clashes with the police when it was rumored that a black cab driver was arrested and killed inside the Newark police station. It turned out that the police had not killed the cab driver but had severely beaten him while in police custody.[54] Regardless, the community's frustration at police abuse and institutional racism resulted in an uprising that lasted for five days. In Newark, twenty-six people were killed, 700 people were injured, and the city sustained more than $10 million in damages, with entire blocks destroyed.[55] The majority of those who were killed or injured were black. On July 14th, the third day of the uprising in Newark, residents in Plainfield also rose up against the poverty and institutional racism in their community. A police officer was killed, and residents acquired weapons from the Middlesex arms factory to protect themselves against the police forces. The governor had declared a state of emergency because of the Newark clashes, a signal many believed gave Plainfield police authority to ransack houses and look for the weapons. Nearly seventy houses were torn apart without a warrant and more than one hundred people were arrested.[56] On July 17, 1967, New Brunswick teetered on uprising when a group of approximately 200 black residents gathered on the corner of George Street and Remsen Avenue. Led by local high school students, the New Brunswick residents protested against unemployment, substandard living conditions, and the treatment of high school students in New Brunswick's public schools.[57] The crowd grew to more than 300 people and there was some property damage throughout the night. The city enforced a 10:00 p.m. curfew and made some arrests, only to have more demonstrations the following evening when some 200 protesters walked to police headquarters to voice their grievances to the mayor, who vowed to improve race relations in the city.[58]

At the same time that protests mounted in central New Jersey, black and Latinx citizens of Camden conducted protests against conditions that had left them penned in congested housing and substandard schools as industry and commerce relocated to the suburbs and middle- and upper-class whites followed. During the 1960s, 28,000 whites left Camden. While Camden lost 48 percent of its manufacturing base, the suburbs around Camden experienced a 95 percent increase in the growth of their manufacturing employment.[59] As happened elsewhere, black and Latinx citizens were prevented from following the jobs by discriminatory real estate and mortgage practices, restrictive covenants, and outright hate practices. Moreover, just as black veterans had been shut out of the GI Bill's tuition grant program, they had also been shut out of the Veterans Administration's and Federal Housing Administration's guaranteed mortgages. Although not available for the Camden area (but including Newark), statistics show that in 1950 in the New York and northern New Jersey metropolitan area, when VA mortgages amounted to 15.5 percent of the total mortgaged properties, African Americans owned only 0.1 percent of them.[60] Stats like these were at the core of the three consecutive years of urban protest in Camden that began in 1967. In August 1971, Camden experienced three nights of large-scale civil disorder as fires, looting, and property damage paralyzed the city.[61]

Conclusion: Hindsight Is Twenty-Twenty Vision

In 2005, Rutgers historian William Gillette published an insightful history of postwar Camden in which he documented the city's transition from a wartime industrial powerhouse to a postwar, postindustrial city. Among the many stories he recounts are those of whites who remember with anger and pain the "riots" of 1971 and the economic and social displacement they felt as Latinx and African Americans "invaded" their city and "destroyed" what for them was "the city that worked."[62] Gillette is careful to note that Camden was not dissimilar from other American cities and that the complaints of whites "cannot be dismissed as simple aberrations."[63] However, he is also careful to mention how African Americans felt. Quoting one of Camden's black leaders, Gillette argues that for blacks who had expected things to change after the war, their experiences with racism were like "a first-time visitor to New York City, who arrives only to find that the Empire State Building has been removed."[64] African Americans had looked forward to the postwar period with hope, but all they found was old-fashioned racism.

Gillette also shows how hard it was for whites to resist blaming inner-city minorities for the turmoil experienced by Camden and similarly situated cities. "Accounts told years after the fact either proceed without knowledge of the large social context that produced black anger at the time or suppress knowledge of those conditions that might have been apparent then."[65] In the 1950s and '60s, Camden was in the grip of what we know today to be deindustrialization, the nationwide loss of manufacturing jobs; suburbanization, the movement of jobs to the outer rims of cities; and globalization, the movement of jobs and services beyond America's borders. Whites in Camden who were caught up in this change, who participated and benefited from it, were not always aware of the larger forces at work or they willfully ignored what was plain to see. Whatever the reason, they blamed minorities for the transformation of life as they knew it. Quoting urban planning scholar Robert Beauregard, Gillette concludes, "Race was increasingly the glue that bound together all of the perceived problems of the declining cities."[66]

The changes that occurred in the nation's cities and across New Jersey were soon to make their way to the nation's institutions of higher learning, including Rutgers. In hindsight, historians now know that the urban uprisings were a manifestation of the northern civil rights movement—agitation against the relatively invisible forces of de facto inequality. But what was not apparent then now looms large. In the immediate post–World War II era, members of the two minority groups who led the protest movement at Rutgers—African Americans and Puerto Ricans—moved to New Jersey looking for opportunity in greater numbers than ever before. Locked out of that opportunity, they, and especially their baby boomer children, forced the issue. In cities around New Jersey they took to the streets and made New Jersey municipalities pay attention. Believing that Rutgers held the key to the opportunity they sought, these New Jersey citizens challenged their exclusion from the student body, faculty, and course curriculums. Eventually, they uprooted the status quo.

2

Rutgers and New Brunswick

A Consideration of Impact

IAN GAVIGAN AND PAMELA WALKER

"What had always bothered me," said Alice Jennings Archibald in her oral history interview with scholars from Rutgers University, was that Rutgers had "no impact" on the "people of color, as well as others" in New Brunswick. By contrast, she thought Princeton "had a great influence on the people in the community," including blacks. But of New Brunswick, she said, "we were a factory town; Princeton was the college town." Archibald was careful to qualify her remarks as "my personal opinion," but as someone who grew up in New Brunswick, she was familiar enough with the city, its institutions, and New Jersey to speak with some authority on the relationship between Rutgers and New Brunswick. After receiving her BA from Howard University, she was forced to teach in North Carolina because town after New Jersey town would not hire her because of her race. The first African American to receive an advanced degree from Rutgers University—from the Graduate School of Education—when she returned to New Brunswick she worked through her church, Mount Zion African Methodist Episcopal, and the New Brunswick Urban League to press Johnson and Johnson, Rickitt's Blueing, United States Rubber, and other factories to hire blacks. These companies, she said, "seemed to have influence." In 1997, when reflecting on the relationship between Rutgers and the city of New Brunswick, she said, "It's only in recent years that I really can see the influence of Rutgers on the community."[1]

If Rutgers could not help the black people in New Brunswick or even provide a model of public policy for the city, it was most likely because both Rutgers and New Brunswick struggled with racial inequality and systemic racism. In the 1960s, while Rutgers was finding a way to increase black enrollment

FIGURE 2.1 Alice Jennings Archibald.

Courtesy of Mt. Zion A.M.E. Church Digital Archives, Alice Jennings Archibald Local History Room, Mt. Zion A.M.E. Church, New Brunswick, NJ

and personnel and transform its Eurocentric curriculum and culture, the city of New Brunswick was reeling from deindustrialization and suburbanization, police brutality, and segregated education, forces that pitted the entrenched white power structure against an ever-growing impoverished black and brown population.

This essay explores New Brunswick during the period of intense transformation at Rutgers University. By exploring some of the developments in the racial landscape of New Brunswick and the nascent left-wing organizing at Rutgers, it aims to shed light on Archibald's observation that Rutgers had "no impact" on the people of color in New Brunswick.

Political Upheaval, Racial Turmoil, and
School Segregation in the City of New Brunswick

Long before her 1997 statement about Rutgers being of little significance to the black people in New Brunswick, Alice Jennings Archibald sent a letter to the *Daily Home News* titled "What the Negro Wants." Among the "wants" were employment opportunities and job training for black New Brunswickers, positive write-ups about local blacks in the *Daily Home News,* and a concerted effort on the part of all New Brunswick residents, blacks and *especially* whites, to end racism and discrimination.[2] This was in 1942—before the sit-ins, free-dom rides, marches, and voter-registration campaigns of the civil rights move-ment. It was before the national legislation that made discrimination illegal and voting a right of every citizen.[3] But in spite of such forward movement, progress on the matters Archibald outlined for New Brunswick was slow to materialize. A brief look at the evolution of New Brunswick's municipal lead-ership, the political turmoil accompanying it, and the educational crisis in the city from the late 1960s into the 1970s suggests why.

Out with the Old, in with the "New Five":
Unrest in a New Era of Governance

"We had no faith in the current administration. So, we ran against them," stated Patricia Sheehan in an interview more than fifty years after that pivotal 1967 election.[4] That administration—an all-male, all-white mayor-commission government—was led by Mayor Chester Paulus, a Democrat. According to Sheehan, the "old guard" had been in office, in one form or another, for more than twenty-seven years. Whereas these men called themselves the "Good Five," others considered their reign a veritable "good ol' boys' club," excluding the voices of women, young folks, and people of color. Their meetings were private, held on "Tuesdays or Thursdays" at the Elks Club on Livingston Ave-nue. Decisions were made behind closed doors without input from community members.[5] Moreover, rumors of rampant corruption scandalized the Paulus administration.[6] Swept up in the national movement of change in the 1960s, New Brunswick citizens took to the polls on May 9, 1967, demanding change.

"A Woman Mayor Chosen in Jersey" was the May 10, 1967, *New York Times* headline after the election of Mayor Patricia Q. Sheehan, the first (and last) woman in New Brunswick history to hold the position.[7] The unprecedented victory was a surprise to all, including the Newark native herself. Running on the progressive ticket to become city commissioner alone seemed such a long shot that the thought of taking the mayoral position never really crossed her mind. At thirty-three years old, the widowed working mother of three small children already had her hands full. The outcome might have been different had she been married at the time of the campaign, but her personal story allowed flexibility for a woman to step into executive leadership. She was, in the eyes of voters, an ordinary white woman trying to raise a family on a single income after the loss of her husband, unconstrained by traditional maternalist expectations regarding the role of women. "Well, my situation was different," she admitted. "I had the advantage of being accepted and respected, plus I had the aura of goodwill because my husband [a city official at the time of his death] was so popular." Moreover, Sheehan notes, "I wasn't part of the 'burn your bra' movement." This act of distancing herself from radical feminism made her a palatably progressive, if largely moderate, candidate.[8]

The election also resulted in other newcomers. Thirty-year-old Aldrage B. Cooper II, the "first Negro commissioner," would later become the first black mayor of New Brunswick in 1974 and served as vice president of corporate affairs at Johnson and Johnson. Carl Valenti, John Smith, and William Cahill completed the incoming "New Five" cohort.[9]

The new mayor and commissioners had determined to govern in a way antithetical to their predecessors. According to Sheehan, the New Five had an open-door policy: "If you wanted to meet with the mayor, the mayor was there." Sheehan and her colleagues also leapt at the opportunity to implement Lyndon B. Johnson's Great Society in New Brunswick. From Job Corps and other Office of Economic Opportunity programs, city officials were eager to fulfill New Brunswick's long-standing need for job training and diverse employment. The diverse "new face of government" was on the path to building trust and creating opportunity in the city.[10]

The goodwill of the New Five, just two months in office, was not enough to stave off the political unrest making its way across the state, most notably in Newark and Plainfield. On July 17 and 18, 1967, "hate flames" erupted in downtown New Brunswick, days after the deadly Newark uprising. African Americans in New Brunswick took to the streets to protest ongoing second-class citizenship in the areas of job discrimination, housing, and segregation after major civil rights victories. On the first night, the *Daily Home News* reported that "small bands of rampaging Negro teen-agers" strategically vandalized stores in downtown New Brunswick. They allegedly tossed bricks and trash cans through glass windows and overturned two cars, setting one on fire. Four fire bombs were thrown in the direction of Roosevelt school, but they did not ignite.[11] Even white youth, according to a report in the *New York Times*, participated, throwing a "Molotov cocktail through the window of a plumbing supply store in a Negro neighborhood."[12] In all, thirty-two adults and eighteen juveniles, all African Americans, were arrested and taken into custody that night. The damage was alarming, yet city officials and authorities "agreed that it was definitely not a 'criminal insurrection' of the type seen in the bloody rioting in Newark."[13]

July 18 saw another night of unrest. City administrators believed the outcome of the "near-riot" could have been much different had de-escalation tactics not been utilized. Mayor Sheehan chose a communicative, conciliatory approach rather than force. Even though New Jersey governor Richard Hughes was just a phone call away, Mayor Sheehan insisted, "There were not going to be any national guardsmen in New Brunswick. Period." The election convinced Sheehan to see the city from a different perspective. The support garnered during the campaign translated to her as a vote of confidence and thus an investment in seeing *all* of New Brunswick as her constituents, as her own. "These were our people," Sheehan stated. "You have to respect the people, wherever they are and whatever they are doing." Furthermore, as newly elected officials, Sheehan and the New Five did not "feel bound by tradition." Mayor Sheehan, utilizing the clergy, radio, and black officers, avoided a "full-scale riot" through reason, communication, and refraining from violent force.[14]

Lieutenant John "Honey" Brokaw and Commissioner Aldrage Cooper served as surrogates for the mayor as well as trusted ambassadors to the black community. Mount Zion AME Pastor Rev. Henry Hildebrand encouraged protesters to leave the streets and to take "their problems to the conference table."[15] Their advocacy was crucial to the de-escalation. Their names, however, are absent from the 1967 Kerner Report on Civil Disorders, which praised New Brunswick and Mayor Sheehan for averting a major crisis. "Using a bull horn," the brief account in the report read, "Sheehan went out onto the steps of the [police] station and asked that she be given an opportunity to [correct] conditions." Eventually, voices called out, "She's new! Give her a chance!" Agreeing to communication rather than protest, the crowd dissipated.[16]

Ordinary New Brunswickers remember the event in less than historic terms. According to Annette Robinson (pseudonym) and Cynthia Flowers (pseudonym),[17] the near-riot was little more than a "scrimmage"—in their minds, it "didn't amount to anything." Part of their dismissiveness of New Brunswick's nights of protest was the scale and magnitude of the uprisings in other cities. "There was a real riot there . . . in Newark," said Flowers, "and it wasn't just the kind of things that people went though at the time. It affected people psychologically." Robinson, then a college student, and Flowers, an elementary schoolteacher, did not retain extensive details about the New Brunswick event. They recall the curfew and a "brick through a storefront," but both consider the "near-riot" language and the celebration of the chief executive overblown. On the other hand, Robinson and Flowers do remember well how the *notion* of a New Brunswick riot was visualized and became the reason behind white flight, urban renewal, and the opening of a new, suburban, mostly white high school.[18]

Although the Kerner Commission's report praised Mayor Sheehan for saving New Brunswick from total destruction, many in the local white community wanted to save the city from Sheehan and the New Five. A reflection piece written nearly two years after the "near-riot" claimed that the one-hour conversation that Sheehan had with protesters was "the night they gave the city away." The "anti–New Five" contingency "maintain[ed] stoutly that the new commissioners 'gave in' to lawless black youths who, the previous night, rampaged through the business district, smashing store windows and engaging in looting merchandise." Instead of law and order, disgruntled citizens accused their mayor of "begging" hundreds of protesters to end the disruption.[19]

No Longer Veiled: Racial Tension in New Brunswick Made Plain

The decision to negotiate with black protesters had ramifications on New Brunswick politics in the late 1960s and into the 1970s. March 1969, a month that saw Rutgers faculty, administrators, and the Board of Governors negotiate major adjustments in policies toward African Americans,[20] was especially combustible in New Brunswick as Mayor Sheehan and the commissioners faced demands from newly formed conservative-right organizations as well as from black high school protesters. At a meeting in mid-March, the Concerned and Responsible Citizens (CRC), an all-white group frustrated by the mayor's concessions to African Americans, presented a list of demands for the "Protection of White Equal Rights" (POWER). Among their desires was a request for veto power, new police hires, and a curfew for New Brunswick residents.[21] These demands alone were enough to rile the community; however, racist and disparaging comments from Officer Jesse Biczi were a catalyst for internal conflict in the police department and at New Brunswick upper schools. According to reports, Biczi stated that the United States was being "overtaken from within" and in his many years on the police force "he had not found one good Negro." Biczi also bolstered an antigovernment stance on gun rights, encouraging the more than 700 CRC meeting attendees "not to register their firearms with the police."[22]

Biczi's remarks had serious consequences, setting off a chain reaction throughout the city. Eight black policemen, including Lieutenant John "Honey" Brokaw, a beloved officer and government-to-community liaison, resigned after hearing the divisive comments. A statement written by Brokaw on behalf of the black officers read: "We feel that his statement and conduct put us in an untenable position and we can no longer do our jobs as policemen effectively. The reason behind this being that as black police officers our characters have been impugned and we can no longer command the respect of fair-minded blacks and whites." Moreover, Brokaw added quite frankly, he and his fellow officers "find it very difficult to perform our responsibilities, working side by side with an individual who has publicly declared himself a racist."[23] Biczi was suspended by Police Chief Ralph C. Petrone and later apologized to his black colleagues and the black community.

It is unclear whether Biczi's degrading words about African Americans and the subsequent resignation of black officers sparked conflict at upper schools in New Brunswick or if they simply added fuel to a smoldering fire. Nonetheless, just a few days after the turmoil at the police department, a "full-scale riot" erupted at New Brunswick High and Junior High Schools. On the morning of March 18, approximately 250 black teens and 350 white teens were having segregated forums on racial tension when 100 black teens interrupted the white forum. The school had apparently been plagued by racially charged scuffles and fights for days; the forums were meant to bring about a peaceful resolution. The altercation resulted in forty broken windows at New Brunswick High and Junior High. Officers—including the newly resigned black policemen—were called in to respond to the scene.[24] Lieutenant Brokaw and others took to the local radio airwaves at WCTC to urge young black youth to "cool it." "[The black cops] did a helluva job," one onlooker praised.[25]

Following the uprising at the junior and senior schools, both schools were closed the following day. That night, parents, city officials, and educators met to discuss how the students could coexist peacefully in the community. "We have got to work out how we are going to live in this community, black and white—it's not going to be black versus white, and it can't be young versus old," said Mayor Sheehan. Mrs. Mildred Small, a black community member in attendance, argued that the children were not the center of the problem. "It's we adults," stated Small. "We have poisoned the minds of young people for years. We are racists—all of us—don't blame the policemen. Don't blame it on the children. Blame it on the adults."[26] The 1968–1969 school year ended quietly. The school board worked to make some concessions, infusing African American and Puerto Rican history into the curriculum; however, the racial and political climate remained tense into the 1970s.[27]

The School Crisis and the End of the New Five Era

By 1970, during Sheehan's mayoral reelection campaign, backlash against the New Five was heightened because of the events of the previous year. Sheehan remembers at least seventeen candidates running against her in the reelection. Her main opposition was Ralph Muehlig, an independent whose campaign motto was "Save Our City." With this, Muehlig promised the law and order that many New Brunswick conservatives believed was absent from the New Five's agenda.[28] It was a nasty campaign; fear tactics and name-calling ran rampant. In the end, Sheehan "soundly defeated" Muehlig in the 1970 election, affirming public confidence in her record and the New Five.

In 1973, when Sheehan was appointed by New Jersey governor Brendan Byrne to a state-level position, Aldrage B. Cooper II became the first black mayor of the city. When it came time for election in 1974, Cooper was unable to squeeze out a victory; he was defeated by Richard Mulligan, a powerful attorney who was well "established in the white community." Cooper and Sheehan both agreed later, in separate interviews, that racism and the abysmal racial state of affairs influenced the outcome of the election.[29]

No question, the school crisis, which had taken place between Sheehan's reelection and Cooper's formal mayoral campaign, was an important factor in the declining popularity of the New Five candidate. As historian Chris Rasmussen meticulously notes in the article "Creating Segregation in the Era of Integration," racial turmoil at New Brunswick Junior and Senior High Schools and the suburbanization and population growth of the majority-white North Brunswick township paved the way for twin movements that advocated for "local control" of education in New Brunswick and North Brunswick rather than "regionalization." Initially, the black and Latinx community in New Brunswick wanted to maintain an integrated school system, but in time they began to favor community control over school consolidation and busing. They hoped to have greater positive influence on the curriculum of students of color in the community.[30]

Prior to 1973, white students from North Brunswick and Milltown were bused to New Brunswick upper schools. But during the years of tension and unrest, the racial makeup of New Brunswick High declined from 79 percent white in 1968 to 60 percent white by 1973. Although the state commissioner of education negotiated with local education boards to ensure that the opening of a new high school in North Brunswick would not "segregate" schools, when North Brunswick High School opened in 1973, there was an exodus of more than 700 white students, making New Brunswick High a majority minority for the first time in its history.[31] Students were encouraged to go to schools in their municipal district, which meant white students were the predominant demographic in North Brunswick High and students of color made up the vast population of New Brunswick High (by this time any whites still living in New Brunswick proper were sending their children to private schools).[32] Community control of New Brunswick schools ultimately did not serve the best interests of black and Latinx students as black institutional and organizational infrastructure withered in the mid-1970s.[33]

The 1960s and 1970s also saw the obliteration of the downtown business sector, which had a detrimental impact on people of color as well. Longtime New Brunswick resident Anthony Marchetta attributed this decline to the development of enclosed shopping malls, while others say that the late '60s near-riots encouraged college students and the white community to steer clear of the area.[34] City officials celebrated the commitment of Johnson and

Johnson to the area and the creation of the New Brunswick Development Corporation (DEVCO), but had little interest in investing in the black community.
City leaders like Sheehan, who advocated for Johnson and Johnson to stay in
central Jersey, and Cooper, who later became an executive for Johnson and
Johnson, saw these organizations as crucial players in the plan to revitalize
the city, bringing back traffic that the area had lost.

This was the beginning of gentrification in the eyes of many downtown
black New Brunswickers. Like Alice Jennings Archibald, who remembered
Rutgers having no impact on New Brunswick until the latter years of the cen-
tury, Cynthia Flowers had memories of the city administration kowtowing to
Johnson and Johnson, Rutgers, and "the hospitals" (Robert Wood Johnson and
St. Peters)—"that was the pecking order"—toward the end of the millennium.
According to Flowers, local blacks were left out of the decision-making process
when it came to the city, and even when there was black leadership in office,
Annette Robinson stated, "blacks in power displayed a sort of nepotism" that
hurt the larger public and often distanced them from the greater black community. According to Flowers and Robinson, the mentality was "I might be
your color, but I ain't your kind."[35] Although they believed that the African
American community in the city had not always advocated for themselves and
that there was a breakdown in the community structure after the civil rights
movement, the women also believed the decline in the African American population was systematic.[36]

Statistics substantiate their claims. In 1960, the black population was 15.6
percent and climbed steadily until it reached 28.5 percent in 1980, peaking at
29.6 percent in 1990. Within twenty years, however, these numbers were cut
in half. In 2000, the percentages were down to 23 percent, and by 2010, the
census revealed that the black population had dropped to 16 percent.[37] The
ebb and flow of the black population in New Brunswick from 1950 to 2010 is
telling and perhaps reveals, if not a systematic removal of blacks, a forced
migration out of the city due to a lack of jobs, the declining education system, reduced housing, and a downtown revitalization that sought little input
from the communities of color who lived there. Indeed, more work needs to be
done, particularly in the realm of oral history with black New Brunswickers, to
fully understand the effect this era had on minority communities in the city.

In sum, although more research might prove Archibald wrong in her "no
impact" assessment of Rutgers and New Brunswick African Americans, it does
appear that during the 1960s and '70s, Rutgers and New Brunswick traveled
very different roads to racial reconciliation. While Rutgers adopted measures
to increase the numbers of blacks enrolled in every part of its university, the
city of New Brunswick "solved" its racial problem by making the city less desirable for African Americans and decreasing their numbers.

The Left in New Brunswick in the Late 1960s and Early 1970s

On August 10, 1971, a group of about a dozen women gathered outside a corner drugstore in downtown New Brunswick. It was a sunny day and, according to the protest's chronicler, a hot one. The assembled women ogled passing men all afternoon, at times exchanging barbs with hostile pedestrians. Their goal: show men what it was like to be objectified. When asked by a passing man why the group was there, one reportedly responded, "Why do you think we're protesting? You like to look at girls. We like to look at cocks. But so far I haven't seen much worth looking at." That day and the next, this group of working women came together to challenge everyday chauvinism in full public view of the "Hub City." The story, captured by photographers and recorded in the alternative monthly newspaper *All You Can Eat* (*AYCE*) on August 27, 1970, was evidence that despite its often reactionary politics, New Brunswick had a left wing that worked consistently for causes not adopted by the mainstream right or center.[38] Although Alice Jennings Archibald did not think that Rutgers had an impact on New Brunswick's "people of color, as well as others," it wasn't for want of trying on the part of a few groups and individuals at the university.

In fact, Rutgers University, as other essays in this collection make clear, contained hotbeds of organizing, and not all activists on and off campus were students. New Brunswick's left movement was rather amorphous. Not all of its participants were as bold and public as were these women; in the late 1960s and early 1970s, a wide range of styles, tone, tactics, and organizing principles were adopted. Nevertheless, although small and disparate, a left-leaning movement that straddled the "town–gown" line did exist, and the radical periodical *All You Can Eat,* produced by writers affiliated with Rutgers—students or former students—offers a window into overlaps and divides between a Rutgers-centric movement left and broader currents in the social and political struggle. By reading the newspaper's content as well as understanding its social background and composition against the backdrop of major changes in New Brunswick and central New Jersey, a number of features of the political life of the university and community come into focus. First, there was no hermetic seal dividing campus struggles from more general trends of left-wing activism. Second, New Brunswick and the central New Jersey region, which was covered by *AYCE,* had an active and vibrant left that appears as a meaningful whole in the alternative newspaper. At the same time, though they tried, the collection of community-based organizations that the mostly young, mostly white crowd built did not achieve the stated goals of multiracial organizing, despite a well-developed rhetoric that envisioned revolution in such terms. Third, in New Brunswick itself, the participant-journalists of *AYCE* also offer a glimpse of grassroots resistance to urban renewal and the crises that produced housing, educational, and economic insecurity.

The *AYCE* and Social Movement Building
in and around Rutgers and New Brunswick

The *AYCE* newspaper was perhaps the clearest link between Rutgers students' on-campus activism in and around New Brunswick and the broader world of social movement activism and organizing. Its editorial staff was firmly ensconced in that world and consisted, according to its own discussions of the origins of the newspaper, of current students and alumni. In the early issues, especially 1970, correspondence to the newspaper was sent to a campus mail address and current Rutgers students authored many pieces. Although white, the editors saw the paper as "an underground paper, a paper that comes from the community, for the community."[39] The staff saw their project as one that mixed political education and mutual aid, offering for the city of New Brunswick and state of New Jersey a platform for alternative, radical, and revolutionary politics.[40]

The politics represented in the paper ran the gamut of early 1970s radicalisms. United under a general rubric of socialism, the paper sought to portray multiple struggles for liberation and justice in New Jersey. Editions in 1970 devoted significant attention to black organizing, especially Black Panther Party organizing and persecution. The *AYCE* editions in the fall of 1970 closely followed the Revolutionary People's Constitutional Convention in Philadelphia and reported at multiple points on the trial of Ericka Huggins and Bobby Seale in New Haven, Connecticut. Its focus on black politics and organizing extended beyond formal groups; early reporting included a number of scathing pieces on prisons and police violence, their tone a combination of essayistic reflection and active investigative reportage. One, a reprint of a Liberation News Service article on the community response to a mass police shooting of black protesters in Asbury Park, a town on New Jersey's Atlantic coast, received a full two-page spread.[41] As the paper developed, the range of topics expanded, although the paper never dropped its focus on black organizing. Over time, the women's, Puerto Rican, and gay movements joined center stage.

While attentive to off-campus issues of repression, the pages of *AYCE* were also filled with writing on a wide array of on-campus social movement activities. One topic that received significant focus and investigative writing was the connections between Rutgers and the Vietnam War—a central focus of New Left organizing more generally and a major concern among all students.[42] Coverage of Rutgers's institutional connections to war research and weapons development, as well as to ROTC, attacked the university for abetting the American empire and for the destruction its wars wrought. Alongside the university, Johnson and Johnson stands out as a repeated target of *AYCE* and activists.[43]

AYCE also tackled off-campus issues, such as the New Brunswick High School crisis of 1972. As historian Chris Rasmussen showed in his study of resegregation, New Brunswick's tenuously integrated system was far from safe and responsive for all students, especially those who were black and Puerto Rican. As noted earlier, when whites departed for schools in North Brunswick, communities of color campaigned for more authority over New Brunswick High School. Meanwhile, increasingly reactionary white suburban conservatives agitated against racial integration. In this context, students took to the streets as well as to the pages of *AYCE* to express their own take on the school system.

In *AYCE*'s pages, students and teachers found an alternative outlet to articulate their own experiences of and responses to the crisis in the public schools. Students wrote of their subjection to authoritarian mores. A fourteen-year-old public school student who styled himself simply "A brother" wrote:

> I think, just as you do, that the system shits. School sucks, they literally say, "Bow down and kiss teacher's ass." That is what its [sic] all about. You're the lower class, they're the upper class. They have the power to praise you or crush you. Most likely they will crush you. The student is the innocent bastard who is massacred for showing his inner beliefs and mild hostilities.[44]

Teachers too wrote to *AYCE,* weighing in not on the conflict between white and nonwhite groups but on the undemocratic and oppressive environment in which New Brunswick's increasingly black and Puerto Rican students learned. One self-identified public schoolteacher, who remained unnamed for fear of reprisal, encouraged students to fight back against this system by organizing for themselves. "Civil disobedience does work," the teacher wrote, following these words with concrete suggestions about how to avoid expulsion and retribution from a school district that would target individuals for organizing. In a special eight-page insert to the November 1972 edition, *AYCE* put the focus squarely on high school students as agents of change. In a special edition meant to reach these young people, the newspaper offered both specific resources—such as the phone numbers of high school organizing groups, the ACLU, and the newspaper itself—and painted a portrait of possible futures outside the current system. One essay bemoaned the emptiness of standard curriculums while another exhorted students and readers to break out of the entire framework as it existed, declaring, "Don't be skooled—create alternatives."[45] Yet another featured reflections on "going through school female," an essay that put gender oppression at the center of the struggle for student justice.[46] Operating outside the framework of the broad debate in which

FIGURE 2.2 Front cover featuring photos of New Brunswick high school students, *All You Can Eat*, November 1972.

community leaders engaged, they pointed to different forms of politics, either in terms of class, as the unnamed student quoted earlier showed, or in terms of pedagogy, as the teacher-focused pieces showed, or in terms of gender, as the student-focused essay showed.

That year the schools were not the only target of social movement activism. The swirl of activity represented in *AYCE* shows a vibrant movement scene. In its May 1972 edition, the paper printed a full-page calendar of activities in and around New Brunswick covering twenty-three days of the month and many more individual events.[47] They included tenant-organizing meetings, radical film screenings, Marxist scholarly lectures, New Jersey Student Union trainings at the Rutgers Labor Center, and more. In addition to the events listing, many days included facts of historical significance in the left-wing social struggle—for example, May 1: International Workers' Day; May 2: "1970—Nixon invades Cambodia"; May 4: "1970—Kent State: Four students killed by National Guard Moratorium Day—Local actions against the war"; May 5: "1818—Karl Marx Born, 1970—Jackson State: Two black students killed"; May 9: "1800—John Brown Born"; May 26: "1971—Ericka Huggins and Bobby Seale acquitted in New Haven"; and so on. Listing historical and recent dates of note that marked the lives of radical thinkers, heroes, and contemporary activists, and then following those with a host of social movement activities brought together not only a multifaceted set of activists but also placed them in the context of a long arc of struggle.

In the pages of *AYCE*, a wide assortment of liberation struggles converged into a single frame. As a source, it offers an archive of a left political geography centered on but exceeding New Brunswick. Advertisements for bookshops, activist circles, draft-resistance trainings, film screenings, abortion services, and all variety of meetings and resources and activities abound across the publication. *AYCE* also actively covered strikes throughout the region, including the strike of workers at the air-conditioning factory of Fedders-Norge Corporation in Edison, which began in the spring of 1972, where predominantly Spanish-speaking workers struck for months for higher wages.

Other coverage helped showcase the organizing in which Rutgers and the community members were engaged. For example, coverage of the New Brunswick Tenants Committee, an organization for which there are no organized records, shows what appears to have been a coordinated series of Rutgers-community housing actions in 1972. In a special edition of the paper, *AYCE* gave multipage coverage to renters organizing for improvements to their housing and an end to rent hikes. These included both students in Rutgers housing, especially married students with children, and tenants of privately owned apartment complexes in the city. In addition to providing relatively detailed coverage of substandard conditions and landlord malfeasance, *AYCE* offered concrete advice to readers about how to get involved in the broader

New Jersey tenants movement for rent control as well as giving explanations of existing renters' and landlords' rights. Localized conflict over tenants' rights, shore–town struggles for black communities in the face of rapid gentrification, shop floor fights in auto factories, and distinct black, gay, women's, Native American, Puerto Rican, Jewish, and environmental movement formations—to name a few—all these issues came together in a rush of energy that also included poetry readings, meetups, protests, and parties. *AYCE* narrated the multidimensional life of a diverse left.

But narrating the movement was not the same as building it. And whereas *AYCE*-adjacent projects sought to bridge the generational and racial divide between a mostly white, Rutgers-affiliated group on the one hand, and mostly black and Puerto Rican long-term residents on the other, not all went according to the young activists' plan. Take, for example, the Peoples' Store, a cooperative grocery store that was founded to be community controlled. Founded in May 1970, by March 1971 there was already intense conflict within the collective and between the collective and its neighbors. While all saw the economic impediments to independent operations, they also perceived their failure as one of community—that is, they didn't have it. The store did not last long, and its operators acknowledged their failure to genuinely engage the community.[48]

In sum, *AYCE* does indeed demonstrate the presence of alternative political organizing. Its base was mostly white, Rutgers-affiliated men who were or had been students at the university. The paper also demonstrates that despite lacking a unified program or sustained organization, the bubbling left attempted to launch an alternative to the probusiness, prodevelopment power structure in the city while linking local and regional left activists to national and global struggles. Sadly, though well intentioned, the left made little headway against its opponents as school segregation, gentrification, and conservative politics prevailed in the city of New Brunswick.

The Question of Impact

This very broad and extremely cursory look at New Brunswick and Rutgers in the 1960s and early 1970s not only seems to confirm Archibald's conclusion that Rutgers was only tangentially related to the city but that as far as the city's politics and policies were concerned, Rutgers did not impact black New Brunswickers or other people of color in a way that imparted agency. As the essays in this volume demonstrate, Rutgers had its hands full changing itself. It took massive amounts of negotiating with a faculty, administration, state legislature, and public that were actively resistant to black inclusion. With Livingston College it added an entirely new campus, and on all of its campuses in New Brunswick and Piscataway (as well as in Newark and Camden), it moved, however haltingly, to make people of color integral.

But this did not happen in the city of New Brunswick. Deindustrialization and suburbanization brought more poverty and desperation to black and brown New Brunswickers, and whites and other elites responded with conservative politics, segregation, police crackdowns, and urban renewal. While not always visible, there was a left-wing movement in New Brunswick and Rutgers that evidenced itself through the *All You Can Eat* periodical. Left-wing activities, though, were not enough to hold off the exodus of black Americans from New Brunswick at the turn of the century. Alice Jennings Archibald died at the end of 2002 after living almost ninety-seven years. Unfortunately, she had lived long enough to see the reverse migration of African Americans out of the city of her childhood.

3

"Tell It Like It Is"

The Rise of a Race-Conscious
Professoriate at Rutgers in the 1960s

JOSEPH WILLIAMS

In October 1963, the *Rutgers Faculty Newsletter* published details of a recent development in the civil rights movement that had garnered national attention. No more than three brief paragraphs long, the article informed faculty of the arrest of Donald Harris, a young black activist and graduate of Rutgers University. Harris had been "imprisoned in Americus, Georgia . . . charged with 'incitement to insurrection' and faces the death penalty."[1] Information about a legal defense fund organized by the National Association for the Advancement of Colored People (NAACP) in Harris's honor also appeared in the article, and editors directed faculty to make donations there, as the NAACP worked diligently "to secure the release of the Rutgers alumnus."[2] They also mentioned Rutgers University president Mason Gross's "wholehearted" support of Harris and his deployment of Bradford Abernathy, the university chaplain, to Georgia as a "character witness" in the case.[3] At the state level, the article noted, US senator Harrison Williams denounced "the police brutality and conditions of confinement" endured by Harris. This careful invoking of President Gross and Senator Williams signaled to Rutgers faculty that Harris's defense elicited support at the highest level of the university's governance.[4]

Subsequent issues of the *Newsletter* provided no updates on the Harris incident and readers really gained no sense of just how many faculty members rallied around their former student, through financial resources or otherwise. Yet Rutgers professors almost certainly possessed a keen awareness of the implications that Donald Harris's incarceration held for race relations at the university. Historian Richard McCormick has argued that his detainment "marked the first faint stirring of efforts to increase the black presence on campus. White consciences had been touched. Soon there were signs, however modest in their immediate consequences, that a new issue was slowly forcing itself onto the crowded agenda of the university."[5] Such a transformation entailed a student-led uprising that climaxed into the takeover of Conklin Hall at the Rutgers–Newark campus on February 21, 1969. Concurrent with the black student protest movement on campus, there existed a dialogue about race among faculty members that played out in the *Newsletter* in contentious ways. This essay delves into the debate and examines how faculty discussed race as the civil rights movement advanced and transformed into the Black Power movement by the late 1960s. It considers the individual research faculty produced, their response to the Gross administration's plans to ensure university compliance with new federal and state laws designed to prevent racial bias in higher education, and their response to Gross's efforts to create a new admissions program to serve disadvantaged high school students from the New Jersey communities of Camden, Newark, New Brunswick, and Piscataway.

The Coming of War: Racial Analysis in the Early Scholarship of Rutgers Faculty

Established in the waning years of World War II, the *Rutgers Faculty Newsletter*—renamed the *Rutgers Newsletter* in 1958—operated as the primary university news feed for professors and staff.[6] Passage of the Servicemen's Readjustment Act in 1944, popularly referred to as the GI Bill, commanded the attention of the administration, then under the direction of Robert Clothier. Much of the *Newsletter*'s content transmitted the university's support for veterans as they reintegrated into society. An abridged version of "The Veteran versus the Professor" in the November 1945 edition of the periodical illustrates just how much matters of war and patriotism consumed the administration and faculty. Written by naval lieutenant Gaynor Pearson and edited by Willard Thompson, a professor and head of the Rutgers Committee on Veterans, the article prescribed specific pedagogical standards for faculty members in their interactions with military students. Pearson called for professors, no matter their area of specialty, to acquire "down-to-earth familiarity with the history of World War II, the invasions and the campaigns; a cognition of the individual student's military background and his experiences . . . and, if time permits, the military record of every veteran in his classroom."[7] Those professors best suited to instruct service personnel would not only institute a more veteran-friendly approach but also voice support for the war and avoid "refuge in an ivory tower."[8] The committee's endorsement of Pearson's analysis, which also characterized veteran students as experienced adults reasonably prone to subordination, constituted an unusual willingness on behalf of the faculty to accommodate a subgroup of the student body.

The onset of the Cold War in the 1950s carried heightened expectations for a pedagogy aligned with patriotism. In fact, Rutgers faculty appreciated little autonomy when it came to the question of national devotion. Out of fear of communist influence among its employees and following a growing trend among state governments, the New Jersey Legislature imposed loyalty oaths on public workers. Rutgers adopted the decree in April 1949, and by June the faculty had questions.[9] What did the state mean by *loyalty*? Did the rule apply to current workers or incoming faculty members only? What happened if a professor violated the policy? Pressure from academics forced President Clothier to commission the Trustee-Alumni Faculty Committee in 1949. Composed of one dean, four trustees, and four professors, the group was charged by the president with clarifying university policy on academic freedom.[10] Two years later the committee published its recommendations to the administration in the *Newsletter*. Only when making public statements as "citizens" were faculty members exempt from reprimand.[11] The use of "citizenship" as a qualifier for immunity from a state mandate seemed absurd enough, but the committee attached an addendum that almost certainly elicited laughter from disgruntled professors and without question weakened the exception. Even as "citizens," the committee suggested, it was incumbent upon all professors to "remember that the public may give special credence to his utterances and may judge his profession and this University by his conduct. He should at all times be accurate and exercise appropriate restraint." If found in violation of the policy, professors faced review by their affiliated department.[12]

Around the same time that the Trustee-Alumni Faculty Committee released its report, Clothier outlined a strategic vision that warned of future devastation for Rutgers because of an impending decline in enrollment and high war-related costs.[13] His bleak outlook was not without reason. Swarms of former militiamen who maximized the GI Bill and matriculated at college in the immediate aftermath of World War II suddenly found themselves confronted with the critical decision to reenlist in the armed forces. Like faculty members, many military students had no choice but to return to the battlefield due to federal conscription. Simeon Moss, a 1941 black alum of the university enrolled in Princeton's MA program in history at the time, suffered this fate in 1950 when the government drafted him for the Korean War one year after earning his degree.[14]

The mass exodus of so-called GI Joes from campuses across the nation posed a potential threat to the economic stability of higher education. Fully aware of the looming financial crisis, Clothier implored the Rutgers community to "retrench where retrenchment is possible, to decline to consider new projects except as they strengthen the war effort."[15] To the faculty, he issued an additional warning. It was inevitable, the president predicted, that the nation and the state will summon Rutgers "to place the . . . intellectual resources of the University at the service of the nation, and when that time comes (and it may come soon) we must not be found wanting."[16] Clothier further instructed the professoriate to resolve any internal conflicts certain to surface with "a high order of statesman-like cooperation" and to avoid "petty bickering." At the same time, he warned, the university "must preserve the essential integrity of our faculty."[17]

Clothier's diplomatic address underscored his position as head of a state-funded institution and his moderate approach to US foreign relations in a period of inevitable tumult. It also hinted at the coming of a different conflict, a battle both distinct from and intertwined with Cold War friction. On the eve of the civil rights movement, Clothier declared that Rutgers would commit to "serving all the people of the State without regard to race, faith, wealth or political party."[18] If that single and rather hackneyed line resonated with any of the *Newsletter*'s readers, it almost certainly raised as many questions as the compulsory loyalty oath. With a faculty body completely devoid of black professors, how did the administration plan to implement a racially diverse agenda? Even if faculty anxieties over wartime academic freedom did not extend to racial integration, the two issues overlapped. In the late 1940s and early '50s, loyalty tests went beyond the halls of academia. Under the guise of the Red Scare, the federal government aggressively surveilled black activists and accused them of communist intentions in sometimes highly publicized forums. Scores of African Americans suffered economic reprisal through the loss of employment, but none of this seemed a point of scholarly interest for the faculty.[19] This willful lack of attention to the domestic war waged on African Americans would soon change. Just as the state handed down its own loyalty mandate, the university hired William Neal Brown, a recipient of the GI Bill and its first black professor.

A member of the celebrated Tuskegee Airmen from World War II, Brown enrolled in Columbia University's graduate program in social work after earning his bachelor's degree from Hampton University, a historically black college and university (HBCU) located in Virginia.[20] Immediately after graduation from Columbia in 1950, Brown studied for a doctorate at the City University of New York and settled in Montclair, New Jersey, where he gained employment as a social worker with the Newark Veteran's Administration (VA) office. In this capacity, Brown monitored and supervised student social workers from a trio of colleges, including Columbia and Rutgers. He was so effective in this position that the director of the VA promoted him, and his diligent reputation eventually reached administrators at the Rutgers Department of Social Work. Brown later recounted his experience at the VA—how the job entailed frequent visits "to Rutgers to meet with the people who supervised the students I was working with and I went to a couple of meetings and I enjoyed it." He continued: "Someone who worked at Rutgers said, 'I hear these people talk

FIGURE 3.1 William Neal Brown seated in the center front with military unit in Montclair, NJ.

William Neal Brown Photo Gallery, Rutgers Oral History Archives

when you're not here. I believe they're gonna offer you a job.'"[21] Skeptical of the murmurs, Brown dismissed the messenger until "sure enough, I got a little note one day" from the Graduate School of Social Work inviting him to interview for a position as an assistant professor in 1956.[22] The offer of employment marked the first time the university had hired an African American in any of its academic departments.

Brown only briefly acknowledged the symbolic nature of his appointment, merely exclaiming "I was the first black person hired as a professor . . . I enjoyed working at Rutgers."[23] His modest reaction was still more than what the *Newsletter* printed. For such a historic occasion, the newly minted young black professor attracted little attention from his colleagues. Quite possibly the editors viewed Brown's appointment as a long overdue step in the right direction. Perhaps they simply overlooked the appointment. In any case, the silence mirrored a pattern in the *Newsletter* traceable to its first issue in which racial affairs took a back seat to the problem of war and nationalism even as the federal government's public harassment of black civil rights activists intensified, most prominently with Rutgers alum Paul Robeson.

Through a series of pivotal moments on a national and local stage—Emmett Till's brutal murder at the hands of white southerners in Money, Mississippi, during the summer of 1954; Rosa Parks's calculated refusal to relinquish her seat on a segregated bus in Montgomery Alabama, one year later; and Willie Neal Brown's unprecedented appointment as assistant professor in 1956—the *Newsletter* and faculty remained mum. Yet the dearth of coverage dedicated to racism changed as the civil rights movement advanced. Professors in the law school and the humanities ramped up their analyses of race relations. Under new leadership in the form of the Mason Gross administration (1959–1971) and with mounting pressure from black students, Rutgers also witnessed the incremental hiring of black academics. These factors resulted in more substantial faculty engagement with race. Conversations rose above the "petty bickering" that Clothier had cautioned against but exposed a panic among some white faculty members as a cadre of Rutgers affiliates made the case for a complete overhaul of the university.

Articles in the *Newsletter* during the early 1960s alluded to the rise of an emergent professoriate conscious of race. One item published in October 1960 mentioned law professor David Haber's participation in a conference on the sit-ins that swept the nation after black students attempted to integrate the lunch counter at Woolworth's in Greensboro, North Carolina, several months earlier.[24] Haber's involvement in the meeting seemed a natural extension of his research. His article "The Scopes Case in Modern Dress," jointly published with Thomas Emerson in the *University of Chicago Law Review,* explored problems related to the separation of church and state, freedom of expression, and civil liberties. While not focused on the civil rights movement, the study probed some of the fundamental legal questions at the center of race relations in the mid-twentieth century.[25] In the wake of Haber's death in 2018, Peter Simmons, a former dean in the law school, characterized his colleague as a subversive academic who possessed "very limited patience with bureaucracy, be it law school, Newark campus, or that emanating from New Brunswick." Haber, he said, bemoaned administrative oversight and "firmly believed that faculties were self-governing institutions."[26]

Not all faculty members shared Haber's disdain for the higher-ups even as they waded into the political issues of the day. Brown, for example, marched a few times but summarized his involvement in the civil rights movement as "not very much."[27] At Rutgers, he retained a mild-mannered, nonconfrontational disposition and seldom clashed with the administration. The lone black professor instead filtered his political views through scholarly exchanges. An unexpected invitation to debate Malcolm X thrust the reticent Brown into the spotlight when Harris, then a newly enrolled Rutgers student, met the prominent proponent of black separatism at a Student Nonviolent Coordinating Committee (SNCC) meeting in New York.

Malcolm X had spent two years touring college campuses when he spoke at the SNCC meeting in 1961. His itinerary included visits to Harvard Law School, the City College of New York, and Clark College, among others, and his agenda pitted him against residential or visiting professors in a debate format. Large crowds of students hungry for a radical alternative to the non-violent Christian philosophy of Martin Luther King Jr. gathered at every stop to hear the charismatic activist's rationale behind racial separatism.[28] After Harris drew Malcolm's attention, and with the help of his peers and the local chapter of the NAACP, the energetic and ambitious student managed to secure him for a debate at Rutgers in November 1961.[29] Brown recalled how the law school professor originally scheduled to rebut Malcolm canceled after learning of plans by Richard Nixon to nominate him for a seat on the United States Superior Court should the former vice president ascend to the presidency in the future. "I've been asked not to do this," he recalled his colleague saying. "The students say that you're the person that should be debating him." Brown initially refused the request, but later accepted it out of an affinity with intellectual exchanges.[30]

Two weeks before the event, Brown studied the talking points Malcolm used in his prior debates, which were centered on reparations and community control for African Americans. In his counterstatements, Brown touted the philosophical ideas of writer Langston Hughes, inscribed in the poem "I, Too."[31] Composed in 1926 during the Harlem Renaissance, "I, Too" articulated a black claim to national identity despite racial discrimination. More optimistic than advocates of black separatism, the fictional character in "I, Too" is convinced that the nation's mistreatment of "the darker brother" will someday bear shame for whites. "They will see how beautiful we are," the poet concluded.[32] This idealism contrasted well with the strident cynicism fundamental to black separatist ideology, but it failed to persuade the audience. One student, Edwin Stevens, praised Malcolm's performance, stating that his points "awakened and delighted the apathetic and sleeping among us."[33] Stevens's assessment is hard to discount. Not much time would elapse between the debate and the set of demonstrations that gave rise to black student petitions for greater cultural representation at Rutgers. The Brown–Malcolm X dialogue precipitated a sustained effort by students to overturn racial inequities in every fabric of the university. Most faculty members, unlike the cautious Brown, eagerly joined the fray.

Shortly after the *Newsletter* informed Rutgers faculty of the Harris incident, its editors showcased research on racial issues in a flurry of articles published in the 1963–1964 academic year. On his way to Georgia to attest to Harris's upstanding record, Bradford Abernathy participated in a conference on civil rights at Howard University. In December, the *Newsletter* reported

FIGURE 3.2 Professor William Neal Brown and colleagues in the School of Social Work.

Courtesy of Special Collections & University Archives, Rutgers University

his trip in its "University Notebook" section, which had typically lacked any race-related content.[34] The subsequent issue reported on Harry V. Barnard, a professor in the Department of Education, and his speech on "Race, Religion, and the Kennedy Education Bill."[35] In the February installment of "University Notebook," the *Newsletter* announced Harry Schapiro's receipt of an award from the predominantly black Tenth Street Baptist Church in Camden.[36] Schapiro, a political scientist, had been a staunch advocate for black and Jewish rights both outside of and within the classroom. A former student and later a professor in the Department of Political Science, Jay Sigler remembered how Schapiro's lectures "excoriated racism and anti-semitism and warned six generations of students that law must be founded in justice and that human rights were fundamental to the working of any civilized political system."[37] The radical Charles V. Hamilton, also a political scientist, embraced a similar philosophy.

Considered a pioneer of race, ethnicity, and politics (REP), a subfield of political science, Hamilton coupled his teaching at Rutgers in the 1960s with community activism. In March 1964, the *Newsletter* reported that he had delivered a speech on "Civil Rights Laws: Recent Results and Future Needs."[38] The brief snippet revealed little about Hamilton's ideas, which were expanded on in his groundbreaking work *Black Power: The Politics of Liberation in America* (1967). Coauthored with Black Power activist Stokely Carmichael, Hamilton expressed a need to "speak forcefully and truthfully" as "the whole question of race is one that America would much rather not face honestly and squarely."[39] Bringing racial issues to the forefront of the nation's landscape required a "rejection" of language that alluded to "progress" or cautioned blacks against insurgent behavior.[40] Texts authored by black thinkers considered revolutionary for their time, including Frederick Douglass and Frantz Fanon, underpinned Hamilton's thesis. He insisted that readers regard the book as a "framework," as opposed to a "blueprint," for racial equality.[41]

Hamilton departed Rutgers before the release of *Black Power* but attributed the project's genesis to his early activism in Lowndes County, Alabama, during Carmichael's campaign to secure black voting rights. This work in the South ultimately led to employment at Rutgers when Hamilton's association with Black Power activists drew the attention of the Federal Bureau of Investigation (FBI). Labeled a communist, the outspoken scholar was fired from his teaching position at Tuskegee University. At the suggestion of his wife, Hamilton decided to forgo another position and instead pursued doctoral studies at the University of Chicago, graduating in 1964.[42] He worked at Rutgers University next before leaving for Lincoln University, where he first pitched the idea of a collaboration to Carmichael.[43] Upon its publication, *Black Power,* according to Hamilton's estimates, sold at 5,000 copies per week. Political scientists hailed it as a canonical text in the field, and the book remains a celebrated treatise of black political consciousness.[44]

The monograph's wide reception at the time probably spoke volumes to Carmichael's popularity more than anything else, but its influence in scholarly circles was symptomatic of a new trend in academia. With the rise of the Black Power movement in the latter half of the 1960s, researchers who were invested in a conceptual deconstruction of the race problem upended a methodological approach that had treated African Americans as mere objects of a racially stratified society. They called for studies that centered on the voices and experiences of black people. This new wave of scholarship detracted from white subjects and authenticated the writings of black thinkers in an analysis of race. Quoting the radical political philosopher Frantz Fanon in *Black Power,* Hamilton pressed for the "starting of a new history" in which black intellectuals marshal the collective experiences of African descendants the world over in the name of "Black Power."[45] Trained as a student to believe in limited government—that "government is best which governs least"—Hamilton inverted the idea and insisted that "government is best which governs most."[46] Political science was best studied as a discipline first and foremost concerned with black people. In other words, Hamilton deemed the study of political science synonymous with the study of race and ethnicity.[47] So convinced was Hamilton of the need for scholars across disciplines to subsume the study of black people under already established fields that he challenged Winthrop Jordan about the historian's embrace of African American history. "I told him that African American history was American history," Hamilton recalled.[48]

Had the opinionated political scientist remained at Rutgers, he almost certainly would have quarreled with Rutgers history professor Eugene Genovese as well. Part of an emerging group of scholars engaged in a revisionist history of enslaved blacks, Genovese became the subject of national scrutiny when he openly denounced the Vietnam War and proclaimed a Marxist affiliation at a "teach-in" held in Scott Hall in 1965. While he fulminated against the government, the historian also embarked on a novel investigation of black plantation life. The *Newsletter* documented this activity in 1966 when Genovese delivered a paper, "Rebelliousness and Docility in the Negro Slave: A Critique of the Elkins Thesis," at the annual meeting of the Association for the Study of Negro Life and History.[49] The paper constituted one of the first challenges to historian Stanley Elkins and his work *Slavery: A Problem in American Institutional and Intellectual Life* (1959).

Using methods in psychology, sociology, and history, Elkins had argued that the antebellum South resigned enslaved African Americans to a puerile state, unable to function intellectually or physically independent of the slaveholder.[50] Genovese undermined the characterization by emphasizing what he perceived as the intimate relationships fostered between enslaved blacks and white slaveholders. Based on a Marxist critique, and expanded upon in his monograph *Roll, Jordan, Roll: The World the Slaves Made* (1974), Genovese defined slavery as a form of hegemonic paternalism with whites expecting "the involuntary labor of the slaves as a legitimate return . . . for their protection and direction."[51] Predicated on "mutual obligations—duties, responsibilities, and ultimately even rights," paternalism humanized blacks at the same time that it facilitated their subjugation.[52] The ability to extract value from bondage compelled enslaved blacks to temper their impulse for a violent overthrow of the institution, and Genovese argued that African Americans opted instead for more subtle forms of resistance—sometimes to the point of accommodating the slaveholder.[53]

Historians have since rejected the claims in *Roll, Jordan, Roll,* among them
Rutgers professor Deborah Gray White in her seminal monograph *Ar'n't I a
Woman: Female Slaves in the Plantation South* (1985) and Rutgers alum Stephanie
Jones-Rogers in the more recent *They Were Her Property: White Women as Slave
Owners* (2019).[54] In the 1960s, however, historians praised Genovese's intervention in the larger account of racial discourse during the culture wars that
unfolded in the ivory tower. When the civil rights and Black Power movements
spawned a cultural turn in the humanities, Rutgers faculty, some more successfully than others, tapped into new archives and charted the political, cultural,
and social contributions of African Americans of the past. The works of Harry
Barnard, Charles Hamilton, and the controversial Eugene Genovese forged
a new academic frontier. Analyses of race no longer seemed an anomaly in
faculty scholarship. The *Newsletter*'s recording of race studies, however scant,
added another layer of visibility. Previously mute on racial issues, its editors
broadcasted faculty participation in academic conferences, government task
forces, and community meetings principally concerned with addressing racial
inequities. This coverage drastically increased when the editors reshaped the
periodical in the aftermath of the race riots that devastated Newark and other
major cities across the nation in the summer of 1967.

A (Not So) New Venture:
White Paternalism and Intellectual Panic

On the first page of the September 1967 issue of the *Newsletter* appeared the
headline "Introducing—A New Venture." The article enumerated the *Newsletter*'s success over the past twenty-three years and promised a greater attempt
by the editors "to report more thoroughly on the major changes and policy
decisions in all divisions of Rutgers."[55] Under the new structure, a faculty
review board would oversee the periodical's ideological direction. Editors
also guaranteed frequent reports by state and federal legislators with a direct
impact on the university. This change supplied Rutgers professors with invaluable insight into the political process behind racial integration at the university, but one additional innovation enabled their active participation in the
dialogue. Instead of simply listing research activity in the form of a "University Notebook," as it had done in the past, the editors implemented "In My
Opinion," a column opened to authorship "by faculty and staff members on
matters of general concern." Submissions immediately poured into the *Newsletter*.[56] Still reeling from images of the hot summer in a Newark engulfed in
racial conflict, guest authors used the first few columns to tackle what faculty
referred to as the "urban crisis." This theme was more than momentary, however. Indeed, for the remainder of the 1960s, race emerged as *the* "matter of
general concern" among the professoriate.

George Sternlieb, a research director in the Graduate School of Business, had just completed a study on urban housing market conditions when the US Senate summoned him to provide expert testimony on the factors that led to the Newark riots. For the inaugural "In My Opinion" entry, the *Newsletter* reprinted his statements. Politicians had attributed the incident to long-term racial disparities, but these legislators had misdiagnosed the problem, Sternlieb argued. Black Newarkers lacked access to the forms of "economic elevation which other American ethnic groups have used."[57] Economic repression—not racial subordination—produced the riots. Even scholars who cited poverty as one primary factor seemed amiss when they framed the episode as a fight against middle-class values. Sure, the riots incurred millions of dollars in property damage, but black-owned businesses in every city remained untouched. This strategic targeting of white stores by the protesters indicated to Sternlieb the black community's desire for upward mobility, if only granted the opportunity by those in power.[58] The government had a responsibility to respond, and Sternlieb proposed a new Homestead Act as the best course of action. He reasoned that prior legislation geared toward home ownership created "the first middle-class farmer backbone," and a revised act would almost guarantee the same outcome for the black community.[59] But for African Americans to benefit, they must denounce the propensity for Black Power. In Sternlieb's view, Black Power hampered black prospects of economic mobility through white means.[60]

Sternlieb's confidence in Congress to remedy black economic hardships denoted a trust in the government many black activists had shed by the late 1960s. Few white scholars at Rutgers could understand the level of pessimism at the core of black insurgency. Malcolm Talbott witnessed it firsthand, however, when high school students in central Camden responded with apprehension to the university's pitch for a college tour. In his column "Universities Must Confront Challenge of Urban Ills," the vice president voiced frustration at the persistent "'salesmanship' it takes to convince a child in the ghetto that he could ever belong in these bright new buildings."[61] Determined to engage the residents, Talbott read their skepticism as even more of a reason that the university should refashion itself as an "urban" institution. He praised some of the departments that exemplified the type of inner-city presence he envisioned for Rutgers, including the Graduate School of Education's partnership with the Camden Board of Education and the drama school's efforts to "give these children an inkling of the cultural experiences they have been denied thus far."[62] Talbott especially valued the public school collaboration for seeking community participation "on the assumption that a child's home experience directly affects his performance in the classroom."[63] He urged the university to take this outreach one step further and plaster the label *urban* on some of its facilities. Not only would the designation lead to more federal funding, but it "could truly carve new paths for those seeking to ease the urban crisis" as well.[64]

Rutgers faculty and administration frequently employed the terms *urban, ghetto,* and *disadvantaged* as euphemisms for *blacks.* Although commonly used at the time in academia and in popular culture, their dialogic function in the *Newsletter* reflected much more than colloquial norms. Too grave of a crisis to ignore, the rhetoric conveyed the university's perception of black poverty as an urgent and inescapable intellectual imperative. Talbott and several other professors painted the most alarming picture of black inner-city life. The *Newsletter* contributed to this depiction, such as when it reproduced images from the reading materials used in the Graduate School of Education's Design Urban Education Project. Captioned with the bold headline "TELL IT LIKE IT IS," the photos showed four school-aged black boys resigned to the hazardous conditions of urban play areas.[65]

All told, it would seem that children frolicked in debris-ridden social spaces, youth lacked cross-cultural competency skills, adults failed at parenting, and the entire black community suffered from an intellectual deficiency. These observations, photos, and the accompanying rhetoric spawned a panic at Rutgers. Faculty members urgently championed much-needed vital reforms to the educational system while fearing that an influx of the "disadvantaged" threatened the intellectual rigor of the college. Unable to disassociate the crisis from the character of black students, professors urged the university to act quickly—and cautiously.

As faculty began to signal a willingness to act on issues around race in New Jersey and the country at large, so, too, did students on all three Rutgers University campuses. In February 1968, a group of students concerned about the slow pace of progress toward racial equity approached Talbott and offered their help in recruiting black students, because the university had not been successful in doing so despite implementing new recruitment policies as early as 1965.[66] Called the Black Organization of Students (BOS), the group met later that month with faculty and administrators on the Newark campus to voice their discontent on issues such as low black student enrollment, the small number of black faculty, and the lack of courses and library material of relevance to them.

At the same time BOS leaders first approached Talbott in February 1968, the University Committee on Equal Opportunity issued a statement proposing changes that aimed to admit more "deprived students" from "minority groups," hire staff from minority groups, better train current staff to give attention to "the problems of deprived persons," recruit minority group faculty from both inside and outside academia, develop minority group graduate students into faculty members, and use the University Extension Division and Cooperative

"I'm going up on that roof.
Maybe I can find something
to play with up there."
He started climbing up.

Adam sat down in the back.
He let his little brother
steer with the wheel.

FIGURES 3.3 AND 3.4 An example of the way African Americans were depicted in the 1960s, these pictures and captions are illustrative of the way social scientists portrayed the hopelessness of urban black life, "Tell It Like It Is," *Rutgers Newsletter*, November 3, 1967.

Courtesy of Special Collections & University Archives, Rutgers University

Extension Service to educate the community at large about the importance of equal opportunity.[67] The archive leaves no record of which individuals served on that committee, but it is reasonable to assume that it was composed of faculty members given that its recommendations covered admissions and faculty recruitment, both of which were in the purview of faculty at that time. Yet while the substance of this particular statement largely dovetails with the initial demands of BOS, relations between the administration, the faculty, and the black students on campus would become contentious, with friction over goals and priorities that were not in alignment and differences over implementation and pace of change.

Other units of the university were also moved to act. In March 1968, Livingston professors "voted to place special emphasis upon attracting and educating disadvantaged students." Spearheaded by Robert Zimmerman, a professor in the Department of Philosophy, the plan involved "the use of special programs, lightened course loads and other compensatory activities which may seem appropriate, with an attitude which is critical but flexible."[68] On the Camden campus, the Society for the Promotion of Ending Northern Discrimination (SPEND) produced three white papers and submitted them to the Board of Governors. The studies recommended several improvements to Rutgers–Camden, then the College of South Jersey. SPEND especially highlighted the poor conditions of the science building and advised the university to immediately outline plans for a replacement. The organization also reported that students and faculty members desired interaction with a greater portion of South Jersey and for Rutgers–Camden to evolve into a residential campus.[69]

Their complaints echoed the views of Jay Sigler, the Schapiro eulogist and a longtime professor in the Department of Political Science. Having taught at all three campuses, Sigler wrote a letter to the *Newsletter*'s editors that accused Rutgers of denying Camden students the superlatives typically associated with a "liberal education." Unlike New Brunswick's campus, Camden possessed no "athletic program," no "artistic functions," and no "meeting halls and places at which speakers may meet large groups."[70] Sigler chalked up the university's neglect of Camden to the campus's status as an "urban" and "commuter" school. He argued that the discourse facilitated by New Brunswick faculty in the *Newsletter* offered a narrow conceptualization of both labels, "to the extent that any conception is held."[71] Excessively focused on New Brunswick, a residential campus, many professors equated *urban* with *nonresidential*. He challenged his colleagues to reimagine *urban* for a more inclusive transformation of the university. Fed up, Sigler questioned, "Should we not take account of the fact that most of the students attending Rutgers in Camden come from backgrounds lacking in profound social and cultural values? Should not Rutgers help these students compensate for the weaknesses of their home environments?"[72] His strongly worded letter may have indicted faculty members for their myopic view of *urban,* but nevertheless reinforced the notion of black intellectual and cultural impairment foundational to a revamp of the university.

With an exigent sense of the need to reform both the system and the students, Rutgers faculty continued to broach the topic of racial equality. Many professors inflamed the situation by proffering that the university had, in fact, arrived late to the conversation. In his diatribe, Sigler surmised that programs for the "disadvantaged" already existed at Temple, Drexel, and other area colleges. At least on the question of diverse textbooks, Herbert Kells, the assistant provost of Livingston College, disagreed. Eurocentric curriculums, in addition to a paucity of black students, constituted the standard in a plurality of New Jersey colleges situated in "ghetto" areas. Kells, an experienced higher education administrator, attributed the problems to subpar training for white teachers.[73]

Once again, student leaders stepped in to move the faculty from conversation to action. On April 19, 1968, black student representatives from all three campuses appeared before the Rutgers Board of Governors (BOG) and presented a "List of Grievances and Demands."[74] The list had fourteen items and noted the "grossly inadequate" number of black students, black deans, and black administrators at Rutgers; called for the creation of an Afro-American studies department, a black culture institute, and more representation of contemporary black authors at the libraries, bookstore, and student centers; demanded the investigation of the "discriminatory practices" of the campus patrol; asked for a reevaluation of the grading system and better dissemination of information about tutorial programs; requested a black dormitory and permission to found a black fraternity; sought to rename the student center for Paul Robeson, the "Noblest Black Son of Rutgers," and to formally recognize other black alumni; and called for the creation of a scholarship committee that included black members and a permanent committee of university administrators and black students that would foster ongoing dialogue.

The board agreed in principle that many of the students' demands needed to be addressed, yet left it to the individual campuses to implement them. In a letter to the university provost Richard Schlatter, advertising executive and Board of Governors trustee Charles H. Brower wrote that although the BOS representatives were "over-demanding and less than friendly, I still believe we must look at the situation calmly, and judge what is best for the university."[75] He went on to address each of the fourteen BOS demands, either agreeing they should be feasible for the BOG to meet or, with regard to creating an Afro-American studies department and reevaluating the grading system, agreeing in principle but noting such changes could only be made by the administration and faculty. Interestingly, the only point on which Brower openly disagreed was on the renaming of the student center for Paul Robeson, a change the BOG had the power to make. Robeson's reputation among many Americans had at that time been tarnished because of his supposed support for communism.[76] Brower noted that while he personally had no negative feelings about Robeson, "it would be politically disastrous for Rutgers," which might impede efforts "to do more than a minimum for the Black students themselves."[77] This comment was both prescient and shortsighted. Brower clearly anticipated there would be political hurdles to transforming the university, but his hope that rejecting this one demand might stave off the backlash was quite futile.

Shortly after the BOG meeting, the Rutgers news service issued a press release defending the university's response—past and present—to the question of "Negro participation in the university at all levels," reporting that while things had not been moving as fast as they would like, there had been "substantial progress" in implementing new policies.[78] The structure of the release, which quoted Provost Schlatter, largely mirrored that of Brower's letter. It addressed BOS demands one by one, listing changes that were or would be underway to address concerns about admissions, faculty and staff recruitment, curricular and cultural changes, scholarship funds, academic support, open dialogue with college deans, black student housing, and the creation of a black fraternity. The press release did not mention the students' demand for an investigation of the campus patrol and rejected the renaming of the student center for Paul Robeson, claiming building names were only changed with the support of a "major donor."[79] It closed with a reminder from Schlatter that the February 1968 statement from the University Equal Opportunities Committee referenced earlier was university policy.

The tone of the press release, including Schlatter's statements, was largely matter-of-fact, with no sweeping pronouncements on the importance of racial justice and equity. Yet it is hard to imagine that the assassination of Martin Luther King Jr., which happened just weeks before the black students presented their grievances, did not influence the administration's and trustees' initially positive response to the students after years of foot-dragging. A draft statement about the assassination prepared for Mason Gross called the act "a great loss, not only in the death of a dedicated leader of his people, but also in the irreparable damage to our national prestige and our individual reputations. None of us can escape a share of the blame for this tragedy."[80] Gross expressed here a sense of personal responsibility, and in using the words *prestige* and *reputation* may have been providing a rationale for his own response to black student demands and protests in the years to come.

In addition to their own feelings about the assassination, there is no doubt that members of the Board of Governors and the university administration were listening to the sorrow and anger of students. The predominantly white Rutgers Student Council convened a special meeting in the days after the assassination to honor King's memory, at which they passed several motions intended to achieve "racial harmony in the Rutgers community."[81] A typed copy of the Student Council's statement announcing these motions appears in the archived Mason Gross papers with a handwritten note of unknown origin reading "Motions Applicable at the Board of Governors Level" along with a list of numbers corresponding to seven of the motions.[82] The minutes of that Student Council meeting list all motions passed; the seven motions noted by hand on the statement are starred in pen on the minutes. The starred motions address the creation of an Africana studies department, the establishment of a black fraternity chapter, the creation of dorm space for black students, the suspension of campus groups that had discriminatory policies or engaged in racist activities, the renaming of the student center in honor of Paul Robeson, the issuing of a formal welcome to Paul Robeson should he choose to speak on campus, and the halt of construction on the National Football Hall of Fame until the question of Robeson's membership was "satisfied to the satisfaction of the student body."[83] The similarity between the Rutgers Student Council's motions and the grievances and demands raised by the BOS less than two weeks later are striking and suggest contact between the two organizations. The annotated documents suggest someone in the administration, if not Gross himself, was paying attention to and sympathizing with what they had to say.

Fear that student unrest would result from grief and anger over Dr. King's murder may also have played a role in the decision of the Board of Governors and Mason Gross to strike a cooperative tone with the Black Organization of Students. The Newark uprising of July 1967 was recent and traumatic, and campus violence was happening around the country.[84] Self-identifying as "White" and "Black," two groups of Douglass College students issued separate, strongly worded statements denouncing King's murder and decrying racism. The white Douglass College students committed themselves to continuing King's "militant, non-violent struggle against white racism, at whatever cost" (underlined in original).[85] The black students of Douglass College denounced white apathy supporting white racism and stated, "Black people are being destroyed, exploited, held down and held back, and deprived of all rights and equal opportunities. WE, BLACK PEOPLE, HAVE REACHED A BREAKING POINT" (uppercase letters in original).[86] As was the case that the Rutgers Student Council's motions closely aligned with the soon-to-be-voiced demands of the Black Organization of Students, so, too, did these separate statements demonstrate similarities in style and tone and suggest collaboration. These obvious networks among students would have signaled to university leadership that a student movement was in the making, one they may have hoped to preempt or contain with conciliation.

After the initial pledges of support, the university's efforts toward equal opportunity did continue. The changes were more incremental than transformational, however. Ten "action-oriented committees" were established, composed of faculty, students, administrators, and community members;

three admissions officers were hired to specialize in minority recruitment; and talent search and other special admissions programs were instituted, accompanied by summer orientation and preparatory programs for students admitted through those programs. The university in 1968 hired twenty black faculty members and fourteen black and Puerto Rican staff members, and a recruitment and training program for clerical workers was put into place. New curricular and community programs were instituted, and the university's expenditure on "equal opportunity purposes" grew from a few thousand dollars to $850,000.[87]

Agreeing in principle to initiatives like recruiting black faculty was not as challenging as implementing those initiatives, given the glaring whiteness of the university as a whole. Newly formed partnerships with HBCUs indicated that the lack of faculty dexterity with urban students was on the Gross administration's radar. In February 1968, the Graduate School of Education collaborated with Jackson State University in Mississippi in an attempt to "learn much from the faculty there about how to educate people from deprived backgrounds."[88] Herbert Kells organized the partnership and modeled it after a program at what was then the State University of New York at Binghamton (today's Binghamton University), which he helped to established before coming to Rutgers. Yet Kells also argued that the need to form partnerships with HBCUs or train faculty members to teach black students pointed to racial disparities in faculty hiring. Almost ten years after the university appointed William Neal Brown, the composition of full-time tenure-track faculty members at Rutgers skewed toward white academics. Kells encouraged the university to prioritize faculty diversity, a task undertaken three years earlier only for the Gross administration to dawdle.

Led by Kells and Educational Opportunity Committees on each campus, the recruitment drive yielded a host of black scholars comprising 1.5 percent of the full-time professors. Faculty-exchange programs with North Carolina A&T State University also resulted in an increase of black academics.[89] Pleased with the results, Kells expressed hope that the HBCU partnerships and line items in the budget reserved for faculty hiring would attract even more scholars of color.[90] On the administrative level, Mason Gross lured the young John R. Martin to be assistant provost, charged with overseeing faculty appointments and promotions.[91] The Graduate School of Education also made efforts to increase black faculty presence when it established the Martin Luther King Jr. Lecture Series in October 1968. Eight black scholars visited the university, including Bennetta Washington, one of the few black women faculty members hired, and Samuel DeWitt Proctor, the renowned educator and cultural critic who became the first incumbent of the Martin Luther King Jr. Chair when the university permanently instituted the professorship on the first anniversary of the civil rights icon's death in 1969.[92]

FIGURE 3.5 Professor Samuel DeWitt Proctor advising students Roberta Williams and Nathaniel Boclair, 1972.

Courtesy of Special Collections & University Archives, Rutgers University

Black students had successfully demanded an increase of black faculty, but their protest movement also directly influenced how Rutgers debated race in the *Newsletter.* Opinion columns suddenly turned from a view of black students in need of institutional guidance to a question of student power and dissent in college hierarchies. The shift was inevitable given the widespread feeling of discontent evoked by the politically dominant Students for a Democratic Society (SDS) and the local Black Organization of Students. In the academic year 1968–1969, black students literally seized control of Rutgers, most notably in the takeover of Conklin Hall. Yet their continual insistence on black faculty hiring and their refusal to waver on black studies as a viable discipline disrupted the paternalism that had informed so much of the professoriate's intellectual gaze just as much.

"Whose World?": From Paternalism to Power

Rosemary Park, the vice chancellor at the University of California–Los Angeles, obviously had the student protest movement on her mind when she questioned

"Whose World?" in her address to Douglass students at their Fiftieth Anniversary Convocation in 1968. Reprinted in the *Newsletter,* Park's speech homed in on the politically charged milieu that had engulfed postsecondary institutions as students asserted their rights to define college culture. Park argued that faculty–student relationships had devolved into a state of chaos because both parties "seem to be saying there is no way of communicating today about our vested interests."[93] She encouraged a resuscitation of rational discourse cutting across race, age, and status.[94] Milton Schwebel, dean of the Graduate School of Education, proposed a similar resolution but outright charged faculty members with abuse of power. He likened professors to mothers and fathers responsible for guiding children into independent adulthood. The most successful parents, he noted, allowed adolescents to question the power dynamics inherent to a domestic setting.[95]

Meanwhile, Richard Poirier, chair of the English Department, provocatively suggested that students not only question power structures but also subdue them. His biting column castigated Rutgers as an institution "too often run by fat cats" and dependent on professors with no interest in innovative scholarship.[96] Learning meant that "the university would be a place where curricula are discovered anew, perhaps every year or so."[97] The fact that students in every region of the country had collectively voiced their dissatisfaction with university norms implied that the creative processes crucial to academia had slowed. Poirier concluded that "what would be hoped for is *more* [emphasis his] disruption, and therefore more questioning and answering than one would ever get."[98]

While Poirier chastised dispirited faculty and pushed for students to topple the university, other staff members fiercely lobbied the New Jersey Legislature and Rutgers for more aid to African Americans. At a forum on civil disorders sponsored by the Rutgers Urban Studies Center, an unofficial black caucus group stormed the podium and pleaded for "a State takeover of Newark public schools, funds for black self-development, corporations in ghettos, and the appointment of Negroes" in the governor's administration.[99] In front of the governor and a predominantly white audience, Robert Curvin, an administrator at the Rutgers Community Action Intern Program, blamed black abject poverty on "white racism." The state's meager allocation of resources to urban areas, if any at all, had starved African Americans. Curvin warned that blacks now functioned on "impatience and despair."[100] His language also alluded to a state of emergency in the black community, but it thwarted the image of black urban depravity so fundamental to white characterizations of the urban crisis.

An earlier announcement from the dean of admissions demonstrated that administrators in other sectors of the university sought distance from the problematic rhetoric as well. For the upcoming academic year, the university had admitted more than one hundred students through a special program.

Most of the prospects identified as black. Although the *Newsletter*'s headline read "Rutgers Opens Doors to 150 Disadvantaged Students," the opening paragraph repudiated *disadvantaged, deprived,* and *poor* as terms that "hide, as much as reveal, the grim reality that these are youngsters with good intellectual potential who probably wouldn't have made it to the State University without special efforts by the University to find and enroll them."[101] Hardly a retraction of previous racist language, the statement, to a degree, constituted a notable pivot from the university's premature construction of black students. The new connotation chalked their handicap squarely up to societal neglect. Resources alone, as opposed to a combination of resources and reform, would ameliorate economic burdens in black communities. On top of the new cohort, Rutgers took seriously a study conducted by Warren Susman in the Department of History that implored the university to troubleshoot its liberal arts program and entertain a "special, nonsegregated college" for urban enrollees.[102]

However, in the academic year following the King assassination and after subsequent pledges to further the goals of equal opportunity, the number of African American and Latinx students enrolled at Rutgers University remained abysmally low, a glaring representation of exclusion and inequality. Overall, black enrollment at Rutgers University went from 1.96 percent in 1967–1968 to 2.77 percent in 1968–1969. The largest black enrollment was at Douglass and Newark Colleges, with 4.1 and 4.4 percent African American enrollment, respectively. The lowest was at the flagship College Avenue campus, with black men making up only 1.49 percent of the all-male student body. And although the data for "Spanish surnamed" students were unavailable for the 1967–1968 academic year, "Spanish surnamed" students made up only 0.97 percent of the overall student body in 1968–1969.[103]

Some faculty recoiled at even this modest influx of black and Latinx students and the accommodations the university created to ensure their academic success. The backlash was most apparent in the *Newsletter.* Harry Bredemeier, chair of the Sociology Department, voiced frustration over what he perceived as "an abandonment of academic values."[104] Rutgers had conceded so much ground that students now ran amok throughout the institution. Particularly in the case of race, the university had allowed black students to manipulate white guilt, "'telling-whitey-how-things-look-from-black-eyes.'"[105] More to the point, Black Power had "imprisoned" black students and robbed them of the intellectual promise of higher education. Bredemeier compared black student indignation to a minstrel show and accused white liberals of self-deprecation through an uninhibited overindulgence with black suffering. This fetishization with black suffering blinded whites to the perils of Black Power and forced them to adopt a "defensive anti-intellectualism." The entire university, in Bredemeier's view, had descended into a state of ignorance, an "ominous" sign that administrators must heed.[106]

Less apocalyptic in his column, George Sternlieb nevertheless carried similar concerns. Since his testimony to Congress the previous year, black students had made only slight inroads in their struggle for equality. Yet from his viewpoint, society now fawned over their plight. In the *Newsletter*, Sternlieb lamented the exclusive application of the category *disadvantaged* to racial minorities and argued that blacks had become the privileged, achieving economic progress "at the cost of the lower and lower middle incomed [*sic*] whites."[107] This was an odd assessment given his earlier economic explanation for the urban crisis, but made sense for a public policy professor never sold on the idea of black radicalism as a vehicle for social change. Sternlieb quite possibly found it inexplicable, and unsettling, that a growing segment of the black student body had in fact secured some victories through the use of the strategies of Black Power. Rather than concede the possibility of a faulty thesis, Sternlieb cried foul. As did most whites who balked at black nationalism, he reaffirmed his support of racial justice but concluded that equality in higher education "must involve much more than a simplistic making up of past errors towards blacks and Puerto Ricans—it must also be involved in the welding of white society."[108] Otherwise, special treatment for racial minorities amounted to reverse racism.

Rutgers, of course, had already devoted so much to the "welding of white society." From the dormitories to the classrooms, whiteness pervaded every corner of the university. For an intellectually empowered black student population, whiteness seemed especially egregious in the curriculum. To the dismay of some professors, calls for the establishment of black studies as a separate academic unit increased. Writing to the *Newsletter*, Dean Arnold Grobman vehemently rejected the idea because of its resemblance to "separatism . . . similar to the thoroughly discredited 'separate but equal' doctrine."[109] A better alternative, in his view, entailed collapsing black studies into existing classes. He enumerated several course offerings that had sufficiently achieved this goal. While Grobman's rhetoric reflected the educational philosophy of Charles Hamilton, his case for merging black studies with other disciplines rested on a different theory. Black studies departments, in his estimation, functioned solely to solve the black community's "identity problem of substantial dimensions."[110] In other words, black studies constituted a discipline purposed to fix black people. This problematization of black studies once again reinserted blackness as a crisis into the intellectual imagination of Rutgers's faculty and overlooked the benefits of an Afrocentric major set aside from the country's racist past.

The onslaught of antiblack opinion columns in the *Newsletter* exposed a slightly different panic among the faculty than previously exhibited. White professors felt diminished and their fears of displacement escalated as black students intercepted Rutgers's urban-reform initiative with their own agenda.

Faculty like Bredemeier, Sternlieb, and Grobman wrestled with a barrage of students holding the institution accountable to an equitable racial integration plan. Seeking control over their college experience, black students envisioned more than a pseudo-form of inclusion. They wanted buy-in. The friction forced Malcolm Talbott, the acting dean of the Newark campus, to strike a conciliatory tone. Straddling both sides, Talbott argued that "any study involving people or people-oriented problems in urban areas must include, in some fashion, the participation of those to be studied." Yet he cautioned against equating "participation" with "control."[111] Whereas the bulk of his column referenced black and brown students and urged Rutgers to consider community input, his final paragraph also assured begrudging faculty that the university would include "poor whites" and "all of American society" in its future plans for growth.[112]

Talbott's effort to appease both parties failed. By early 1969, students had grown impatient with the pace of change, and BOS decided to focus its attention on forcing institutional changes. On February 10, 1969, BOS issued a detailed list of demands for restructuring the admissions process that included the removal of the director, Robert Swab, and his assistant, C. T. Miller. They called both men "basically prejudiced," and singled Miller out as being "hostile, derrogatory [sic] and arrogant in dealing with Black applicants."[113] Three days later, Talbott met with department heads at Rutgers–Newark to share BOS's demands and the university's proposed responses to them. He requested they respond in writing if they wanted a faculty meeting on the issue. Of the twenty-one departments and institutes represented, sixteen required no further meeting and supported the university's handling of the issue. Only the departments of chemistry and philosophy asked for a meeting while the remaining three did not respond, suggesting that, at this point, most of the faculty were either in alignment with the university's response or uninterested in actively contributing to its shaping.[114]

Talbott met with BOS students on February 20, 1969, and verbally outlined the university's response to their demands. A day later, BOS alerted him in a letter that his response was "totally unacceptable."[115] On February 24, 1969, more than two dozen students occupied Conklin Hall on the Newark campus; the protesters pledged to stay until their demands were met.[116] Black students in New Brunswick and Camden took actions in solidarity that included dumping trays of food on the floor in the dining hall, refusing to speak with white students and faculty, walking out of classes, blocking up toilets, and even setting small fires.[117] After three days of negotiations between BOS representatives and university officials, the students occupying what they had deemed "Liberation Hall" left the building after securing promises from President Mason Gross that the university would make sweeping changes to admissions practices, with the goal of increasing black enrollment. Talbott

met with faculty in Newark on February 27 to explain the terms of the agreement, but there is no evidence that faculty were consulted or involved in
negotiations before that point, something that would become a major issue
in the coming weeks.[118]

On March 3, representatives of the Newark College of Arts and Sciences
faculty met with BOS representatives to discuss elements of the agreement
considered in their jurisdiction—scholastic standing and admissions—and
also listened to a statement from the admissions committee that was "not
in accord with BOS demands."[119] On March 6, the faculty issued a statement
supporting the goals of creating a statewide system of higher education "to the
end that every holder of a high school diploma shall find that form of higher
education which is best suited to his needs, abilities, and aspirations"—but
voted ninety-five to forty to accept the recommendations of the admissions
committee, not the BOS, effectively repudiating the agreed-upon terms that
ended the protest.[120] This marked one of the first public signs of a fissure
between the faculty and the administration over pledges Mason Gross and
Malcolm Talbott had made to students.

University leadership seemed not to heed this sign of faculty discontent,
and on March 14 the Board of Governors passed a resolution authorizing the
creation of a "far-reaching experimental and even revolutionary program for
educationally and economically disadvantaged students" to be called the
Urban University Program (UUP).[121] The program would at the outset serve
only high school students from Camden, Newark, Piscataway, and New Brunswick who met the New Jersey Educational Opportunity Fund (EOF) standard
for financial need and who would not be admitted to any of the university's
colleges under standard admissions criteria.[122] The EOF had been created
in November 1967 in response to the Newark uprising and provided financial assistance to "economically and educationally disadvantaged" students
through the state's institutions of higher education.[123] But the amount of
money Rutgers was receiving through the EOF at that time was only a fraction of the estimated cost of the newly announced UUP. Moreover, although
its inception was linked to the racial unrest in Newark, no direct mention of
racial or ethnic justice was articulated as part of the EOF mission. The Board
of Governors resolution announcing the UUP also used race-neutral language,
but university leadership did not shy from characterizing it as a program to
help students from racial minorities overcome discrimination and unequal
schooling.[124] In addition, the three cities that were to become the beneficiaries
of the UUP were home to many African American people, particularly the city
of Newark, making it a de facto truth that a large proportion of program participants would be black. Thus, the question of funding for the UUP program
was murky from the start, its focus on the three Rutgers campus cities raised
immediate questions of unfairness in the rest of the state, and its origin as

a product of negotiation between the university and black student activists made it an easy target for those hostile to any race-based affirmative action programs.

There were many critics among the faculty on just such grounds. In an undated statement issued after the March 14 BOG resolution, the Newark College of Arts and Sciences faculty elaborated on its position. It is worth citing the statement at length for a firsthand view of discontent in the faculty. First, the faculty noted its disdain for the way in which the UUP came into existence—"hastily worked out under duress"—and its conviction that faculty needed a role in implementing the UUP to guarantee the "quality of education at Rutgers does not suffer."[125] Second, the statement sought reassurance from the Board of Governors that the "programs and activities for students admitted under regular procedures" would not suffer as a result of the creation of the UUP. Third, the statement called for the proportion of "disadvantaged students under special programs to the number of students admitted to regular programs be the same at all campuses," noting that because of "basic population statistics, the University's new programs will have by far its heaviest impact in Newark," a reference to Newark's status as a majority black city. The juxtaposition of *regular* versus *disadvantaged* students is telling. It indicates a preoccupation with protecting the status quo and fear that the Rutgers–Newark campus would become host to large numbers of underprepared African American students, clearly an unwelcome proposition. The faculty warned that without proportionality across the three campuses and the provision of additional funding to Newark to compensate for any expansion of students, the board would inevitably deny educational opportunities to the children of nondisadvantaged working people in Newark and to many students, black and white, who did not live in Newark and whose parents could not afford either private or residential colleges. Such a step would deny the disadvantaged student a place in a college of quality and at the same time embitter intergroup relations by educating some students at the expense of others.[126]

Implicit in the faculty's statement is the notion that an influx of black "disadvantaged" students would both deteriorate the quality of education at Rutgers and deny the kinds of students who traditionally attended Rutgers in Newark—white students—the educational experience that was their right. By using negative rhetoric filled with warnings that framed the university's efforts as a zero-sum game rather than as an expansion of opportunity to those historically denied it, the Newark College of Arts and Sciences faculty effectively set themselves up as opponents to opening Rutgers to racial, ethnic, and economic diversity in all but the most theoretical terms.

Officially, student–faculty relations were more cordial on the New Brunswick campus than in Newark. Student protests there did not rise to the level of building occupation, and under pressure from black student activists, and presumably to avoid the escalation of disruption, the deans of Rutgers and Douglass Colleges agreed to cancel classes on February 28 and March 3 and 4 to discuss student demands and grievances. Closed committee meetings composed of students and faculty were held throughout the two days, and workshops and cultural programs planned by students and faculty were open to all not involved in those meetings.[127] The actions and statements from the New Brunswick college deans that followed were fairly conciliatory in tone. A press release announced that the Douglass College faculty agreed to twenty-five measures in response to grievances by black students to "improve the education of all students at the women's unit of the State University," noting that "Douglass currently has 115 black students in a student body of 2,779."[128] The Rutgers News Service reported that Dean Arnold B. Grobman of Rutgers College "congratulated both the student body and the faculty for 'significant and extraordinary efforts in taking positive steps toward resolving our problems. But we still have a long way to go,' he noted."[129] Faculty at both colleges made commitments supporting efforts to recruit and admit more black students, hire more black faculty and administrators, and create academic support programs for "disadvantaged" and "inner-city" students. And while both faculties articulated support for the concept of an Afro-American studies program, neither voiced support for a separate department of Afro-American studies, in keeping with what Grobman had written previously in the faculty *Newsletter*.

The spring semester of 1969 did witness at least two faculty members writing opinion columns in the *Newsletter* that rejected reductionist characterizations of black studies. In a direct response to Grobman, history professor Rodney Carlisle argued that "black studies, and particularly Afro American History, are valid fields of academic endeavor."[130] The *Journal of Negro History*, he pointed out, was a "respected" academic publication in the field. Grobman had failed to take the long-standing intellectual infrastructure enabled by the journal and other sources into consideration. Not only was this evident by his own ignorance of black history, but also by his one-dimensional portrayal of black radicalism. For Carlisle, the study of black history demanded, as opposed to dismissed, "rebels and leaders who challenged the white assumptions of superiority and the white system of oppression by direct action, by the search for separate political identity, and sometimes by the use of force."[131] What Grobman perceived as a threat to intellectual rigor, Carlisle viewed as an enhancement. In the narratives of black radical nonconforming "rebels"— Harriet Tubman, Paul Cuffe, Malcolm X—existed a lesson about the importance of black studies as a separate discipline. It meant that whites might no longer expect black people to "simply" assimilate without question.[132]

Samuel DeWitt Proctor joined Carlisle in a defense of black studies. Lecturing his colleagues on the importance of an Afrocentric curriculum, the professor of education reminded them that "since there have been 'white' universities for so long, and all other kinds of de facto separate universities serving ethnic and demographic units, it is time for blacks to cry out."[133] He then enumerated a number of universities built in the name of cultural preservation. In the founding of Brandeis University and Yeshiva University, he pointed out, Jews had coalesced around their culture. Lutherans had claimed St. Olaf, and Catholics had "never entrusted higher or lower education to the majority."[134] Proctor went further. Nearly all the public universities "contained pockets of cultural homogeneity" that disbarred blacks or made obsolete their contributions to the nation. He counted "Ole Miss, LSU, Georgia Tech, V.M.I., and The Citadel" among such institutions, but the faculty must have read his list as an indictment of Rutgers too.[135]

Proctor's view of black studies also undermined Grobman. Black studies had the potential to influence black identity development, he admitted, but it would also fill "a sufficient void in the knowledge and appreciation of the history of American Blacks."[136] The tendency among some whites to misinterpret black separatism illustrated to Proctor exactly why framing African American studies as a corrective to the current curriculum was more generative than wielding it as a psychological cure for the black community. Most whites simply did not appreciate African Americans enough—their cultural, literary, artistic, and intellectual prowess. Proctor understood the problem. How could the dominant race value blackness if the very institution charged with producing informed citizens neglected to fully include the voices of black people? "What we are talking about," he passionately proclaimed, "is an orientation in history, literature, social science, psychology, fine arts, and education that is 'Black.' It means viewing these disciplines from the perspective of a Black student, standing body deep, soul deep, in his own culture."[137]

The philosophy of Carlisle and Proctor directly conflicted with the recommendations of Bedemeier, Grobman, and Sternlieb for black students to eschew an Afrocentric lens. By aligning with the protesters, Carlisle and Proctor also affirmed the students on a level not yet seen among the faculty. Their columns marked a rare occasion in the *Newsletter* in which professors chimed in on race without presenting black students as blemished constituents of the university desperately in need of a social, intellectual, and cultural cleanse. References to historic black rebels like Tubman and culture-producing institutions like St. Olaf provided much-needed historical and sociological context to black students' call for cultural representation in their struggle against white paternalism.

Evidence of the university's gradual embrace of black studies came in November when the *Newsletter* announced that Rutgers had moved closer to offering more courses in "Afro-American Studies."[138] The expansion varied across campuses. Camden and Newark designed new courses without creating a major. The New Brunswick faculty created a major; a sample of the courses included "Race Relations in America," "Afro-American Art," and "Contemporary Social Movements." The program at Douglass College entailed "a world view of the black man, community involvement through field work activity, and special preparation for secondary school teaching." Douglass faculty also hoped that the new major would "bring awareness of the corps of knowledge developed by and evolving about Afro Americans . . . pertinent for students preparing to live in a multicultural society."[139] Still careful to balance black cultural representation with Rutgers's first-rate reputation, Vice Provost Henry Winkler ensured the scholarly community that each program had been designed with the utmost "academic integrity." He also cited academic integrity as the primary reason that faculty on each campus were reluctant to establish a separate department, but promised that such an arrangement was forthcoming.[140]

In addition to growing support for black studies as a legitimate academic field, some faculty members personally rallied to the cause of aiding students who did not have the financial means to attend Rutgers. Associate Professor Lowell A. Douglas proposed that faculty members voluntarily allocate 1 percent of their payroll to a fund for "disadvantaged students."[141] In June 1969, a group of four faculty members penned a letter urging their colleagues to contribute to this fund as a tangible symbol of their commitment to the new opportunity program, which was still severely short of money. They explained that this donation was necessary

> TO CONVINCE THE ADMINISTRATION AND THE BOARD OF GOVERNORS, THE STATE GOVERNMENT, AND THE PEOPLE OF NEW JERSEY, OF THE DEGREE OF SERIOUSNESS WITH WHICH THE FACULTY PASSED ITS MARCH 4 RESOLUTIONS;
>
> TO CHALLENGE THE UNIVERSITY AND THE STATE TO FACE UP TO THE FINANCIAL OBLIGATIONS INVOLVED IN PROVIDING EDUCATIONAL OPPORTUNITIES FOR DISADVANTAGED STUDENTS IN NEW JERSEY;
>
> TO ASSURE THE BLACK STUDENTS, TO WHOM ON MARCH 4 THE FACULTY MADE A COMMITMENT, THAT THE COMMITMENT WAS MADE IN FULL FAITH; and
>
> TO EXPRESS A PERSONAL COMMITMENT TO SOCIAL JUSTICE[142]

This method of fundraising was successful enough that the money provided substantially for initial financing of the Transitional Year Program (TYP), which was a preparatory program embedded in the suite of initiatives that also included the creation of the UUP.[143]

Despite these public signs of support, internal opposition was overwhelming. In a statement bitterly opposed to the university's actions, an ad hoc committee that had been charged in May 1968 with exploring affirmative action options asserted:

> It is our belief that any change in the admissions policy of the University should be responsive to the needs of all citizens and students of New Jersey and should *not* be based, individually or collectively, on race, ethnic origin, economic factors, or geographic location. . . . We strongly recommend that there should be no change in the standards of admission, or Rutgers' academic standards, which would result, immediately or ultimately, in the deterioration of the quality of the Rutgers' degree [emphasis in original].[144]

Of particular contention was the university's decision to transfer Robert Swab and C. T. Miller out of the Newark Admissions Office at the behest of BOS. Staff of the Admissions Office circulated a petition in support of the two men, and several resigned in protest.[145] The ad hoc committee in its report wrote that it "abhor[ed]" the fact the two men were transferred "in compliance with the Black Organization of Students demands."[146] As was seen in the position of the Newark College of Arts and Sciences, the ad hoc committee was fearful of a drop in standards and prestige caused by the admission of black students, was angry at not being included in the process of creating new programs, and was essentially unsympathetic to the project of racial justice if it in any way represented a transformation of the status quo.

Faculty were not alone in their hostility to the initiatives taken by Gross, Talbott, and the Board of Governors. The New Jersey state legislators who controlled the purse strings were extremely angry about what they characterized as the "appeasement" of student protesters, and Republican members, particularly those with an eye on the gubernatorial election, criticized Gross relentlessly.[147] Professing himself interested in the welfare of the students, State Senator Alexander Matturri chastised Gross for "not performing his duties and obligations" by allowing a small group of "militant" students to disrupt the education of thousands of other students.[148] In a letter to a constituent who had written to complain to him about the handling of disruptions at Rutgers–Camden, State Senator Edwin Forsythe asserted that he vigorously disapproved of the use of force, sit-ins, or other disruptive measures in these situations. "Primary to the maintenance of society is order. Without order there can be no justice, not even the freedom to discuss the important problems of our society."[149]

This was the ideological outlook of many of the legislators who controlled educational funding in the state. At the same time that Mason Gross was developing the UUP through negotiations with student protesters, faculty, and administrators on all three Rutgers campuses, legislative support for the EOF was growing. The EOF had come into existence through the Department of Higher Education in 1968, and the same legislators who were openly hostile to the black student protesters controlled funding for it. In a letter to Mason Gross, Rutgers professor Richard McCormick[150] of the History Department outlined the problem facing the UUP:

> As I see it, the legislators have every right to want to know who is in favor of the program. They have obviously had a great deal of adverse reaction from their constituents; they are leary [sic] of supporting something that seems generally to have aroused hostility.
>
> We are asked, in effect, what is the demand? At this point we can not with any confidence say that the faculties of the several colleges favor the program, nor can we count on the students, their parents, or the alumni. If there is support, or even understanding around the state, I am unaware of it.[151]

McCormick had deftly read the reality facing the efforts of Gross to defend programs born out of direct conversation with those to whom it most urgently mattered—the black students of New Jersey who represented themselves, their families, and their community. Ultimately, the legislature expressed its hostility to the programs created through negotiations between university leaders and protesters by refusing to fund them, and instead forced all money earmarked for "disadvantaged" students at Rutgers to be channeled through the EOF budget. By 1972, the grassroots programs had all but given way to the EOF.[152]

Epilogue

Historian Paul Clemens shows that despite sympathy with the cause brought by the black student protesters, Mason Gross was encumbered in his efforts to craft a comprehensive response by negative state and public opinion.[153] This essay has added to the narrative by showing that faculty opposition was another factor limiting the response of the Gross administration. Specially designed initiatives for marginalized populations and black students' demand for greater cultural representation produced a robust dialogue about race among faculty members. The combined opposition to the Gross administration led to the unraveling of a key program, the Urban University Program, which was instituted by Rutgers after direct negotiation with protesters and was eventually replaced by smaller-scale programs supported by the state-advocated Educational Opportunity Fund and financed wholly through state-controlled dollars.

There is no question that this was a blow to Gross, the students, and the countless individuals who had supported and worked for the UUP and the other programs set in motion in 1968 and 1969. However, there is also no question that programs at colleges and universities across the state funded by the EOF have had a positive impact on participating students. Today the EOF is widely viewed as New Jersey's leading program to support low-income, first-generation students with scholarships, counseling, and academic support. Historians laud this reform as one of the great achievements of the civil rights movement at Rutgers.[154] And indeed, the program has made a material difference in the lives of New Jersey students, primarily students of color. According to the Rutgers EOF website, the program has served more than 20,000 Rutgers graduates during the past five decades.[155] Statewide, the EOF serves more than 13,000 students each year with grants between $250 and $2,500 per year, and data show EOF students graduate at higher rates than their low-income peers in New Jersey and fifteen other states that report data on opportunity programs.[156]

Black faculty and administrative recruitment increased alongside the growth of the black student population through the EOF. The *Newsletter* announced the appointment of Blenda Wilson as assistant provost in May 1969. Cheryl Wall was appointed as a lecturer in the Department of English in 1972, and Cheryl Clarke, then a graduate student, taught courses there as well.[157] Their appointments came just as women across higher education demanded gender equality. Even as second-wave feminists disrupted male labor bias in higher education, black women composed only a small fraction of the faculty and administrative hires reported in the *Newsletter.* Proctor's suggestion that academia reshape courses on Western civilization "to an understanding of Man through the eyes of Black people" belied, in some respects, the extent to which academics, subconsciously or otherwise, expected male normativity in intellectual circles and curriculums. Still, a combination of black student protest, administrative programming, and faculty intervention compelled and altered a discourse on race at Rutgers in the 1960s. Filtered initially through white paternalism and prevailing ideas about black deficiency, the conversation quickly shifted to black autonomy and cultural representation by the end of the decade. Nevertheless, the feminist movement of the 1970s and the lack of black women professors signaled that the full narrative on race had yet to be told.

4

Black and Puerto Rican Student Experiences and Their Movements at Douglass College, 1945–1974

KAISHA ESTY, WHITNEY FIELDS, AND CARIE RAEL

In the late nineteenth and early twentieth centuries, women's colleges emerged to offer women the opportunity of higher education that had been denied to them since the establishment of the first colleges and universities in North America.[1] In turn, black women sought placement at these institutions and experienced double exclusion from colleges based on race and gender. Previous studies on the first black women at Douglass College, once known as the New Jersey College for Women (NJC), revealed the names, aspirations, and activities of students such as Julia Baxter-Bates (NJC '38), who researched and coauthored the winning brief in the historic *Brown v. Board of Education of Topeka*.[2] This essay's focus is on those who came in the decades after World War II but before the late 1960s.

These women of color were agents of change in the culture of the institution and, by extension, in the white racial image of the "Douglass woman." This essay presents the insights, challenges, and everyday experiences of black and Puerto Rican women who had to navigate Douglass as racial minorities and who wittingly and unwittingly expanded the image of the "Douglass woman." It explores the networks of subtle protest and antiracist resistance that they created as a civil rights consciousness ever so slowly emerged on Douglass's campus in the 1960s. By looking at the campus culture as it was revealed in campus newspapers, this essay shows the challenges that confronted early black and brown students and how they navigated them. By the late 1960s, the entrance of more minority students made it easier for young black and brown women to advocate for what they needed. Still, as revealed here, the groundwork laid by those who had persevered through the late 1950s and early 1960s made the work of the latter generation easier.

Ambassadors for Their Race and the Image of the "Douglass Woman"

Black women who enrolled in Douglass in the postwar years and early 1960s confronted an image of the "Douglass woman" that was racially coded as white and middle class. For Julane Miller-Armbrister (DC '74), the traditional "ideal 'Douglass woman' was one who was well-rounded, well-read, [had] good manners, [and was] sophisticated from a social standpoint as well as from an academic standpoint."[3] The "Douglass woman" had been constructed so that she possessed a distinct quality that equipped her to "go from tea to sports."[4] Strict customs such as curfews and "Cooper skirts"[5] in the dining hall and "appropriate dress" (modest dress) in classes, chapel, and during visits to downtown New Brunswick revealed the college's institutional investment in traditional codes of gender. "Courtesy," explained a 1961 edition of the orientation guide the *Red Book*, "should be a natural part of a Douglassite's life. You should be aware at all times that you are a representative of Douglass and that your actions will be interpreted as such by members of the community."[6] Although Douglass offered a progressive path in higher education as *the* state college for women—meaning that it welcomed students from families whose incomes were more modest than those who sent their girls to elite private schools—the institutional ideal of the "Douglass woman" remained tethered to conservative notions of femininity and womanhood, ideals that the black woman's history of labor and sexual exploitation had excluded her from.

Since most Douglass students before World War II were white Anglo-Saxons, this ideal was hardly challenged. Until 1938, no confirmed African American woman graduated from what was then the New Jersey College for Women.[7] Julia Baxter Bates (NJC '38), known as the first confirmed black woman to graduate from NJC, gained entry through an administrative oversight: Because of her fair complexion, she was initially mistaken for a white woman.[8] Bates was forced to live off campus, allowing NJC to maintain a whites-only policy in the intimate sphere of its dormitories. Although Jewish students expanded the boundaries of the Anglo-Saxon and Christian image of the "Douglass woman," black students were severely underrepresented at the state college for decades. The few that gained admission forged their college experience from the purview of a "Bee"—the nickname given to commuters, whether that was their desire or not. It was not until a year after the end of World War II, in 1946, that Evelyn Sermons Field (NJC '49) and Emma Andrews Warren (NJC '49) became the first two black students permitted to live in the dormitories at NJC.[9] As historians Miya Carey and Pamela Walker have argued, by enacting a "respectable" form of blackness, these early African American Douglass students began to expand the image of the "Douglass woman."[10]

Whether consciously or not, the few black students who attended NJC and later Douglass in the two decades after World War II served as ambassadors of their race. Encircled by the systemic racism that sustained the white racial image of the "Douglass woman," black students "felt an obligation to be successful, to live up to their predecessors and set a standard so other African Americans would be" admitted.[11] In 2015, Wilma Harris (DC '66) recalled feeling "obligated to be effective, to be successful because I was here on the shoulders of the Evelyn Sermon Fields, Yolanda Macks and the Inez Durhams and the Bernice Proctors—so I could not screw up." Harris continued, "They had gone through so much that I had to do right and besides that I wanted Douglass to be able to accept other black students. So if I was a major screw-up they'd say, 'Oh no, we're not gonna do that anymore. Remember that Harris child.'" Harris felt the pressure that had from time immemorial been put on the striving class of African Americans. She added, "I did and I still feel an obligation that whatever I'm doing, I'm doing it in the name of my race because I have to—my mother said you have to be twice as good to be considered half as good."[12]

For black and white prospective students, Douglass was a highly reputable and sought-after school. "If you were a woman in 1962 and you wanted to go the state university," explained one former student, Douglass "was the only game in town because Rutgers College didn't admit women until '72."[13] Importantly, as the state college for women in New Jersey, Douglass offered an affordable alternative to private college tuition or out-of-state schooling. It attracted young women from a variety of socioeconomic and regional backgrounds—a meaningful factor for its largely poorer and working-class black students. But whether supported through tuition assistance, scholarships, or private funds, the women who attended Douglass prided themselves on the public recognition of their intellectual merit.[14] This fact took on a distinctive shape among Douglass's black students. Understanding the high stakes of acquiring a degree in a racist and sexist society, graduates such as Evelyn Sermons Field (NJC '49), Bernice Proctor Venable (DC '62), Golden Elizabeth Johnson (DC '65), M. Wilma Harris (DC '66), Juanita Wade Wilson (DC '66), and Betty Davis (DC '66) entered Douglass with a strong sense of determination and drive toward individual and collective success. They forged a sisterhood based on friendship, mentorship, and support while challenging policies around campus. Unlike their white peers, black women understood that their success at Douglass determined the course of future black representation at the college.

By virtue of their enrollment at Douglass, black students subverted longstanding white ideas of the innate intellectual inferiority of African Americans while they also changed the idea that college was for acquiring "culture"

Bernice Joan Proctor
A.B. Spanish

FIGURE 4.1 Bernice Proctor Venable, *Quair Yearbook*, 1962.
Courtesy of Special Collections & University Archives, Rutgers University

only. Black students at Douglass understood their labor potential on different terms than their white counterparts. In the North and South, the racially discriminatory and sexist labor market left few options for African American women.[15] As in the South, black women in New Jersey were accustomed to working either as domestics in other people's homes or as factory hands. As Harris (DC '66), from Paulsboro, New Jersey, remembered:

> My mother worked. All of her friends worked. All of the black women worked, because they needed the income to support the family. So, it wasn't an expectation that I was going to be Muffy and Buffy and sit around and play Bridge all day and go to lunch, like I do now as a retiree.[16]

The presence of black students inevitably pushed the boundaries of the white "Douglass woman" image. At the same time, however, black women used the "Douglass woman" ideal to reclaim and construct a respectable and professional black womanhood. "If you were going to do anything honorable, not dirty, like your nails wouldn't be squished down [or] you[r] hands wouldn't be all blistered," Harris said, "you'd go to college to do that."[17] In a corporeal description of the inevitability of menial and arduous labor for black women with no college education, Harris, like other black students, saw their education as a ticket for survival, dignity, and economic freedom.

The Douglass promise had a powerful impact on the way black students navigated their college experience as well as their memories of their time there. For example, in a 2007 interview, the late Evelyn Sermons Field (NJC '49), a distinguished alumna, explained that a shared value in women's education unified the students at NJC. "Whoever came, I'm sure, had families like mine, who felt that you're a human being first and then a woman, and so you had to learn," Field affirmed. "You had to be educated and so I think that we all sort of felt that education, in and of itself, was valuable. And I was happy to be here [NJC] with them, a lot of others felt that in some way," she added.[18] In language such as "you're a human being first," Field gestured to an environment where evading gender discrimination with white women mediated racism. Field also remembered Douglass as an experience that instilled her with lifelong confidence and grit. "As for me personally," she highlighted, "what I felt that Douglass gave me was the opportunity to realize that as a woman, and even as a minority woman, as they say, 'You can do anything that you want to do.'"[19] From Field's perspective, there was no white racial image of the "Douglass woman"; the "Douglass woman" did not have a race.

Yet Field's 2007 recollection of racial irrelevancy belied the challenges that she and other black students faced at NJC and Douglass. In 1946, Field and Emma Andrews Warren became the first two black students permitted to live in the dormitories at NJC.[20] The integration of NJC dormitories was not a given: During their freshman year, in 1945, Field and Warren commuted to campus from their respective New Jersey towns of Somerville and Plainfield. The desegregation of NJC housing occurred at the urging of student members of the History, Economics, Political Science, and Social Science Club (HEPS). In a wartime era with international and domestic race relations debated widely in public, HEPS students sparked a conversation around race relations on campus. In December 1943 they created the Racial and Minorities Relations Committee and stated that its "primary purpose is to better relations between racial and minority groups on campus, [and] our secondary aim is to carry this program further into the community and the nation."[21] HEPS members expressed that they were interested in getting "to know people of other backgrounds."[22] Their concern was that the policy of prohibiting African Americans from living in dormitories marginalized black students and limited interracial interaction, and thereby fostered an educational experience that was itself segregated.

Desegregating housing on Douglass was emblematic of so much more than just letting black and white young women share accommodations. For example, the expense of room and board was an effective tool for policing campus residency. Without financial aid, black residency would remain severely limited. HEPS students understood this and figured in efforts to secure financial backing for their proposal. Among other sources, HEPS solicited funding from units of the National Association of Colored Women's Clubs to cover Field's and Warren's room and board.[23] Additionally, the initiative that student members of HEPS took to integrate NJC dorms was telling. According to Field, "The students were very active in this movement. But they also did not really reveal to any of us any of the, you know, the problems."[24] In essence, slow, gradual desegregation in the late 1940s took place without much organizational input from black students; this was a factor that shifted vastly by the late 1960s as more black students arrived and spoke for themselves about where they wanted to live.

The initial integration of the dormitories at Douglass revealed residuals of prejudice. Field and Warren were paired together in a dorm. The assumption or demand that the only two black women living on campus share the same room reflected a deep-rooted fear of racial "intermixture." As historians have noted, the long history of the "miscegenation" taboo and analogy reached beyond explicit heterosexual interracial relations to other forms of black–white intimate interactions, both sexual and nonsexual.[25] With an equally long history of black women working as live-in domestics in white homes, the prejudice here appeared to rest in black and white students sharing the private space of a dorm as social equals.[26] Desegregating university housing, if only minimally, did not guarantee greater cultural exchange between black and white students on a campus that remained overwhelmingly white. Lastly, by permitting a micro form of segregation within student housing, HEPS and the university merely pushed a door ajar, setting in motion a gradual process of desegregation. Until 1962, all black students at NJC and Douglass who lived in campus housing were paired by race.[27]

By Field's recollection, desegregation took place in the absence of a black support network. "I guess in a way we were sort of an experimental group really," Field suggested.[28] Field could not recall experiencing hostility from her white peers at the time, although she heard years later that a student gave up her assignment in a room when her parents learned that there were black women living in the house.[29] "But those things weren't revealed at the time," Field noted.[30] By this account, white NJC students were not openly confrontational or aggressive with their racism. Rather, antiblack prejudice took the form of apathy, indifference, and distancing oneself from black students. In their senior year, Field and Warren received the inaugural Senior Service Award from NJC. This award was given "in recognition of what we had done while we were here," explained Field, and "the influence we had upon attitudes and practices."[31]

The award, and Field's understanding of it, speaks volumes about NJC in the immediate postwar years. It exposed the scrutiny that Field and Warren experienced as deviations from the all-white "Douglass woman." Put differently, the award indicates the extent to which Field and Warren were being scrutinized and whether their behavior and demeanor passed muster. Moreover, inasmuch as the award was a service award, one might consider some of the assumptions and expectations of NJC toward its few black students as representatives of their race. Integrating dormitories on white students' and NJC's terms, for example, was award-worthy "service work." The effort that Field and Warren put into influencing "attitudes and practices" as students surely benefited future generations of black Douglass women, but it was extra labor and a burden nevertheless.

Field built a prolific career as an educator and civil rights activist in her postgraduate years. She became a founding member of the Black Alumnae Network (BAN) and held many offices, including that of president of the Associate Alumnae of Douglass College.[32] Through these efforts, Field pushed the boundaries of the white racial image of the "Douglass woman," widening the door for more active and vocal black student representation. For example, Bernice Proctor Venable (DC '62) specifically identified Field as her mentor and credited her with advising her to enroll at Douglass in 1958. Venable was active in the student government and Rutgers University Choir.[33] She served as house chair of Jameson Hall where "approximately 95 percent" of the women were Jewish, and she also worked as a "waitress of waitresses."[34] Like Field, Venable felt that "these activities helped her character and instilled a sense of 'I can do it.'"[35] She recalled enjoying some of the rituals of the college, "from wearing her white gloves to important events, to attending Voorhees Chapel and the Sacred Path Ceremony."[36] Venable's ability to immerse herself in campus activities is demonstrated in her remarks; this ability was undoubtedly made possible by the efforts of the few black students, like Field and Warren, who preceded her.

Yet the road to racial equality and equity at NJC/DC was long. As Venable explained, in the late 1950s and early '60s there still wasn't "a whole lot of cohesiveness."[37] Along with her roommate, they made up "two of four black women, the others were upperclassmen."[38] Describing the enduring segregated social landscape of the NJC/DC campus, Venable noted: "Folks tended to stick together, by race, ethnicity, at first; then, as time passed, by the major fields selected."[39] In the mid-twentieth century, as a highly publicized civil rights movement swept the nation, racial politics at NJC and Douglass appeared to equally embrace and resist the changes of the era. Responding to their own sense of isolation and building on the footprints of former students, black women forged a sisterhood that overtly defied the white racial image of the "Douglass woman."

Together Alone

In an environment that was largely indifferent to their presence, black women were "together alone."[40] Juanita Wade Wilson (DC '66) described a feeling of "loneliness of searching for oneself in blackness in a sea of whites."[41] Like Field, Wilson affirmed that "there was no overt racism" during her years at Douglass.[42] This was not because whites openly accepted black students but "because there were so few blacks on campus—we didn't matter."[43] As Wilson continued:

> Isolation was our index of systemic discrimination . . . there was no mention of black authors in classes, interested students [had] to form their own reading groups. . . . Many came from all-black high schools, which had nourished them in the old-fashioned way—counseled by adults who cared. By contrast at university, the attitude was more, "you're here, so what?" There were no mentors.[44]

By Wilson's account, the admission of a few black students was both insufficient and potentially harmful to the students themselves. Without resources, mentors, and a curriculum that included black scholars and subjects, black women faced an educational experience that differed radically from that of their white counterparts. The dearth of support and the drive to succeed motivated black students to build a network of their own.[45]

Although their class and background contexts varied, one thing African American students had in common was their experience of Douglass as a white space. Some, such as Wilma Harris (DC '66), came from small, segregated towns like Paulsboro, New Jersey. Harris recalled knowing of the existence of an active Ku Klux Klan chapter not far from her hometown. Realizing that she would not return to Paulsboro to live, she was delighted to see even the few black women at Douglass. Although she did not see the other black members of her class every day, she recalled that when she did, "it was such a warm and caring feeling."[46] Others, like Betty Davis (DC '66), hailed from more urban areas. Born in Washington, DC, Davis grew up in Jersey City and East Orange, New Jersey, where she attended a racially integrated high school. This difference in background mattered. One of Davis's first impressions of Douglass College was that "it was very white."[47] Although many of New Jersey's cities such as Newark were more racially diverse, white students who came from smaller, segregated towns and rural parts of the state arrived at Douglass having had little to no close contact with black people. "Most of the people that I lived with . . . I think all of them in that house had never been that close to a black person before," Davis explained. "A lot of them were from the far reaches of New Jersey, like South Jersey and Northwest Jersey and stuff, so they hadn't been exposed to black people."[48] For Davis, white students' lack of exposure to black people led to awkward interactions and added to the overall feeling of a "very white" campus.[49]

The alienation that black students felt at DC was driven by external and internal forces. If white students' lack of prior contact with black people facilitated uncomfortable interactions, black students who came from segregated schools also struggled to adjust to DC's white campus. The experience of Barbara Morrison-Rodriguez (DC '71) provides an example. Coming from Washington, DC, where she had attended a segregated primary school, middle school, and high school, Morrison-Rodriguez recalled being socially unequipped to handle Douglass's whiteness. Speaking of her segregated experience prior to Douglass, Morrison-Rodriguez noted, "That kind of apartheid is hard for people to understand, where you have such a complete racial separation. But that's what Washington, DC, was like."[50] She recalled that "when I came to Douglass, you could have put me on freight to Siberia for the kind of experience that I felt. I actually went into a clinical depression the first month that I was here. I felt so isolated and so totally disconnected."[51] She did not go to the dining hall, she did not leave her room—all in anticipation of what *might* happen. "I was not gonna give anybody an opportunity to call me a nigger or to offend me. . . . So I withdrew."[52] Although white Douglass students were "nice and cordial" and "wonderful," Morrison-Rodriguez also recalled how after two months she had decided to leave but that Wilma Harris and the lone black faculty member, Professor Cecelia Hodges Drewry, talked her into staying at Douglass. In hindsight, she is of course appreciative of her degree and her time at Douglass, but in 2015 she reflected on what was sacrificed for integration. We gave up "that warm, nurturing, loving environment that we had from our families, our churches and our schools . . . that protected us from a lot of ugliness."[53]

There were also socialization differences that contributed to black students' feeling of alienation at Douglass. For example, Harris came from a family and black Baptist church community that paid a lot of attention to maintaining a "respectable" appearance. Thus, for Harris, it was a given that she would dress up for her first day at Douglass. "Well, I had this little blue dress on and gloves on," Harris explained. "I was like, 'Oh, God.' Nobody else did. They all had jeans."[54] Harris felt the consequence of her impractical outfit; it made moving in harder than it had to be. "You had to schlep this stuff up and down two flights to get to your room."[55] Reflecting on the experience without regret, she noted that where she came from, respectability "was important."[56] Harris also felt that the "food at Douglass was not the food that we had grown up on." Again, the lone black professor, Cecelia Hodges Drewry, came to the rescue by regularly inviting them to meals at her home.[57]

Other black students wrestled with fundamental cultural differences. In 1963, Jamaican international student Beverly Chisholm wrote in the *Caellian*, the Douglass newspaper, about customs that were unfamiliar to her. Coming from St. Hilda's Diocesan High School, a small girls' school in Brown's Town, Jamaica, Chisholm was accustomed to sleeping in "long dormitories with 10 to 40 other girls."[58] Chisholm also wrote that "in general there was much more formality and discipline at my former school than I have seen here."[59] Chisholm's gesture to a culture of permissiveness was likely alien to her educational context. With the independence of Jamaica occurring the previous year, in 1962, Chisholm's educational background reflected the strict and punitive British culture that governed colonial Jamaica.[60]

As different as their socialization was, black and white Douglass students shared the belief that men did not have a monopoly on intellectual matters. However, for black women, this challenge was often compounded by intraracial dynamics that overlaid an already racist culture. Although the ideal of the "Douglass woman"—one valued for her intellect and not simply her marriageability—was appealing to black women, color made a difference. For example, Harris recalled that colorism and the belief that she would never get married drove her to enroll at Douglass. "My uncle, my mother's younger brother, told me I would never get married because 'why would anyone want to marry someone who looks like you?'" explained Harris.[61] "Fortunately, or unfortunately," she continued, "that's been a guiding principle. I better excel at what I do because no one's going to be out there taking care of me because no one's going to marry me and Uncle Bobby wouldn't make that up."[62] In her predominantly black home community of Paulsboro, New Jersey, Harris experienced discrimination and devaluation from fellow African Americans because of her medium to darker skin. As she described:

> Unfortunately, that's where I learned about discrimination and segregation, was from others [sic] blacks. . . . Light-skinned blacks were obviously better than dark-skinned blacks because I guess master loved their mother more than master loved our mother. You had to have flowing hair. You had to look like Lena Horne.[63]

Colorism in Harris's family and church community had a profound impact on her sense of self-worth. It appeared, then, that for some black women, academic success at Douglass College offered a rejection of negative past experiences as well as an escape from the prospect of menial labor in their future. As Rosalind Carmichael, a dark-skinned African American woman (DC '72), recalled, "To be bright, you had to be light skinned and have money."[64] Such past experiences, as in Harris's struggle with colorism, also informed the black students' commitment to each other as part of a sisterhood at Douglass. Speaking in an interview conducted in 2018, Harris asserted that because she "rejected" colorism, she couldn't recall the skin tones of her black peers, "whether they were vanilla, caramel, or ebony."[65] She also noted that "if those [colorist] comments were made, they didn't stick in my mind later. . . . I don't remember those kinds of conversations."[66] The apparent absence of colorist tensions among black students at Douglass suggests that they made a conscious or subconscious effort to establish a unified sisterhood within their small network.

The formation of community emerged as much from material necessity as it did from alienation and isolation. In an era before the emergence of the Afro hairstyle as a symbol of the Black Power movement's cultural and political message and aesthetic, black Douglass students relied on each other to straighten their hair and style their bob cuts. Incoming black students quickly learned that Golden Elizabeth Johnson (DC '65) owned a straightening iron. This essential tool was used on rotation by all the black students at Douglass. With schedules that included swimming classes as a condition to graduate,[67] black students faced the added burden of managing their hair between classes to maintain what was deemed a trendy and more "respectable" appearance.[68] Because black students could not wait until the weekends or the occasional home visit to style their hair, they used Johnson's straightening iron to groom themselves before their next class. Johnson was also remembered for the guidance she provided. Patricia Felton-Montgomery (DC '68) remembered an occasion when she and the white male student with whom she was discussing campus NAACP matters were confronted by white males who approached them with hate signs. Johnson made it her business to not only comfort Felton-Montgomery but also to find out who the haters were so that she could make the proper contacts that ultimately forced these white men to apologize. Felton-Montgomery remembered that she looked up to Johnson. "She was like the great mother even though she was a student like me. . . . It was because of the personality, the fortitude, the self-awareness of Golden . . . that she was appreciated not only by us but respected by others."[69]

The community created by black students admitted to Douglass in the early 1960s contributed greatly to the growing diversification of Douglass College, and, by extension, the image of the "Douglass woman." Their mentorship especially helped to sustain new black students admitted in the mid to late 1960s. In 1968, 115 black women were admitted to Douglass—the largest proportion of black students in the university's history. While it was a small percentage of the overall class of 2,860, this black student body entered with the benefit of an established network of support among its black upperclassmen. Julane Miller-Armbrister, who joined Douglass in 1968, remembered meeting upperclassmen such as M. Wilma Harris (DC '66) and C. Maxene Vaughters-Summey (DC '70). "They were there for us," Miller-Armbrister explained in a 2019 interview. "They mentored us. And they tried to, you know, make sure we were there to get an education, and that we realized sort of what was riding on us as the largest black class coming in."[70] Black upperclassmen made sure that black freshmen understood all the hard work they had put in to make their opportunity possible. As Miller-Armbrister recalled, these mentors "talked to us about different professors, grades, all that kind of stuff."[71] In short, while the entire freshman class received a general orientation from Douglass College, black upperclassmen rounded up black freshmen for a "black orientation." Like Miller-Armbrister, many black students credited this informal system of support with their ability to thrive and demand more representation at Douglass.

The community forged by Douglass students was facilitated by the only black professor at Douglass as well as by black people in and around New Brunswick. Professor Cecelia Hodges Drewry of the Department of Speech and Dramatic Arts invited students to meals at her house. Students bonded with each other as they traveled to and from her home together and ate meals there. "Dr. Drewry," Wilma Harris said, "has a very special place in my heart."[72] Juanita Wilson (DC '66) also remembered that Drewry was someone "very special." Said Wilson, "We were only children" and Drewry "provided us with a home away from home" and "with intellectual inspiration." Drewry helped them understand what was happening in the United States, said Wilson, and gave us "an understanding of the time."[73] Patricia Felton-Montgomery (DC '68) remembered that besides Drewry, the black dining room staff was solicitous. Recounting the care they provided, she recalled that because the staff felt that she was way too thin, "they would make sure that I had loads of food." She also remembered that members at one of the churches would occasionally invite them to dinner. "They would make big Thanksgiving kind of dinners for us as long as we would go to church." Their gestures of compassion were even more appreciated than the dinners. "Sometimes when you would feel lonely and away from home they would hug you and kiss you and tell you how proud they were of you and tell you that they wanted you to succeed."[74] It is not surprising that Miller-Armbrister (DC '74) had similar memories. She recalled a black couple with the last name Johnson who owned a soul food restaurant in New Brunswick that black Douglass students would frequent. "Even though we had meal tickets you know and stuff, we would go there and eat. And if you missed a meal or had no food, you could always go to the Johnsons' restaurant," explained Miller-Armbrister.[75] The welcoming environment and informal pay structure (they would let students eat even when they couldn't pay) of the Johnsons' soul food restaurant showed the importance of spaces where black Douglass students could enjoy traditional black food as well as a respite from an overwhelmingly white campus. "I always endeavored to try to go back and give them something," Miller-Ambrister added. "I look back at it now: that was their way of giving back."[76] The Johnson couple's downtown New Brunswick soul food restaurant would not have been alien to most of Douglass's black students, who came from predominantly black communities. With close-knit communities forged across extended families, friends, church sisters and brothers, and neighbors, the Johnsons' soul food restaurant offered a vital "home away from home." This sense of community offered Douglass's black women a foundation to make meaningful change for themselves and future generations.

Early Puerto Rican Students at Douglass

The isolation of Puerto Rican women at Douglass was even more profound than that of the black students. In the 1970s, the very few who matriculated at Douglass created a cross-campus community with the newly admitted Puerto Ricans at Livingston College. However, the few who arrived at Douglass in the late 1960s had to weather the same "mostly white" environment as the African American women, and had to do so in the absence of a Puerto Rican campus community.

Before the late 1960s, Puerto Rican students, like African Americans, remained a very small minority of the student population. In 1926, the New Jersey College for Women admitted its first Puerto Rican students, Carmen Martinez and Emilia Caballero (NJC '30).[77] However, it took another forty years and student pressure for Douglass to purposefully admit Puerto Rican students and it did so through its Special Admissions program.[78] The Special Admissions program allowed students who were perceived to have the potential to succeed but did not have the required standardized test scores to be admitted.[79] This special admission process stemmed from a direct response to pressure from the Black Organization of Students, which formed in 1967 to address issues regarding race, particularly the low admission rates of minority students.[80] Despite student pressure, Douglass College admitted only two Puerto Rican students in the fall of 1967.[81]

One of those students was Gloria Soto (DC '71), who was born in Aguadilla, Puerto Rico.[82] Her mother and nine siblings migrated to Perth Amboy, New Jersey, after her father found work as a migrant farmer before becoming a factory worker. Community connections in Puerto Rico had relayed to Gloria's father that Perth Amboy was a good place to settle in the United States.[83] Gloria recalled that her family was one of the few Puerto Rican families in Perth Amboy.[84] Both of Gloria's parents found work in local industries.[85] Her mother, Milagros Soto, made costume jewelry at the Sobel Brothers factory and her father worked at an insulation manufacturer called Philip Carey Manufacturing. Like many of the jobs available to black and brown people, factory work exposed workers to dangerous industrial conditions. Soto's family was no exception; her father passed away from cancer after long-term asbestos exposure.[86]

Being Hispanic in a predominantly white community was difficult because of language barriers and prejudice. Tracked into lower-performing classes, Soto and her siblings found limited educational opportunities. Moreover, her family experienced unsettled living conditions, including eviction threats.[87] To combat the multiple forms of discrimination and the economic and educational barriers, Soto's father and other Puerto Rican families formed a social club called El Pepino and created their own community support system.[88]

Gloria Esther Soto
Spanish — French

FIGURE 4.2 Gloria Soto, *Quair Yearbook*, 1971.
Courtesy of Special Collections & University Archives, Rutgers University

As a child Soto developed rheumatic fever, leaving her with limited physical agility. In spite of the family's reduced financial resources, she remembered fondly how her father bought her a violin from a pawn shop and paid for weekly lessons.[89] She learned to play and, with the help of an African American teacher named Austin Gumbs, she auditioned and applied to Douglass College as a music major, which she later switched to French and Spanish. With the help of financial aid, Soto became the first sibling in her family to attend college.

Much like the experiences of African American women, Gloria Soto recalled the culture shock in attending Douglass. Nevertheless, she made friendships with women from different backgrounds who exposed her to new cultures and customs. Despite being an honors student in high school, the French and Spanish major recalled struggling academically in the first year, something she attributes to the isolation and shock that came with being one of only two Puerto Rican students in the entire college. As a work-study student, she worked as a waitress in the dining halls, an experience that further ostracized her. "Some students saw you as fellow student and some saw you as help," she remembered.[90] It was horrible serving food to women who "thought you were beneath them. . . . It made me feel lesser of a person."[91]

Looking for a better environment, Soto made her way over to the Rutgers College Avenue campus. There she participated in antiwar protests. She did not want her grades to suffer and, significantly, she did not want to "hurt her parents" so she kept her participation to a minimum.[92] Still, she recalled the Rutgers campus as more liberal than Douglass's. Characterizing Douglass as "conservative," she described rules and expectations reminiscent of earlier decades when Douglass College upheld the ideal of the "Douglass woman."[93] Like the remembrances of black women, Soto recalled having to go to dinner in skirts, having a monitored curfew, and having to entertain men only in designated lounge areas.[94] At Rutgers she could socialize with men at "mixers" and frat parties on College Avenue.[95] Soto also recalled going to Princeton on a bus to socialize and attend football games—anything to be away from Douglass.[96] When she looked back on her years at Douglass and reflected on the "Douglass woman," she could honestly say, "I don't know that there is just one definition of the Douglass woman. . . . I see a Douglass person as being multifaceted. It wasn't just one cookie cutter. It's a lot of different things to different people depending from where you as a person come from."[97] Having defied the rigid and conservative expectations of the college, Soto felt that she embodied what it was to be a Douglass woman.

Diane Maldonado (DC '71) entered the same year as Soto as the second Puerto Rican student admitted at Douglass in 1967.[98] Like Soto, Maldonado entered Douglass as a "special admit" student. In fact, out of the five Puerto Rican students admitted from 1967 to 1969, three were "specially admitted students," despite the fact that their high school grades and extracurricular activities qualified them in the regular admittance category.[99] Diane Maldonado viewed the "specially admitted" status as a way to demean and discredit her intelligence. Reflecting on this status she stated, "It makes you feel stupid and dumb."[100] She expressed how being specially admitted left her with a stigma and made her feel less competent than her peers despite having the qualifications to be admitted through the normal process.

Maldonado graduated with honors from Perth Amboy High School, but she recalled being "scared as hell" when she arrived at Douglass. Both Maldonado and Soto participated in a two-week summer program prior to starting

Diane Socorro Maldonado
Spanish Education

FIGURE 4.3 Diane Maldonado, *Quair Yearbook,* 1971.

Courtesy of Special Collections & University Archives, Rutgers University

college at Douglass in the summer of 1967. This preparatory summer program was created by the Equal Opportunity Board, a group made up of students, faculty, and administrators dedicated to serving the needs of minority students.[101] The summer program was intended to "academically and socially prepare the students for college life."[102] Both women found the program useful socially and found comfort in meeting another Puerto Rican student prior to the start of the semester. After meeting in the summer program, Soto and Maldonado decided to room together at Douglass in their sophomore year. Seeking to support other students of color at the university, Maldonado joined the Financial Aid Committee for the Livingston campus in the 1968–1969 academic year.[103] Looking back, Soto also recalled that the summer program had heightened her awareness of the lack of other Puerto Ricans on campus. She decided to do something about it as well and subsequently partnered with the Educational Opportunity Fund (EOF), which formed in 1968 as part of a state mandate, to encourage Hispanic high school students to consider applying to Douglass.[104]

Over time, Maldonado noticed an incremental increase in the number of Latinx students as a result of the efforts of the EOF program.[105] The Educational Opportunity Fund—a program designed to increase the enrollment of and give financial and academic support to underrepresented students—had mandated it.[106] Although Douglass admitted no Puerto Rican students in 1968, in 1969, two more were admitted.[107] Virgen Veléz (DC '73) was specially admitted in 1969, despite attending a preparatory school in Vermont on a scholarship. Veléz only stayed at Douglass for one semester. She later transferred to Mercer County College.[108] And Zaida Josefina "Josie" Torres (DC '73) arrived the same year.[109] Josie worked with the four other Puerto Ricans at Douglass and other Puerto Rican students across campuses to pressure the administration to recruit more Puerto Rican students.

Puerto Rican students often experienced the same kind of alienation as black students. Diane Miranda (DC '71), who entered Douglass in 1967, recalled that her roommate expressed shock that Diane was not black. Her roommate believed her to be black based on a photograph that Diane had sent her over the summer. Diane recalled, "When I walked into the room she was kind of relieved, although I never hid the fact that I was Puerto Rican, she seemed to be shocked."[110] Racial tensions were also felt in the classrooms where Puerto Rican students expressed dismay that professors assumed they did not understand English.[111]

A special issue of the *Caellian* published in 1973 took an interest in the "racial dilemma" facing Douglass. Putting blacks and Puerto Ricans in the same category, a student journalist noted how "Douglass is no different in implementing racist tactics. Minority students, particularly blacks and Puerto Ricans, are forced to adjust to white institutionalism."[112] One suspects that there was some cross-networking between black and Puerto Rican women at Douglass but there is no written or oral evidence of it. We do, however, know that in 1969 and 1972, black and Puerto Rican women, respectively, got their own residence spaces, and that by the early 1970s they were networking to bring black and Puerto Rican studies to Rutgers, as well as more minority faculty and administrators.[113] In 1974, the Douglass student publication *Black Voice/Carta Boricua*—an African American/Puerto Rican publication—ran its first issue. Previous to this, *Carta Boricua* and *Black Voice* published singular intercampus newsletters.[114]

Douglass, Desegregation, and
Student Protest in the Early 1960s

There were no known Puerto Rican students on campus during the early civil rights movement so we do not have their remembrances of how the civil rights movement manifested itself on the Douglass campus. However, there are hints that apathy about black rights predominated. For example, when Douglass students gathered on October 14, 1958, for a Government Association (GA) meeting, they were more preoccupied with the Douglass cheerleading team than with the Youth March for Integrated Schools taking place in Washington, DC, that weekend.[115] The nationally organized march received only a brief fifteen minutes of discussion. According to one member of the Douglass GA, civil rights was simply not their problem. Although another delegate stressed the international implications of desegregation, other members felt they had little stake in the issue. The following Thursday, the *Caellian* published a student's editorial account of the meeting, and the editorial suggested that students coordinate plans and transportation to the march. The writer called for more political organizing on campus, a need that they warned should not be pushed aside for the sake of a successful football season.[116] This unidentified student was clearly frustrated with the apathetic classmates who, with "deep conviction" thought that, "since the problems of segregation belonged to the South, we from the North should not involve ourselves." The writer used the opportunity to draw attention to New Jersey's de facto segregation and concluded, "We, the college students of the United States, are important in that we can and should involve ourselves in this attempt to end segregation. We all believe in equality and yet how many of us are willing to do something about it?"[117]

The poor turnout for the march seemed to indicate where Douglass students stood on desegregation. Twenty-nine Douglass students had expressed interest in attending the march.[118] However, as the bus departed for Washington, DC, on October 25, only five Douglass students were on board.[119] One participant questioned readers: "Could this minute representation indicate that most of the Douglass students are apathetic about segregated schools? Are we more interested in the Saturday night date or cheerleading than this national issue?"[120] Another letter argued that while necessary, the single Youth March was not nearly enough.[121] The reactions to the desegregation march were not unique. A pattern of outrage, debate, and silence emerges from student writings. As evidenced by the Youth March correspondence, indifference was one of the many themes reflected in the campus newspaper in the late 1950s.

Indeed, the seeming disinterest was the impetus behind the May 12, 1960, gathering at the Rutgers Student Center for a discussion organized by white students titled "Segregation in the North."[122] "Is there discrimination in this University?" someone asked the panelists. Rutgers professor Dr. Walter

Bezanson did not feel qualified to answer, although "he suspected that there was." Another person asked, "What can a Northern white student do to help?" Robert Curvin, a black Rutgers student who would subsequently work for the university in community relations, directed students to the recently formed Rutgers-Douglass chapter of the NAACP. Additionally, Charles Ray, the director of Neighborhood House in New Brunswick offered the Urban League of New Brunswick as a good organization for white students to address discrimination. One of the final questions stirred the most tension. A white student proceeded to ask "why Negro students always seemed to sit together and never mix."

Five black women from Douglass College "jumped to their feet" and did not hesitate to answer the question directly. One explained that she had been the only black student in her class since grade school. She realized then that she "could not have any relationship with her 'quote schoolmates' that might extend beyond 3 p.m. Monday through Friday or at any time during the weekend." The students she had befriended were those that she had the most in common with. Another black student explained further: As freshman in September, she and the other Negro girls consciously avoided "bunching up" to dispel any notions that their fellow students might have about self-isolationism. However, indicating the pressure that "fitting in" added to their lives, she continued, "We got tired of being crusaders and decided to be friends."[123]

As more black women entered the college in the late '60s, the pressure to allay the anxiety of white students who were otherwise indifferent to black issues decreased, but integrating Douglass in the early 1960s fell pretty squarely on the shoulders of early black students. For example, Bernice Proctor Venable (DC '62) was engaged in civil rights activism on and around campus. She worked in collaboration with the local chapter of the NAACP to fight discrimination against black students, and in 1961, Venable proposed a motion to "alter the present system of off-campus room allocation."[124] Steve Leeds, vice president of the NAACP chapter and chairman of the Housing Committee, criticized the system as discriminatory toward black students. The system consisted of a directory of prospective private landlords who listed available accommodations for Douglass students to rent. Applying directly, black students were often denied accommodations. Venable and the Housing Committee of the NAACP called for the university to take a stand against landlords who discriminated against its black students. They proposed that the university screen landlords to ensure that they adhered to the civil rights of prospective tenants. Landlords who discriminated, the committee argued, "should not be listed or if currently listed be removed."[125]

The push to fully integrate the Douglass dormitories was also driven by black students in collaboration with the Housing Committee of the NAACP. On the front page of the November 17, 1961, publication of the *Caellian,* an article reported on the end of "dorm bias" at Douglass College. Student contributor

Harriet Bloch declared, "There will be no racial segregation of incoming fresh-man [sic] with reference to the assignment of roommates, commencing September 1962." She continued, "The College Hall administration has requested the Admissions Office not to furnish them with any information indicating . . . the race or color of incoming freshmen."[126] According to the administration at Douglass, there was no awareness that the existing policy of pairing students by race was "unsatisfactory to the Negro students on campus." Even though the issue of racial integration was a national concern, the administration stated, rather disingenuously, that "last spring was the first time it had been brought to their attention."[127]

Although the university made strides toward full integration, the manage-ment of this new policy was conducted in a manner that appeased white racist sensibilities and dehumanized its very few black students. The public commit-ment of the institution did not always match the private actions of some of its figures. For example, the administration reassured the NAACP Housing Com-mittee that, "should any student or parent be dissatisfied with this situation, they will be informed that this is College policy. There will not be a transfer of roommates; the dissatisfied student will either have to commute or resolve her difficulties."[128] Yet word of mouth between white students who befriended their black roommates suggested otherwise. Admissions officers solicited per-mission from the white parents of students who were assigned to room with black students. Juanita Wade Wilson learned that the parents of her white roommate, Lydia Agnoli, received a call from the university. Wilson's parents did not. Betty Davis (DC '66) recalled learning about the policy much later in her time at Douglass. Her white roommate's family received notice of this plan and was asked if they would consent—which they did. "My parents weren't asked if it was okay if I was paired with a white student, which I found really interesting," Davis stated.[129] Neither the parents of the black students nor the black students themselves were informed. Although an interracial pairing was a nonracist move, the college administrators' handling of this new policy rein-forced ideas of the inferiority of African Americans and remained indifferent to the feelings of their black constituency.

If the desegregation policy was not described as an "experiment" officially, it was certainly viewed that way among white students. Like the dorm deseg-regation efforts involving Evelyn Sermons Field and Emma Andrews Warren in the 1940s, the university tracked the progress of the experiment as the black students were left uninformed. Although Wilma Harris learned decades later that she was a member of the inaugural class of this new desegregation policy at Douglass, the sense of being tracked as part of an experiment was felt by some of the black students at the time. As Betty Davis explained, "I can remember being stopped a couple of times [and someone] asking me was that working out okay, and that's when I [said], 'Yeah.' Then someone explain[ed] to me, 'Well, this is the first year that this has ever been done. This is an experiment, and we're trying to see if it's going to work."[130] Although Douglass College set in motion a gesture toward desegregation, the attitude of this person who explained the policy to Davis suggests that the university was ambivalent in its commitment.

As the "experiment" progressed, Douglass's African American students became involved in other civil rights activities. Bernice Proctor Venable (DC '62) was one of the first to circulate and sign a petition protesting the arrests of one hundred Tennessee students who participated in lunchroom sit-in strikes for desegregation in 1960.[131] She was also one of the students to participate in the Douglass prointegration protest that occurred on February 29, 1960, in front of the Student Center.[132] Like the 1959 Youth March for Integrated Schools, Venable and others urged the Douglass Government Association to protest the arrests of activists and support the strikes.[133]

Mirroring the campus apathy discussed earlier, the petition drive had a low turnout. Those who did participate voiced their disapproval of the campus response. Some pondered how the fight against school inequality could be met with shrugged shoulders and silence. Segregation was not just a "southern phenomenon" but was also a local northern fight. Housing discrimination occurred across northern and western cities, with escalating tensions around access to public housing and the practice of redlining in urban neighborhoods.[134] As the civil rights movement gained traction across the South, some northern students pushed for efforts to combat discrimination in their own communities. As Douglass students reminded their colleagues, "For those who did support the petition drive, there are many other ways to channel our protest: there is a semi-segregated housing situation here in New Brunswick and segregated fraternity houses in New Brunswick. And perhaps a contribution to the NAACP to fight the impending lawsuits would also give some direction to our energies."[135]

Throughout the early 1960s, students and faculty often referenced the NAACP, the New Jersey Urban League, and the National Student Association (NSA) as vessels through which to channel activism. Students constantly cautioned against inaction: "Any further silence will be an indication of acquiescence on the Douglass campus to a rather distorted American behavior on civil liberties."[136] Indeed, the Rutgers-Douglass NAACP had formed on campus in the spring of 1960 under interracial leadership, and the Douglass *Red Book,* the yearly handbook of information for students, listed descriptions and activities of the organizations committed to informing "students of the problems affecting the Negro and other minority groups through programming such as lectures, concerts, and fundraisers."[137] Additionally, students had the opportunity to join the campus chapter of the Congress of Racial Equality (CORE). This interracial organization fought against racial discrimination in admissions, student housing, and student employment. Going beyond the campus community, the few who got involved collaborated with New Brunswick activists who worked on voter-registration drives.[138]

Reflecting the tenor of the national civil rights organizing of the period, the NAACP and CORE would become the two most active political groups on campus in the early 1960s, but the National Student Association (NSA) also urged campus action. When Martin Luther King Jr. and college students were arrested during a sit-in demonstration in Atlanta, the NSA pressed students and the Douglass GA to support King and the Student Nonviolent Coordinating Committee (SNCC).[139] In 1960, the Rutgers-Douglass NAACP organized a pre-election day demonstration after a nationwide appeal from SNCC.[140] The purpose was "to call attention to the denial of voting rights in the South and to the need for meaningful civil rights actions." Rutgers students Joe Barry and Ed Kenton arranged plans to march from the Student Activities Center, then known as the Ledge, to the Middlesex County Courthouse on Bayard Street with protest signs and posters.[141]

Douglass students had the opportunity to attend lectures and events that not only put the black struggle front and center but that also illuminated the looming ideological fissures in the movement as well. For example, black Douglass student Barbara Washington (DC '63) was the president of the Rutgers-Douglass NAACP in February 1962 when the organization sponsored Malcolm X to speak on campus.[142] While introducing Black Nationalist Malcolm X to the stage, Washington boldly clarified that the NAACP was in no way affiliated with the separatist ideas proposed by Malcolm X and the Nation of Islam. The NAACP, Washington said, seeks the advancement of colored people through integration.[143]

Interestingly, Washington resigned from her position as Douglass-Rutgers NAACP president shortly after Malcolm X's campus visit and there is no way to know what, if any, impact the Malcom X visit had on her resignation; however, by the next semester, the vice president, black Douglass student Rita Murphy (DC '64), presided over the organization's meetings. During its first meeting in the fall, more than fifty Rutgers and Douglass students gathered and "adopted a motion to write to the National Office of the NAACP stating their sympathy with James Meredith."[144] Meredith had been denied admission to the segregated University of Mississippi in 1961. He insisted on his constitutional right to attend the public university and enlisted the support of the NAACP Legal Defense Fund to sue the school. Meredith was the first student to integrate the University of Mississippi in 1962. He did so after the Kennedy administration stationed the state guard and federal troops on campus to quell white student uprisings against desegregation.

As encouraging as was most of the campus activity surrounding the James Meredith case, there were also some disquieting reactions. For example, the *Caellian* published one reader's letter titled "How to Prove You(r?) Liberality in 10 Easy Steps" (signed "Mas' Charlie and Uncle Tom"), which included the snide advice "Be able to say in all sincerity: 'Even my best friend is a Negro,' and 'Be nice to all Negroes so they will know how liberal you are, but be very careful with Negro boys or they may think you want to date them.'"[145] Others were not amused and decided to refocus their energies to start a weeklong SNCC fundraising campaign on the Douglass campus to pay salaries, bail fees, and administration in the SNCC Atlanta office.[146]

Little did they know that recent Rutgers graduate and SNCC organizer Donald Harris (RC '63) would soon spur the campus to action. As the women of Douglass College started the fall semester and settled into dorms and new classes, urgent news seared across campus headlines: "Jail Term Continues for Civil Rights Champion; Violence and Demonstrations Continue in Georgia."[147] On August 8, 1963, Harris was arrested in Americus, Georgia. He and fellow SNCC members Ralph Allen and John Perdew, along with CORE member Zev Aelong, had led a meeting at Friendship Baptist Church and were arrested for insurrection. Harris had started working with SNCC in the summer of 1962, conducting voter-registration drives in Georgia locales including Albany, Lee County, and Americus. By 1963, he was a full-time staff member for SNCC, and by that summer was imprisoned indefinitely.[148]

The summer of 1963 was tumultuous as the attacks and police brutality against black children, students, and activists mounted. Two weeks after Harris's arrest, Martin Luther King Jr. delivered his "I Have a Dream" speech in Washington, DC, one bus ride from campus, and by September 15, 1963, four young girls—Denise McNair, Carole Robertson, Addie Mae Collins, and Cynthia Wesley—were murdered in the bombing of Birmingham's Sixteenth Street Baptist Church.

All this permeated the campus atmosphere and while so much of it seemed a southern issue, the incarceration of Donald Harris brought the fight for civil rights to Douglass's doorstep. Some Rutgers-Douglass students decided that apathy to murder, violence, and police brutality could no longer be tolerated on campus. The black Douglass and Rutgers students immediately organized "Birmingham Week" on campus and aptly titled its theme "Action against Apathy." The 1963–1964 school year witnessed a flurry of demonstrations, protests, and panels on campus that were without precedent.

The protests against apathy were led mostly by Rita Murphy, who headed the Don Harris Co-ordinating Committee. Murphy urged her fellow students and colleagues to support Harris:

> I would like to see the Don Harris case become the personal crusade of every member of this college community. To do this we must send letters and telegrams, make contacts wherever we can. Building a national awareness campaign is not an easy job, but it can be done with the help

of every one of us. Please help us organize your ideas to make Don Harris of vital national interest. Every day let's be able to say, "We did a little something to free Donnie." Did you do something today? Are you going to do something tomorrow? When are you going to start moving?[149]

That same month also marked reporting on the Birmingham church bombings, and students organized a rally.[150] The Action against Apathy rally drew a reported 1,200 students to Voorhees Chapel. During the event, participants signed a petition that was sent to the attorney general in support of Harris.

As encouraging as was this activism, the energy did not last and the concern about apathy once again reared its head. One student questioned, "Are students genuinely concerned with the plight of the American Negro? Or are they merely sympathetic with the Harris case?" This writer suggested that students were invested strictly for themselves—for the "joy of united spirit, the feeling of self-righteousness." The student was dismayed when he realized that "one student feared that Harris might be released as a result of Tuesday's hearing and next week's rally would be cancelled. . . . Perhaps," he averred sadly, "ralliers [sic] need to be reminded of their cause. . . . Civil rights is not a football game."[151] Another student, A. Greenbaum, questioned why more Rutgers and Douglass students did not attend. "Surely there could not have been apathy in the air—or was there?" he asked. With the question "do we need the imprisonment of a graduate of Rutgers University as an excuse to call for action,"[152] he queried the sincerity of Rutgers students' commitment to the general cause of civil rights.

African American students could not afford to lose sight of the causes for which they organized. Douglass student Joyce Carrington (DC '66) reflected:

I sat in Alexander Hall, thoroughly perplexed and confused, saying to myself, "I don't believe it . . . I don't believe it." Gov. Barnett was on my side????!!! Me a Negro! Was he actually saying he was for freedom!? Democracy!? I had to applaud him, for so was I. Did I actually hear him repeating those precious words that people are entitled to the pursuit of happiness? I again applauded him, as many others did. But I had forgotten for a moment that when he spoke of "people" or "states' rights," he didn't mean me. He didn't mean me because I was a Negro! And as we all know, Negro citizens of Mississippi, 42 percent of those whom he "represents," don't have states' rights because if they did Gov. Barnett would see no difference between states' rights, civil rights and human rights.[153]

The low turnout for Harris's on-campus visit after he was released from jail that November was surely a disappointment for those who had invested in his release. Of the estimated 250 students (in comparison to the 1,200 who turned out in September) who attended his speech, one disheartened student wrote: "Perhaps it was the deluge of midterms that kept the once-enthusiastic from Chapel Wednesday night. We would like to think so. It would be unfortunate if they have forgotten so soon."[154]

After the Harris case concluded and the activism on campus seemed to subside, a black Douglass international student from Jamaica, Lucille Dukissette, once again evidenced the stake black students had in the black freedom struggle. Pointing to student indifference to the 1965 voter-registration campaigns in Selma, Alabama, she wrote a letter to the *Caellian* titled "Smoldering Protest":

> Has anyone found the time to read the *New York Times* lately? If you did, maybe you've noticed something about a place called Selma, Alabama. Oh, but you should have noticed it! It has been in the papers for the past few weeks, although you might think it is not quite as important as the Congo episode or the sending of troops to Vietnam. Anyway, if you happened to have noticed, just how do you feel? Horrified, angry, or indifferent? I am angry, not only because I am a Negro, but because I am a human being and I cannot stand to hear of human beings, people like you and me (yes, they have red blood like yours) being mistreated.[155]

Others joined the sentiment of that edition and encouraged students to march on Washington. Ultimately, eighty students attended the March 14 Washington march to denounce police brutality in Selma, Alabama. Joyce Carrington (DC '66), an African American organizer of the spontaneous campus movement, thought the demonstration was a success. "It was precisely national indignation—30 demonstrators in Walhalla, Mch., or 300 in New Brunswick—that applied the last-minute pressure to bring about the federal action. The demonstration truly awoke the consciousness of America. The only way the government can know the feelings of the nation is if they are demonstrated publicly in all possible ways."[156]

As much as they wanted students to get fully involved, and as powerful a statement that people like Carrington thought students could make, activist Douglass students had to be satisfied with a status quo that was characterized by indifference with occasional spurts of energy. An article in the March 1965 issue of the *Caellian* spoke volumes: "After Apathy, What?"[157]

Late 1960s Activism and the
Gender Tension Accompanying It

In the years between 1965 and 1975, there was a palpable and radical shift in the movement for civil rights across the country. Increased violence from white opposition to black civil rights gains and unmet demands led to changes in the strategies and sentiments of black activists toward the movement for

social change. After 1965, the philosophies of Black Power and black nationalism predominated in the freedom struggle, and the shift was especially apparent on college campuses, where the urgency of the new era inspired students
across the nation to demand increases in black and brown student enrollment, more courses and faculty that reflected their own histories and communities, and campus spaces where students of color could build networks and
support each other. Students across Rutgers campuses harnessed the energy
of national student movements to work for their own and future students'
educational rights.[158]

In 1966, black Rutgers and Douglass students decided that the existing
campus organizations could no longer accommodate their expanding perspectives on activism and Black Power. In December 1966, Douglass and Rutgers students formed the Student Afro-American Society (SAS) with Frank
McClellan (RC '67) as president. In a 1968 editorial to the *Caellian,* black Rutgers student and second president of the SAS Gene Robinson (RC '68) declared,
"Integrationism, a 50-year movement, has failed to achieve . . . respect for the
average black man. . . . The 10 years of the 'Civil Rights Revolution' benefited
largely the small black middle-class 'black bourgeoisie.' So the integrationist
movement has clearly failed to aid the black masses."[159] Black Power, Robinson determined, was the only way to achieve black self-determination. Much
like the college NAACP chapter, Douglass and Rutgers students worked across
campuses to invite speakers to campus, organize rallies, and write editorials
on Black Power.

Rutgers men and Douglass women worked together for a year before they
clashed. In 1968, Gene Robinson issued an executive order to limit SAS membership to Rutgers students. Robinson said, "Next year's SAS leaders, whether
through a committee or presidential system, can of course decide to be coed";
however, "most SAS male members feel there will be less social antagonism
and more practical efficiency without girls around, at least for the rest of the
semester."[160] Shortly after announcing the separation of SAS, Gene Robinson
issued an apology to black Douglass students. Although he did not spell out
the details of the fissure, his mea culpa seemed sincere:

> I would like to offer my fullest and sincerest apology to the Douglass
> Afro-American community for my intemperate, if unintended, outburst
> at the last SAS meeting. It was not my intention to insult black wom-
> anhood in any way, shape or form. All I can do now is to pledge myself
> never to repeat such unfortunate action and continue to work fulltime
> in the best interest of the Rutgers-Douglass Afro-American and total
> communities. "To err is human, to forgive is divine."[161]

Although sources on the causes of the split at Rutgers are absent, gender
friction was not uncommon on campuses across the country. This is because

for many African Americans, *Black Power* became synonymous with the lib-eration of black men from the emasculating effects of racism. Though many women were prominent, they had not been able to use all of their talents and hold leadership roles in the nonviolent direct-action phase of the movement, and when the movement transitioned to black nationalism, men, as professor and activist Angela Davis wrote, were determined "to push women into the background."[162] When political scientist Charles Hamilton did his 1960s survey of black student activism across the country, he found that on many cam-puses, "some of the males, sensitive to the theory of black male emasculation, argued that leadership roles should be assumed by men—especially in such matters as occupying buildings, negotiating with school officials, and talking to the press."[163]

Whatever the reason for the split, Douglass women were quick to respond with an organization of their own—the Douglass Black Students' Committee (DBSC). The group elected Karen Predow (DC '70) as its first chairman, and its subsequent activism demonstrated not only that Douglass's black women could advocate for themselves but also that they could and would make the white campus a place where they could thrive.

One of the first things the DBSC did was demand courses on African Americans. Black students like Rosalind Carmichael (DC '72) refused to accept the same Eurocentric education that they received in high school. Born in Fayetteville, North Carolina, and having attended high school in the South, Carmichael was frustrated by the education she received. As she noted in a 2015 interview: "The whole education in the South was Eurocentric, definitely. By the time I got to Douglass, I knew all the folks. I knew the writers. I knew everything. I didn't know anything African American. But in terms of Euro-centric education, I was in."[164] Carmichael became active in the DBSC and was elected as one of its presidents. In 1969, in response to negotiations with the DBSC, the Douglass faculty approved the creation of an African American studies program.[165]

No longer willing to be subjects in the Douglass experiment in interra-cial living, black students in the late 1960s demanded—and through the DBSC received—a space of their own. This eliminated a lot of the problems black students had with "fitting in." As remembered by Carmichael, some of her black friends struggled. She explained, "I don't know why. They had problems with roommates. They had problems with residency. They had a lot of prob-lems."[166] In 1969, along with acceding to the demand for increased enrollment of black students, Douglass founded the African American Residence, or Black House. It should also be noted that in 1972 Douglass established Casa Boriqua, a residence and cultural house for Puerto Rican students. Established along the lines of the foreign-language houses, these spaces were not just residence halls but places where cultural events took place as well.

FIGURE 4.4 Karen Predow seated with Professor Rhoda Goldstein in 1971. They are discussing *Black Life and Culture in the United States* edited by Goldstein, which is comprised of lectures from her Douglass course on black culture that Predow helped to advocate for as president of the Douglass Black Student Congress.
Courtesy of Special Collections & University Archives, Rutgers University

The DBSC worked with activists across all the Rutgers campuses. In February 1969, in coordination with the takeover of Conklin Hall in Newark, the DBSC organized a black student protest in the cafeteria.[167] As Carmichael recalled, the black student activists positioned themselves strategically at different tables throughout the cafeteria. "At a certain time, all of us were supposed to take our plates, which was full of food. We didn't throw them. We just put them over on the table like that," Carmichael explained.[168] The students refused to move. They then announced: "We want black faculty. It's as simple as that. You're going to have to do something."[169] Making their voices heard in the largely "quiet," apathetic campus of Douglass, black students also walked out of classes, yelled at instructors, locked bathroom doors, and clogged drains. They distributed leaflets charging that the university had ignored their problems. "Blacks can no longer tolerate this," they declared.[170] In response to the demonstrations, besides committing to an African American studies program and the residence house, Douglass committed to reserving ninety-six

FIGURE 4.5 Students in the Black House.

Courtesy of Special Collections & University Archives, Rutgers University

spaces for black students, hiring fifteen black faculty during the following two years, and hiring a black assistant dean, a black counselor-in-residence, and black professionals in admissions and financial aid.[171]

As tangible as these outcomes were, sometimes the activism of Douglass women yielded intangibles. Julane Miller-Armbrister related an instance of self-reflection that tilted to the side of a burgeoning black feminist consciousness. For example, she remembered that during a demonstration in front of a segregated white fraternity housed on George Street, black Douglass students joined black Rutgers men in solidarity. Angered by the protests, white fraternity students holding bats gathered on the porch of the house, threatening physical violence. In that moment, Miller-Armbrister looked around and noticed that the line of fire consisted mainly of black women. The visual of a virtual wall composed of black women between an aggressive white fraternity and black Rutgers men generated a moment of pause for Miller-Armbrister. She remembered thinking, "What's wrong with this picture?"[172] Miller-Armbrister got out of the line and stood by the black Rutgers men, who, in the midst of the demonstration, reconfigured themselves and stood face to face with the white fraternity. "But I just remember that one 'aha!' moment," Miller-Armbrister reflected.[173] This kind of an "aha moment" by no means sought to undermine the tireless organizing efforts of black Rutgers men. Still, it was an example of a fleeting scene that brought attention to the underlying gender tensions within the struggle.

Conclusion: The Legacy of Douglass

Douglass alumna Barbara Morrison-Rodriguez (DC '71) started at the college in 1965. In her sophomore year, she married and took a hiatus from school. When she returned to campus in 1970, Douglass College was a different place. Morrison-Rodriguez described a palpable shift in black students' attitudes. Between 1968 and 1969, she described how attitudes had changed from "Thank you so much for the opportunity, I'm happy to be here" to "You ought to be glad I'm here." Barbara Morrison-Rodriguez thought to herself, "What has happened on this campus?"[174]

What had happened on campus was the Black Power movement.[175] In the late 1950s and early '60s, black students from Douglass experienced racism, intense isolation, and depression on campus. They made of it what they could and bonded with their Douglass peers on the basis of gender rather than race. Most remembered Douglass positively. However, there was no consistent civil rights activity, only occasional concentrated spurts of activity. Because they did not find support from the college, they continually turned to each other for guidance. If there were Puerto Rican students in the early 1960s, Douglass did not document it. Given what we know of the life of black students, Puerto Rican women would probably have experienced even more isolation than black students. In the late 1960s, however, both black and Puerto Rican students began to carve out their own institutional spaces.[176] During the black student movement at Douglass, students put pressure on the college to recruit more students of color, helped develop a black studies program, brought civil rights leaders and speakers to campus, pushed the school to recognize the legacies of black alumni, and engaged in student activism beyond Douglass. Black and Puerto Rican students laid the foundations for the creation of their own movements and social spaces, and in so doing they changed the image—indeed the very definition—of the "Douglass woman."

PART II

Student Protest and Forceful Change

A History of Black and Puerto Rican Student Organizing across Rutgers University Campuses, 1950–1985

The historic era of the 1960s and 1970s illuminates a seismic shift in the political, social, and economic fabric of the United States. Massive civil rights campaigns were launched and protests held against police brutality and the Vietnam War, and the large-scale activism of young people challenged the systems of inequality, racism, and economic exclusion faced by black and brown people across the country. Young people converged on the South to confront antiblack violence and Jim Crow segregation and to advocate for voting rights, and activists in cities demanded access to fair housing and equal employment in a growing postwar economy. As urban uprisings spread across the nation in the wake of Martin Luther King Jr.'s and Robert Kennedy's assassinations, Camden and Newark, New Jersey, figured as vital nodes in the fight for economic and racial justice. The Rutgers University system grew during this era and did not escape the movements for equality and access happening in each campus location and from an increasingly diverse student body. In a shift from the trickle of black and Puerto Rican students admitted and graduating from Rutgers in the 1950s, civil rights legislation and pressure from black and brown communities increased the number of students of color at Rutgers and forced the university to reckon with its historic lack of diversity and resources for these students.

There is much to cover in this volatile and dynamic era. These essays are set in the context of the national movement of black college students pushing predominantly white universities to attend to their demands for increased diversity and a curriculum reflective of their communities.[1] This section focuses largely on the histories of Rutgers–Newark and Rutgers–Camden, the establishment of Livingston College at Rutgers–New Brunswick, and the creation of black student organizations at all three, in particular concentrating on the efforts of black and Puerto Rican students to wrest support and inclusion from Rutgers administrations. These essays cover pivotal events in Rutgers's history of racial reckoning, including the Conklin Hall takeover, and chronicle the tangible changes in curriculum, student body, faculty, and staff that black and brown students fought for and initiated. The 1969 occupation of Conklin Hall by the Black Organization of Students (BOS) and negotiations with the Rutgers administration resulted in policy initiatives like the Urban University Program and provided a rationale for the Educational Opportunity Fund Act that had been ratified by the New Jersey state legislature months before the February takeover. According to historian and former Rutgers dean Richard McCormick, the Educational Opportunity Fund Act "was among the first of its kind in the nation . . . [and] set forth policies to encourage participating institutions to recruit disadvantaged students, provide them with financial assistance, and offer them appropriate supportive services."[2] It was the students' fortitude, courage, and thoughts of the future that brought opportunities to prospective Rutgers students of color.

Each essay in this part delves into the specific context and history of Rutgers–Newark, Rutgers–Camden, their respective law schools, and Livingston College at Rutgers–New Brunswick to bring attention to the lives and experiences of black and Puerto Rican students on these campuses and the obstacles they faced. Equally important, each piece showcases the growth of black and Puerto Rican student organizations from which students launched demands and from where they created spaces for mutual support, collaboration, and activism, including the Black Unity League on the New Brunswick campus, highlighted in chapter 7.

The section begins with "A Second Founding: The Black and Puerto Rican Student Revolution at Rutgers–Camden and Rutgers–Newark," which spans the 1950s to the 1970s and documents the consolidation of the Newark and Camden law schools and the establishment of Rutgers–Camden from the South Jersey Law School and the College of South Jersey in 1950. This remarkable essay covers significant ground, examining each campus's institutional origin and the first black students' insistent demands to be included in and supported by the scholarly promises of the university. By the late 1960s, Rutgers–Newark and Rutgers–Camden saw increasing activism and direct action from students demanding that admission programs recruit students of color, provide financial support through the law school, and hire more black faculty and staff. The 1969 occupation of Conklin Hall by the BOS made national headlines in the midst of other black student movements across the country demanding courses and faculty that reflected their histories and perspectives. In the aftermath of the Newark uprisings of 1967, the events at Conklin Hall rightly demanded significant attention. But campus activism did not limit itself geographically. Equally important is the essay's focus on the founding of Rutgers–Camden, the black and Puerto Rican student organizing there, the relationships between student and community activism, and the ongoing troubled relationship with the university. Its growth in the 1970s displaced black and Puerto Rican residents in the city of Camden in the wake of the Camden uprisings of 1969 and 1971. Often overshadowed by the national coverage of Conklin Hall events, black and brown students at the Camden campus made explicit the connections between their place in the university and the struggles of the local populations by taking over the College Center in February 1969. The essay "Equality in Higher Education: An Analysis of Negative Responses to the Conklin Hall Takeover" exposes the resistance to black activism from Rutgers administrators, white students, faculty, and local citizens.

A shift to the 1970s occurs later in this section, in the essays exploring Rutgers–New Brunswick's relationship with a growing black student population and the establishment of Livingston College and its vision to serve a largely black and Puerto Rican student population. In "The Black Unity League: A Necessary Movement That Could Never Survive," we learn about the Black Unity League (BUL) in New Brunswick, which sought to draw the various black campus organizations under one umbrella. Founded in 1968, the BUL focused its efforts on the establishment of a black studies program, the creation of a Black House that would serve as a site for organizing and cultural programming, and the end to police harassment of black students. Serving twenty-four demands to the Rutgers administration, the short-lived BUL set the foundation for imagining sites and spaces in the university for black students to create a meaningful home at Rutgers.

In tandem with black students demanding recognition as stakeholders in the university vision, Rutgers, under President Mason Gross, embarked on a major financial campaign to vastly expand the university. Out of this expansion came Livingston College, a school that would be coeducational and "fulfill a vision of multiple liberal arts colleges within a larger university." The administration's vision for Livingston included "[decentralized] education, . . . a curriculum that would engage students from the start with the problems of the contemporary world, and . . . create physical spaces that would connect learning and living."[3] The final essay, "'We the People': Student Activism at Livingston and Rutgers College, 1960–1985," tells the stories of a diverse group of black and Puerto Rican Livingston students who created the Puerto Rican Studies Department; fought police brutality; and established black arts programming and curricula, a black women consciousness-raising group, and black fraternities and sororities—all while holding divergent and sometimes opposing views of what black identity was and how to support Puerto Rican students in this era. With the creation of the group Black United to Save Themselves in 1969, tensions between the black students' and the administration's visions and ownership of Livingston College mounted during various meetings. Black and Puerto Rican students sought support for dedicated spaces within Livingston to explore what it meant to be black and brown at Rutgers and in the world, while the administration appeared to be more concerned with the image of Livingston as a "minoritized" part of Rutgers University and the public impression of this image.

Taken together, this section highlights the tireless work of black and Puerto Rican students and community members in making the university accountable to their needs and to the needs of future students of color who would make Rutgers their academic home. Through the turbulence of the 1960s and 1970s, Rutgers necessarily shifted and adjusted to the rigorous pressure of students who considered the needs of their urban communities and fought for what they needed to succeed.

5

A Second Founding

The Black and Puerto Rican Student Revolution at Rutgers–Camden and Rutgers–Newark

BEATRICE J. ADAMS, JESSE BAYKER,
ROBERTO C. OROZCO, AND BROOKE A. THOMAS

"We, as black students, fully support the position taken by the black students at Rutgers undergraduate school," wrote students from the Rutgers–Newark Law School in their official position statement on the "siege of Conklin Hall." "We have a direct investment," they continued, "in the problems associated with the presence or absence of black students at the undergraduate facility." Parallel to the goals of the black undergraduates who had taken over one of the main buildings on the campus of Rutgers–Newark, the primary objective of the black law students who produced the statement was to increase the number of black lawyers. Specifically, they hoped to produce black lawyers in order to represent the black community of Newark that they believed had been subjected to an "essentially racist legal system," a truth recently made all the more tangible by the urban rebellion that had swept across the core of the city. Moreover, in the statement, they also concerned themselves with issues they had with the policies of the law school, including its admissions process and the "aggressive recruitment of black undergraduates." They ended their statement by asserting that the "Newark annex of the undergraduate school was built upon the homes of displaced black people." Consequently, they argued that the university owed a "special duty to the black community," which they further reasoned had undoubtedly not been fulfilled, "especially with regard to making available to the black community the total benefits of state education."[1]

The statement from the black law students at Rutgers–Newark signifies the commonalities among the students—undergraduate, graduate, and professional—across all three campuses of Rutgers–Camden, Rutgers–Newark, and Rutgers–New Brunswick, who boldly demanded that the university "reflect and serve the people of their communities."[2] As Rutgers continued to expand across the state of New Jersey through the creation of additional campuses, the push to expand and enhance these campuses came into direct tension with the needs of the surrounding communities. Like other institutions during the period who used the language of urban renewal to displace poor urban communities, the university sought to expand and enhance its campuses at the cost of destroying urban black communities. However, the actions of the university along these lines were called into question by black and Puerto Rican students as well as members of the black and Puerto Rican communities that surrounded the university campuses. Often working in solidarity, these groups challenged the university to acknowledge its social and moral responsibilities to the communities in which it was located.

Akin to actions taken on campuses across the nation in the late 1960s, student and community protests at Rutgers were part of the larger spirit of the moment. In 1969, as students at Rutgers–Camden and Rutgers–Newark took part in bold protests to highlight the urgency of their demands of the university, there were also confrontations between students and universities at the City University of New York (CUNY), Berkeley, Cornell, and Howard. Part of what historian Martha Biondi labels "the black revolution on campus," the students at Rutgers were part of a wave of students across the nation who questioned the mission of higher education and brought the struggles and the politics of the modern black freedom movement onto campus.[3] Taking on the ideology of Black Power, they helped transform Rutgers into one of the most diverse campuses in the nation. Their actions also reveal a critical chapter in the long history of educational institutions serving as a central site of black and Puerto Rican activism, particularly during the transition from calls for integration to demands for educational equity.

This essay explores the beginnings of Rutgers's law schools and the experiences and efforts of law students of color in activating changes in admissions and matriculation at these institutions. Echoing other national student movements, law students of color demanded space and support to enter the school and legal profession. This essay also focuses on the founding of the Rutgers–Newark and Rutgers–Camden campuses and the student movements that evolved in response to the urban uprisings in Newark and elsewhere, with particular attention to the liberation of Conklin Hall in 1969. Reflecting on the university's position in the community, state, and nation, Rutgers students of color from all campuses set in motion policies enabling more inclusivity and access for generations to come.

Rutgers University–Newark's Beginnings

In 1946, the Rutgers School of Law in Newark emerged out of the merger of three law schools. The first of these law schools—the New Jersey School of

Law—was founded in 1908; the second and third, the South Jersey Law School and the Mercer Beasley School of Law, were both founded in 1926. In 1933, the Mercer Beasley School of Law and the Newark Institute of Arts and Sciences merged to form the University of Newark. Three years later, in 1936, the University of Newark would merge with Dana College, the Seth Boyden School of Business, and the New Jersey Law School to form a unified University of Newark. By 1936, the new university had formed three divisions, one of which was a law school. During the next ten years, this University of Newark–affiliated law school would deal with issues of accreditation and financing.[4] The onset of the Second World War also saw enrollment at the law school drop drastically. Although the school was able to rebound by the end of the war, calls from the state legislature to unify state education would reopen discussions about a merger between the University of Newark and Rutgers, the newly minted State University of New Jersey.[5] On July 1, 1946, a merger between Rutgers University and the University of Newark was enacted. University administrators had two main goals with the founding of the Rutgers University School of Law in Newark. In addition to providing the state with a fully accredited law school, the merger also represented an opportunity for the existing law school to ensure economic stability and an increased prestige through its affiliation with the larger state institution.[6] With the idea that the law school would function best if separated from the other units in the college, it moved to a "three-story Victorian mansion on 37 Washington Street" and was renamed the Rutgers University School of Law.[7]

Four years later, Rutgers University merged with the South Jersey Law School in Camden, New Jersey. From its inception in 1926, the South Jersey Law School served as the counterpart to the Mercer Beasley School of Law in Newark. After the merger of the two law schools, faculty served both campuses and both locations served as two divisions of one law school. However, in the 1950s, Rutgers–Camden had a much lower enrollment than its counterpart in Newark and the administration debated whether it should remain open. After an intervention from the state legislature, the Camden branch remained open through the 1950s. By 1961, the Camden branch began to grow and in 1967 the Rutgers School of Law–Camden became its own independent institution, autonomous from the Rutgers School of Law–Newark.[8]

Each law school served different populations of students; the Camden site pulled from the south end of the state and the Newark site pulled from the north end. Consequently, the experiences of students of color at the two institutions were not the same. But just as the black law students in Newark made connections with their undergraduate counterparts, similarities can be drawn across both campuses. In the years following the merger, the law school in Newark grew due to the influx of World War II veterans. Of the 391 students enrolled in the law school by 1946, more than 80 percent were veterans.[9] Although there were some women students present, as Paul Tract-enberg points out, the majority of students enrolled at the law school were white men.[10] However, in this early period of the law school's existence, there was a small contingent of black students matriculating at the institution.

On November 19, 1949, the *Chicago Defender* published an article under the headline "2 Negro Girls Pass N.J. Bar." The article announced that "two colored girls were around the 134 persons who successfully passed the New Jersey Bar examination last week. Miss M. Bernadine Johnson, 26, and Miss Martha C. Belle, 25, will be the first women of their race to be admitted to practice in this state."[11] Marie Bernadine Johnson was the daughter of J. Bernard Johnson and Maime Cooper Johnson, and was born in 1923, the same year her father moved from Gordonsville, Virginia, to Trenton, New Jersey, where he was admitted to the New Jersey State Bar. Six years later, the Johnson family had eventually settled in Newark.[12] In 1944, Bernadine Johnson graduated from Howard University with an AB degree in sociology. Three years later, she and her classmate Martha Belle would enter the newly formed Rutgers Law School in Newark. Martha Cecil Belle, later Martha Belle Williams, received her bachelor of arts from Upsala College and later resided in Montclair, New Jersey.[13] Around the beginning of her law school career, Belle was one of twenty-eight US representatives to a World Christian Youth conference in Oslo, Norway. After law school, she served as a chairperson on the board for the Young Women's Christian Association in Montclair.[14] In 1949, Bernadine Johnson entered into a law partnership with her father's firm, and in 1955 she was appointed to the US Senate Subcommittee on Juvenile Delinquency for two years. By 1961, Johnson returned to Newark as Marie Bernadine Johnson Marshall, after her marriage to future Rutgers professor of management Richard D. Marshall. In May 1961, she was the first woman to be appointed to the Newark Alcoholic Beverage Control Board.[15] Together, M. Bernadine Johnson Marshall and Martha Belle Williams were some of the earliest, if not the first, black women to graduate from the newly formed Rutgers Law School.

It is difficult to determine exactly how many black students matriculated at the law school and graduated before the late 1960s. A perusal of the Rutgers–Newark yearbooks reveals a succession of black students after the graduation of Marshall and Williams in 1947. Between 1949 and 1964, the yearbooks reveal approximately sixteen black students.[16] Each year seems to have averaged about one to three black law students. Within this fifteen-year period from 1949 to 1964, the class of 1963 had the most black students, with four graduating from the law school. These students arrived at Rutgers from a range of undergraduate colleges and universities that included Rutgers College and historically black colleges and universities (HBCUs) such as Howard and Fisk Universities. Almost all of these students were men, with one black woman, Barbara Ann Morris, in the 1953 yearbook. In addition to the black students, there was also the presence of the black law school spouses in the law school community. In the 1963 yearbook, Gloria Buck, wife of student Milton Buck ('64), was listed as secretary of the club for law school wives.[17] The presence of the wife of a black law student in what was most likely an auxiliary organization is representative of the ways in which black law students and their families were active in the law school community in Newark. In addition to the presence of black students, in 1955 the law school at Newark also hired its first black faculty member, Clarence Clyde Ferguson Jr., who was a graduate of the Ohio State University and Harvard Law School. Ferguson departed Rutgers–Newark Law in 1962 and would later work in the State Department. He also spent six years as a professor, then dean, at Howard University.

Amid the arrival and departure of Ferguson and the collection of black law students and their spouses, by 1967, Rutgers School of Law in Newark was still a "quite traditional, predominantly white school."[18] The lack of diversity in the institution became even more apparent as the Newark campus as a whole continued to expand. In September 1966, the Newark law school moved to a new fifty-thousand-square-foot structure. Named for New Jersey Supreme Court justice Henry E. Ackerson, Ackerson Hall was the first building erected specifically for the law school at Newark. The construction and move to Ackerson Hall was representative of the university's strong commitment to the growth of the law school, which by 1966 was only twenty years old.[19] Although the expansion of the law school was great for the university, as with its undergraduate counterpart, it was also representative of the growing disparity between the students who attended Rutgers–Newark and those in the neighborhood around it. As Tractenberg asserts, the law school at Rutgers–Newark was a "nearly all-white institution whose predominant mission was a traditional one: to prepare white lawyers to serve white clients mainly in commercial matters."[20] A little short of one year after the move to Ackerson Hall, in July 1967, the city of Newark erupted into urban rebellion.

A New Era for Black Students

Tensions in the black community of Newark had been increasing for years. As the black population of the city grew, its access to economic development and adequate housing stagnated. Meanwhile, incidents of police violence became routine. This situation created an atmosphere in which the black community felt that institutions were not performing effectively and social issues were not being adequately addressed.[21] Then, on the evening of July 12, 1967, the arrest and beating of a black taxicab driver by the police was the spark that ignited a rebellion. As leaders of community organizations tried to calm down the growing crowd around the police precinct where John Smith, the taxicab driver, was being held, frustrated citizens started smashing windows, throwing bricks, and looting.[22] By the following day, the mayor had been pressured to call in the State Police and the National Guard. Alongside the local police, the State Police and National Guard would actually fan the flames of the rebellion, shooting looters on sight and destroying the property of black businesses spared during the initial looting. The rebellion finally ended when the governor removed the State Police and National Guard.[23]

In the aftermath of the rebellion, the state commission, like many commissions before it, located the roots of the rebellion in the effects of poverty, tensions between the police and the community, and governmental corruption.[24] With the eyes of both the state and federal governments turned toward Newark, leaders in the black and Puerto Rican communities prepared a united front of organizations with various missions and programs in an attempt to address some of the fundamental issues the black community felt sparked the rebellion, including the proposal to build a medical school in the Central Ward that would displace an African American neighborhood.[25] Ushering in a new era of militant black politics that set the stage for the election of Newark's first black mayor, the rebellion helped generate a surge in black and Puerto Rican activism, of which the black students at the Newark campus were a crucial element.[26] In fact, the activism of black students at Rutgers–Newark created a significant moment in the narrative of Black Power in Newark.

Inspired by the zeitgeist of the uprising, the dean of the law school and, arguably, of black law students, although not mentioned in the official documents, worked proactively to address issues of racial disparity in the law school. In a memo dated April 17, 1970, Rutgers Law dean Willard Heckel wrote to Rutgers president Mason Gross and enclosed a brochure for the newest program at Rutgers Law. Heckel deemed this the "single most urgent task" before he left the deanship.[27] Willard Heckel's urgent task was to raise funds for the second year of a new program aimed at increasing the number of minority students matriculating at Rutgers Law. In his request for financial assistance, Heckel further asserted,

> If we are to be a nation committed to the rule of law, then those who feel oppressed—the poor and the black—must feel that they have the resources to move society through peaceful procedures. To do this, they must feel that they have the trained professional manpower to bring about peaceful change through the legal process.[28]

Between 1960 and 1967 the law school in Newark had graduated 1,000 students, but only twelve of these students had been African American. Moreover, Heckel's memo also asserted that "less than 2% of the nation's lawyers are black and less than 100 of the 8,000 members of the New Jersey Bar are black." With these data and on the heels of the recent urban rebellion, the Rutgers Law administration sought to implement a new program to alter the university's demographics. In their argument regarding the creation of this new educational opportunity program, the law school's administration stated, "Recognizing its social obligation to train more lawyers from minority group backgrounds, the faculty of the Law School has established special standards of admission and is developing special education programs to assure a minimum of minority group students in each class commencing in the fall of 1968."[29] This plan would become known as the Rutgers Law Minority Student Program.

In order to implement this plan, the administration began with a targeted identification and recruitment effort. First, the school added racial designations to the application and increased the allotted number of spaces in its first-year class from 150 spaces to 155 in order to make space for more minority students. Second, Rutgers Law contacted the "Negro colleges and the Woodrow Wilson Teaching Interns for recommendations of students interested in legal careers."[30] They also contacted faculty in New York, especially at the City College of New York, because they believed it was probably "the single largest producer of Negro college graduates in the country."[31] Consequently, in May 1968, as the law school worked to fundraise and plan for the program, it announced that seventeen black students had already been admitted to the law school.[32] Fourteen were admitted unconditionally and, as the law school's administration saw it, were "equally divided between southern students from segregated educational backgrounds and northern students from integrated backgrounds."[33] Five of the admitted students were from HBCUs, three were graduates of Rutgers College, one student was admitted from Douglass College, and the remainder came from as close as the City College of New York and as far as Auburn University in Alabama.[34] By the start of the 1968–1969 academic year, the law school had admitted three more students—a total admission of twenty students into the Rutgers Law Minority Student Program.[35]

It must be noted that of those initial seventeen students, three were admitted conditionally. These three students were rejected "with a promise that their applications would be reconsidered if they be admitted to and successfully complete the CLEO summer program at Emory University."[36] The Council on Legal Education Opportunity (CLEO) began in 1964 when the vice dean at Harvard Law School, Louis Toper, convened a group to discuss ways to encourage black students to study law. The outcome of this discussion was the creation of an eight-week summer program at Harvard University for forty students, a majority of whom were juniors from historically black colleges and universities. From there, similar pilot programs were launched at Emory University, the University of Denver, and the University of California–Los Angeles. In 1968, the program was established as the first national program to coordinate and recruit students to participate in what was essentially a pipeline program for minority students to enter law school.[37] CLEO was a significant program because it offered black students the opportunity to gain more preparation before entering law school. At CLEO summer institutes, students were exposed to the workload they could expect in law school by taking classes from first-year law curricula. It also worked to aid in the recruitment of students who would not have qualified for law school based on their LSAT scores or grade point average but did well in the summer institute.[38] Lastly, the program also offered students the financial support to gain these experiences to help facilitate their admission and entry into law school.

As with CLEO, the Rutgers Law Minority Student Program (RLMSP) also deemphasized the LSAT. The admissions criteria for the minority student program gave less weight to this test and paid more attention to personal references and prior experience in business or civil rights work. The average LSAT score for the minority students who entered the program in May 1968 was 442, compared to an average of 610 for the previous first-year class, in 1967. Ultimately, reducing the significance of the LSAT and boosting the significance of other admission criteria resulted in a diverse group of minority students who came from a range of colleges and universities and professional backgrounds. For example, John Mayson, who was admitted unconditionally, attended Southern University and Livingston College and had worked as an accountant for three years before starting at Rutgers Law in 1968. Hamlet Gore, a graduate of North Carolina A&T, had been out of college for six years, and Stafford Thompson of the City College of New York worked as an engineer before arriving at RU–Law.[39]

The actual academic program at RU–Law, developed by both minority students and faculty, gave students two options for course of study. In addition to a two-day preorientation, students could elect to take the usual course of study or to waive a first-year course in property law for a four-hour seminar that would be more introductory, and the program also offered tutoring and other support. Of the twenty students who began the program in the fall of 1968, ten elected to take the traditional course of study and the other ten chose to defer the property course.[40] At the end of the first year, fourteen RLMSP students who would have been excluded under the usual standards were considered to have "proven themselves fully qualified to study law at the Law School" under the same standards as their counterparts.[41] The most significant conclusion of the first-year pilot program was the argument that the LSAT was not "a valid predictor of first year law student performance of black students."[42] Moreover, the creator of the first-year evaluation recommended that the data from the first year of the RLMSP program be submitted to the educational testing service and that the "implication of possible discriminatory operation of the LSAT be brought to the attention of the Association of American Law Schools at the winter meeting, 1969."[43] For the Rutgers Law School administration, the greatest issue concerning the enrollment of minority students in law school was the LSAT. By deemphasizing that exam, the college administration found that black students could and did do just as well as their white counterparts.

In many ways the RLMSP program was seen as a successful and progressive move by the law school in Newark to increase the admission of black law students. Moreover, these early discussions of the LSAT are significant when considering minority student testing at all levels of higher education. In addition, the founding of the Rutgers Law Minority Student Program coincided with changes in the law school curriculum. In 1968, the Association of Black Law Students (ABLS) published an "Indictment of the Rutgers Law School Community" that resulted in an overhaul of the law school curriculum.[44] The law school added seminars about legal representation of the poor, social legislation and urban poverty, and consumer credit and the poor.[45] The addition of these courses suggests that, in the wake of the Newark rebellion, the law school was working in step with RLMSP to create a curriculum. But for all the potential progress the program was making, there was tension between students and the administration about the sustainability of the program.

Several years after the establishment of the RLMSP and the curricular changes, minority students at Rutgers Law School in Newark questioned the sustainability of the program. In a statement from the ABLS, they explained, "Whether the program was created out of tokenism, fear of reprisal from Newark's black population, or a heartfelt desire to alleviate the problems of the black community within the state of New Jersey is for the most part, unimportant." Instead, they posited that the important part was the potential success or sustainability of the program. By the mid-1970s, black students charged that there were two central problems facing students in the program: funding and admissions. In a March 1970 funding brochure, the law school asserted that in the 1968–1969 academic year, $26,880 had been awarded to the initial RLMSP students. Eight students had been awarded $2,000 in scholarship money, seven had received $1,000, and the rest had received lesser amounts. Tuition and fees were listed as $500 per year. Where the university had allocated $9,000 for the students in the program, the New Jersey Educational Opportunity Fund (EOF) allocated $8,500. The remaining funds came from alumni donations, CLEO, the Office of Economic Opportunity, and the Scholarship, Education, and Defense Fund for Racial Equality.[46]

Although by the following school year the program had tripled that funding amount, as the 1970s progressed, students maintained that this funding had been reduced and they were struggling for financial stability. Tuition had risen to $840 dollars, increasing along with the cost of living in Newark.[47] The most significant cut in this funding was through the EOF. As the ABLS explained, the funding had dwindled to $1,500 per student and according to a statement from university president Edward Bloustein, it would remain so.[48] This cut in funding meant that students were having to take part-time jobs or bank loans in order to subsidize their matriculation in the program. As a result, minority students were "subjected to a tremendous psychological burden, faced with foraging literally for their next meal, and at the same time worrying about property or Torts."[49] In addition to these financial problems, students also claimed that the admissions program for the RLMSP needed to be reexamined. At the outset of the program, the committee making financial and admission decisions had consisted of faculty and minority students. However, by the mid-1970s, the admissions process had shifted to that of another law school dean who was also in charge of the regular admissions. The ABLS charged that Dean John Hanks had been allowed to "accept and reject individuals on the basis of his own narrow judgement without benefit of council from minority students or faculty members."[50] As a result, the ABLS demanded the hiring of a full-time program director to oversee the admissions process of the program. Ultimately, the students reasoned that it was not that the program was unsuccessful—there was evidence to support that progress had been made via the program—but the question that loomed was sustainability.[51]

Change for Camden Law School

At the same time that Newark students were working to create change on their campus, black law students in Camden made efforts to transform their law program. In 1970 and 1972, the Black Law Students Union at Camden (BLSUC) sent the university administration two sets of demands. On November 17, 1970, the BLSUC sent their demands to Dean Russell Fairbanks and O. Theodore Reid about financial aid. They argued that "a triangle of frustration existed on this campus between the dean, the scholarship committee, and the financial aid office."[52] Students charged that there were no guidelines to receive scholarship monies and their scholarships arrived late. Consequently, black students were not only unable to pay bills or purchase books but their concerns about funding were impacting scholastic performance. Ultimately, this 1970 set of demands sought to clarify and alleviate the stress students felt over funding. Two years later, Camden law students sent a second list of demands to faculty that reiterated their concerns about funding and listed a host of other issues students were facing on campus.

They argued that it was not simply enough to admit students without support. Black students needed support from the administration in order to be successful. Since Camden and Newark law schools operated separately, there was no counterpart to the Minority Student Program in Camden. Whereas minority students in the RLMSP could take advantage of tutoring and an orientation in Newark, minority students in Camden did not have those options. In their proposal for supportive services, Camden students demanded that the institutions develop a program that would offer a two-week orientation, create a minority admissions committee, and hire a part-time instructional advisor. They argued that the program would aid in the strengthening of law school skills for "educationally handicapped and minority students." Moreover, they proposed that the program should emphasize legal writing and test taking and support students with counseling and tutoring on an individual basis. Lastly, the creation of these tutoring programs could become work-study opportunities for second-year students. Additionally, Camden law students demanded the recruitment of more minority professors and an ombudsman to mediate between black students and the administration.[53]

In step with black students around the country, black law students made demands on Rutgers that would force the university to do more than essentially integrate. For Newark students, the development and implementation of the MSP signified that the law school's administration recognized the disparities between the city of Newark and the College of Law. Their discussion of the LSAT and its effects on student success, for example, was significant in illuminating the hindrances black students faced in the admissions process. Moreover, the efforts to connect with programs like CLEO emphasized the mission to increase the number of black students in the law school. But without financial support or consistent oversight to advocate for minority students on the admissions committee, which was potentially impacted by personnel changes in the university, the program was not sustainable for black students. Similarly, the demands by law students in Camden further echoed the demand for the university as a whole to do more to support full inclusion. Without a program like RLMSP, students at Camden argued that they needed more institutional support to continue in law school. Students demanded equity, not simply integration. The creation of programs like that in Newark represented positive change, but without efforts to create educational equity, these programs were not sustainable and the law school's commitment to create more black lawyers was dishonest. Given the history of black law student activism at Newark and Camden and their demands for inclusion and equity, it should be no surprise that undergraduates at these campuses made similar efforts to shape and take ownership of their Rutgers education.

Rutgers–Newark, Black Undergraduates, and Black Power: The Liberation of Conklin Hall

In the wake of the Newark rebellion of 1967, Vickie Donaldson started her matriculation as an undergraduate at Rutgers–Newark.[54] Before the start of the fall semester, Donaldson had opted to take a Spanish class at Newark Preparatory in the summer so she would not have to take the course during her first academic year at Rutgers. This decision meant she had a firsthand understanding of the violence of the uprising because she rode the bus through the midst of it each day to get to class. Donaldson was originally from Florida, where she had been active in local civil rights activities—which undoubtedly helped her navigate the tensions of the moment and cultivate skills she later used as a student activist at Rutgers.

In the fall, after what seemed like many days on campus, Donaldson finally saw another black student and was immediately invited by Richard Roper to attend the next meeting of the National Association for the Advancement of Colored People (NAACP). According to Robert Curvin, a 1960 graduate of Rutgers–Newark, the Rutgers–Newark chapter of the NAACP was founded by Bill Payne and Curvin to encourage students to get involved with the civil rights movement. Both men had been active with the NAACP in high school and they believed the organization could be used to leverage more support for the civil rights movement on campus. The RU–Newark chapter of the NAACP sought to be more progressive than its citywide counterpart. The citywide chapter cooperated with leaders in the city government, whom many members of the black community saw as corrupt.[55] During the tenure of the NAACP on campus, it did take a more militant position than the city chapter, including inviting Malcolm X to campus.[56] Additionally, as Roper demonstrated during his chance meeting with Donaldson, the NAACP also served a social function as a space where the small number of African American students on campus could meet and be in community.

However, in the aftermath of the uprising, an event that signaled a larger political and ideological shift in the modern black freedom movement in Newark, Donaldson, as well as many of her peers, had sharp critiques of the NAACP. Not explicitly seen as a protest organization taking part in the movement for black freedom, the NAACP was considered too conservative by many students, including Donaldson, as demands for civil rights gave way to calls for Black Power.

The move away from the NAACP was formulated around a call for a new organization. This new organization became the Black Organization of Students (BOS). Formed in the fall of 1967, the same semester that Donaldson began her matriculation at the university, the formal purpose of the organization was "to foster an awareness and an understanding of the changing role of the black population both on and off campus."[57] Distancing itself from older language ("colored") and ideologies of black identity and activism to emphasize their ideological standpoint, the name BOS signaled the group's collective shift toward a more radical agenda. Although members of BOS espoused a diverse array of political and ideological standpoints, the organization had a collective desire to create change on the campus of RU–Newark and a shared vision of responsibility to the black community of Newark.[58]

A key element of the mission of the new organization was leveraging their position as students to extract resources from the university to benefit the black community of Newark. At the time, the demographics of Newark were shifting as the black community grew, but the demographics of Rutgers–Newark did not reflect this shift. Accordingly, the main goal of the BOS was to convince the university to not only accept more black students from Newark schools but also to establish connections with schools in black neighborhoods to ensure that students saw Rutgers–Newark as a reasonable choice to pursue their secondary education. This effort was rooted in the larger background of social and political change in Newark.[59]

With these ideals in mind, the members of BOS worked from the fall of 1967 to the spring of 1969 to convince the administrative leadership of the university to change the admissions process. BOS members were assisted in their efforts to change institutional policy by Bessie Nelms Hill, the first African American person to serve on the Rutgers Board of Governors, starting in 1965. Prior to serving on the Board of Governors, Hill worked for forty years in the Trenton School District as a teacher and guidance counselor—experience she would use to guide the members of BOS as they formulated their demands of the university. Insisting on clarity, both ideologically and grammatically, Hill challenged BOS members to work through their anger and frustrations to deliver a clear message to the university, recalled Vivian Sanks King (RC '70), a member of BOS and a 1970 graduate of Rutgers–Newark, who described the group's meetings with Hill.[60]

Members of BOS delivered their carefully constructed messages to the university whenever the opportunity arose. Calling for changes in the admissions process, for the hiring of more black professors and staff, and for the university to establish programs focused on the study of the black experience, they met with the vice president of the Newark campus, Malcolm Talbott, sent representatives to faculty meetings, and made presentations at meetings of the Board of Governors. However, their efforts resulted in little institutional change.[61]

Consequently, during the 1969 spring semester, a subset of the members of BOS who had grown tired of the endless back and forth with the university about admission standards voted to take over Conklin Hall. Unable to convince the Board of Governors of what they saw as the moral responsibility of the university to educate the members of the community in which it was located, they hoped their actions could communicate the urgency of their demands to the university. Conklin Hall was an ideal choice because they had access to both the floor plans of the building and an understanding of when the night guards came to check the building.[62]

After deciding on the location, they established rules, including no firearms, and agreed to let a handpicked group of community-based organizations know about their plans to take over the building. In the early morning hours of February 24, 1969, a select group of twenty-four members of BOS entered

FIGURE 5.1 Black Organization of Students member placing protest banner on top of Conklin Hall.

Courtesy of Special Collections & University Archives, Rutgers University

Conklin Hall and refused to leave until the university met their demands. Climbing to the roof of the building, they unrolled a huge banner that declared the building "BOS Liberation Hall." The image of BOS activists on the roof, holding up a Black Power salute, would grace the *New York Times* the next day.[63]

Negotiations with President Mason Gross started on the first day of the protest as both protesters and counter-protesters rallied outside the building. Ignoring the calls of lawmakers, white students, and fellow administrators, Gross did not call in the police but instead met with a group of negotiators including Richard Roper, who now worked for the Department of Higher Education; Peter Jackson, a member of BOS; Robert Curvin, the faculty advisor of BOS; and Vice President Malcolm Talbott.[64]

Arguably one of the most spectacular moments of the takeover actually took place outside of Conklin Hall as supporters of BOS clashed with counter-protesters. The BOS protesters had chained the doors shut to prevent anyone from entering Conklin Hall. On February 26, 1969, counter-protesters used a telephone pole as a battering ram in an attempt to break down the doors. The counter-protesters' most vocal leader was Anthony Imperiale, who was noted for advocating for white self-defense during the rebellion. He would also become a politician well known for race-baiting.[65] Members of local community organizations, including the Newark Area Planning Association (NAPA) and the Committee for a United Newark (CFUN), protested outside in solidarity with BOS and came to the students' defense.[66] Several BOS members had relationships with these local organizations, in particular Joseph Browne, the chairman of BOS. Browne was active in the larger Newark activist community and was seen by Junius Williams, the chairman of NAPA, as his "second-in-command."[67] In addition to NAPA and CFUN, members of the Black Panther Party, the local welfare rights organization, and members of black student organizations from other institutions also protested in solidarity outside Conklin Hall during the takeover.[68] Their solidarity with the takeover was meant to publicize the urgency of the policies that were needed and that would affect not only the students at Rutgers but also the entire black community of Newark.

After occupying the building for three days, in the early morning hours of February 27, the protesters left the building because they believed there had been a signed agreement with President Mason Gross that resolved their demands, particularly the ones related to changes in admissions.[69] However, the celebratory moment would be undercut once the members of BOS came to understand that several demands in the signed agreement with Gross could not be enacted without the approval of the faculty. And, as Joseph Browne pointed out in retrospect, the support of the faculty had always been "mushy and BOS had done little to court their support."[70] Moreover, Peter Jackson, one of the main negotiators for the BOS, questioned whether there was ever more than a mere verbal agreement between President Gross and the protesters.[71] These key facts would ignite another battle between the liberators of Conklin Hall and several groups of university stakeholders.

Several days after the takeover ended, it was reported that President Gross signed a copy of the transcript of the negotiations as opposed to signing the demands. Browne declared that the signature on the transcript as opposed to the agreement was an act of "bad faith."[72] Then, on March 6, the faculty rejected the agreement that university officials had made with the BOS related to changes in admission standards. The core demand of the BOS under debate

FIGURE 5.2 Black Organization of Students protester holds "Rutgers White Oasis" sign during the Conklin Hall takeover.

Courtesy of Special Collections & University Archives, Rutgers University

was that any African American student who graduated in the top 50 percent of their class would automatically be accepted to Rutgers. After the meeting, Talbott said that he believed President Gross and Talbott had agreed to this demand during the negotiations with the BOS during the takeover.[73] Nevertheless, the faculty had the power to vote down any changes made to admissions policies—a power the vast majority of faculty used to communicate their disapproval of the way President Gross had handled the negotiations.[74]

The failure of the faculty to agree to the demands proposed by BOS served as just one voice in a concert of cries deriding the actions of the liberators. These other voices of dissent included BOS members who believed their parents would not approve of their actions if they took part in the takeover, black students who felt the university was making adequate progress related to race, conservative members of the community who believed the police should have been called in, and faculty who resented President Gross for not discussing the demands with them. The actions of the students who took over Conklin Hall were seen as extremist and unproductive by many campus and community members.[75]

However, BOS had made its demands in a moment when government officials were motivated to listen to the demands of urban communities in the hope of curbing further urban unrest. Therefore, although the demands of the BOS may not have been honored by the faculty, they did inspire change on higher levels. On March 14, the Board of Governors voted to establish a program to open the doors of the university to "all economically and educationally disadvantaged students" in Newark, Camden, and New Brunswick.[76] This program would become the Urban University Program. Embodying the idea that the university had a responsibility to the communities in which it was located, an idea emphasized in the demands of the BOS, the program provided a range of supportive services meant to allow students from Newark, Camden, and New Brunswick who did not meet the complete admission standards a chance to not only attend Rutgers but become successful there as well.[77]

Viewing the new program as their program, BOS members helped provide the supportive services students needed to be successful at Rutgers.[78] Yet despite these efforts, the program was short-lived. The funding for the program was tenuous from the start, the faculty did not fully support it, and students in the program struggled academically.[79] Instead the Educational Opportunity Fund (EOF), which like the takeover itself was a response to the changing political and social terrain that emerged after the Newark rebellion in 1967, became the main mechanism used to diversify the student population at Rutgers.[80] A state-funded program that provided financial and academic assistance to students from economically disadvantaged backgrounds, the EOF has helped generations of students from minority communities graduate from Rutgers.

The Birth and Expansion of Rutgers–Camden

As the dramatic events at Conklin Hall grabbed *New York Times* headlines in 1969, a similar protest was emerging in Camden. Although the activities of Newark's BOS have garnered more attention from historians, undergraduate students in Camden became equally energized in the late 1960s. They organized the Black Student Unity Movement and staged their own dramatic protests to draw attention to the educational needs of Camden's black community. Their organizing—and their vision for a more inclusive urban university—is particularly remarkable considering that the Camden campus enrolled only about twenty black students total (in comparison, 148 black students enrolled at Rutgers–Newark during the 1968–1969 academic year).[81]

The emergence of Rutgers's South Jersey campus and its expansion in Camden provides an important background for understanding Camden students' demands, tactics, and aspirations for the college, which called for increased enrollment of black students and presented a vision for reshaping the university's relationship with its urban host community. The Camden campus became part of Rutgers in 1950 when the South Jersey Law School and its undergraduate division—called the College of South Jersey—merged with the state university. The undergraduate school initially kept the moniker Rutgers University College of South Jersey, but the growing campus would come to be known simply as Rutgers–Camden.

The 1953 edition of the *Mneme* yearbook revealed four buildings that defined the locality of the college during the early days of its merger.[82] By 1958, approximately 1,300 full- and part-time students made up Rutgers–Camden's population. Although enrollment of first-year students continued to see growth, the number of graduating students stayed steady until 1958, when the graduating class almost doubled from the previous year.[83] As enrollment continued to increase, the trustees and the administration confronted the issue of physical expansion. At this time, debates began about the alternative routes for growth: The institution could expand into what the administrators and trustees described as the "deteriorating neighborhood" of Camden, or the university might consider moving its location to a more suburban environment.[84] Racial undertones permeated the content of these debates and would come to mirror the conflicts between elite institutions and their surrounding urban communities who did not benefit from the presence of these universities.

In the aftermath of the Newark uprising and urban rebellions across the country, Camden officials sought federal funding to develop and "renew" the city after the postwar decline in industry and white flight to the suburbs. In the same moment, community activists worked on rebuilding and restoring cities for the benefit of African Americans and other people of color who comprised the majority of these urban populations.[85] The "urban renewal" movement meant different things to community members and to Camden politicians. Like other parts of the state, black and Puerto Rican families had moved into Camden for employment opportunities and to build stable communities in the 1940s.[86] After the decline of war industries in the 1950s, black and Puerto Rican families faced diminishing employment opportunities and housing that priced them out or proved substandard and unsafe. This decline, coupled with the disappearance of city-centered businesses and amenities, forced families of color to organize against thoughtless and exclusionary city development.[87] The tensions between Camden city officials and communities of color played out in several ways throughout the 1960s and 1970s.

Al Pierce entered city politics at the beginning of these urban renewal efforts. A graduate of the College of South Jersey, a war veteran, and a native of East Camden, Pierce led the charge of "redeveloping" the city by successfully winning a 1959 election for one of the five at-large commissioners on the basis of the "Save Our City" platform he created.[88] Quickly appointed "mayor and director of public safety," Pierce took control of "[cleaning] up the city." Obsessed with "law and order," Pierce first targeted Camden's informal economies like gambling, bringing increased police presence to black and brown neighborhoods.[89] Alienating an increasing population of African Americans and Puerto Ricans, he ran for reelection in 1961 on the same platform while including Elijah Perry—"the first African American to run for city-wide office"—and other people of color, including Mario Rodriguez, the first Puerto Rican to run on the city ticket, to show inclusiveness and an attempt at coalition governing with representation from across the city's wards.[90] However, the critical moves Pierce made to rebuild the city caused increased tension with the black and Puerto Rican communities. For residents of color, housing and employment needs remained marginal or ignored by efforts to build up downtown and put roads and highways where they would split these communities physically apart and alienate them from their community businesses.

These efforts provoked wide backlash from community members of color and their allies from local churches. Alongside local chapters of national organizations such as the NAACP and the Congress of Racial Equality (CORE), the Black People's Unity Movement (BPUM) was established in Camden to "[push] for fundamental changes in how African Americans were treated by both the public and private sectors."[91] BPUM energized young student activists such as Benjamin Ortiz and Malik Chaka (Michael Edwards), whose leadership would ignite protests at Camden High School and at Rutgers.[92]

Increased policing, denial of fair and adequate housing, and exclusion from redevelopment plans led Camden's residents of color to form alliances with local and national civil rights organizations and invited Black Power movement activists to assist with strategies to fight displacement and abandonment. Like other parts of the country, people of color in urban areas fought back. In Camden, tensions came to a climax on September 2, 1969, when reports of police brutality brought hundreds of black protesters into the streets. The city's chief of police, Harold Melleby, refused to meet with the protesters, and policemen clashed with the crowds. This violent night claimed the lives of two people: a white police officer and a fifteen-year-old black girl named Rose McDonald, who was by all accounts an innocent bystander.[93] The brutal beating of a Puerto Rican man by Camden police on July 30, 1971, elicited another uprising. As news spread about the beating of Rafael Rodriguez Gonzalez (erroneously identified in the press as Horacio Jimenez), Camden's Black Power activists and Puerto Rican nationalists banded together to organize marches and sit-ins demanding police accountability, with Rutgers student Gualberto Medina emerging as a key leader in the movement. After weeks of protests, Mayor Joseph Nardi's failure to take the community's demands seriously fueled the fire; on August 19, 1971, protesters once again clashed with the police, beginning when officers assaulted hundreds of demonstrators with tear gas and dogs.[94] The uprising lasted several days and resulted in deaths, injuries, and arrests of protesters. What was at stake was the community-led actions and activism that pushed back on Camden officials' efforts to revitalize the city while forsaking and inflicting violence upon its black and Puerto Rican residents. Rutgers–Camden's complicity in the displacement of these communities of color necessitates further exploration.

Well into the 1960s, the city leadership continued their goals of urban revitalization and gentrification while displacing black and Puerto Rican people. And although the Camden Housing Agency began developing new housing projects, applications by black and Puerto Rican families were being denied.[95] Ultimately, Rutgers–Camden played an integral role in the efforts to "revive" the city and was responsible for dislocating black and Puerto Rican residents. In several communications between the city of Camden and the college, decisions were made to move forward with the expansion of several lots around the school without consideration for the local neighbors—in particular, the Cooper-Grant community, a working-class community that had historically been composed of black and Puerto Rican residents.[96] In a memorandum of intent to expand, Rutgers University detailed its plan to acquire an additional nine blocks, primarily situated within the Cooper-Grant community.[97] Although the Rutgers University administration took on the expansion project through a relationship based on good faith, the subsequent communications detailed decision-making that often did not take into account the needs of the local community. Working with Camden Regional Legal Services, the residents of the Cooper-Grant community brought their concerns about the expansion to Rutgers administrators. However, the university had no legal right to enter into an agreement with the community. Having gone back and forth, the university officially decided to expand into the surrounding community with no intention to develop residential housing as previously promised in dialogues coming from Camden officials.[98] And even though Rutgers University would continue to be held accountable to the local community by Rutgers–Camden students and community members, the university would eventually proceed with its expansion after a lawsuit, *People of Cooper-Grant vs. Rutgers University and the City of Camden,* was judged in favor of the university on July 17, 1978.[99] The consequences of this invasive expansion on Camden's residents of color was long term and devastating. Simply acknowledging Rutgers's complicity in displacing and dislocating community members does not redress the decades of neglect and suffering black and Puerto Rican residents bore at the hands of the city government, white residents, the police, and the university, despite attempts by student activists to address these concerns within Rutgers–Camden.[100]

Demands of Black and Puerto Rican
Students at Rutgers–Camden

It was in the context of these debates about urban renewal that black and Puerto Rican students began to organize for change at Rutgers–Camden in the late 1960s. Young activists formed the Black Student Unity Movement (BSUM), which was an outgrowth of the local organization BPUM that had emerged in Camden in 1968 under the leadership of charismatic Black Power activist Charles "Poppy" Sharp. Malik Chaka, a Rutgers sociology student, was one of the central founders of BPUM with Sharp. Chaka worked to turn the BPUM into the most influential black community organization in Camden, and he brought Black Power politics to Rutgers when he cofounded BSUM as a campus offshoot of BPUM.[101] Other Rutgers students were also inspired by Sharp and his politics. Marie Downes recalled, "We were very vocal against injustice in the black community. We wore our Afros, we wore our daishikis, and picketed businesses that discriminated against black people."[102] Black student activists at Rutgers–Camden also included Roy Jones, Tom Warren, Myrna Williams Thompson, Oliver Thompson, Aaron Thompson, and Cheryl Amana-Burris.

The members of BSUM saw a divide between Rutgers and its surrounding urban community. In 1968, Rutgers–Camden remained the smallest of the university's campuses, enrolling 1,150 full-time students; only about twenty of them were black. Whereas Camden's population was nearly 40 percent black, the Rutgers–Camden student body was more than 98 percent white. Furthermore, the majority of the white students did not reside in the city. Rutgers–Camden was a commuter campus with no residence halls, and it drew students from the predominantly white suburbs in Camden County, Gloucester County, and Burlington County. If these students invested their time and energy into community programs, they did so in their own suburban neighborhoods after they left campus. Many professors did not live in Camden either. The handful of black students, on the other hand, were mostly Camden residents and were deeply concerned about the social problems facing the city. Because they were involved in community organizing in Camden, these students grew increasingly angry at the town–gown divide and the university's lack of investment in the city's black youth.

Similar to their BOS counterparts in Newark, BSUM members attempted to make their case to the administration but grew frustrated by the lack of progress on issues that mattered to them most—recruitment of and support for black students and Rutgers's obligation to its surrounding community. On February 10, 1969, BSUM published a list of twenty-four demands that articulated a vision for a more inclusive, community-engaged university.[103] Students delivered the list to the administration, demanding the university's compliance within one week. They also mimeographed and distributed the list of demands around campus, urging conscientious white students to stand with BSUM. Interrupting a political science class, Roy Jones, one of BSUM's leaders, spoke passionately to the students about the relevance of a college education in a time of national turmoil. "An urban university should be, as a consequence of its location, actively concerned about its neighboring community," said Jones. He accused social scientists of being "more interested in abstract theory and correlational statistics" than in understanding the real problems facing their fellow man. He continued:

> Education here does not relate to the community, nor is its theoretical composition applicable to the neighboring community. This university must begin to bring into focus the practical day-to-day uses of scholarship, creativeness, and equipment it clumsily misuses. The community must be given an active place in this university's educational structure. A university's relevance is questioned when its application of social and physical sciences does not move in the direction of solving historical, social, environmental and related injustices. Irrelevance vaporizes the atmosphere here and stifles the educational process.[104]

Jones concluded by telling students, "More than ever today, relevance must be sought after."[105] How might this relevance to the neighboring community be achieved? BSUM's demands included the establishment of an urban education program as well as revising the curriculum in sociology, political science, education, and psychology to place an emphasis on field work and outside research. This way students could gain hands-on experience outside the classroom while putting their college education to good use in the city. BSUM also demanded that "student teaching be done within Camden City proper" rather than in suburban schools. Moreover, BSUM sought to make a Rutgers education more relevant to black youth by demanding the establishment of a black studies department and the creation of a library collection of books by black authors as well as periodicals and audiovisual materials about African and African American life and history. They wanted this collection to be named for Dr. Ulysses S. Wiggins, a well-respected leader in the African American community in Camden and longtime president of the local NAACP branch who had passed away three years prior.[106] Many of the BSUM demands were aimed at significantly increasing the enrollment of black students from local schools and then providing support services to ensure their academic success, including the hiring of more black personnel at the college.[107]

On February 11, 1969, one day after presenting their demands, BSUM began a series of meetings with a group of faculty and administrators. The students agreed to accept three monthly reports on the university's implementation of the demands, the first report to be issued by February 17. When the office of W. Layton Hall, dean of the college, issued its first official response to the students on February 17, BSUM members surmised that the university was reticent to fully commit to meeting their demands. The activists decided to escalate their protest actions. They interrupted an outdoor meeting of the Student Council and publicly burned the administration's response, declaring it unacceptable. BSUM members then demanded to meet directly with President Mason Gross.[108]

As President Gross prepared for his visit to Camden, the BOS in Newark initiated their dramatic takeover of Conklin Hall. On February 26, 1969, while the "Liberation Hall" banner hung from the roof in Newark, Gross left negotiations in Newark to meet with BSUM in Camden. At a private meeting with the student activists, Gross gave the students the impression that he supported their demands. But an hour later, when Gross addressed the wider college community at a public meeting, BSUM members were dismayed and angered by what appeared to be Gross's backtracking. Student activists realized that a verbal understanding with the administration could be dismissed if they lacked a written agreement.

Knowing that the Conklin Hall takeover was already putting the national spotlight on Rutgers's relations with its black students, BSUM decided to strike while the iron was hot. At ten o'clock that same night, two dozen activists entered the College Center on Fourth and Penn Streets and vowed to occupy the building until they received a written statement from President Gross confirming the verbal agreements made earlier in the day.[109] The protesters used chains, furniture, and fire hoses taken off the walls to barricade the four entrances to the building and spent a quiet night inside. The morning of February 27, 1969, a crowd formed in front of the building as students began to arrive on campus, and local black activists from BPUM and from other schools came to support those who had taken over the College Center. As in Newark, the sentiment of the crowd split between BSUM supporters and counter-protesters, and university officials worked to keep tensions from boiling over into open confrontation. Dean of Students Barry M. Millett hoped to avoid involving the Camden police.

Yet the occupation in Camden differed from Newark in one important aspect. The protesters who took over the building included not only students but also several Camden activists who were not enrolled at Rutgers, such as Sherwood Saunders, a Camden High School senior and chairman of the youth arm of BPUM. Another protester was Benjamin Ortiz, a twenty-year-old Puerto Rican activist who had led hundreds of Camden High School students in BPUM-supported protests the year before.[110] Their involvement illustrates the strong link between Camden's BPUM and the Rutgers protesters. The handful of black students at Rutgers–Camden simply could not have accomplished the takeover without the help of their allies in the broader Camden community. But the involvement of nonstudents also put the protesters at greater risk because of New Jersey's Public Law 981, which made it a state violation for nonstudents to interfere with the operation of a New Jersey school or college.[111] The involvement of nonstudents opened the door for the Camden police to act even if the university officials did not want them to enter the campus. Realizing the added risk that their presence inside the building brought, the nonstudents eventually left the College Center.

Around noon on Thursday, February 27, the protesters received a written statement from President Gross agreeing to most—though not all—of their demands.[112] After occupying the building for fourteen hours, BSUM members declared success and walked out, holding up their fists in the Black Power salute. The BOS occupation in Newark ended around the same time. Classes at Rutgers–Camden were suspended until March 5, giving the campus community three days to meet and discuss implementing the BSUM demands in a range of forums, including a meeting of the college's faculty where Roy Jones and Malik Chaka appeared to plead their case again.

Rutgers–Camden faculty eventually voted to endorse the spirit of the BSUM demands while expressing reservations about several points.[113] Two of the twenty-four demands proved particularly problematic for faculty. Demand number one at the top of the list read, "We demand that all racist faculty be removed from the university."[114] Black students were tired of the blatant discrimination that some professors practiced in their classrooms. The college's point-by-point response to the students failed to acknowledge the problem, stating, "The College does not know and cannot identify members of the faculty who can be labeled racist." Instead of firing racist faculty, the dean of the college suggested that a "seminar on the subject of racism" might suffice. Many of the faculty were outraged that President Gross issued a statement agreeing to students' demands without consulting the faculty body. Gross did not mince words, closing his letter with this remark: "Let me reiterate my own conviction that there is no place in American democratic society for people who practice racism and that as the administrative head of the University, I will file charges against any Faculty or Staff person when there seems to be evidence that he is a racist."[115] Camden faculty were dismayed by the president's statement. What about due process? What about academic freedom and professors' rights to hold conservative views? Appearing at a faculty meeting, Malik Chaka explained that "as for the firing of racists, this doesn't mean that any professor with conservative views should be fired." Chaka argued that students were more concerned with professors' discriminatory *actions,* such as bias in grading, which were, after all, illegal under the Civil Rights Act of 1964. And yet professors' views on race were not unimportant in the classroom. BSUM students did not want faculty to preach hate in front of the blackboard. "If Nazis are graduating from the college after four years here, the faculty have failed," Chaka told the meeting.[116] The faculty eventually passed a resolution conceding the point, but reminding students that "Academic Due Process" would be followed "in the event a charge of racism is brought against a member of this faculty."[117]

One final point became so controversial that the faculty simply could not endorse it. This point touched on the issue of the names and images that adorned the campus, a reminder of Rutgers's founders, heroes, and loyal sons and daughters. BSUM demanded that Camden's brand-new "library addition be named after Brother Paul Robeson."[118] Black students longed to see their heroes' names on campus spaces, quietly signaling from the walls that "you belong here." As one of Rutgers's most accomplished alumni—scholar, athlete, performer, and global activist possessed of uncompromising integrity— Paul Robeson seemed like the perfect choice to the students. But many in the faculty could not fathom putting Robeson's name on the building, and this demand was brushed aside.[119] Twenty-two years later, it would finally come to pass, and another generation of Rutgers–Camden students would see Paul Robeson's name emblazoned on the front of the building when the library was renamed in his honor in 1991.[120]

Historians' appraisal of the BSUM takeover has been mixed. Richard McCormick concluded that tangible results fell short compared with the new programs that were implemented in Newark and New Brunswick as a result of the protests of 1969.[121] His assessment hints at the long-standing disparities between the three campuses of the state university, with Rutgers–Camden often getting the short end of the stick regarding resources. But there are multiple ways to look at the legacy of black protest at Rutgers–Camden.

The BSUM takeover of the College Center was not the end but rather the beginning, inaugurating an era of persistent student activism that reshaped Rutgers–Camden. "Our actions in 1969 served as a catalyst to move the university from an exclusive suburban enclave to an inclusive, very diverse urban

FIGURE 5.3 Roy Jones speaks at the 2016 symposium "Beacons of Light: The Black Student Protest Legacy at Rutgers–Camden."

Courtesy of Special Collections & University Archives, Rutgers University

university model," Roy Jones reminded the audience at a 2016 retrospective event on campus.[122] Recalling the BSUM protests in 2001, Marie Downes also agreed that "being a catalyst for change" was their biggest accomplishment. "Three decades ago as university students," said Downes, "we learned that if the individual doesn't summon the courage and step forward and take action when action is needed, then nothing will change."[123] The legacy of the BSUM protest went beyond Rutgers—it shaped a generation of leaders, many of whom would invest years of their lives into teaching at Camden's schools, running local libraries, fighting environmental injustice in the city, and otherwise using their education (in and outside the classroom) to generate positive change for their communities. Moreover, historian Laurie Lahey argues that the BSUM protest presented a key turning point for African American and Puerto Rican relations in Camden because BSUM integrated Puerto Rican activists into the group. These activists included Gualberto Medina, Benny Galaf, and Angelo Carillon, all of whom would later play a role in Camden community organizing and the protests that would erupt in 1971.[124]

On March 4, 1971, Puerto Rican students across all the Rutgers campuses submitted a list of multiple demands that mirrored each college's needs for

FIGURE 5.4 Malik Chaka speaks at the 2016 symposium "Beacons of Light: The Black Student Protest Legacy at Rutgers–Camden."

Courtesy of Special Collections & University Archives, Rutgers University

supporting their student populations. The Puerto Rican students of the Camden community submitted a list of sixteen demands that captured similar grievances expressed by black students two years earlier.[125] BSUM member Gualberto Medina served as the student representative of the Puerto Rican students of Camden, along with his peers Walter Martinez from Livingston College, Zaida J. Torres from Douglass College, and Rolando Cruz from Rutgers College.[126] Puerto Rican students insisted that the university develop a Puerto Rican studies program, establish more intentional practices of admitting Puerto Rican students into the university, and hire more Puerto Rican faculty and staff at all levels of the institution. Moreover, they insisted on the development of space specifically for Puerto Rican students, as well as the use of Rutgers University facilities for Camden's black and Puerto Rican community.[127]

The publication *Black Voice*, later renamed *Black Voice/Carta Boricua,* was used as a means of communication among the black community and communities of color at the multiple colleges in New Brunswick starting in 1969.[128] Similarly, black students in Camden created the newsletter *Khuluma* to bring the black community together. This collection of writings and flyers for local events continued the engagement with Black Power on and off campus and was distributed throughout the Camden community. Black students were called upon in the issues to strengthen and hold on to a black identity that was constantly being challenged by the university.[129] Students found means of communication other than protests and rallies that often had a larger reach with those outside of the university.

Therefore, using multiple organizing methods, students during the late 1960s and early 1970s pushed the university administration to support their proposals. The student movement at Rutgers University after this period brought its own challenges, including the shift in Rutgers's presidential leadership in 1971 from President Mason Gross to President Edward Bloustein. Despite the minor and major obstacles the students faced, several demands they had made were met by developing funding line items for personnel and resources requested by students with the assistance of the local community and a few faculty on campus.

Conclusion

In many ways the Educational Opportunity Fund represents the legacy of the student revolution on the Newark and Camden campuses of Rutgers. In 2019, the EOF and the Conklin Hall takeover both celebrated their fiftieth anniversaries.[130] And the histories of both the BOS and the EOF are linked in the institutional narrative used to explain how Rutgers–Newark transformed into the most diverse campus in the nation.[131] However, the progressive narrative of university leaders simply embracing the ideals of the takeover and using the EOF as a mechanism to create a more inclusive university belies the fact that the takeover of Conklin Hall should be understood as a fundamental event not only in the history of Rutgers, but in the modern black freedom movement as well. Fighting for educational access and pushing the central issue of the debate beyond integration to equity of opportunity and resources, the BOS members who voted to take over Conklin Hall helped usher in a new era of black politics

Similarly, the creation of the Minority Student Program at Rutgers Law School in Newark is also a piece of this larger narrative. The creation of the RLMSP and the demands made by students in the mid-1970s to change the program also represent a push by black students for more than integration. The demands of black law students at Camden and Newark are reflective of larger demands for equity in higher education. Their demands represent the call for an institutional understanding of the hindrances black students experienced in their efforts for higher education. Moreover, these demands represent the self-determined zeitgeist of black students to shape higher education on the graduate and professional levels.

Now in its fifty-first year, the RLMSP continues to support the matriculation of minority students at the law school and into the legal profession. The current program ensures this commitment to minority education by keeping many of the same aspects as in the original program. The RLMSP offers students a two-week summer orientation, a first-year legal skills study group, and opportunities for paid summer internships.[132] Moreover, the program and the law school work to connect with the Newark community through the establishment of legal clinics that aid in cases involving immigration and receiving asylum, wrongfully convicted prisoners, protecting victims of domestic violence, and a host of other legal issues that disproportionately impact racial minorities.[133] With the program established at Rutgers–Camden, this mission has now spread across the state of New Jersey.

Given the challenges that ensued with the transition of leadership from President Mason Gross to President Edward Bloustein, black and Puerto Rican students continued to stand assertively in their demands. Similar to the narrative of Rutgers–Newark but often overshadowed by the Conklin Hall takeover, for people of color at Rutgers–Camden, this transition was one that included both their experiences on and off campus in partnership with community members. Several of the demands that the black and Puerto Rican students made were met by the addition of personnel and programmatic monies to the existing and new fiscal year budget in 1969. During his tenure, President Gross was adamant in allowing students to speak up about issues they believed the university was facing and sought to deal with the protests without involving the local police forces. He negotiated with the members of BOS and BSUM and pledged to address their concerns, which included the expansion and revamping of the EOF program as a central aspect of minority recruitment, access, and retention. Students also gained resources for academic and cocurricular initiatives that were intended to meet the holistic student experience on campus. Through their demands, students were able to continue building a black and Puerto Rican student experience as the university continued to grow and evolve.

Although the student revolution that took place on the campuses of Newark and Camden are seen as successes and even hailed as the second founding of the campuses, the fundamental change at the core of the students' demands has had an uneven track record. At the core was the insistence that the university acknowledge and engage its social and moral responsibilities to the communities of color in which it was located, an ideal the university has struggled to live up to in spite of its recent focus on the need for both diversity and inclusion. As black and brown communities in Newark again face displacement through the processes of gentrification, university projects have both quickened the pace of the process while also trying to lessen its shock. Nevertheless, the potential displayed during the student revolution at Rutgers during the 1960s and 1970s continues to shape student activism into the present, and in this sense, the revolution was a success. In shaping the early narrative of these institutions, black and Puerto Rican campus activists succeeded at centering their experiences as a central aspect of the history of Rutgers University. And as Rutgers became even more racially and ethnically diverse, the institution would find itself again in a similar place, having to contend with and try to redress the reality that communities of color have historically been disenfranchised at Rutgers University.

6

Equality in Higher Education

An Analysis of Negative Responses to the Conklin Hall Takeover

KENNETH MORRISSEY

The Conklin Hall takeover was a protest at Rutgers University–Newark organized by a group of African American students known as the Black Organization of Students (BOS). The goal of the protest was to rectify procedures that made the Rutgers University–Newark campus 95 percent white despite the fact that it was located in a city and a ward that was predominantly black.[1] In order to rectify the perceived inequality, the BOS presented a list of demands to the Rutgers administration on February 6, 1969, that they hoped would increase the odds of black students being accepted into the university. Their list of demands included the dismissal of admissions administrators Robert Swab and C. T. Miller, the employment of black students and faculty members in the admission's office, curbs on the ability of the university to dismiss a black student before they completed at least three semesters of work, and the institution of rules that allowed black students to erase their first academic year. The BOS also demanded the automatic acceptance into Rutgers of any black student who earned a degree from a Newark high school, the establishment of a Black studies institute, and the creation of financial aid packages to pay for tuition and tutors.[2] When these demands were not met, BOS members organized an occupation of Conklin Hall on February 24, 1969. Soon after the initial occupation, protests occurred on Rutgers's New Brunswick, Douglass, and Camden campuses to show solidarity with the protesters. The BOS protest eventually ended about three days later on the morning of the 27th, when President Mason Gross worked out an agreement with the students. Under the agreement, the admissions officers were to be transferred to other duties and more black personnel and faculty were promised, as were remedial programs, scholarships, and a black studies program. The issue of admissions was left for further negotiations; President Gross assured BOS members that their demands required faculty approval. Although the occupation ended on the 27th, negotiations continued into March, and on March 14, the Board of Governors, while not agreeing to a full-blown open admissions program in which every graduate of a Newark public high school would be admitted to Rutgers, did create an Urban Universities Program that, with its remedial and scholarship programs, attempted to implement a plan that would bring more black students to Rutgers. Throughout the confrontation, President Gross maintained that while he did not agree with the tactics used by BOS members, he thought that their criticism of the university regarding admissions, faculty, and curriculum were just and merited consideration and resolution.[3]

Although history has judged the Conklin Hall takeover as a positive turning point in Rutgers's road to diversity, the letters sent to Rutgers University president Gross show that a large portion of the white student population, alumni, state congressmen, and concerned citizens had major qualms with the protest by the Black Organization of Students and the university's seeming acquiescence. Bernice Rosenzweig, a Rutgers undergraduate who in 2002 conducted an archival study of the event, described how the protest was "met by a great deal of opposition by white students, who were angered by the disruptions, although some sympathized with the demands of BOS."[4]

This essay confirms Rosenzweig's findings, showing that the vast majority of letters sent to Gross criticized how he chose to compromise with the protesters. The few letters of support were vastly outnumbered by those more critical of the fact that he did not call in the police or use force to remove the students, or even impose disciplinary penalties on the students. Out of the letters stored at Alexander Library in the collection called "Inventory to the Records of the Rutgers University Office of the President (Mason Welch Gross), 1936, 1945–1971," there were eight folders across boxes 33 and 34 that were filled with negative responses to Mason Gross, and only one folder in box 34 that was filled with positive ones. Additionally, even a large portion of the positive letters were not sympathetic to the BOS protest, but instead empathized with the difficult situation that Gross had to navigate.[5] This essay analyzes these negative letters and examines the trends in their responses.

Angry Letters to President Mason Gross

Although almost all of the letters to Gross were angry, they fall into different categories of anger. For example, a number of letter writers claimed that Rutgers's response to the protest was "undemocratic" because black students served only the needs of the few (African American and minority students) over the many (Caucasian students). Letters that argued this viewpoint

FIGURE 6.1 President Mason Gross.
Courtesy of Special Collections & University Archives, Rutgers University

usually emphasized that the protesters only represented a very small portion of the student body. An anonymous letter writer who went by the pen name "Betrayed" told the university's president that he had "stabbed in the back 80% of the Rutgers–Newark student population."[6] "Betrayed" clearly had a different conception of what was wrong with the university. While BOS protesters probably thought that the university's main injustice came from its refusal to admit more African American students from economically disadvantaged areas, "Betrayed," unconscious of white privilege—or perhaps because of it—argued for the privileges of the majority. The angry letter writers who deployed this argument justified their viewpoint by claiming that they were more democratic than BOS members. Erwin Perkins wrote Gross to tell him, "I believe that the U.S. is still a democracy with consideration given to minority groups but still ruled by majority process."[7] In his letter, Perkins did note that "consideration" should be given to minority groups like the BOS, but later pulled back on this assertion when he claimed that "majority process" should triumph in most situations. His letter indicated his belief that the BOS protest violated this process because it served the needs of a few African American students over the mostly white student population. Writers like Perkins found democracy and classically liberal principles about majority rule incompatible with the protection of minorities from the majority.

Another group of writers accused the black protesters of racism because they believed that standards would be lower for minority students than for the rest of the applicant pool. One angry mother of a rejected Rutgers applicant wrote the university's president to ask him, "Why the double standard? Are not my civil rights being denied also?"[8] Letters such as this one by Shirley Martin argued that minority students were given advantages that they (or in this case their children) were not privy to when they applied to Rutgers. They seem to suggest that these advantages created a "double standard" that would admit less qualified students over more qualified ones due to their skin color. Inherent in this belief was a quid pro quo mindset—the idea that to give more opportunities to one group, opportunities had to be taken away from another. Martin, and others like her, did not empathize with the plight of black students because they felt that they were being discriminated against by Rutgers University.

A conservative organization on campus, the Young Americans for Freedom, went further—it declared the BOS's proposal to be "racist-extremist demands," as did a white mob that approached Conklin Hall during the building takeover with a telephone pole intended to ram open the doors.[9] And the *Observer* (the Rutgers–Newark student newspaper) ran an article that compared the BOS to Hitler youth.[10] These critics of the black student movement refused to even consider the idea that admissions procedures were not "neutral." Although many of the angry letter writers accused the BOS of reverse discrimination, the goal of the BOS protest was to give an opportunity to those who might not have previously received one.

In an attempt to legitimize their claims, many letter writers highlighted their "alumni," "parent," and/or "taxpayer" status when they first addressed President Gross. Charles Rannells Jr. displayed this strategy when he wrote, "I speak as an Alumnus, taxpayer, and parent of a Rutgers Student."[11] This common opening suggested the vested interest so many had in the affairs of Rutgers University. Some felt so strongly about their investment that they sent letters to then governor Richard Hughes in hopes that as President Gross's boss, he would force Gross to be more assertive. Mario Battista, for example, wrote in his letter that he had "forwarded to Governor Hughes [this letter] which amply expresses my views on your handling of the present crisis at Rutgers."[12] Like the protester who marched in front of Conklin Hall with the sign "WE PAID—WE WANT IN," a large number of parents felt that the BOS had no right to take over a building or cause the university to suspend classes.[13] They felt that because they directly contributed to the university through their taxes and tuition payments, they should have some control over university policy. Most considered Gross's policies to be, at best, ineffective and, at worst, spineless. He was derided as gutless and meek. Said a Cape May Republican county congressman in a telegram to the governor: "If Mason Gross hasn't enough guts to do his job, let's get someone who will."[14] Republican State Senate president Frank McDermott declared that "the meek surrender to the demands of a handful of dissatisfied students makes a mockery of the university's authority." "Abject surrender" was what McDermott called it.[15] Dr. Benjamin J. Macchia made his point by writing to the university's president in red crayon. "Dear Mr. Gutless—Plain cowardice bowing to 20 lousy militant bastards."[16] Letters that expose this viewpoint show the undeniable link that many people draw between effective leadership and masculinity. In their minds, an effective male leader would never "bow down" or compromise with those challenging the existing hegemony. One could realistically assume that Dr. Macchia thought that a real man would not tolerate such disobedience, that the ideal leader would stand up and slap down anyone who tried to take over Conklin Hall. To not act as they wished proved to them that Gross was too weak to be an effective president, and thus had to be replaced by a stronger, more capable man.

The angry letters never reflected the possibility that Gross might have been sympathetic to, or at least recognized, the BOS members' right to protest. Take, for example, the "too weak" argument put forth by a writer dubbed "Club 35." He could not see why Gross would negotiate with the protesters. In capital letters he bluntly asked, "WHO IS BOSSING YOU OR ARE YOU AFRAID[?]"[17] Letter writers like "Club 35" assumed that Gross was just too weak to enact his true intentions because they never considered the BOS arguments to have any merit. As suggested by Dr. Macchia, the militancy of the protesters infuriated a few letter writers. The militancy argument was usually used to paint the BOS protesters as enemies of the university. E. Peterson attempted to employ this tactic when he wrote, "These militants have surrounded you."[18] The language that the letter writers used made the protesters appear to be more like an invading force rather than a group of student activists. Those who had opposed the protesters were perceived to be the defending army. Their cause was supposedly a righteous one; they presumably thought they were fighting to protect their very way of life. By tying the "militant" argument to "communism," Gross's opposition cemented the notion that Rutgers was being invaded by illegitimate outside forces. Macchia made this point when he claimed that capitulation made the university the "Rutgers School of Communism."[19] Given that Vietnam and the Cold War were national backdrops to the Conklin Hall takeover, with Americans receiving daily battlefield reports on America's war against the North Vietnamese communists, the "communist" argument was a salient one.

So was the "ethnicity" argument. The late 1960s was a period of population turnover in American cities. As middle-class whites and industries hastily abandoned cities for the suburbs, ethnic minorities were often left to fight for the increasingly scarce resources metropolitan areas generated.[20] Not surprisingly, ethnic minorities often found themselves opposing each other, and the letters sent to President Gross reflect this. An example was illustrated by a man named Seamus Smith on behalf of a fictitious organization called the Irish Residents Insisting on Saner Happenings (IRISH). Smith (if that was his real name) sent Gross a list of demands mirroring the BOS demands that was aimed at improving the lives of Irish Rutgers students. Many of these demands were intended to mock African American demands for black studies. One called for the "junking of all textbooks erroneously failing to refer to Jesus Christ, George Washington, Abe Lincoln, George Washington Carver, etc. as IRISH."[21]

Seamus Smith was not the only student to use his ethnicity to ridicule the BOS demands. G. A. Hale similarly demanded "rights" for people of Baltic origin, requiring for example that "two administrators of Baltic origin are placed at each branch of the university."[22] Clearly, both Smith and Hale saw no merit in African American student demands. An anonymous Douglass student expressed a similar sentiment another way. In an editorial letter to the *Caellian,* the student newspaper, titled "Americanize or Leave," the writer said that black students were knocking at the wrong door of opportunity. "It's not the United States [they] want. [They] want Africa!"[23] Neither Smith nor Hale, or even the anonymous Douglass student, gave much consideration to the fact that, by 1969, Irish and Baltic peoples were not discriminated against to the same extent as African Americans, and had largely been accepted into the dominant white homogenized culture, something that had not happened and perhaps would never happen to African Americans.[24]

A majority of letter writers (including letters to newspapers) wanted Gross to implement harsh punishments on the Conklin Hall Liberators (the name participants gave themselves). "This is no way for a university to conduct itself," said Assemblyman Ralph Caputo, who accused Gross of "bowing to student blackmail" and "falling beneath student pressures." Caputo claimed, "University officials should act like persons in responsible positions."[25] A. T. Gough, another letter writer, felt the same way: "To prevent further outbreaks of this kind, I feel that swift measures must be taken."[26] The sentiments expressed in this quote were probably the most prominent of all the ideas presented in the anti-Gross letters. Beyond the "swift" qualifier, Gough did not specify what "measures" needed to be taken against the protesters. This lack of specificity suggests that he might not have considered the possible consequences of such harsh action. Gross, on the other hand, responded to the inquiries regarding his decision to negotiate, including one from the state legislature, by stating firmly that "the administration had made it quite clear to the university community that disruption in any form, whether it be occupation of a building, blocking of a building, or the invasion of classes or offices, is a violation of University regulations."[27] Gross went on to argue that calling the police "inevitably leads to violence and greatly intensifies the gravity of the situation." Several times he asserted the legitimacy of the BOS complaints, saying that black students were probably right about the university's foot-dragging on admissions of minorities; when asked how he would answer the charge that he had been blackmailed by the students, he responded, "I would ignore it."[28]

However, most letter writers were of the opinion that Gross should have been more like Notre Dame's president, the Reverend Theodore Hesburgh. They cited his "15 Minutes and Out" policy wherein after "15 minutes of mediation," students were given the choice to either desist or face expulsion.[29] Francis R. McAlonan, for example, specifically called on Gross to follow Notre Dame's example in his letter. "Couldn't you take a page out of . . . Reverend Hesburgh's book in handling these matters?" he asked.[30] An Essex County Democratic senator agreed, saying that "we must take a firm stand now."[31]

Many of the anonymous letter writers offered no argument but instead resorted to name-calling and blunt ridicule. One of the more direct writers wrote to Rutgers's president to tell him, "I think you *STINK*."[32] Another, less mean-spirited message made its point by awarding Gross a fake medal that was claimed to have been sent by the student body. It read, "Nobody of the Year Award."[33] Many of the respondents expressed fear that lowering the admission standards for the so-called economically disadvantaged would reduce the overall academic quality of the school. Susan Gahs Luthman, for example, wrote, "If carried to its ultimate end [the BOS demands] will depreciate the value of our degrees earned in the past as well as the degrees earned by students in the future."[34] Luthman thought that employers would eventually believe that Rutgers graduates were woefully unprepared to enter the work world, and would thus think less of anyone who earned a degree from Rutgers. As a Rutgers graduate herself, Luthman feared that this outcome would damage her own chances at gaining future employment. She had little confidence that black students were as competent as their white counterparts.

Some letters exposed a latent elitism and other writers thought the BOS demands would never end. With seemingly little regard for the social implications of his remarks, E. J. Palma told Gross, "Higher education must be regarded as a privilege for those who have earned it and not as a right which is due them by mere graduation from high school."[35] R. Santor wrote that by negotiating with the protesters, the university essentially "establishes a terrible precedent."[36] Santor, and others like him, believed that the Conklin Hall takeover was the first in a long line of protests. It was, in their opinion, a negative harbinger of things to come.

For sure, this was how Robert Swab and C. T. Miller felt. The BOS explicitly demanded that "there be an immediate removal of admissions director, Robert Swab, and his assistant, C. T. Miller." Black members wrote that Swab's admissions figures "reveal his inefficiencies as admissions director"; that he had "failed to sufficiently comb Black high schools for applicants from ghetto areas"; that both Swab and Miller were "basically prejudiced"; and that Miller was "extremely hostile, derogatory and arrogant in dealing with black applicants."[37] Swab and Miller categorically rejected this characterization of themselves and their work. A March 4 press release clearly spelled out their feelings on the university's decision. Swab and Miller noted that they had "placed our trust in the University Officials who were acting in our behalf."[38] Although they were both reassigned to head admissions at the College of Nursing and Pharmacy and at the Rutgers Business School, they felt that the university had betrayed their "trust," or at the very least misled them as to how they would compromise with the BOS protesters. As employees of Rutgers University, Swab and Miller felt that they deserved more loyalty from Gross, who, they felt, made them look guilty. Said Swab, "The action of the university in acceding to the demands concerning us without any substantiation whatsoever has placed us in an extremely untenable position, and coming as it does amidst the rash of reckless charges and confusion, can only be construed by the public as an inference that we were in some way guilty."[39]

Swab and Miller wanted to clear their names of the charge of racism. In their attempt to salvage their reputations, they cited a previous job evaluation that stated: "Both Robert Swab . . . and C. T. Miller . . . have done a conscientious job in their efforts to recruit disadvantaged high school students—black as well as other youth—for Rutgers–Newark."[40] Swab used this quote to show that the university's representatives had previously thought that neither he nor Miller were racist in their admissions policies, and that their position had somehow hypocritically changed since this assessment of their job performance.

Given the predominantly negative assessment of President Gross's handling of the entire affair, Swab and Miller garnered a lot of support. Just as unprecedented as the black student takeover of Conklin Hall was the walkout of the entire clerical staff in the admissions office. They vowed not to return until Swab and Miller were reinstated in their original jobs.[41] In a petition to President Gross, the staff expressed their fear and frustration. "How can any of us feel secure in our jobs after what has happened [to Robert Swab and C. T. Miller]?"[42] Those who signed this petition clearly empathized with the plight of the diminished admissions administrators. For them, capitulation to the BOS meant that black students could potentially remove anyone who was not sympathetic toward African American demands.

Looking Back

Decades after the protest, the dominant view of the Conklin Hall takeover has transformed into a much more positive depiction. Such a change in perspective goes to show how drastically public opinion can change on an issue or event over a long period of time. Forty years after the end of the Conklin Hall takeover, the protesters were welcomed back onto campus as heroes. In her article "Rutgers–Newark Marks 40th Anniversary of Conklin Hall Takeover," Kelly Heyboer quoted then Rutgers president Richard McCormick, who exclaimed, "You are heroes. . . . You're back where it all began. We are deeply proud of you."[43] All the returning protesters were much better received by the students and public in 2009, and again in 2019, than they were back in 1969.[44] When they were originally on campus, they were shunned and scorned by the vast majority of the student body. There was a seemingly endless stream of letters and memos asking President Gross to disperse and punish the protesters. A majority of the student body was extremely angry that Gross chose to tolerate and negotiate with the BOS. However, the reaction seemed almost entirely flipped forty and fifty years later. This massive change in perspective was largely due to the BOS members and their demands emerging on the right side of history. Heyboer's article states that "today, Rutgers–Newark ranks as the most racially diverse public university campus in the nation."[45] The goal that the BOS sought to accomplish back in 1969 had been mostly achieved at Rutgers–Newark. The student body was no longer completely dominated by a white hegemony; they now bragged about being one of the most diverse campuses in the entire country. The opinions of the angry letter writers have fallen out of favor in mainstream society. There still is such a thing as white privilege, but it is not what it was back in 1969, at least on Rutgers's campuses. Even though the angry letter writers may have initially dominated popular public opinion, over time, the BOS protesters eventually won out. The goal that the BOS sought to accomplish in 1969 had been mostly achieved at Rutgers–Newark. The student body is no longer completely dominated by a white hegemony and is one of the most diverse campuses in the United States.

7

The Black Unity League

A Necessary Movement
That Could Never Survive

EDWARD WHITE

Throughout the 1960s and the early 1970s, radical change was pressed upon American society. The civil rights movement gained incredible momentum and this movement had resonated with young students on America's college campuses. During this time, numerous black student groups emerged in and around Rutgers–New Brunswick. Ultimately, all of these organizations shared many of the same goals and missions. They were created in order to address issues such as recruitment and retention of black students, safety on campus, and a lack of cultural awareness and expression, among many other issues. College campuses were still significantly and predominantly white, and these organizations offered a space that was familiar and relaxing for young black students.

Shortly following the passage of the Civil Rights Act of 1964, the Rutgers–New Brunswick campus attempted to accommodate all black student organizations. Rutgers was supportive of most endeavors that these organizations sought to pursue. Concerns were raised at meetings called to discern whether the university met the requirements of the new federal act. Black student organizations used their freedom to expand and seek new members. Initially, the relationship between Rutgers–New Brunswick and black student organizations was sound. However, over time those relationships began to strain.

Throughout 1970, Rutgers's attitude toward black organizations made a turn for the worse. Campus patrol became more aggressive and were directed to specifically target black organizations. Rutgers's actions were consistent with the larger federal attitude toward black organizations such as the Black Panthers. On a federal level, the surveillance of black bodies became widespread and there was an overarching distrust of black people by law enforcement. One particular student organization, the Black Unity League, became subjected to surveillance as it struggled against an increasingly oppressive Rutgers administration.

Prominent members of various black student organizations realized that they could become more effective if they pooled their resources, knowledge, and influence. This eventually led to the formation of the Black Unity League (BUL). The BUL at Rutgers University was founded in 1968 by a small contingent of black students who wanted to draw the influence of these various black student organizations together. Collectively, this new organization challenged the university to create a safer and more conducive learning environment for the many black students in and around New Brunswick. The BUL appealed to university administrators on behalf of the entire black student body and was created because Rutgers University was "deficient in meeting the social and political needs of the black community at the University."[1] They intended to use their larger numbers and increased influence to attract and retain more black students to Rutgers University, as well as petition the university for investment in their interests.

One of the first acts of the BUL was the issuance of twenty-four demands to the university on behalf of the black student body. Some of the key demands included the following:

> We demand that all racist faculty be removed from the University.
> We demand that a Black Studies Department be established.
> We demand that this University hire more black personnel other than faculty.
> We demand that a black dormitory and recreation building be completed within the next year and a half.
> We demand that graduate schools be established in other fields of scholarship besides Law and Education.
> We demand that the community be granted access to existing University facilities.
> We demand that class loads are to be reduced for professors.
> We demand that a course in Racism be instituted.
> We demand a pay increase for professors and non-professionals.[2]

Many of the demands made of the university were specific to black students. However, there were quite a few demands, such as reducing class loads for all professors and increasing pay for both professors and nonprofessional employees, which were intended to improve the university overall.

The BUL made it known to the university that their organization was not one of exclusion. Rather, it was an organization intended for inclusion and the furtherance of the university for all students. Any student could become a member of the BUL. The only rule listed in the charter of the organization was that all members of the league had to vote on the acceptance of new members.[3] Although the BUL did not maintain records of their members, it is possible that the organization did not only consist of black students but also progressive students of any race.

Establishment of the Black House

The Black Unity League focused its early efforts on the acquisition of a house in order to have an established location where black students could organize and hold events. The BUL was founded under the vision of a united black community on the Rutgers campus. A major component of this would be the establishment of a location where black students could live, work, and learn together. In 1969 the BUL petitioned the university for a location to hold meetings and events, live, and study.[4] The BUL wanted to model their location after the success of the "Black House" at Wesleyan University in Connecticut. The Black House there was successful in bolstering black student recruitment and diversifying culture at their university.

Rutgers University conducted a study in 1968 in response to the multiple requests for black student housing from the BUL and other organizations and students. The extensive study compared various aspects of college life for black students who lived in all-black student housing versus those who did not. In Clothier Hall, one floor was established for black student housing. This study found that only 18 percent of black students who lived on this particular floor in Clothier Hall received three or more warnings for misbehavior in the residence hall. This statistic was compared to the 29 percent of black students who received three or more warnings elsewhere.[5] The study revealed multiple reasons for this disparity, including that students were more likely to interact with their housing advisor if they were of the same race, and that black freshmen tended to adjust more quickly to college if they were immersed with other black students. This Rutgers study concluded that it would indeed be beneficial for incoming black students to live in segregated housing.[6]

The Black Unity League and its members understood the benefits of surrounding incoming freshmen with an environment they were familiar and comfortable with. A major goal of the BUL was to attract more young black students to Rutgers and raise graduation rates. The members wanted to acquire a space in which black students could visit and engage with each other and study in a comfortable setting. That wish became a formal request to the university from Michael Muse, the first chairman of the Black Unity League, in 1969.[7] The request was sent from the league to Dean Earle Clifford, who then formally requested a space for the Black Unity League from Assistant to the President Maurice Ayers. Ayers originally intended to offer the BUL space within an academic building for the league to conduct meetings. However, following the unwavering support of Dean Clifford, Ayers and the university agreed to find a suitable property for the league.

Initially, Rutgers administrators enthusiastically supported the establishment and use of the Black House, as it came to be known at Rutgers. Correspondence between elected members of the Black Unity League and the dean of students was always cordial and requests were taken seriously. Dean Earle Clifford and Maurice Ayers immediately began to search for a site close to campus to establish the Black House and identified 17 Bartlett Street, located less than a block away from College Avenue and which currently serves as the office for fraternity and sorority affairs.[8] This location was ideal for the organization. It was close to campus, which would encourage black students and guests to visit the house, but it remained off campus, which would allow the BUL to engage with the New Brunswick community—a central goal of theirs.

Rutgers administrators worked swiftly to fulfill the Black Unity League's request for a Black House. The building at 17 Bartlett Street was originally intended to serve as office space for faculty of the Geography Department.[9] However, at the behest of Dean Clifford, the university decided that 17 Bartlett would serve as the Black House, and a new location would be found for the Geography Department instead.

The issue of the Black House was discussed at a meeting of the deans, and there were only a few valid concerns noted in the minutes of the meeting. Maurice Ayers voiced his concern about the establishment of the Black House being a separatist movement. He was concerned that the establishment of a Black House would be in violation of the Civil Rights Act of 1964. However, the Black Unity League had already addressed this concern in their formal request for the Black House. It was not to serve as a place to remove themselves from the community but rather as a place from where to engage with the community. Also, the league noted that all members of the New Brunswick and Rutgers community were invited as guests to the Black House, as long as they followed the same rules that applied to all regular members. The other concern raised at the meeting was whether the BUL would outgrow the space available at 17 Bartlett Street and require a larger building in a short time. There were no outright objections from any of the deans present, and once their concerns were addressed, they immediately began work on the Black House.[10]

Michael Muse, chairman of the Black Unity League, was in constant communication with Dean Clifford throughout the process of establishing the Black House. He sent Dean Clifford a list of amenities that the BUL requested to be purchased for the house on 17 Bartlett Street. Included in this request were multiple desks and chairs, one hundred stacked chairs (for event purposes), a snack bar, three beds, a television, and African artifacts, among other decorations. They also requested two electric typewriters and a printing press.[11] The BUL was allotted $4,000 for furnishing the house, which meant forgoing some of the items on their list. The cost of renovations to the house was estimated to be $8,276.40.[12] Dean Clifford gave guidance that the Black House was to be available for BUL occupation by August 1969. The initial request for a Black House came in February 1969. In roughly half a year, Rutgers renovated, furnished, and opened a Black House to be used by its black students and the community.

A Turning Point

Between August 1969 and August 1970, there was very little correspondence between the Black Unity League and any members of the Rutgers administration. It is probable that the league was content with their new accommodation. An ad hoc committee was formed by the chairman, Michael Muse, which delegated individuals to roles such as building supervisor and event coordinator.[13] The BUL likely spent their time during this year hosting cultural events in an attempt to attract new members to their organization. The lack of interaction between the Black Unity League and Rutgers officials suggests an atmosphere of cohesion and contentment. There were no negative events that required Rutgers to contact the organization. Likewise, there were no attempts by Rutgers to stifle the operations of the BUL or the Black House, actions that presumably would have caused the league to write Dean Clifford. For an entire year, all seemed well with the relationship between a primary black student organization in New Jersey and its host, Rutgers–New Brunswick.

The first notable documented event involving the Black Unity League or the Black House and Rutgers University occurred on August 30, 1970. It is likely that as the new school year approached, the Black House began to host larger events in order to attract attention to their organization from incoming students. At this particular event, a Sergeant Rosshirt from campus patrol reported:

> Approximately 60 blacks converged on Bartlett Street between College Avenue and Sicard Street, creating a disturbance by sitting on cars, trespassing on private home porches and verbally taunting him [Rosshirt] to come outside of Campus Patrol Headquarters and "be taken care of" as a policeman.[14]

The report submitted by Sergeant Rosshirt concluded that the people on Bartlett Street, ranging in age from nine to thirty-five, were attending an event at the Black House and had no supervision. Sergeant Rosshirt also concluded that a majority of the people causing the local disturbance were from the surrounding New Brunswick community and were not Rutgers students. A Black House community engagement event had caused trouble for the first time in a year of operation. Rutgers responded with understanding and tact. Michael Borden, the campus patrol chief, wrote to Robert Ochs requesting that he ensure all events at the Black House be supervised for the benefit of the Black Unity League itself. Chief Borden feared that if events like the one on August 30 continued to occur, residents of Bartlett Street would "rebel" against the Black House, hindering further events and placing community cohesion in jeopardy.[15]

The early fall semester in 1970 was riddled with campus patrol reports involving incidents with fraternities. One such situation was noted on September 29, 1970, in the local newspaper with the headline "Rutgers, City Consult to Halt Noisy Dancing."[16] In this incident, hundreds of people took to the streets around College Avenue, spilling out of overcrowded fraternity houses. Traffic could not navigate the streets and campus patrol vehicles would have been unable to respond to potential emergencies. This event was such an ordeal for the university and the city of New Brunswick that President Mason Gross and Dean Earle Clifford met with the mayor and other city officials to discuss the affairs of Rutgers's fraternities. The newspaper mentioned that during this meeting, Dean Clifford praised the actions of one particular fraternity, the Black Unity League.[17]

Despite having been inappropriately labeled as a fraternity by the local newspaper, the Black Unity League's behavior on September 29 was exemplary. Rutgers officials had notified fraternities and other student organizations, including the BUL, that they needed to end their parties early and send their guests home. Fraternities along College Avenue ignored warnings from the university and continued their partying past three in the morning, resulting in countless phone calls and complaints from residents of New Brunswick. Dean Clifford made it known at his meeting with New Brunswick officials that guests and members of the Black House had cooperated with the university and campus patrol on September 29. The Black House had shut down their event and sent their guests home immediately following the first warning from campus patrol.[18]

Primarily because of what happened on September 29, Rutgers vowed a stricter policy toward fraternities. This policy extended to events that were held at the Black House. Fraternities and the Black House were expected to strictly enforce their limits on guests, and guests were not allowed to be outside of the houses or gather in the streets as they had on September 29.[19] The university's policy was to be directed at all student organizations on campus, and campus patrol became assertive in their approach to fraternity parties and events.

Despite the good behavior of the Black House on September 29, their standing with campus patrol and the university was compromised. Instead of commending the Black House and the BUL for their cooperation, campus patrol began to disproportionately target the Black House. One particular campus patrol directive ordered a patrolman to check the Black House at two in the morning every day.[20] There were no such documents or directives to be found that pertained to any of the fraternities or other off-campus residences or organizations. Campus patrol had specifically targeted the Black House under the ruse of their new policy for fraternities.

At this point, Rutgers administrators, including the Black Unity League's former advocate Dean Clifford, began to involve themselves more with the operations of the Black House. In a response dated March 24, 1971, to a letter from Dean Clifford, James Jeter, the secretary of the BUL, outlined in detail the operations and purpose of the Black House.[21] Clifford had provided integral support for the foundation of the Black House and had been familiar with the BUL for years prior to this letter; the dean's request for this information from the league denotes a problem or a shift in Rutgers's perspective on the Black House. Dean Clifford was no longer familiar with the Black House or its expanding membership. The year of silence between Rutgers and the Black Unity League while it was establishing the Black House seems to have proven detrimental to their relationship. Without a positive and sustained relationship between the university and the organization, it was easy for the university to target the Black House—even though it was the fraternities that had caused the initial trouble.

As more time passed, the university's demeanor toward the Black House and the BUL became increasingly aggressive. After the campus-wide incident on September 29, the university began to severely pressure the Black House throughout 1970 and into 1971. The university demanded records of all events that had been held at the Black House during the summer of 1970.[22] There are no other records contained within Dean Clifford's transcripts or campus patrol reports with similar requests for any other student organization. The new chancellor of the Black Unity League, Raymond Holmes, made it known that the league was willing to comply with the university's request. However, he demanded a reason for the request from Dean Clifford.[23] The records show that Raymond Holmes never received a reply from the dean that explained his reasoning, and it is likely that Holmes never sent a detailed accounting of events from that summer.

Campus patrol records show that there were only two formal complaints made against the Black House during the summer of 1971. The first incident came in the form of a typical noise complaint. A New Brunswick resident had notified campus patrol at 6:30 p.m. that the Black House had been making noise "throughout all hours of the day."[24] Patrolman Day was directed to conduct periodic checks on the Black House. During these checks, Patrolman Day reported that he had not once heard noise coming from the Black House. The second report arrived on August 24, 1971. In this incident, Patrolman Fernandes witnessed a person entering the Black House carrying a suitcase and speakers.[25] The patrolman recorded that the person appeared to have the intent to set up residency in the house. During the entire summer of 1971, only two reports were filed involving the Black House, both resulting in no damages or serious repercussions; nevertheless, the relationship between Rutgers and the Black House at 17 Bartlett continued to sour.

In the summer of 1971, a contradictory notice from the university was directed toward the Black House. Earle Clifford notified the Black Unity League that they had to close the Black House at midnight every day. Any persons found within the house would be considered trespassers.[26] Earle Clifford made it clear that if the BUL attempted to test this new regulation, it could result in the loss of 17 Bartlett Street for the league. It is important to note that two years prior, while paying for furnishing the house in 1969, Rutgers had purchased beds for use in the Black House.[27] Rutgers administrators knew that the BUL used the Black House as a residence, but now they contradicted themselves in their policy change.

The most outrageous and drastic change to university policy occurred on August 26, 1971, two days after the suitcase-and-speakers incident recorded by Patrolman Fernandes. On August 26, the associate vice president of student affairs, Ralph Taylor, notified the Black Unity League that any person found on the premises of 17 Bartlett Street after 2:00 a.m. would be subject to arrest as a trespasser.[28] Ralph Taylor acted in the absence of Earle Clifford, who was on vacation during both of the August incidents. However, Earle Clifford upheld this new policy upon his return to Rutgers. Although there were no records of arrests made at 17 Bartlett Street, the new policy severely restricted the intended use of the Black House. Records of the Black Unity League ceased after August 1971.

It became very clear by then that Rutgers was targeting the Black House. The amount of pressure that the university had placed on the BUL hindered the members' ability to fulfill many of their original goals for black students and the community. One major goal of the Black House was to provide a safe and relaxing environment for black students to study and socialize. Under the new Rutgers policy, the Black Unity League could not provide this relaxing environment when their building seemed to exist under constant surveillance from campus patrol and had to operate with restricted time limits. Rutgers's own 1968 study showed the countless benefits of providing housing for black students.[29] Now, in 1971, the university seemed to be doing everything in its power to destroy the only semblance of official black student housing.

Surveillance

During the time period that the Black House existed, from 1968 to 1971, the FBI surveillance program known as COINTELPRO was in full effect. This program, officially named the FBI Counter Intelligence Program, targeted American political movements and radical organizations such as the antiwar movement, the civil rights movement, and the Black Panther Party, among others. Students were not excluded from this targeted list of the FBI. One student organization in particular, the Student Nonviolent Coordinating Committee (SNCC), entered the crosshairs of the FBI.[30] The Black Unity League may not have been targeted by the FBI, but due to the actions of Rutgers, its members suffered many of the same effects of surveillance, as discussed in Simone Browne's book *Dark Matters.*

The effects of surveillance on students are detrimental to their ability to learn and perform well in the classroom. Browne lists the effects of surveillance as "nervous tensions, insomnia, fatigue, accidents, lightheadedness, and less control over reflexes . . . [and] nightmares too."[31] The Black Unity League wanted to provide a service for black students that would both make their transition to college easier and offer an environment conducive to learning. Any progress that the league made between 1968 and 1971 was effectively reset and even worsened by the surveillance of black bodies conducted by Rutgers's campus patrol. Black Panther leader Huey P. Newton explained the consequences of policing:

> Constant surveillance [is] incompatible with a free society. Restriction of associational expression is likely to become, in practice, an effort to suppress a whole social or political movement. History and experience warn us that such attempts are usually futile and merely tend to obscure the real grievances which society must, if it is to survive, face squarely and solve.[32]

This quote from Huey P. Newton's doctoral dissertation applies to the situation found on Rutgers's campuses in the late 1960s and 1970s. The Black Unity League was founded in part because of a lack of political representation for black students in the Rutgers community. For the first few years, the BUL accomplished that goal. The league successfully pressed the university for black interests included in their list of twenty-four demands, which led to their greatest success, the acquisition of the Black House.[33] However, by 1971, Rutgers had effectively suffocated one of the most active and successful—yet little known—black student organizations on campus.

Rutgers slowly and surely tightened the noose on the Black Unity League until the organization could no longer survive. The BUL dared to face the real problems that society experienced, and it created problems for them within the university and in much of the surrounding community. The league directly confronted race issues on Rutgers's campus but the disruption to the status quo was too much for Rutgers. The radical thoughts and demands of the league caused distrust and contempt among many Rutgers administrators. This conflict ultimately led to the ever-increasing surveillance of the Black House, which stifled their ability to engage in political discourse with Rutgers. American campuses are typically viewed as places where students are encouraged to challenge their preexisting views and discuss different schools of thought. Rutgers essentially forbade these activities for members of the Black Unity League through its aggressive surveillance tactics.

The Black House's Legacy

The Black Unity League was formed at Rutgers in an attempt to bridge the disparity in treatment between black and white students. The league was well versed in the issues of black students and became the largest advocacy group for correcting those issues on Rutgers's New Brunswick campus. The league grew quickly in its early years of operation as young black students eagerly sought to engage with Rutgers and the community. For some time, the BUL afforded students the ability to do exactly that. However, Rutgers continually tightened their grip on the league's ability to engage with the community and even function as an organization.

The Black Unity League set out to change the landscape of Rutgers and New Brunswick. They sought a safer and more diverse environment for all students to learn and challenge their preconceived societal standards. Initially, Rutgers seemed to champion this idea; they afforded the BUL many resources and worked rigorously to aid the league. The greatest resource Rutgers allotted to the BUL was the property at 17 Bartlett Street that came to be known as the Black House.

The Black House was created at a time when it was both needed most and yet incapable of longevity. The atmosphere in the United States in the late 1960s and early 1970s pitted white authorities against black people nationwide. During this time, the FBI Counter Intelligence Program was used to subversively surveil black bodies across the country. Even after the passage of the Civil Rights Act of 1964, black people were deadlocked in a struggle for fair and equal treatment from all forms of authority. This struggle was also fought on Rutgers's campus by members of the Black Unity League.

The Black House became unfairly associated with fraternity houses and became a matter of undue attention from Rutgers and the campus patrol. Ironically, as Rutgers vowed a stricter policy on fraternities, the Black House, which was far from being a fraternity house, was the only organization to face any form of retribution. By 1970, the Black House was under nearly constant surveillance by Rutgers and the community. This effectively negated any progress that the Black Unity League achieved during the first few years of their existence. BUL members and their guests no longer felt safe and could no longer promote the interests of minority students because they were occupied with simply preserving the existence of their organization.

The legacy of the Black House is one that has remained an integral part of Rutgers's history, although the Black House itself has been forgotten by most.[34] The Black Unity League, through its use of the Black House, encouraged inclusion, political activism, learning, and a sense of community. Many of the goals that the league pursued have been achieved, and the new generation of students at Rutgers have continued to pursue the ones that have not—yet. Rutgers may have stifled the Black Unity League in the early 1970s, but its ambitions and the sacrifices of its members continue to be instrumental in the lives and struggles of black students today.

8

"We the People"

Student Activism at Rutgers and Livingston College, 1960–1985

CARIE RAEL AND BROOKE A. THOMAS

"Livingston College Will Have No Ivory Towers"

Named for William Livingston, the first governor of New Jersey during the American Revolutionary War, Livingston College opened its doors in the fall of 1969 with 627 students. In the opening class, 146 students were black, 25 were Spanish-speaking—categorized as foreign—and 449 were designated other, meaning mostly white.[1] At the dedication of the Livingston campus, Shirley Chisholm, the first black woman to win a congressional seat, spoke directly to the black student demands. She stated, "True integration exists not just in terms of race, but in terms of coming together—a respect for different cultures. It exists in the realization that integration is not a melting pot, but a salad bowl."[2] According to one of the incoming freshmen, Margaret "Margie" Rivera, Livingston represented a campus that sought to bring together a diverse set of students, faculty, and staff that encouraged a shared learning community with the pursuit of academic innovation and excellence.[3]

Livingston from its outset would be different from the other schools and colleges on the New Brunswick campus. Not only would it be a coed institution, but its founding mission seemed to challenge inherent notions of what higher education could or should do. If the traditional aim of a college education had been "to give the individual student the intellectual skills necessary to understand his society and the professional and technical skills to contribute to it," Livingston College asserted a mission that sought to complicate who that student was and what technical or professional skills they learned. In its inaugural catalog for the 1969–1970 school year, Livingston College was

FIGURE 8.1 President Mason Gross and Dean Ernest Lynton at Livingston ground-breaking in 1967.

Courtesy of Special Collections & University Archives, Rutgers University

described as a "new and distinctly contemporary-minded college of Rutgers University." It proclaimed to incoming students that Livingston College would "have no ivory towers."[4] It could not, as the catalog went on to state, because "cities are decaying, many of our fellow men are starving; social injustice and racism litter the earth; weapons of awesome destruction threaten our existence."[5] From the start, Livingston College was designed as a "multi-racial college" that emphasized the coming together of racial minorities and students from lower socioeconomic backgrounds. Livingston's catalog asserted that in the "revolutionary and bewildering" times in which it was founded, understanding and mastering radical change had become a necessity. This "radical change" was more than gaining knowledge of the technological advances, computer innovations, and the encroaching "information age" to come. Radical change also meant becoming informed about racial polarization in cities, considering the moral and medical questions of prolonging life, learning the politics of activism, and hearing the radical intellectual voices of the time. As a result, Livingston sought to create academic spaces to support the future "urban sociologists, the political scientist, the economist, the city planner and the community organizer" who could solve these issues.[6]

Livingston College was in many ways forged by the momentum of the historical moment in which it was founded. The college opened its doors only nine months after the takeovers in Camden and Newark and three years after the rebellion in Newark. It sought to be a college that served racial minorities and students from lower socioeconomic backgrounds. In its inaugural catalog, the college declared a "special commitment to disadvantaged students . . . [because this] country has not provided equal opportunities to all its citizens and has deprived many of them of their sense of self-worth. This is true of the urban and rural poor and particularly true of Black Americans."[7] At its outset, Livingston, at least ideally, had the goal of being socially and politically relevant in the context of the late 1960s and early 1970s. It sought to create a space where students could gain an education that would support their professional goals, and it would help solve and potentially fix the problems the administration believed students from these backgrounds experienced. Intentions aside, the idea behind Livingston was experimental—its intention was to create a college environment that would produce leaders who could tackle the social problems of the world. Its announcement that the college would have no ivory towers was significant because it indicated who this college would serve and what it sought—in theory—to accomplish.

Despite the claims that Livingston represented a space with no ivory towers, it was remembered by students from the first graduating class of 1973 as a place of "mud and ivory towers."[8] It is noteworthy that the campus was built on the former land of Camp Kilmer.[9] Isolated from the other campuses, this former militarized space came to house one of the most diverse student bodies in a white institution for its time.[10] The layout of housing at Livingston was divided by three quads. The architecture of the quads included "long windowless and pictureless corridor[s]" that seemed to students to be "the acme of institutionalization" because it mirrored prison and psychiatric hospital construction.[11] Despite being a newly constructed campus, the facilities experienced frequent flooding, power outages, and lack of hot water.[12] The school opened unfinished. The medical center was poorly staffed and underfunded, leaving students to feel "like you were going to die while waiting for the Health Center."[13] One black student commented on the conditions by asking one to "imagine waking up during the night with an upset stomach. You go over to the health center and it's closed. Or maybe there's a nurse there but she can't do anything for you and has no power to refer you to another student health center across the river where you can get help. What can you do? You're in the middle of nowhere."[14] The lack of facilities and resources left students feeling isolated. "You gotta take a 25 minute bus ride just to get a beer," declared a Livingston student to the *New York Times.* "There's nothing to do on campus, with no place nearby to go," said another.[15] Elia Vecchione, a graduating student in 1973, wrote the following poem in remembrance of her time at Livingston:

> Livingston College—the flood of the years, not long in existence, yet
> covered with tears.
> A place of enlightenment where no one can learn.
> That from the walls of prejudice no one can turn.[16]

The conditions at Livingston embodied both experimentation and racial tensions. The housing quads emulated society's segregated housing, where Quad III, which was predominantly black and Puerto Rican, came to be known as "the ghetto"; Quad II was "the suburban area of the campus"; and Quad I became "Livingston's answer to Woodstock."[17] This newly formed campus carried with it the old prejudices and attempted to contain and isolate the frequent student uprisings. Nevertheless, students were able to take this newly constructed and conceived space and shape their education through constant struggle and organization.

Social Movements on Campuses: 1969 into the 1970s

Inspired by the Black Organization of Students (BOS) and their work around issues of representation and institutional support from Rutgers, a group of Puerto Rican students convened a few weeks after the Conklin Hall takeover and formed the Puerto Rican Organization (PRO). Outlining their support of the black student movements in Newark, the PRO attempted to hold the Rutgers administration to past promises to change the university's policies that neglected the needs of Puerto Rican students. In the spirit of the BOS, they demanded better recruitment and retention of Puerto Rican students, work-study opportunities, and recognition of the accomplishments of María Blake, a recruiter hired for the Newark campus.[18] Both the BOS and the PRO included in their demands the end of neglect and discrimination in addition to institutional support.

In 1969, sixteen out of eighteen students involved in the Educational Opportunity Fund met and issued a new set of demands that led to the creation of the Puerto Rican studies program at the Livingston campus in 1970.[19] One of these students was Margaret "Margie" Rivera. Rivera was born in Perth Amboy, New Jersey,[20] and was the first in her family to go to college.[21] She described attending Livingston as a "rude awakening."[22] Students intended the program to be a space where students could "learn about their cultural and political history and how these were translated into their daily lives." She and other students believed Puerto Rican studies would help in understanding the political, social, and economic dynamics of the time.[23] Students asserted,

Maria Canino
Associate Professor

Carlos Pineiro
Assistant Professor

Puerto Rican Studies

Vilona Perez
Secretary

FIGURE 8.2 Puerto Rican Studies Department, *The Rock Yearbook*, 1978.
Courtesy of Special Collections & University Archives, Rutgers University

"We believe that the Puerto Rican and Third World communities are faced with a basic condition of survival as entities in the United States. As Puerto Ricans, we affirm that the space and time which we have wrested within the universities, must be utilized to . . . confront the university on issues of significance to the continuity and cohesiveness of the Puerto Rican presence within its walls."[24] These principles guided the students, faculty, and staff to push for the creation of the Puerto Rican studies program and attempted to strengthen it despite the meager resources allotted from the university.

In 1970, the university hired María Josefa Canino as the founding coordinator of the new program. At the fortieth anniversary of the program's creation, Canino recalled how "Puerto Rican studies proponents broke ground in defining new terrain for the academy."[25] But she recalled the limited resources given to the program and the lack of administrative support. For example, the university allotted the program one half-time secretary, Vilma Perez, whom Canino described as her cochair—despite her having the title of *secretary*—because of her immense contributions. The university also granted the program one teaching assistant, Luis García, who worked ten hours a week as a graduate student, and one adjunct professor, Juan Angel Silen.[26] Five courses were offered, and a total of 125 students were registered in 1970.

Despite these meager resources, the organization accomplished some extraordinary feats in its first year. In addition to founding and staffing a newly formed program, the PRO organized and strengthened the department by creating a plan of operation, created three new courses for the 1971–1972 academic year, and continued to recruit new students. The student group Unión Estudiantil Puertorriqueña (UEP) organized the first Puerto Rican festival in New Jersey at Douglass College in 1970.[27] The program also secured a $60,000 John Hay Whitney research grant to conduct groundbreaking research on the conditions of Puerto Rican migrant farmworkers in southern New Jersey.[28] Dr. Luis Nieves Falcón, who founded the Department of Latin American and Caribbean Studies at the University of Puerto Rico, later published the findings from this research as *El Emigrante Puertorriqueño* in 1975.[29] One of the students who worked on this project was Luz Towns, mother of songwriter, actor, and *Hamilton* creator Lin Manuel-Miranda. Towns was a part of the 1969 incoming class of Livingston and participated in the newly formed Puerto Rican program while there. She graduated and later attained her doctorate in psychology.[30] The influence of the Puerto Rican program continues to grow well beyond the initial incoming class of 1969–1970.

1971–1972

The 1971–1972 academic year entailed continued and immense growth for the Puerto Rican studies program. At the start of the academic year, 190 students registered, and a second full-time faculty member was assigned to assist in program management. More adjuncts were hired to teach Puerto Rican program courses, and they were able to secure faculty outside of Livingston College to serve as affiliated faculty.[31] The growth of the program was sustained by the volunteer efforts of these outside faculty to teach courses. During this time, the program also established a scholarship fund for Puerto Rican students.[32] Students played an integral role within the department by providing serious evaluations of courses and instructors. They pushed for courses to be taught in the Puerto Rican House, and the student group UEP established a Puerto Rican library. Students continued to work on the migrant farmworkers grant and participated in another groundbreaking initiative when Professor Carlos Piñeiro attained a Ford grant to research and publish unreleased documents pertaining to Puerto Rican history.[33] During this academic year, the Puerto Rican program initiated the Prison Project, where volunteers met weekly with Puerto Rican prisoners at Trenton State prison, teaching poetry, music, history, and cultural classes; holding discussions about the Puerto Rican community; and providing tutoring.[34] At one meeting, singer/guitarist and adjunct professor Suni Paz Johnson performed for the Trenton prisoners.[35] The program also established El Teatro Guazábara under the direction of Professor Víctor Fernández Fragoso, the first Puerto Rican student theater group in New Jersey.[36] They wrote and performed about the Puerto Rican experience and were part of the course on Puerto Rican theater taught by Professor Fernández Fragoso.[37]

The program's accomplishments also extended beyond the continental United States. The UEP petitioned the program to put on a series of conferences and lectures that centered on topics of colonialism,[38] and more than 700 students attended the conference and lectures on campus and in Puerto Rico.[39] The study trip included eleven students and two faculty who went to Puerto Rico during intercession,[40] and was intended to provide a "first-time experience for students who had never been to the island."[41] The connection to the island was very much a part of the curriculum and culture of the Puerto Rican studies program.

The Puerto Rican studies program became an international resource for innovative Puerto Rican education. During this year, the program established resources and outreach for high school students and recruited from New Jersey high schools.[42] Additionally, the program was consulted to assist high schools both in New Jersey and out of state in the development of Puerto Rican studies curricula.[43] The program continued to be a much-utilized resource for shaping other programs throughout the United States, including in Puerto Rico, in the years that followed. In 1972, Canino and Livingston College assisted with the City University of New York's (CUNY) proposal for a center for Puerto Rican studies and research in CUNY's graduate center.[44] Additionally, in 1972 the Department of Sociology and Anthropology of the University of Puerto Rico wrote to María Canino asking for guidance to help a student of theirs who had been accepted to the CUNY doctoral program in anthropology.[45] The amount of outreach that the Puerto Rican program and coordinator María Canino engaged in during the first precarious years of the program was astounding.

1972–1973 and Later

During the next school year, the Puerto Rican studies program achieved more milestones to institutionalize and accredit its curriculum within Rutgers. The program established a thirty-two-credit concentration and drafted proposals for Puerto Rican studies to receive departmental status. As the department gained official status, María Canino became the first department chair. Student registration rose to 272 students and the budget increased to $2,285.[46] During this time, courses began to be cross-listed with nine other departments, supporting an interdisciplinary course of study.[47] At the end of the year, the first class of Puerto Rican students graduated from Livingston College. Five graduates were Puerto Rican studies majors and five other students majored in different areas.[48] The 1973 yearbook featured a dedication to the students from faculty and staff: "We have all worked hard at treating each other as equals in this community, and now you join the small ranks of Puerto Rican college graduates. You are much needed."[49] This letter exemplified the immense need and impact of students, faculty, and staff in shaping the direction of the Puerto Rican Studies Department.

The department continued to excel after the graduation of the first class. Another $30,000 grant was obtained by Professor Ralph Ortiz from the National Endowment for the Humanities to produce an exhibit with El Museo del Barrio in New York showcasing Puerto Rican artists.[50] In 1973, María Canino created a new education program with Spanish-speaking women at the Clinton Correctional Facility for Women in New Jersey. She persuaded the prison to not charge the inmates for any calls made to members of this volunteer program. By 1974, students were able to visit the prison in Clinton to teach Spanish-speaking women in person.[51] The expansion of this new prison educational program also allowed for inmates to visit the Livingston campus.[52]

Despite the formation of the Puerto Rican Studies Department and tremendous accomplishments in the initial years of the Puerto Rican program, conditions at Livingston proved precarious and divisive. Registered students increased to 368 students, yet the budget decreased to $2,000.[53] Poor living conditions on the Livingston campus continued to rouse student action. On November 5, 1973, a group of black students occupied the office of acting dean George Warren Carey, demanding the resignation of Dean Luis Nieves from the Department of Student Affairs.[54] Dean Nieves, who was of Puerto Rican descent, had installed gates in the Quad tunnels without consulting the student body. Additionally, the black student group blamed Dean Nieves for the removal of black students and staff from student affairs positions.[55] Puerto Rican students were also at odds with the Puerto Rican faculty and staff over this issue, sowing divisions between them.[56] The black students presented a total of forty-three demands that included an appeal for better conditions in the health center, requested the creation of a student center, and opposed the need to show identification to be on campus.[57] With the exception for the call for Nieves's resignation, 350 black, Puerto Rican, and white students supported the demands by the occupying students. Subpar and isolated living conditions and poor campus resources continued to frustrate students. One student stated, "The blacks are organizing the demands, but the frustrations have been felt by all."[58] The 1974 yearbook memorialized images of broken washing machines, cockroaches in sinks, an empty library, and broken chairs.[59]

Tensions rose even higher in March 1973, when two Puerto Rican students were beaten, spit on, and sexually assaulted by campus police.[60] Instances of police brutality resulting in mass unrest provided a violent backdrop for this time period in New Jersey. In addition to the Newark and Plainfield riots four years earlier, in 1969, Camden had also experienced moments of violent unrest in response to police brutality. Also in 1969, after police beat a young black girl, an uprising ensued in Camden that lasted a week and resulted in the fatal shooting of a young girl and a police officer.[61] In 1971, the Puerto Rican community rose against the police after they shot and killed a Puerto Rican motorist. The 1971 uprising in Camden lasted for two days, which led to the police shooting two more Puerto Rican youths and an officer dying after he stepped on a downed electric wire.[62] The 1973 case of police brutality at Livingston College occurred against this backdrop of larger clashes with police in New Jersey.

On Friday, March 23, 1973, William Hernandez and Consuelo Rivera were stopped by campus police for moving two pieces of furniture from the South Tower to House 34, also known as the Puerto Rican House.[63] The police tied them up by their hands and feet, spat on them, yelled racist slurs at them, and beat them. Rivera stated that Detective Robert Franz then proceeded to sexually molest her while he "searched" her.[64] Ms. Rivera requested to be searched by female police officers instead, who then proceeded to spit on her and assault her. The two students suffered psychological trauma in addition to bruises, contusions, a fractured nose, and kidney damage. They were taken to the Piscataway police station, where they were not read their rights nor given phone calls, and they were held overnight. This act of terror enraged the Livingston College community. The following Monday, the assaulted students met with a group of students and faculty from the Puerto Rican Studies Department and drafted five demands: (1) the immediate suspension without pay of the four officers involved pending a hearing within one week, and immediate termination if allegations against them were proven; (2) a requirement that students must compose 50 percent of any decision-making panel concerning student incidents with police; (3) the creation of a student faculty board to review campus patrol officer candidates and review their performance; (4) the development of a "workable and responsible" procedure for students charged with criminal acts to receive legal assistance of their choice; and (5) payment by the university for damages to Rivera's car caused by the campus patrol during the incident.[65] The students and faculty took their demands to President Edward Bloustein in Scott Hall after a rally with other outraged campus members. Bloustein agreed that the evidence against the officers was credible enough to suspend them—but with pay. He refused to meet with students personally and instead relayed this information to Department Chair María Canino. Students and faculty were at odds over how to handle the situation.[66] They attributed the divide to having "no channels of communication" and a lack of confidence in the process of justice seeking, which resulted in a wedge in the relationship between the students and faculty.[67]

The impasse between the students and university forced students to protest in front of the police station in Piscataway, where they cut the US flag from its pole and tore it to shreds. The university accused the protesters of acting like a lynch mob, which only further enraged the group.[68] Multiple protests continued for three days while students and faculty created a steering committee to continue to push for their demands.[69] The committee set up in the Puerto Rican House, where they told students they could call if they needed any resources. The steering committee made sure to remind students, however, that the phone in the Puerto Rican House was tapped.[70] Fifty-two faculty members also created an ad hoc committee for justice, at which they decided to cancel class to host meetings on how to move forward and address their issues to the university.[71]

In July 1973, the charges of simple battery against the officers were dropped by the Piscataway court.[72] Rivera and Hernandez then accused the officers of assault and battery, but these charges were also dropped. Meanwhile, the students themselves were facing charges of assaulting the police officers and possessing twenty-five grams of marijuana.[73] The court and university hearings for the students resulted in a mistrial because they were unable to establish the students' guilt or innocence. The four officers were given their jobs back, and the campus patrol fought the university to become armed by introducing Bill 764 to the New Jersey State Senate, which passed.[74] This bill effectively turned the campus security patrol into a fully armed police force.[75] The next year, the lesser known Puerto Rican Newark riots occurred, which lasted for three days with violent unrest.[76]

During this perilous and uncertain time in New Jersey, the Puerto Rican Studies Department at Livingston College continued to recruit, retain, and educate as many students as possible. In 1974, the department registered 294

FIGURE 8.3 Mural commemorating the police brutality event on Livingston campus, *We the People Yearbook*, 1974.

Courtesy of Special Collections & University Archives, Rutgers University

students and taught eighteen courses. It was this year that Dean Emmanuel Mesthene threatened to eliminate the entire Puerto Rican Studies Department.[77] The faculty was reduced to only one full-time faculty member, which did not include founding coordinator and first chair María Canino. The Livingston UEP student group was left fractured and weakened from fighting the police brutality incident.[78] In retrospect, the department remembered their biggest achievement during this year was survival.[79] The following year, the department reached an agreement with Dean Mesthene that ensured its continuation.[80] Additionally, the department was able to secure control over its own budget, hire a full-time secretary, and find dedicated office space.[81] María

Canino was hired back, part time.[82] These were significant wins in a time defined as one of retrenchment and conservatism.

The university continued to cut departmental budgets and maintained a "revolving-door policy," which resulted in only 2 percent of all Rutgers employees being Puerto Rican.[83] The accusations of employment discrimination by the university against its Puerto Rican employees were confirmed in a study conducted by the Puerto Rican Congress of New Jersey in 1977. Additionally, the Puerto Rican Congress of New Jersey claimed that Puerto Rican students faced administrative barriers that prevented them from attending, finding that in 1976, 489 Puerto Rican students were admitted, but only 137 actually enrolled because of these administrative obstacles.[84] The congress organized a protest on the Old Queens campus and wrote to President Bloustein with an offer to serve as a liaison between the university and their Puerto Rican employees and students.[85]

The years from 1976 to 1980 were years of rebuilding and reflection for the Puerto Rican Studies Department. Divisions emerged between the Department of Puerto Rican Studies and the UEP student group.[86] Students, faculty, and staff went on three-day retreats in 1976, 1977, and 1978 to review the curriculum and the program's progress and assess the history of the department and their strengths and weakness over the years.[87] The department adapted to shifting demographics in New Jersey by changing the department name to the Puerto Rican and Hispanic Caribbean Studies Department under Professor Miguel Algarín.[88] The fact that the Puerto Rican Studies Department survived and adapted to become the Latino and Caribbean Studies Department today is a testament to the students, faculty, and staff who persistently organized, protested, and strengthened their department over the years despite the climate of repression, administrative barriers, and violence. Their efforts and accomplishments during these years left a legacy of activism and centered the education of Puerto Rican students at Livingston College.

"Peace Be with You, Black Students"[89]

In his discussion of black student protest on campus, former Rutgers University dean and professor of history Richard McCormick argues that black students at Rutgers were experiencing a number of concerning issues on campus by the late 1960s and early 1970s. These issues included over-policing, few black cultural activities, issues with financial aid, and a lack of black faculty. But, as McCormick asserts, one of the most profound issues facing black students at Rutgers was the feeling that black students were "at best tolerated and more commonly resented."[90] With the exception of black student involvement in athletics, McCormick argues that "scrawled racial epithets, hostile stares and overbearing attitudes reminded [black students] constantly of their alien status."[91] Consequently, McCormick argues that black students took "little part in predominantly white campus organizations and instead focused on their own sororities, fraternities, political and cultural organizations and living groups." He asserts that "they sought to create for themselves a separate and protective environment."[92] McCormick does not indicate what these spaces looked like or to what degree black students might have participated in multiracial student organizations. His statement does, however, point to a significant aspect of both the black student experience and black student activism on campus.

As the number of black students increased on Rutgers campuses across New Jersey, so did a variety of issues facing these students. They responded by creating social, political, and cultural student clubs and organizations that allowed them to find and create community and discuss the issues they faced on campus and how they would respond to them. Although black students at Livingston College were no different in creating space for themselves than at the other campuses, Livingston College was founded in a different context than the other campuses in the New Brunswick–Piscataway area. Livingston College was the only Rutgers University campus that black students did not integrate in the late 1960s. Additionally, it was the only one that proclaimed a special mission, at least in theory, for minority students. By 1974, 30 percent of the Livingston College student body was composed of black and Puerto Rican students.[93] Despite the increased numbers of minority students, this collegiate site was not without problems. Black students at Livingston faced many of the same issues as their New Brunswick and Douglass College counterparts. But by building on the possibilities that Livingston College offered as an experimental college, black students at Livingston worked to create the campus they wanted to see. This section explores the creation of various clubs and organizations on Livingston's campus in its earliest years, which reveals the ways that black Livingston students viewed and used spaces on campus as incubators to develop a larger political, cultural, and social consciousness.

One way in which Livingston College offered the room to cultivate a social and political consciousness was through the intellectual opportunities created by faculty and staff. In an April 1971 memo to Provost Richard Schlatter, Dean Ernest Lynton explained that the Livingston College faculty chamber had voted to change "Afro-American studies" from a program to a department. Lynton said that the change in title would "formalize what has been our intention since the inception of Livingston: to build a strong curriculum in Afro-American studies."[94] Lynton asserted this move was an essential element to the college's commitment to complement the other programs at Rutgers and Douglass Colleges. With a goal to "develop analytic skills as well as provide the student with a body of knowledge of the black experience in this country and the world," the courses offered within the African and Afro-American Studies

Department were taught by faculty from a range of academic disciplines.[95] Patricia Graham (LC '72) experienced this intellectual space firsthand. She recalled the experimental premise of Livingston as the reason for her transfer from Rutgers–Newark in 1969. Her decision was made in part because of the advice of Rutgers–Newark professor Clement A. Price. She recalled, "I talked to Dr. Price often and he said, 'Well, Patricia . . . why don't you transfer to this brand-new campus, Livingston? . . . Maybe you'll enjoy it.'"[96] She continued, "It was labeled as a social experiment. . . . They're bringing together famous artists and writers, and they're going to be the professors. They're going to have all these cultural events tied to the academics and new courses, a few black history courses, women's studies courses, courses about your community, environment and health care and things like that."[97]

An urban planning major, Graham recalled taking a number of courses that exposed her to the very ideas Professor Price discussed with her before her transfer. Graham took a course by black arts movement poet Sonia Sanchez titled "Black Women." In the 1971–1972 course catalog, Sanchez's course was described as a class that dealt with "the experiences, historical and current, of Black Women." Sanchez's course offered a broad study of black women's experiences from a range of religious, social, economic, and political backgrounds.[98] Graham recounted that, in addition to appreciating the invited guest speakers like Vertamae Smart-Grosvenor,[99] she did not fear that professors would not understand her—or even fear the professors themselves. Graham remembers her class with Sanchez as being a comfortable space where, in addition to Sanchez cooking for students, she also exposed students to a variety of scholarship and literature and created an environment that supported student development. Graham's experiences in Sanchez's class would later impact her own teaching at East Stroudsburg University, where she used the methods of her former professor with her own students.[100]

Along with "Black Women," the course listings in the 1971–1972 course catalog for Afro-American studies ranged from "The Afro-American and U.S. Politics" to "Institutional Racism," "Literature from the Black Perspective," and "Afro-American Music." Additionally, African studies offered courses in elementary Hausa and Swahili, African folklore and tradition, and the course "African Political Thought." In the early 1970s, Livingston's faculty included leading writers, activists, and filmmakers like Sonia Sanchez and Toni Cade Bambara.[101] Livingston provided the curriculum not only to serve its black students but also offered the courses to students at all Rutgers campuses. As a result, Livingston provided the most variety of African American and African history courses within the tri-campus area.

In addition to her experiences with renowned black studies professors, Graham remembers the opportunities Livingston College opened for off-campus enrichment. For an African American history course titled "Research

Techniques," Graham traveled to the Schomburg Center for Research in Black Culture in Harlem, New York. There, Graham worked on a research paper about Ghana's first president, Kwame Nkrumah. While in New York, she explored Harlem bookstores and restaurants before ending the day at her professor's apartment for dinner where each student "was given something to prep" before their class session began.[102] Though not a long distance from campus, this experience allowed Graham to interact and engage with resources outside of the university classroom. As a part of her urban planning major, she worked with "a pretty well-known lawyer in New Jersey" who was Latinx and had students engage in research about community issues.[103] In regard to her paper, Graham approached the professor and said that she was "concerned about health care for America" and wanted her research to reflect that. Consequently, and under the guidance of that professor, Graham traveled to hospitals in New Brunswick and Newark to conduct research for her project. Taken together, Graham's experiences reflect Livingston and its faculty's mission to "connect the campus to the community and to expose students to social, legal, and political issues at home and in society at large."[104]

In addition to the domestic trips that Graham experienced, Livingston students were also offered the opportunity to travel abroad. In December 1969, Willie J. Smith, of the Livingston Division of Urban Studies and Community Development, wrote to secure eleven places in the 1970 American Forum for African Study program in Ghana. The allocated spaces were for students who "had demonstrated an interest in African Studies and [were] involved in the college's Urban Studies Program."[105] The American Forum was a private, nonprofit organization established in 1967 by Melvin Drimmer and C. Eric Lincoln.[106] Under the direction of the Institute of African Studies at the University of Ghana, the American Forum for the International Studies Africa program conducted a summer program.[107] The program was designed to "communicate a better understanding of the Afro-American past . . . and give the student a broadened base from which to relate Africa's heritage and culture to American Society."[108] Livingston was selected because of its identity, at least from the perspective of organizers, as the new experimental school of Rutgers University.

Although correspondence from Melvin Drimmer to President Mason Gross and then Provost Richard Schlatter reveals tension over Rutgers's financial commitment to actually send its students abroad, the creation of the Afro-American studies program and other similar programs at Livingston that included opportunities to travel abroad illuminates the cultural and political consciousness cultivated in Livingston classrooms by faculty. As exemplified by the range of courses and research assignments, black students from varying backgrounds had the opportunity to learn not only more about the world around them but also about the experiences of black people in the United

States and in the diaspora. Livingston students, however, did not simply depend on faculty to create space and opportunity for them, nor did they let faculty completely direct their ideas. In parallel with faculty efforts, Livingston students created their own spaces in which they could find support and an outlet for their ideas and expressions. The creation of these cultural, social, and political clubs and organizations allowed black students to articulate how they saw themselves and how they envisioned the Livingston College mission.

Black Student Arts and Culture at Livingston

On a cultural level, black students at Livingston created a variety of spaces in which they could express varying identities. A plethora of student groups emerged in the late 1960s and early 1970s articulating a rich diversity of black arts and cultures. These groups drew students together to share life, art, music, and experiences and offered forums for debates and consciousness-raising. From African dance and drumming to black Greek organizations, black students actively manifested their interests on the Livingston campus.

Under the heading "Yours in Blackness" in *Livingston in the Retrospect, 1969–1973*, William Bellinger (LC '73) explained the origins and purpose of the Weusi Kuumba Dancers and Drummers he founded in 1969. Bellinger explained that the formation of the troupe served to promote "a language, a mode of expression, which addressed itself to the mind, through the heart, using related, relevant and significant movements" to ultimately "portray a heritage, a culture, conceived, and felt by our troupe."[109] The Weusi Kuumba Dancers and Drummers traveled and performed widely, both close by, at nearby Somerset County College, and as far away as Malcolm X University in Chicago and Boston University. They donated all the proceeds to support black students majoring in community development and for research about sickle cell anemia.[110] Established on the zeitgeist of black cultural nationalism and expressions of blackness of the early 1970s, the Weusi Kuumba Dancers and Drummers is just one example of the ways that black students sought to express themselves culturally on the Livingston campus.

Whereas the Weusi Kuumba Dancers and Drummers articulated a particular cultural expression, the Black Women's Consciousness Group (BWCG), founded in 1970, sought to raise black social and political consciousness on campus. BWCG member Diane Brown said that the *conscious black woman* "is a woman who is aware of her oppression as a Black person and a woman. She also realizes that she has to explore, along with other women who are similar to her, different possibilities of their struggle and draw conclusions based on their experiences, both distant and common."[111] Brown's statement illuminates the ways in which the black women in the BWCG were using these spaces to think about the intersection and impact of race and gender in their lives and to explore the decisions they made in relation to these identities. As

YOURS IN BLACKNESS

FIGURE 8.4 Kuumba Dancers perform, *Livingston in Retrospect Yearbook*, 1973. *Courtesy of Special Collections & University Archives, Rutgers University*

the author asserted further, "Black women are an integral part of the Black experience. The women's liberation movement effects [*sic*] the consciousness of all women, of all ethnic backgrounds, therefore putting Black women in 'double jeopardy' in terms of her race and sex."[112] As a result, the members of the BWCG argued that it was time for black women to organize and deal with the social issues facing them at this moment. Additionally, the BWCG sought to work "within the Rutgers University Complex" and develop an agenda that would empower black women and black students at large on Livingston's campus and across all the Rutgers campuses.

In order to accomplish this, the BWCG worked to "awaken women" at Livingston by offering programs that would stimulate discussions among black students and provide opportunities to engage with speakers on campus. For example, between 1970 and 1974, the BWCG held four Spring Festivals at Livingston College. The 1973 festival focused on the Livingston campus and its community specifically; the 1974 festival broadened those horizons. In the April 1974 edition of the *Black Voice* newspaper, the BWCG cordially invited students to their fourth annual Spring Festival—its theme: "Day of Black Love." Diane Brown (LC '75), coordinator of the event, stated that the goal was to "set up relationships with the surrounding community by putting on programs that focus on the political, economic, and social conditions of Black PEOPLE."[113] Scheduled to begin at 1:00 p.m. in the Livingston College gymnasium, the program included an inmate prison-reform panel, a poetry reading, a performance by the Black Liberated Gospel Choir, and a fashion show. Additionally, the festival featured two black women speakers, Bibi Amina Baraka and Halima Toure. Baraka was scheduled to speak about the roles of black men and women in community development, and Toure would speak about marriage in Islam. Although the programs were free, the day concluded with a dinner for which the BWCG accepted dinner donations of one dollar, which went toward the Black Scholarship Fund.[114] These forums not only served as a site for students to discuss how to respond to issues with the administration but also to larger issues facing them as citizens of the world in which they lived.

The Weusi Kuumba Dancers and Drummers and the Black Women's Consciousness Group existed alongside a host of other social, political, cultural, and preprofessional organizations formed at Livingston College by 1974. Besides these two organizations, Livingston students could join the West Indian Students Organization, Black United to Save Themselves (BUST), the Black Aesthetic Club, and the Black Student Psych Association. These organizations allowed the space to forge community around cultural expressions, to discuss social and political issues, and to share knowledge and engage around coursework. As a result, through these organizations, like their counterparts around the country, black Livingston students worked to articulate a consciousness among black students that made them aware of the larger social and political issues in the world around them.

These discussions, however, were not without debate. As students confronted a variety of topics, it became apparent that there were differing ideas about what kinds of spaces black students should create. In September 1974, an anonymous article appeared in the tri-campus Rutgers student newspaper the *Black Voice* headlined "Message to Black Students." Drawing from poet Gil Scott-Heron and keyboardist Brian Jackson's song "Peace Go with You, Brother" from the 1974 album *Winter in America,* the article began:

Peace be with you, Black students—all of you; be you be anxious freshman, the apprehensive senior, the obnoxious graduate student; be you nationalist, Nation of Islam, Pan Africanist, radical liberationist, Black Feminist, accommodationist, black anglo-saxon or warrior. Peace go with you.[115]

But like Scott-Heron's bluesy song, this extension of peace was not without a larger message.[116] For the writer, black students across the tri-campus area (Rutgers University and Livingston and Douglass Colleges) needed to develop and assert a black consciousness that still spoke to "the revolutionary liberation of Black people"[117] Whereas the Weusi Kuumba Dancers and Drummers and the BWCG invited members to explore their heritage and social consciousness, other black student clubs and organizations had different missions and goals. This diversity of the black student body at Livingston, as the anonymous author in the *Black Voice* illuminates, resulted in debates about what black student consciousness and activity should look like on campus. The debates over the subsequent arrival of black Greek letter organizations at Livingston in the early 1970s reveals a poignant example of differing ideas around black identity throughout the campuses.

By the mid-1970s, three of the "Divine Nine" black Greek letter organizations (BGLO) had arrived in the tri-campus area.[118] It should be noted that BGLOs were chartered in a unique way at Rutgers University. Because Rutgers University itself was composed of campuses in different cities and because each BGLO had its own rules regarding how chapters could be chartered, some BGLOs had established chapters on Rutgers campuses in Camden and Newark prior to the 1970s. By 1977, five of the nine BGLOs and two black social fellowship organizations had chartered chapters at Rutgers University, including Livingston College.[119] By the late 1970s and early 1980s, the tri-campus area would see the addition of the Zeta Phi Beta sorority and the Phi Beta Sigma fraternity on campus as well. In addition to BGLOs, Livingston College also saw the charter of a chapter of the social fellowship Groove Phi Groove, which established a chapter in October 1972 for interested black men on campus.[120] Groove's sister organization, Swing Phi Swing, also established an undergraduate chapter of the fellowship for black women at Rutgers College in the early 1970s. Groove Phi Groove and Swing Phi Swing represent a different tradition than BGLOs. Formed in 1962 and 1969, respectively, Groove Phi Groove and Swing Phi Swing's mission was expressly more political and was the antithesis to the perceived conservatism of BGLOs. Groove and Swing embraced black cultural nationalism and critiqued BGLOs in their mission and programming.[121]

As black Greek letter and social fellowship organizations began interest groups and established chapters on campus, they quickly announced their missions. When announcing their charter in a 1974 editorial in the *Black Voice*, the Eta Epsilon chapter of Kappa Alpha Psi viewed the creation of the letter organization at Rutgers as "not just another Black Fraternity, but as another

FIGURE 8.5 Swing Phi Swing members, *We the People Yearbook*, 1974.
Courtesy of Special Collections & University Archives, Rutgers University

vital instrument for Black People and the Black Community."[122] They hoped, as they continued, "to work alongside other organizations to aid in the better-ment of minority people on the college campus and off the college campus."[123] This sentiment was echoed by the Kappas and other black fraternities on campus as they sought to combine social activities with community-minded organizing. Similarly, but with a pointedly different organizational mission, Groove Phi Groove and Swing Phi Swing, the black social fellowship organiza-tions on campus, also worked to support both the Rutgers and New Brunswick communities. In April 1974, the two organizations held a voter-registration drive in order to bring awareness to the upcoming local mayoral race while also allowing the "fellowship to go beyond the purely social level."[124] In addi-tion to the fraternities and social organizations themselves, the auxiliary or "sweetheart" organizations on campus also took up community programming

FIGURE 8.6 Omega Psi Phi Fraternity members, *We the People Yearbook*, 1974.
Courtesy of Special Collections & University Archives, Rutgers University

as a part of their work. In October 1973, "the twenty-two sisters" who made up the Omega Pearls hosted a Valentine's Day party for children at a local day care.[125] Events such as this, Pearls president Edythe Haygood explained, sought to create community connection but also hold up their founding principles: womanhood, scholarship, and love of Omega Psi Phi.[126]

Love for the fraternity aside, the mission of all these organizations—the black Greek letter organizations, the social fellowship groups, and other black student organizations—sometimes clashed and tension resulted. What was the role of a black fraternity or sorority when their students were focused on political and social issues both on campus and around the world? In her recollection, Patricia Graham said, "Sororities were just a little self-serving to us, and fraternities, because we were a little bit more political [and] interested in the politics of the day."[127] In an editorial in the *Black Voice* titled "Black Fraternities: A Socio-Political Perspective," Gregory Burke echoed a similar sentiment. He argued that the problem with these organizations, particularly fraternities, was their relevancy at that moment. In earlier times, black students entered Rutgers University in smaller numbers and reflected the particular homogeneity at Rutgers and Douglass College. This homogeneity was forged through what Burke argued was the intersection of middle-class identity and blackness. In this way, Greek letter organizations became a relevant space for black students to find and create support on campus before the 1960s.[128]

But "on the wings of student activism in the late 1960s, the new dominant type of Black student [appeared] who was [an] educationally and/or economically disadvantaged student . . . from urban-core areas and possessed strong geo-cultural identifications [that] led to social heterogeneity in the community."[129] Increased numbers of black students meant, according to Burke, that there were a variety of student wants, needs, concerns, and responses to a diversity of issues. Class difference was also a central problem with Greek letter organizations because of organizational hierarchy and membership costs. In Burke's view, students coming from oppressed environments were ultimately recreating cycles of oppression for incoming black students through the "pledge" process. Lastly, the sweetheart organizations associated with the fraternities were a "crude imitation of the male chauvinist's placing of the female in the aristocratic south." These organizations were challenged by black people and, more specifically, black women on campus, but not by black fraternities.[130]

In response to Burke, a "Brother Henry C." wrote an editorial for the *Black Voice* in support of black fraternities. Brother Henry C. argued that the basic aim of these organizations was "to promote social and political awareness and betterment."[131] Brother Henry C. did admit that "some of the organizations have not lived up to their doctrines and are not helping the community in great steps," but these organizations had the potential to do so.[132] Where Burke claimed that these organizations kept students from studying or that only students from higher socioeconomic backgrounds sought to participate, Henry C. asserted the opposite. Brother Henry explained that students from all backgrounds were interested in and participated in these organizations. Moreover, fraternities and social fellowships promoted unity and high scholastic achievement. For Brother Henry, fraternities were a melting pot of students that could support both students and their communities.[133]

Left out of these conversations was the place of black sororities on campus. In 1973, Annette Williams affirmed that although there were no sororities at Rutgers and Douglass College before 1973, that was changing for black women at Rutgers University. Her article announced plans to charter a chapter of Alpha Kappa Alpha sorority. Under the sponsorship of Theta Phi Omega and Doris Reid of Douglass College, the new Alpha Kappa Alpha chapter would be open to black women at Rutgers, Livingston, and Douglass Colleges once they created an interest group of twenty young black women. Williams proclaimed, "With the establishment of the various fraternities within the University where Brothers find certain prestige and social status, it is only natural to highlight that the sisters of the university want a sorority where they too can find the same fulfillment." She explained that not only "could the sorority give a sister a feeling of prestige, but also something to work toward." For Williams, the arrival of sororities to campus was potentially self-affirming for black women students of the Rutgers tri-campus community.[134]

Ultimately, the differing perspectives about the impact of black fraternities and sororities on campus are reflective of the ongoing debates and tension among black students about identity and political purpose. These debates also represented how the students saw themselves in the larger movements and in their efforts for cultural expression, and showed how black students shaped the campus for themselves. The creation of these student organizations and clubs allowed students to host programs and bring performers and speakers to campus that embraced their interests and ideas.

Defending Livingston's Vision

As black students debated among themselves what the conscious black student at Livingston looked like, they also had to contend with alternative ideas about the image of the college. In 1974, the same year the BWCG sought to awaken black women and two new chapters of black Greek letter organizations were chartered, other student organizations sought to advocate on behalf of black students with the faculty and administration. Originally calling themselves the Organization of Black Unity, Black United to Save Themselves (BUST) was organized in 1969 with the motto "To promote a peaceful co-existence between the minority students and the total student population."[135] Between 1969 and 1977, BUST organized a variety of events, including Homecoming Week with the first homecoming king and queen pageant; a coffee hour for black faculty, staff, and students; a program to support Assata Shakur, hosted by Ossie Davis; and, in combination with other organizations, a "Black Week."[136] Black Week, similar to Homecoming Week, was a week of events hosted by BUST dedicated to celebrating black culture and students. In addition to these activities, in October 1974, BUST included two meetings with faculty and administration as a part of their efforts to build "a working rapport."[137]

The first meeting was held with the Black Faculty and Staff Association at Lucy Stone Hall on the Livingston campus and sought to create new academic opportunities for students. The second meeting was held in Quad II with the newly appointed dean of the college, Dr. Emmanuel Mesthene, and spoke to tensions about the identity of the college. Chaired by Livingston students and BUST steering committee members Richard Husband and Damon Keeling, the meeting with Dean Mesthene focused on a number of issues. In addition to asking for clarification about Mesthene's statements regarding the difference in the needs of "nontraditional" and "traditional students," BUST representatives also questioned Mesthene's qualifications to serve as dean of a college "designed for minority and working-class students."[138] Before his arrival at Rutgers, Emmanuel Mesthene worked in research at the Rand Corporation from 1953 to 1964 before earning his PhD from Columbia in 1964. His other professional experience included serving as an editor at Bantam Books and teaching at Adelphi and Columbia Universities. Prior to arriving at Rutgers, he served as a faculty member at Harvard University's Business School from 1964 to 1973.[139] For BUST representatives, this background ran contrary to the larger goals and aims of Livingston College. As it proclaimed at its inauguration, Livingston College was a college "without ivory towers" that created space for racial minorities and students from lower socioeconomic backgrounds.[140] The question regarding Mesthene represented black students' desire for administrators with a professional background that could support that mission. In short, although Mesthene was qualified for the position on paper, students questioned whether his professional experiences, which included work at several Ivy League universities, could support the experimental space that students and faculty had created at Livingston.

This tension was further emphasized by the efforts of BUST representatives to gain clarification on another statement made by Mesthene regarding the college's image.[141] "Members of B.U.S.T.," asked Willie Webb and Soneni Bryant, "for the purpose of clarification, What did the dean mean by the statement, 'Livingston is in need of a new image'?"[142] Mesthene's reply, described as "evasive" by Webb and Bryant, was that his comments referred not to the black image of the college but to the "sloppy academic performance of Livingston."[143] For BUST representatives and for other students, this question surrounding Livingston's image was an important one. The conversation between the dean and BUST members further intensified while discussing the Livingston gymnasium. The gymnasium served as a significant site for black student organizing and programs in addition to its role as the home of the Livingston Panthers basketball team, sometimes referred to as the Black Panthers. In the 1970s, the gym was the site of the BWCG's Spring Festivals, speeches by Julian Bond and Dick Gregory, and concerts by popular black artists like Bootsy Collins.[144] The importance of the gym to BUST members was also emphasized in their questions at the meeting, specifically about the hiring of more black staff in the gym. Mesthene responded, however, that the administration had received complaints from white students about feeling intimidated in the gym.[145] BUST member Damon Keeling pushed back, arguing, "Blacks are intimidated by the entire university system, [and] the university system is not responsive to our needs and feelings of intimidation."[146]

This standoff between Dean Mesthene and members of BUST represents the tensions about what Livingston College meant to students and administrators and about how the college was perceived by the other Rutgers campuses. Students forged alliances through the creation of campus groups and challenged, discussed, and organized against the administration for downplaying their experiences. Additionally, they used these spaces to hold public social programs and events as a means to create and nurture a supportive community. These students played a significant role in shaping college life across the campuses. As Patricia Graham remembered, "Of course, the kids from the other campuses would come to our affairs at Livingston's campus, because it was coed and they had a lot of social things at Livingston."[147] With its larger number of black students, the intellectual spaces it offered, and the social and political organizations centered there, Livingston College served as a significant site for black student events, programs, and activism.

At the same time, where black students saw campus spaces like the gym as a positive space, Mesthene's comments reveal a different perception from the administration. In his inaugural address in September 1974, Mesthene said that the college had "virtually no credit left in the eyes of the University and the State" and that the "Board of Governors are prepared as early as this year to declare the Livingston experiment a failure."[148] Moreover, even the *New York Times* penned an article in 1974 with the headline "Livingston: Image a Problem."[149] Quoting Provost Kenneth W. Wheeler, the *New York Times* wrote, "The public seems to think that Livingston is all black. . . . The public also thinks Livingston is not a safe place to attend."[150] Although Wheeler argued that these statements were inaccurate, this problematic image of the college loomed large and was only compounded by other issues facing the still-evolving campus. As students continued to voice concerns over policing, specifically the arming of campus patrol, other matters were raised about the grading system, funding from the Educational Opportunity Fund, and tensions with President Edward Bloustein's administration.[151] Additionally, Livingston's structure, which focused on providing a nontraditional educational space, seemed to be cracking as both faculty and students demanded more support on campus.

As Livingston College continued to grow and develop throughout the 1970s, so did the disparity between the founding mission of the college, the demands of minority students, and actual institutional support. The founding mission of Livingston College was to support black students as they sought a university that would encourage their political ideologies, cultural expressions, and social gatherings. With a myriad of programs designed to assist any student interested in black American or African American history, culture, politics, or language, ideally black students could use the classroom to learn about subjects that they were directly affected by. At the same time, students created extracurricular forums to further discuss, problematize, or introduce ideas to each other. Through performances or public talks, students expressed a variety of ideas to each other. Although they debated what the collective spaces should look like, the common consensus was that the development of consciousness among black students about issues on campus, in the community, and around the world was necessary to their survival. But as students worked to shape the campus in the ways they wanted, they ultimately confronted the changing ideas about the experimental college that was Livingston. During the final years of the 1970s, declining administrative support for the vision and institutional goals of Livingston College and its students significantly influenced the trajectory of the institution.

Conclusion

By the 1980s, Livingston College began to shift away from its initial identity as an experimental college. As scholars Paul Clemens and Carla Yanni assert, this was due in part to a continued lack of structural organization and support. From its inception, Livingston had suffered from major structural issues that ranged from student and academic life to the campus architecture and layout. Additionally, by the 1980s, Rutgers University had moved to a consolidated department model. Clemens and Yanni note that "consolidation broke the connection between faculty and departments and reworked the academic landscape of the New Brunswick and Piscataway campuses."[152] Previously, each college had independent departments. This new model consolidated faculty into single departments on either the Livingston, Rutgers, or Douglas College campuses. Because Livingston College "was perceived as the most isolated and least desirable home for consolidated departments . . . it thus lost out in the musical-chair politics that sent specific departments to specific campuses."[153] This shift in the departmental organization, tuition increases, and the larger lack of organization direction contributed to a shift in Livingston's ability to create a nontraditional educational space. As a result, some scholars argued that although Livingston offered a significant amount of opportunity, it ultimately fell short of its goals.

Livingston College, as an institution, did indeed move away from its initial student and academic goals toward a more traditional college setting and in that way it did fall short of what its founding deans set out to accomplish. However, Livingston's legacy remains thanks to the tireless efforts of students, faculty, and staff from over the years—the most notable example being the Puerto Rican Studies Department, now known as the Department of Latino and Caribbean Studies and in its thirty-seventh year. This department is a testament to student, faculty, and staff activism and their dedication to the education of students of color at Rutgers despite constant defunding from the university. Moreover, the inclusion of student voices in the University Senate and the Board of Governors is also a testament to Livingston student efforts to have the students be a part of the decisions made at the administrative level.[154] Success, then, is found in the struggle of Livingston students and faculty to create the intellectual, political, and social spaces to support students of color. Puerto Rican and black students seized on the mission of Livingston College and utilized campus spaces to celebrate their histories, amplify their voices, and find reprieve from the racism and other indignities they faced as people of color. By creating or joining clubs and organizations, they combated isolation from the New Brunswick campuses and created communities for themselves, for students of color from other Rutgers campuses, and for the larger New Brunswick and Piscataway communities. Puerto Rican students also forged relationships in their homeland of Puerto Rico and among the broader Puerto Rican communities in New Jersey. Like their counterparts in student movements around the country in the 1960s, black and Puerto Rican students at Livingston reimagined higher education by creating spaces for themselves that reflected their intellectual interests and cultural heritage.

PART III

Making Black Lives Matter beyond Rutgers, 1973-2007

MIYA CAREY

Throughout the 1960s, black and brown students brought the black campus movement to New Brunswick, Newark, and Camden.[1] They advocated for policies that increased minority enrollment and culturally relevant course offerings and social spaces.[2] Much of the activism traced in part 2 focuses on race relations on campus. Part 3 of *Scarlet and Black: Making Black Lives Matter at Rutgers, 1945-2020,* however, shows the expansive vision and reach that blacks and other students and faculty of color held regarding activism. Against the backdrop of Black Power, the anti-apartheid movement, and the culture wars, faculty, staff, and students of color extended the boundaries of campus activism in the latter part of the twentieth century. They argued that the university was responsible for cultivating racial equity and held the university accountable for creating a more just and equitable campus *and* world. This meant attacking systemic racism from the banks of the Raritan to the shores of South Africa and addressing the ways in which institutions of higher education have historically perpetuated it.

This section begins with Joseph Kaplan's "'It's Happening in Our Own Backyard': Rutgers and the New Brunswick Defense Committee for Assata Shakur." Here, Kaplan chronicles the arrest and nationally publicized trial of black activist Assata Shakur. In May 1973, Shakur and her comrades were pulled over on the New Jersey Turnpike outside of New Brunswick. The traffic stop turned into a deadly shootout that ended with the deaths of activist Zayd Shakur and State Trooper Werner Foerster. Kaplan's essay chronicles how a network of local activists and Rutgers students, faculty, and staff rallied around Assata Shakur, a controversial figure, during her trial in the city of New Brunswick. Organizations like the New Brunswick Defense Committee for Assata Shakur worked as the political counterpart to Shakur's defense team, helping to build community support and apply pressure to the judicial system. All eyes were on New Brunswick during the trial, which drew attention from the American and Soviet press. The essay offers a much-needed glimpse into the ways in which residents of the small city and black Rutgers affiliates engaged with black radicalism and viewed their role in the movement for black liberation.

Whereas student activists at Rutgers in the 1960s focused primarily on institutional change—namely, the creation of ethnic studies programs and the recruitment and retention of students and faculty of color—the student activists of the 1970s and 1980s looked outward. Students in this era drew a connection between racial equity on campus and global racial justice. They held the university accountable for its role in perpetuating injustice and its duty to solve the issue. One of the most prominent social justice movements of the twentieth century was the anti-apartheid movement. As early as the 1960s, activists from around the world launched a global movement and called for the end of apartheid in South Africa. American college students formed a vocal contingent of this movement, calling for their universities to divest from companies with financial ties to the apartheid regime. Rutgers students were among those calling for their institution to divest. The divestment movement at Rutgers was a multiracial one. As the university became increasingly diverse, there were more opportunities to socialize and organize across racial and ethnic lines. This cross-racial organizing was not without its difficulties. In "Fight Racism, End Apartheid: The Divestment Movement at Rutgers University and the Limits of Interracial Organizing, 1977–1985," Tracey Johnson shows the limits and possibilities of interracial organizing. Is cross-racial solidarity possible? Johnson argues that although the multiracial divestment movement at Rutgers was ultimately successful, it hampered the creation of interracial movements on campus that followed.

Like the divestment activists in the 1970s and 1980s, student organizers in the 1990s drew from a long legacy of campus protest at Rutgers. The university was thrust into the national spotlight in 1995 when remarks made by President Francis Lawrence months earlier went public. In a faculty meeting in the fall of 1994, Lawrence suggested that African American students performed poorly on standardized tests because of a hereditary deficiency. His remarks, which harkened to the biological determinist claims made by Richard Herrnstein and Charles Murray's conservative text *The Bell Curve* (The Free Press,1994), set off a firestorm of reactions on campus, in the state of New Jersey, and across the United States. In "'Hell No, Our Genes Aren't Slow!': Racism and Antiracism at Rutgers during the 1995 Controversy," Meagan Wierda and Roberto C. Orozco are less interested in whether Lawrence was a racist and meant what he said. Rather, the authors are concerned with, first, what his statement can tell us about the long-held relationship between race science and the academy in America. Second, they narrate the efforts of faculty and students of color to use the incident as a springboard to protest and make demands that the administration not only say that they are committed to diversity and inclusion but also put into place concrete policies that create a truly equitable environment.

The final essay in this section analyzes yet another statement made about black Rutgers students. This statement, however, came from outside the university. In "'Pure Grace': The Scarlet Knights Basketball Team, Don Imus, and a Moment of Dignity," Lynda Dexheimer recounts the statement made by "shock jock" Don Imus in 2007 about the Rutgers women's basketball team. Imus drew sharp criticism with his description of the Scarlet Knights as "nappy-headed hos." Although cultural commentators, regular citizens, and the Rutgers administration admonished Imus for his racist comments—some even arguing that that he should be fired—Imus supporters invoked the First Amendment and argued that the radio show host was well within his rights to express his opinions, even if those opinions were racist and sexist. But what about the women at the center of the controversy, the Scarlet Knights and their coach, Vivian Stringer? Rather than focusing on whether Imus was racist, these women shifted the direction of the national discourse by highlighting the pervasive racism and sexism that black women had experienced across time.

In his commencement address to the class of 2016, President Barack Obama praised Rutgers as a diverse institution. He declared Rutgers as a space where "America converges." He highlighted the fact that Rutgers students came from a variety of racial, ethnic, and socioeconomic backgrounds and experiences. For Obama, Rutgers symbolized both the gains that America has made in terms of inclusion and equality and the possibilities of the nation. He framed diversity as an asset.[3] But thinking beyond diversity, America converged at the university in important and often explosive ways in the late twentieth and early twenty-first centuries. Those who voiced their support for Assata Shakur, protested for divestment from South Africa, called for the resignation of President Lawrence after his "bell curve" remarks, and argued for Don Imus's firing in the wake of his "nappy-headed hos" comment demonstrated that calls for racial justice on campus were linked to broader debates about race and gender taking place nationally and abroad. Furthermore, they forced Rutgers to reckon with a larger question: What role should the university play in society? Indeed, this is a question that American colleges and universities continue to grapple with today.

9

"It's Happening in Our Own Backyard"

Rutgers and the New Brunswick Defense Committee for Assata Shakur

JOSEPH KAPLAN

At 12:45 a.m. on May 2, 1973, Assata Shakur, Zayd Malik Shakur, and Sundiata Acoli were traveling southbound on the New Jersey Turnpike from New York City to Philadelphia when they were stopped by State Trooper James Harper. The ostensible reason for the stop was a faulty taillight, but given the three young African Americans' involvement with the New York branch of the Black Panther Party, it is possible that Trooper Harper was already aware that the white 1965 Pontiac Lemans was carrying a group of black militants. Upon stopping the group around exit 9 near New Brunswick, Harper called for backup, which arrived minutes later in the person of thirty-four-year-old Werner Foerster. What happened next is highly disputed, but a shootout left Zayd Shakur and Trooper Foerster dead, while Harper ran for a nearby state police headquarters and Sundiata Acoli and Assata Shakur fled down the highway. The next thing Shakur recalled, she was being kicked and punched as she struggled to breathe from a gunshot wound that had shattered her right clavicle. She hazily recalled officers screaming, "Which way did they go?" and telling her, "Bitch, you'd better open your goddamn mouth or I'll blow your goddamn head off!"[1] Thus began one of the most polarizing and racially charged legal cases of the late twentieth century.

Assata Shakur is a larger-than-life figure—an underground activist, political prisoner, fugitive prison escapee, and political asylum recipient in Castro's Cuba. While her story has been memorialized by artists and activists for years, it has received little treatment in historical scholarship.[2] For that matter, much more is known about the shootout on the turnpike and the trial that followed than about the role of Rutgers students, staff, and New Brunswickers in the story of Assata Shakur. The case placed New Brunswick as a key site of post–civil rights black radicalism, law enforcement politics, and even Cold War rivalry. Recall Alice Jennings Archibald's observation, echoed in chapter 2 in this volume, that Rutgers had failed to impact New Brunswickers of color and held little "influence on the people in the community" throughout much of the twentieth century.[3] This time, however, Shakur's trial galvanized Rutgers affiliates and locals to come to her aid. Despite intimidation from police and more immediate concerns about access to housing and jobs, many ordinary people in the New Brunswick community and students and faculty at Rutgers, primarily black women, rallied to Shakur's aid as part of the New Brunswick Defense Committee for Assata Shakur. Although Shakur was ultimately convicted, activists affiliated with the defense committee and those not affiliated with the group demonstrated, "trial-watched," and generally caused disruptions throughout the proceedings, making her trial a key moment in New Brunswick's political and racial history. This essay traces the Shakur trial from the perspective of Rutgers and the local community.

The Turnpike and Conservatism in the Hub City

The shootout on the turnpike occurred at a moment when the political landscape of New Brunswick and the United States as a whole was in flux. By the early 1970s, New Brunswick had begun to move from the liberalism of the "New Five" toward the right of the political spectrum. The New Five, ushered in with the election of Mayor Patricia Sheehan in 1967, sought to bring progressive change to city government with the inclusion of women and people of color in elected positions. The Sheehan administration also worked to strengthen transparency and communication between the municipal government and its constituents. However, the "near-riot" that engulfed New Brunswick on July 17 and 18, 1967—spurred by black New Brunswickers' ongoing struggle against employment, housing, and educational segregation—and Sheehan's subsequent response to it signaled the beginning of a conservative backlash against liberal government. Detractors argued that Sheehan's strategy of listening to protesters and not calling in law enforcement against them was a sign of weakness and evidence that Sheehan condoned actions such as looting and vandalism.[4]

New Brunswick's move toward a more conservative politics coincided with the rise of the New Right in the United States, which was solidified with the election of Republican President Richard Nixon in 1968. *New Right* refers to the newly rebranded Republican Party made up of social conservatives and Southern Democrats who had changed parties. It coalesced around a law-and-order platform—a reaction to the increased militancy of the Black Power–era activism and urban rebellions that swept across the United States in the late 1960s. The "tough on crime" policies and rhetoric that emerged from this platform increased the power of law enforcement, disproportionately targeted black and brown communities, and took a more punitive approach to addressing crime.[5] Radical activists such as Shakur, who was a former Black Panther and at the time a current member of the fledgling Black Liberation Army (BLA), an underground anticapitalist militant organization that engaged in armed resistance, would have been a state target.[6]

The impacts of the growing conservatism of New Brunswick's government coupled with national crackdowns on radical black activism and growing police power were made clear on the turnpike that night. The New Jersey Turnpike was known to be a particularly hostile place to all black motorists. While researching his book *Looking for America on the New Jersey Turnpike,* Rutgers professor Angus Gillespie received a letter from a former student who recalled that during their time working at a Howard Johnson's on the turnpike in the early 1970s, "the state troopers on the Turnpike were known as bigots/rednecks/civil rights violators," and "blacks . . . had a much higher chance of being pulled over and searched and harassed than your average citizen."[7] Shakur acknowledged as much in an address titled "To My People," which Evelyn Williams, her aunt and lawyer, managed to smuggle out of the Middlesex County Workhouse and distribute to local radio stations. In her message, Shakur apologized to her fellow revolutionaries for taking the turnpike. "I should have known better," she reflected. "The turnpike is a checkpoint where Black people are stopped, searched, harassed, and assaulted."[8] Given the high levels of surveillance that all black folks faced on the turnpike, it was no surprise that these three avowed revolutionaries were stopped by hostile white officers that night.

By situating this story within the context of the growth of conservatism locally and nationally, it becomes clear why black Rutgers students, staff, and New Brunswickers stood in solidarity with Shakur. In addition to the uprising of 1967, residents had witnessed the rise of "white power" organizations, deindustrialization, struggles for local control of schools, and police violence against black citizens throughout the late 1960s and early 1970s.[9] As the essays in part 2 of this volume demonstrate, this was also a moment of institutional change at Rutgers. Students held the university accountable for creating a more racially equitable environment for themselves and for faculty. For black residents of New Brunswick and black Rutgers faculty, staff, and students, the shootout and subsequent trial was a larger manifestation of the racial violence and discrimination that they endured within their city and within the institution. At the same time, they believed in Shakur's vision of black liberation.

Organizing a Defense

News of the shootout polarized the already fractured community of New Brunswick, but it did not take long for activists to come together to defend Shakur and Acoli from what they were sure would be a railroading in court. In October 1973, just days before the trial was set to begin, Angela Davis appeared at a Princeton University conference sponsored by the New Jersey ACLU where she urged students to protest the upcoming trial. Based on her own experiences with the justice system, she told the crowd of five hundred, "I know what it's like to be a political prisoner. . . . The only way we're going to scratch the surface is by building a unified movement, especially among women."[10] Clearly, black women answered Davis's call, for they were among the majority of those in the Rutgers and local community that came to Shakur's defense.

One of the most active and committed activists for Shakur's freedom was Cheryl Clarke, a burgeoning poet from Washington, DC, who had come to Rutgers to get her master's degree in English. At the time of the turnpike shootout, she was working for Middlesex County while taking courses at Rutgers. Clarke initially heard about the shooting through the press, but soon became interested in the case when activists began coming in from New York to protest. Sometime in mid-1973, Clarke was approached by Frieda Grier, who told her, "Look, we need to show some solidarity with this sister. It's happening in our own backyard. Let's find out what we can do."[11] Grier and Clarke became founding members of the New Brunswick Committee for the Defense of Joanne Chesimard and Clark Squire (the given names of Shakur and Acoli), a political counterpart to their legal defense teams and the local counterpart of the defense committee in New York.

The defense committee in New Brunswick was primarily composed of women, some of whom were students at Rutgers. Originally consisting of just a handful of people, the committee used their connections with Rutgers to leverage support for the case. On Halloween of 1973, Grier and Clarke, along with Domine Pittman, Brooks Sunkett, and Marge Woods, conducted a question-and-answer session on local AM radio station WCTC's *Forum for Progress* show, and a transcript was reprinted in the Douglass College newspaper *Caellian*. The program covered a range of issues related to the case, including the racism of state troopers on the turnpike, police intimidation of New Brunswick's black community, and logistical questions about the incident. The article showed that the defense committee was reaching out to Rutgers students with "areas of campus designated for donations for the trial. Pamphlets are being given out on what's going on at the trial. Rallies are being planned, as well as shows provoking community awareness."[12] The small committee used whatever resources it had at its disposal. It got its message out over the radio and in student newspapers, even though, as Clarke recalls, "We really

FIGURE 9.1 Protesters march in "Free Assata" rally in New Brunswick.
Courtesy of Special Collections & University Archives, Rutgers University

considered ourselves in the community, not so much at Rutgers." Clarke, who worked for Middlesex County, also says she did "a lot of Xeroxing for Assata on the county's dime."[13] The *Caellian* article concluded by telling those interested in supporting the defense committee to call the Douglass Black House, indicating that black students at Douglass were actively involved in the defense at this early stage.

The defense committee's support extended to carpools to Morristown, where Shakur was being held, to offer support and to ensure that she was not being mistreated in her fragile state. Acoli and Shakur's trial was delayed until February 1974 due to contentious change-of-venue motions, as well as other cases based on spurious charges that Shakur faced in New York. However, in late January it emerged that Shakur was pregnant, the father a codefendant in a case in New York. Evelyn Williams announced Shakur's pregnancy and called for her case to be severed from Acoli's for her health and safety. Shakur eventually gave birth to a healthy baby girl, but the severing of the case had consequences for both her and Acoli. The committee reminded those taking part in the carpools to "be aware that the already hostile behavior of the New Brunswick police toward black people will be heightened."[14]

In March 1974, Sundiata Acoli was convicted for the murders of both Trooper Werner Foester and Zayd Malik Shakur, despite that fact that Trooper Harper admitted to firing the shots that killed Shakur. This was possible because of a New Jersey state "aiding and abetting" law that allowed the state to charge a suspect with any additional crimes that resulted from the initial criminal act. Acoli was sentenced to life plus thirty years for the shooting. While it is not the intent of this essay to relitigate the case, it must be noted that there were major inconsistencies in Trooper Harper's testimony that led to the verdict.[15] With Acoli successfully convicted, the state turned its attention to Shakur. After spending the first year of her child's life fighting court cases in New York, all of which she won, Shakur finally returned to New Brunswick in late 1976 to face trial for the crime that had just sent her comrade to prison. This represented a new phase in the case, and many community members redoubled their efforts to free Shakur from what they saw as a politically motivated trial.

1976: The Fight Continues

Between the time of Acoli's conviction and the beginning of Shakur's solo trial in New Brunswick, Shakur was incarcerated without bail even though she had not been convicted of any of the other crimes of which she was accused. Despite the gauntlet thrown down by the state, Shakur remained hopeful, partly thanks to the committed action of women in the community like Cheryl Clarke and Martha Pitts. Pitts was a nurse from Newark who dedicated herself to the cause of Shakur's and Acoli's freedom, traveling between New York and New Brunswick to recruit new members for the defense committee. As Shakur later recalled of Pitts, "Year after year, she endured humiliating searches, police surveillance and police harassment to make sure [I] had a visitor, to make sure someone cared."[16] Women like Clarke and Pitts were instrumental in not only publicizing the case but also clearly had a personal impact on Shakur's spirits as she endured multiple hostile trials. In a 1975 interview with the group Women Against Prison, which took place in her cell at Rikers Island, Shakur expressed her gratitude to these stalwarts, saying, "I want to thank the people who have supported me, and the people who have come to court for me. My message to them is: keep on struggling."[17] And this is exactly what they did. Although Shakur had already endured six grueling trials by 1976, her supporters in New Brunswick had just begun their struggle.

In late 1976 the trial loomed, and Shakur's allies kicked their advocacy into high gear. On October 21, famed radical lawyer William Kunstler spoke at the Rutgers gym before an estimated 400 to 700 people, mostly students. Kunstler decried the corruption of law enforcement and pointed out that "while murderers like Richard Nixon walk around . . . a few blocks from here in the basement dungeon of Middlesex county jail, is a woman with no criminal record who has been denied bail."[18] In covering the speech, the New Brunswick *Home News* solicited the opinion of Middlesex County sheriff Joseph DeMarino, who took exception to Kunstler's characterization of the jail basement as a "dungeon." He argued that the twenty-two-by-forty-four-foot

FIGURE 9.2 Poster for William Kunstler's speaking engagement in defense of Shakur (Kunstler was held in contempt for his comments during the event), *Daily Targum*, October 20, 1976.

Courtesy of Special Collections & University Archives, Rutgers University

cell was "larger than some homes," and that "she has 'more than any other prisoner in the country.'"[19] In contrast to DeMarino, the black-owned *Baltimore Afro-American* had reported on Shakur's conditions months earlier and noted that the basement of the all-male facility where Shakur was housed lacked proper ventilation and sunlight. Moreover, it reported that "she is on a 24-hour solitary confinement basis and is denied TV, social encounters, movies or work options," and, "as a Muslim, she must often limit her daily food consumption to milk and cold cereal since pork . . . is often on the menu."[20] These were the conditions Kunstler decried and DeMarino tried to spin. Ultimately, Kunstler's diatribe before the assembled students and community members was an attempt to create political support for legal actions calling for the amelioration of Shakur's conditions of confinement. In retaliation for his speech, Kunstler was charged with contempt for violating court rules. The charges were dropped a month later.

In December a group of women from the Rutgers community started the short-lived feminist newspaper *LABRYS*. The group published the first edition out of pocket without university funding, and the trial issue was dedicated to Assata Shakur. Rutgers student Sondra Korman, who founded the fledgling paper, explained that "we want to make students aware of her trial and generate support for her predicament."[21] The issue's lead article, "Assata Shakur: Strength behind Bars," was written by Cheryl Clarke and focused on the deplorable conditions of Shakur's confinement. Clarke stressed that political support for Shakur was key to ensuring a legal victory, arguing that Shakur's previous acquittals showed "that support of the people, now wise to the fatal capriciousness of the American institution of justice, forced truth from absurdity."[22] The inaugural issue made an impassioned plea for public support by showing how critical it was for Shakur's chances in court and connecting her case to civil liberties writ large. Clarke and the women behind *LABRYS* saw Shakur's incarceration as a prime example of the government's hostility toward poor black women as well as a threat to their own right to dissent.

Clarke noted that "anyone who supports Assata and other incarcerated political prisoners is a target of the government also," which was why after Angela Davis gave a speech in support of Shakur in New Brunswick that summer, "the car Angela was riding in was stopped by the New Brunswick police for a so-called 'routine check.'"[23] That Davis was targeted illuminates, again, how the conservatism of the city posed a threat to black radicalism within its borders.

As Angela Davis's appearance in New Brunswick made clear, Shakur's trial encouraged a range of prominent supporters to make the trek to the Hub City. The New Brunswick Defense Committee for Assata Shakur (now reflective of her name change and the severing of the cases) solicited the support of prominent black women poets, thanks in part to the influence of Cheryl Clarke and the resources of the university system. Clarke recalled that the committee "got Jayne Cortez and Audre Lorde involved. There was another woman who got involved with us. Her name was Hattie Gossett. She taught at Livingston for a while."[24] Cortez and Gossett were both at Livingston College at the time, and they, along with Lorde and Clarke, represented some of the most talented poets of the era. Lorde was particularly inspired by the strength she saw in Shakur. According to Clarke, "Lorde read her poetry for the benefit of several political defense fundraisers in New York and New Brunswick,"[25] and it was during this time that she wrote her tribute poem "For Assata," which was published in her 1978 collection, *The Black Unicorn* (Norton, 1978).

The Trial

Shakur's solo trial in New Brunswick was set for January 1977. As early as January 5, the *New York Times* reported that "a number of militants and members of the underground press have been seen in town and on the campus of Rutgers University here."[26] Jury selection began on January 17, and from the outset it was marked by protests and controversy. National Jury Project polling data showed that, before the trial, a full 70 percent of Middlesex County residents had not only heard of Shakur but believed her to be guilty as well.[27] Thus the media had pronounced Shakur guilty before the trial even began, and white New Brunswickers' memories of the "near riot" a decade earlier fueled law-and-order rhetoric that conflated black militancy, urban uprisings, and street crime into an undifferentiated threat to white citygoers. Despite these prejudicial factors, Judge Theodore Appleby rejected motions for changes of venue on the basis of potential bias, and the defense team quickly exhausted their peremptory challenges. In the end, the jury was all white, composed of seven men and five women, and, according to Shakur, contained "two friends, one girlfriend, and two nephews of new jersey state troopers," leading her to conclude that the "so-called jury selection process was the biggest farce in legal history."[28] As the defense team battled with Judge Appleby, Shakur's supporters formed "a picket line of about 50 young persons . . . chanting 'Free Assata,' 'Free All Political Prisoners,' and 'Stop the Trial'" outside the courthouse in the frigid winter weather.[29] The courthouse pickets, hostile encounters between defense and judge, and highly dubious legal proceedings would become par for the course in this emotionally charged trial.

Perhaps nothing set the tone of the trial more clearly than controversy over an alleged bomb threat on the second day in court. The defense protested the highly visible and heavily armed security, arguing that this further prejudiced the jury into believing that their client was a dangerous criminal. Kunstler had risen on the first day of proceedings to exclaim, "You'd think we were dealing with a wild animal that demands security of this nature."[30] Sheriff DeMarino argued that the heightened security was necessary because of unspecified bomb threats as well as threats made against the lives of both Shakur and Kunstler. Although the threats against Shakur and Kunstler never materialized, this was not an unthinkable proposition given that there had been a visible neo-Nazi presence at Shakur and Acoli's initial trial.[31]

The trial gained national prominence as a result of the litany of figures who threw their support behind Shakur as well as her colorful and well-known lawyer Evelyn Williams, but in mid-February the case went international when the Soviet news agency TASS sent a reporter to New Brunswick to cover the events. In a sort of meta-reporting, the *Home News* noted the presence of the

FIGURE 9.3 "Free Assata" advertisement, *Black Voice/Carta Boricua*, November 2, 1976.

Courtesy of Special Collections & University Archives, Rutgers University

Soviet agency and interviewed its reporter, Vladimir Baydashin. When pressed for the reason that a Soviet news outlet would be interested in the case, Baydashin responded that "it gives a good example of the judicial process in this country. She's a human being, colored, a poet, an intelligent person, and that's why she's interesting."[32] Baydashin's article was dispatched to the eight thousand members of the agency throughout the socialist world. Soviet propaganda often featured images of violence against African Americans and stories about racism and discrimination at the hands of the federal and state governments in an effort to delegitimize America's claim as the beacon of democracy and to gain political allies for their side in the Cold War. The decision to send Baydashin to cover the trial of Shakur, a black woman targeted by the state for her radical activism, was a strategic choice.[33]

Thanks to the CIA's Foreign Broadcast Information Service (FBIS), an open-source intelligence department within the agency, Baydashin's article was translated into English. The article was strident in its criticism of the case, claiming that the state was hoping "to make short work of this Negro activist" and noting that "racist feelings, encouraged by the authorities, are particularly strong in this city."[34] The article also reported on the "mass demonstration" outside the courthouse and quoted "Sharrol Clark [sic], member of the Assata Chacourt [sic] Defense Committee," as saying that "the purpose of the demonstration was to demonstrate solidarity with Assata."[35] Although the Soviet press had their own agenda for covering the story, namely to document injustice in the United States to deflect criticism from their own government, the article became another venue for the defense committee to generate support for Shakur's case. Soviet outlets would continue to publicize Shakur's story as a means of shaming the United States and distracting from its own abysmal human rights record, marking New Brunswick as a notable site of Cold War racial politics and propaganda.

As the trial pressed on, conflict between the judge and Shakur's legal and political supporters became increasingly combative. The day after the TASS article was printed, Beatrice "Bebe" Watson was thrown out of court by Judge Appleby. Watson, a Trenton State College graduate and founding member of the National Coalition to Defend Assata Shakur, was removed from the courtroom for allegedly passing out "propaganda leaflets." When one of Shakur's attorneys, Lawrence Stern, protested that evicting Ms. Watson was a deprivation of her right to take part in a public trial, Appleby thundered back, "She has no rights in here that I do not give to her."[36] Shakur recalled in her autobiography that Appleby "claimed that he was a 'stickler for the decorum of his courtroom,'" adding that his courtroom contained "plenty of decorum but not a bit of justice."[37] Kunstler spoke to the media after leaving the courthouse, claiming that the incident "reflects [Appleby's] continued bias toward the defendant on every level," which was why "we moved to disqualify him from the beginning."[38] With fading hope for a fair trial, Shakur's defense team again solicited support in the court of public opinion.

On the last day of February, the Paul Robeson Cultural Center and the Rutgers Committee for Democratic Rights sponsored a benefit performance for Shakur. The program featured Shakur's lawyers as well as playwright Amiri Baraka and actor Arthur Burghardt. Baraka and Burghardt drew a crowd to the event, and Shakur recalled that Newark native Baraka was an active supporter of her cause throughout New Jersey. Lennox Hinds, Shakur's lawyer in her civil suit against the conditions of her confinement and president of the National Conference of Black Lawyers, claimed that he was being "'harassed and intimidated' for speaking out against trial proceedings and in support of Joanne Chesimard."[39] Hinds faced potential disbarment in the state of New Jersey for comments he made at a press conference on January 20, where he called the trial "a legal lynching and a kangaroo [court]" after Judge Appleby refused to allow an investigation into allegations that the offices of the defense team had been bugged.[40] Shakur's defense lawyers also spoke about the hostility of the judge toward their client, citing Kunstler's own contempt charges from his speaking engagement at Rutgers in October as well as the removal of Watson from court earlier that week.[41]

The performance at Rutgers may have helped drum up political support for Shakur, but it certainly did not calm the tensions between the judge and Shakur's backers. Just two days later, the courtroom erupted into near chaos as Appleby ordered a spectator, possibly a New Brunswick resident, to be removed for refusing to take off his hat. As the man was forcibly removed from the building, Shakur exclaimed, "This is a damn shame."

Appleby ordered the sheriff's officers to "remove anyone who's violent," to which Shakur replied, "There was no one who was violent at all!"

"Sit down!" the judge shouted at Shakur.

"You sit down," she snapped back, "you're doing this deliberately to harass anyone coming into this court."[42]

After a brief period of calm, another Shakur supporter rose in the back of the court and asked to be allowed to speak. He was also removed, setting off another testy exchange between Judge Appleby and the defense team. As the two sides went back and forth hurling invectives at each other, yet another spectator rose and exited the courtroom, declaring, "It's a travesty. I'm glad I saw it with my own eyes."[43] After a wild day in court, Shakur complained of feeling ill and was escorted from the building, apparently in tears. In the midst of this hostile atmosphere, Judge Appleby denied the defense team's motion to subpoena FBI director Clarence Kelley and Senator Frank Church to introduce evidence from the FBI's Counterintelligence Program (COINTELPRO) on behalf of their client. This ruling was highly significant because several black radicals charged in conspiracy cases in the early 1970s were eventually exonerated by evidence released through Freedom of Information Act requests that proved they were targeted by the intelligence community. Denied this potentially exculpatory testimony, Shakur's defenders continued to fight with the limited legal and political tools available to them.

Courtroom disruptions were another way for the community to show solidarity with Shakur, both to document the unfair proceedings and to show her that she had political support. Although the identities of these "disrupters" are unknown, it is possible that they were New Brunswick residents or Rutgers students. Regardless, they highlight one of the myriad ways that students or local citizens could have engaged with the case and expressed their support of Shakur and the black radical political stance that she represented. Disruptions, however, may have made an already hostile judge even more unyielding. This became apparent when Appleby ignored one of Kunstler's most ingenious legal arguments.

Days after denying testimony about COINTELPRO, the judge waived Kunstler's motion for a dismissal on the grounds that the state's case against Acoli had implicitly exonerated Shakur. Anticipating a potential challenge to Acoli's conviction, Middlesex County assistant prosecutor William Welaj had submitted a brief that claimed "attempting to attribute the killing to Chesimard was not viable."[44] The brief went on to say that although "Chesimard could have been shown to have been in the immediate area, the testimony and evidence would have virtually eliminated her as the principal."[45] Despite the state's admission in the Acoli case that Shakur could not have been the person who shot Trooper Foerster, the judge allowed the case to move forward on the basis of the New Jersey "aiding and abetting" law. With a hostile judge, an unsympathetic jury, a lack of expert witnesses willing to testify on behalf of an alleged cop killer, and the rejection of their best legal arguments, the defense appeared increasingly futile and protesters became agitated.

The trial dragged on, and supporters continued to protest even as it became clear to them that the fix was in. On March 15, in the midst of the defense's case, five Brooklyn women were arrested for spray-painting "Free Assata" and "Stop the Lynching" on the county welfare building near the courthouse. The women were arrested after they were found passing out handbills calling for Shakur's freedom in downtown New Brunswick.[46] Among the five women was twenty-one-year-old Susan Rosenberg, a radical student who later became involved with the May 19th Communist Organization, which worked with the Black Liberation Army. Seven years later, Rosenberg was arrested in New Jersey for her alleged involvement in Shakur's escape from prison, charges that she was acquitted of. However, Rosenberg did receive a fifty-eight-year sentence for weapons possession (sixteen times the national average for such offenses).[47] Rosenberg was among several activists involved in

Shakur's defense who would be surveilled, harassed, or investigated for their suspected role in her escape.

By March 25, Shakur's defense team and supporters had done all they could, and it was left to the jury to determine her guilt or innocence. Even as the jury deliberated, Shakur's supporters continued their picket outside the courthouse. However, the odds had been stacked against her from the start, and after three days of deliberation, the jury returned a verdict of guilty. Shakur was convicted of the murders of both Trooper Foerster and Zayd Malik Shakur as well as assault with the intent to kill Trooper Harper, illegal possession of weapons, and armed robbery of Foerster's gun.[48] As the jury read the verdict, Shakur interrupted them, saying, "You are racists—yes, you are."

Judge Appleby ordered her to be silent, but she continued, "You are unfair. You abuse the law. I haven't taken part in this trial from the beginning. I knew it was racist. I knew it was unfair."

At that, Appleby ordered the sheriff to "remove the prisoner," to which Shakur retorted, "The prisoner will walk away."

As she exited the courtroom, several of her supporters got up and walked out with her, some shouting obscenities at the judge. One frustrated man exclaimed, "I don't want any part in this lynching."

After Shakur left the room, Kunstler continued to argue with the judge, and finally Appleby told the shaggy-haired lawyer, "It's over and I don't have to put up with arguing with you anymore. I'm glad it's over."[49]

Pickets surrounded the courthouse the next day, but the verdict was in: Shakur was sentenced to New Jersey's mandatory life term for intentionally killing a police officer. This ended one of the most contentious political trials in the nation's history, let alone that of New Brunswick. Recalling the trial in her autobiography, Shakur regretted even participating, claiming that "by participating, I participated in my own oppression. I should have known better and not lent dignity or credence to that sham. In the long run, the people are our only appeal."[50]

Aftermath

After the verdict, some black Rutgers students saw the trial as a sham and evidence of the corruption of the American judicial system. The Rutgers University newspaper *Black Voice/Carta Boricua* ran a full-page segment asking students their opinions of the conviction. Most of the students expressed detailed opinions that showed that they had followed the case closely. Douglass student Sabina Morrow noted, "I don't see how she could have gotten a fair trial with the types of things that went on in the courtroom. The judge was clearly on the side of the prosecutor."[51] Rosalind King, another Douglass student, claimed, "It was a sham from start to finish. I attended court several times. The racism was very obvious."[52] Chuck Chaplin, a junior at Rutgers, offered his take on the problems of the case, arguing that "the burden of the trial was on Chesimard to prove her innocence while purportedly we believe that the suspect is innocent until proven guilty. The evidence could not place a gun in her hand, yet she is convicted of firing that same gun."[53] The students, all black, saw the trial as a clear miscarriage of justice and displayed a sophisticated knowledge of the case and its inconsistencies. Although these students obviously had strong feelings about the case, one Douglass student, Renee Carter, lamented that there were not "more Black people there to give their support because I think it would have had more bearing on the case."[54] Carter called the verdict "depressing," but claimed that it had inspired her to attend law school to do something about the racism of the legal system.

One of the reasons that more black people did not participate in the protests was the level of racial animus that the case exposed in New Brunswick. As early as 1973, the defense committee argued that "black people know that their community is cased by police more than the white community," and that "the extension of repression by the police is very obvious."[55] While clearly many black students and community members cared deeply about Shakur's fate, the repression that white supporters like Rosenberg were subject to was only magnified for black activists. Cheryl Clarke recalls, "I had to deal with the FBI for at least three years after Assata went to jail and especially after she escaped." Clarke recounted police stopping and harassing her friends as they drove to meet her for a picnic at Johnson Park on the banks of the Raritan River. Then one day the FBI showed up at her doorstep in New Brunswick asking for information. As she remembers, "I think that was the first time they confronted me. Then, when I moved to Highland Park, they followed and stopped the mother of the woman I was living with, just fucking harassing. Of course, she was horrified."[56] The FBI even went so far as to visit Clarke's parents' home in Washington, DC, where her mother promptly told them off for questioning her loyalty as a taxpaying citizen. If the FBI and local police went to such lengths to harass and intimidate a respected artist and intellectual like Clarke, it is unsurprising that many ordinary black people in New Brunswick chose to refrain from direct action even if they had followed the case with interest.

Moreover, the trial of Assata Shakur coincided with major changes happening in New Brunswick. Given the quotidian struggles being waged over redevelopment, education, and the allocation of municipal resources in which all black residents had a serious stake, it is unsurprising that the reaction to the highly sensationalized trial of a black freedom fighter from out of town was muted. Even if most black residents saw the injustice of trying a black woman for the murder of a white trooper on the notorious turnpike in front of an all-white jury, many people were simply too preoccupied with protecting their families from the more glacial forms of racial discrimination represented by redevelopment and school segregation. In the context of a massive reorganization of the black community driven by corporate avarice and weak-kneed neoliberal political leadership, forces Shakur had dedicated her life to combating, many black residents would have been disheartened by her conviction, but few surprised.

Conclusion

Thanks to an accident of geography, New Brunswick became a major site of conflict when Black Power icon Assata Shakur was arrested on the New Jersey Turnpike and tried in the city on hotly disputed charges. Although the case drew international attention, it was a Hub City story. The defense committee, local residents, and Rutgers students voiced their support for Shakur and engaged with the case in many different ways. Their responses to the shootout and subsequent verdict were a culmination of frustration at an increasingly conservative and suppressive local government. Furthermore, Rutgers students who actively voiced their support for Shakur highlight the expansiveness of student activism in this period. Black students were not only concerned about the recruitment and retention of black students and faculty or the creation of black studies courses; they also believed that their activism should transcend the bounds of the campus.

The legacy of the Shakur trial remains embedded in the landscape of New Brunswick. More than forty years after her trial and subsequent escape from the Clinton Correctional Facility for Women in New Jersey, Shakur appeared again on the New Jersey Turnpike. This time, however, it was her "wanted" image emblazoned on digital billboards dotting the toll road. In 2013, the FBI added Assata Shakur to its "Most Wanted Terrorists" list, the first woman to be included. She is referred to as Joanne Deborah Chesimard on that list. The FBI uses these billboards to urge motorists to report tips regarding crimes and sightings of criminal suspects and convicted fugitives. The Route 18 overpass on the New Jersey Turnpike, known as the Werner Foerster Overpass, was dedicated to the state trooper that stopped Shakur and her companions on that fateful night in May 1973. That she is labeled as a "domestic terrorist" and that her "Most Wanted" billboard coexists with the Foerster overpass on the turnpike is telling. It not only reveals the ongoing conflicts between the federal government, law enforcement, and black radicals, but also the contested nature of Shakur's legacy in New Brunswick and beyond.

10

Fight Racism, End Apartheid

The Divestment Movement at Rutgers University and the Limits of Interracial Organizing, 1977–1985

TRACEY JOHNSON

The anti-apartheid movement, part of the broader decolonization movement that spread across the African continent, began in the United States in the late 1960s on the heels of the black student movement. With the rise of black studies, a tangible result of the black student movement, came the introduction and proliferation of diaspora studies, a subfield of black studies that examines the experiences and intellectual and cultural connections of people of African descent across the globe. Diaspora studies, coupled with the continued relationship between black radicals and pan-Africanism, fostered an interest in anti-apartheid and later stoked the divestment movement among students.[1] Proponents of divestiture wanted universities to abandon their investments in corporations that supported the South African economy. They argued that economic support for South Africa led to the continued oppression of South Africa's black majority, who had no voting power, were impoverished, lived in a segregated society, and were victims of racial violence.

The 1980s witnessed the height of the divestment movement on American college campuses. Rutgers was among the most active campuses in the struggle. Anti-apartheid activism at Rutgers took various shapes throughout the 1970s and 1980s, including marches, sit-ins, and hungers strikes, among other tactics.[2] The divestment movement began at Rutgers in the late 1970s with the creation of the Coalition in Solidarity with Southern African Liberation (CISSAL). This umbrella organization took a multipronged approach to protest that included written information campaigns, lectures, and picket lines. CISSAL's goal was to not only raise awareness about the system of apartheid, but total divestment as well.

FIGURE 10.1 A multiracial group of Rutgers students rally for divestment.
Courtesy of Special Collections & University Archives, Rutgers University

In 1977, President Edward Bloustein, with the support of the University Senate, the Board of Governors, and the Board of Trustees, agreed on a policy of partial divestment. This decision emerged from a debate that began during the spring 1977 semester. That semester, the University Senate forwarded two reports. The major report, penned by economics professor Sidney Simon, argued that divestiture could detrimentally impact black South Africans. Rather than divest and lose their voting privileges within certain corporations, he argued that Rutgers could use its corporate votes to pressure corporations. The minority report, authored by Leila Sadat, a student member of the University Senate, questioned the effectiveness of Simon's voting argument and called for divestiture. The University Senate sent the majority report back to the committee. After multiple hearings, the senate recommended partial divestment. The terms of this policy included an individual examination of each corporation to assess their labor practices and operating procedures in South Africa. The university would divest based on the findings of the individual investigations. By the fall semester of 1977, both the Board of Governors and Board of Trustees accepted the proposal. Student protesters were not alone in their push for total divestment. Faculty members also criticized the position, framing partial divestment as immoral. Bloustein, however, contended that "entanglement with money connected to South Africa was more pervasive than people realized, and that the board had taken the

FIGURE 10.2 Students at anti-apartheid rally at Rutgers.

Courtesy of Special Collections & University Archives, Rutgers University

most constructive approach to the problem."[3] As this essay shows, debates about total divestment raged on into the 1980s.

Students in the anti-apartheid movement came from a rich tradition of student organizing across Rutgers in the 1960s. However, the divestment movement at Rutgers that emerged in the late 1970s was quite different from the student movement that occurred in the prior decade. Namely, the anti-apartheid movement at Rutgers and other college campuses was multiracial—it brought together minority students and predominantly white "New Left" students. Historian Matthew Countryman, who was involved with the anti-apartheid movement at Yale University as an undergraduate, noted, "The divestment movement spawned more attempts to build campus multiracial coalitions in eighteen months than had occurred in the previous decade."[4] The same held true at Rutgers. In 1984, students formed the multiracial Rutgers Coalition for Total Divestment (RCTD). As the name implies, the RCTD, like other student-led organizations across the United States, called for the university to divest itself from all corporations invested in the South African economy. Multiracial coalition building at Rutgers, however, ultimately proved to be just as difficult as convincing the administration to totally divest.

Relationships between black, brown, and white students in the RCTD were fraught with racial tension. Interracial tension within the divestment movement was not unique to Rutgers. Rather, it was a fixture of the nationwide campus movement. Countryman recalled how "as black and Third World students we found ourselves in fundamental disagreement with white students over tactics, agendas, and decision-making structures."[5] At Rutgers, these clashes were most evident in the 1985 takeover of the Rutgers University student center and its aftermath, as well as the campaign to bring Jesse Jackson to campus. Testimony from black students in the movement, organizational papers, and reports from the campus newspaper the *Daily Targum* reveal that the primary issue at the center of this conflict was white students' inability to see the connection between confronting racism on campus and ending apartheid in South Africa, as well as their failure to grasp the importance of this link.

The divestment movement was unable to foster a cohesive multiracial coalition, which caused black students to question the efficacy of interracial organizing. Still, it is important to highlight that anti-apartheid activists were ultimately successful in achieving their goal for the university: total divestment from corporations that supported the South African economy. Anti-apartheid activists forced the university to reflect on its global responsibility as an American institution and reckon with its commitment to create a more just and inclusive world. This is a crucial part of the movement's legacy.

CISSAL and the Early Phase of the Divestment Movement at Rutgers

In the late 1970s, Rutgers students formalized their role in the divestment movement with the creation of the Coalition in Solidarity with South African Liberation (CISSAL). This student-led group was composed of a mixture of students and faculty from various minority student organizations across the three New Brunswick campuses, including the West Indian Student Organization, the African Student Congress, the Pakistani Student Organization, the Black-Hispanic Graduate Students, and the Committee in Solidarity with the People of El Salvador. CISSAL took a multifaceted approach to organizing. First, it produced and disseminated written information campaigns to raise students' awareness about apartheid. The goal was to grow a student movement that would "demand that Rutgers University divest itself of all stock in corporations" invested in South Africa.[6] Second, CISSAL sponsored lectures. One of their largest events was a university-wide forum titled "Struggle and Repression in South Africa."[7] The keynote speaker at the event was Andrew Manqunte Lukele, an outspoken dissident who had been exiled from South Africa.[8] After the forum, students organized a rally and picket line for divestiture on the Cook/Douglass campus. Lukele put a face to the black South

FIGURE 10.3 Flyer for student "sleep-in" at Rutgers.

Courtesy of Special Collections & University Archives, Rutgers University

Africans who suffered from the apartheid regime and galvanized the students across all the campuses to protest in the name of divestment. These information campaigns and lectures took place in 1977, prior to the largest student-led anti-apartheid demonstrations.

The third part of CISSAL's strategy highlighted the similarities between black South Africans' lives under apartheid and African American struggles for liberation. The group compared South African apartheid to racism in the United States to not only make the South African situation more relatable to students just learning about apartheid but also to critique continued discrimination against African Americans on US soil. In an undated informational packet about apartheid, CISSAL referenced the antibusing protests that took place in Boston from 1974 through the 1980s. Antibusing protesters, the majority of whom were white mothers, protested court-ordered school desegregation and the busing of African American students to white schools. White students also engaged in antibusing protests, which at times became violent, such as the conflict between white and black students at South Boston High School.[9] CISSAL wrote, "It is racism that drives white students to attack Black school children in Boston when they demand the right to a quality and integrated education."[10]

Perhaps the coalition wanted to draw a parallel between the violence met by black students fighting for educational equality and culturally relevant education in America and the schoolchildren who took part in the Soweto uprising. In 1976, black South African students living in Soweto organized a demonstration to protest the Bantu Education Department's order for the compulsory use of Afrikaans in their schools. It has been estimated that between three thousand and ten thousand students participated in the demonstration that began on June 16 and lasted for nearly ten days. Police opened fire and unleashed tear gas on the peaceful protesters. The official death toll has been reported as 174 blacks and 2 whites. Thousands more black South Africans were wounded.[11]

The coalition also used images in their pamphlets and leaflets to allude to the parallel struggles experienced by black people in the United States and by black South Africans. Images of black men in shackles harked back to American chattel slavery. One leaflet featured a call to readers to "End Apartheid!!!" Under this declaration was a well-known image of an enslaved black man, kneeling and in chains. By placing this image specific to antebellum America underneath the call to end apartheid, students in CISSAL bound the struggles and fates of African Americans and black South Africans together, and hoped to provoke an emotional response among students familiar with the history of chattel slavery. As members of the first post–civil rights generation, these students also drew their enthusiasm for anti-apartheid from their experiences of the black freedom movement of the 1960s.[12]

While invocations of slavery and civil rights struggles could have inspired students from a variety of backgrounds to join the anti-apartheid movement, many white students suffered from cognitive dissonance. As the movement grew in the 1980s, it became clear to black and brown students that although white students wanted to take part in dismantling the system of apartheid in South Africa, they ignored and simultaneously perpetuated racism at Rutgers. This led to rifts within prodivestment groups.

Protest   Rutgers   investments   in
South Africa

MASS DEMONSTRATION
FRI. APRIL 12TH AT 12:30 P.M.

in front of Brower Commons

on College Avenue

Skip Classes
Be There

Sponsored by:

African Student Congress

Busch Minority Affairs Council   African Heritage

Organization of Third World   Peace Center of Central Jersey
and Minority Students

Pakistani Student Organization

Organization of Arab Students   Democratic Socialists of America

Black – Hispanic Graduate Students
YGAP
African Students Organization

Puerto Rican Students Organization   100 Black Men

Committee in Solidarity with The People of El Salvador

FIGURE 10.4 "End Apartheid" flyer.

Courtesy of Special Collections & University Archives, Rutgers University

Racial Tensions in the Rutgers Coalition for Total Divestment

The anti-apartheid movement at Rutgers continued to expand in the 1980s. The Rutgers Coalition for Total Divestment (RCTD), created in 1984, was larger than CISSAL. It was a racially diverse student organization composed of other student groups including the Committee on South Africa, the Busch Minority Affairs Council, the Organization of Third World and Minority Students, the

Black and Hispanic Graduate Student Association, and the African Student Congress.[13] This multiethnic, multiracial group of young people joined forces to exert pressure on the Rutgers administration during a time when students at other universities persuaded their institutions to divest.[14] RCTD's diversity turned out to be one of the group's largest challenges. In his monograph on youth activism, scholar Sekou Franklin described racial tensions that arose when black student leaders within the anti-apartheid movement across the United States "challenge[d] their white counterparts for their resolute opposition to racism abroad, but disregard for confronting similar racist behavior in the United States."[15] The RCTD faced similar issues.

The RCTD organized a twenty-four-hour-a-day occupation of the Rutgers University student center in response to the university's decision to only partially divest from corporations that had business dealings with South Africa, which did not go far enough for the students who wanted total divestment. Approximately one hundred students took part in the occupation that began on April 12, 1985. RCTD members renamed the student center the Nelson Mandela Center and protested there for thirty days. The sit-in marked the first private controversy that the RCTD weathered.

Nearly one year later, the *Daily Targum* published an article that featured accounts from RCTD members detailing moments of racial discord within the organization during and after the sit-in. The article captured both sides of the argument and the resentment within the coalition. Lisa Williamson, now known as the author Sister Souljah, was a student activist and member of the Rutgers Coalition for Total Divestment. She told the *Daily Targum* that white animosity against black students began after the election of a steering committee that was set up to "organize food and health supplies, police protection, administrative interaction and community input." Of the seven elected members, six were black and one was white. Williamson claimed that white students immediately contested the results and that some even cried. She believed their emotional reactions to the election results stemmed from racism. Williamson said, "The white students realized they had empowered the black students to run things . . . and though they couldn't pinpoint why, they felt they themselves should be running things."[16]

The white students interviewed for the article saw the situation very differently than Williamson did. Lisa Sherper, a junior at Rutgers College, claimed that not all members of RCTD were "invited" or present at the vote on the steering committee. Whereas Sherper claimed that the majority of members present for the vote were black, Williamson argued the opposite, stating that "there was not a majority of black students at the election. White students elected the blacks—it was not that the vote was fraudulent in any way, they simply did not like the results."[17] Whatever the truth may have been, this dispute highlighted the difficulty of cross-racial alliances in organization building, leadership, agenda setting, and strategizing.

There seemed to be more cohesion and understanding between the black and Latinx members of the RCTD. While most demonstrators at the 1985 sit-in at the Nelson Mandela (former student) Center, were white and Latinx, black students seemed to appreciate the participation of the latter more. Black members felt that the Latinx students "expressed solidarity" with African American students without imposing or trying to take the lead. Students of color resented the white leaders and members of RCTD for what they saw as a lack of sincerity based on their insufficient knowledge about apartheid. Williamson described how the white participants at the sit-in decided "on a wing and a prayer [that] this is what they wanted to do."[18] Williamson also put forth that "if most of those white students were given a quiz on the simple facts of South Africa, they would fail academically."[19] Much of the interracial tension stemmed from the fact that black students believed they should lead the movement and the RCTD, not white students.

Black and brown members believed that some actions taken by white RCTD members had the potential to sabotage the movement. During the sit-in, white members of RCTD relayed important information to the protesters, despite the fact that undercover police were rumored to have infiltrated the sit-in.[20] Had police overheard any sensitive coalition plans, it could have curtailed activities to pressure the university to divest. White students used the low numbers of African American participants in the sit-in to question their commitment to the divestment movement and the group. Williamson explained the low turnout among black students at the sit-in by arguing that, if the black students *had* attended en masse, they felt that "there would've been banging heads and clearing out, rather than toleration by the police and administration."[21] Williamson's comments suggest that the majority of the tensions within the RCTD came from white students' lack of understanding of their privilege and the different set of circumstances that black members and other students of color faced.

Although the tensions within divestment groups were kept hidden from the public until Rutgers severed all of its investments tied to South Africa, the stories of group hostility that surfaced highlight much about race relations among the post–civil rights generation at Rutgers, and the United States more generally. The wave of African American students entering previously segregated institutions of higher education did not erase decades of institutional discrimination or automatically change the hearts and minds of white students and faculty.[22] Furthermore, the black and brown students of the post–civil rights generation entered college at a moment when the Republican-led federal government targeted critical educational legislation like affirmative

FIGURE 10.5 Student wears Crush Apartheid sign at rally.

Courtesy of Special Collections & University Archives, Rutgers University

action, which was designed to make higher education more equitable and accessible for historically marginalized groups.[23] Overall, black students in the movement felt that they were victims of white hostility.

After the election of the predominantly black steering committee, some members of the coalition created a proposal for structural reorganization. In a preface to the proposal, a member listed only as "MK" asserted that the proposal was "in no way an attempt to discredit the existing leadership . . . but [to] address a problem that threaten[ed] to destroy the RCTD." The "problem" was that the coalition structure as it stood was not representative of *all* coalition members.[24] The "colorblind" proposal, as it was touted, was the "product of some 45 hours' worth of meetings, discussions . . . and hard work" by a multiethnic and racially and gender-diverse group.[25] One of the individual proposals brought forward was that future decisions of the coalition should be made by at least 60 percent of RCTD members. This proposal was meant to ensure that, unlike the previous election, future elections could not happen without the presence of the majority of members. This was a direct response to white members' claim that the previous elections were held without their knowledge or attendance.

Unsurprisingly, the proposal upset black students in the coalition. They believed that the proposal for a new permanent structure was rooted in racism and jealousy. White members, on the other hand, had become tired of being labeled racist, and thought that racial discord within the group would eventually bleed out and affect the entire movement. At the beginning of the proposal, student "MK" wrote that the issues of racism in the group were "too pervasive and complex to be addressed in terms of personal experiences and histories" and that the issues should be addressed by a task force instead of dominating the focus of RCTD—time that could be better spent on organizing programs and events for divestiture.[26] Another white member, Christine Kelly, argued that black students were all too quick to label coalition politics as *racist,* which in turn "neutralized many previous supporters of the proposed 'Constitution'" and stunted the progress of the group.[27] Kelly wrote a letter to the members of the RCTD that defined *racism* and explained when she thought the term should be used. She concluded the letter by stating, "It is inconceivable, however, that any conclusion concerning the nature and dynamics of racism in the movement, the country, the world will be reached before the next agenda item."[28] Although Kelly's suggestion comes off as an attempt to silence black students in favor of a singular focus on the coalition's anti-apartheid efforts, she claimed her suggestion "can be attested to by the diversity of Black scholarship on the issue."[29] In short, racism is too complex a subject to handle and resolve within the confines of the meeting space. Instead, Kelly called for a committee on racism within the RCTD. These suggestions bureaucratized valid concerns of RCTD's minority members.

White members of the RCTD continually proposed setting aside the issue of racism within the group to focus on its anti-apartheid efforts. This silencing of black students highlights the irony of white students' obsessive efforts to end racist practices abroad while ignoring how they themselves participated in racism at Rutgers. The proposal for structural change to the RCTD called for a vote on spokespeople. Student "MK" expressed the need to increase the credibility of the coalition by working "with the system"—something black student members of RCTD did not want to do.[30] Williamson stated that any cooperation with the administration was useless because the goal of the coalition was "total divestment."[31] Student "MK" also argued that previous spokespeople had misrepresented the RCTD to the press and thus the public, and therefore the coalition's press committee should be reorganized.[32] In return, Williamson believed that the proposed reorganization of the press committee stemmed from white members' jealousy of the black members. She said that "the whites accused [them] of being celebrities" and white members became hostile when "they were confronted with a black leadership that was competent, and they were angry with our successes."[33] One such success Williamson earned was securing Jesse Jackson to speak at Rutgers—an attempt first made by white students, who, according to Williamson, began to complain about Jackson only after he agreed to come at her request.

The Jesse Jackson Controversy and
Black–Jewish Relations at Rutgers

The sit-in at the Nelson Mandela (student) Center drew national attention, and Jesse Jackson was among the first and most well known of the political figures who agreed to come and speak in support of the protesters' efforts. His planned visit caused controversy on campus and highlighted racial and ethnic tensions between the black, white, and Jewish communities at Rutgers. During his 1984 presidential campaign, Jesse Jackson labeled Jews as "hymies," an ethnic insult against Jewish people, and New York as "hymietown."[34] Jackson's comments, coupled with his support for Palestine, made Jewish and non-Jewish liberals alike question their support for him. More controversy followed when Nation of Islam leader Louis Farrakhan, an outspoken Jackson supporter, defended Jackson by declaring to Jackson's Jewish critics that "if you harm this brother, I warn you in the name of Allah, this will be the last one you harm."[35] Although Jackson denounced Farrakhan's comments, he did not denounce Farrakhan's support, which made his apology ring hollow to the Jewish community. When Jackson announced his plans to come to Rutgers to support the sit-in in April, more than a year after his comment controversy, many students decided to speak out.

Jackson's presence at the sit-in appeared contradictory to certain members of Rutgers's Jewish community. In a letter to the editor titled "Jackson Racist," Joseph Aronds, a Rutgers student, called for a boycott of Jesse Jackson's visit and argued that his invitation contradicted the aims of the divestment movement on campus because "Jackson actually represents everything demonstrators should be rallying against: discrimination, racism, and violence."[36] Aronds went one step further and brought up his concerns to the RCTD; he said that the group "should have courted a more caring figure, like civil rights activist William Kunstler," a famous Jewish radical attorney and activist.[37] Despite these critiques against Jackson's presence at the sit-in, there were many Jewish students who set aside their concerns about Jackson for the greater good of the divestiture movement.

Some students recognized the advantage of Jackson's participation at the rally because it would garner a lot of publicity and put more pressure on the university to divest. In a letter to the editor of the *Daily Targum,* two Jewish students, Miriam Aronoff and Martin Goldman, called on the Jewish community to attend the rally in order to help mend the rift between the black and Jewish communities. They believed the conflicts that arose in the wake of Jackson's planned visit "might overshadow the cause for which so many people are fighting."[38] Other articles written in the *Targum* by Jewish student journalists mirrored these pleas to end the conflict, because the benefits of having Jackson, in their opinion, outweighed the negatives. *Targum* writer Eleanor Levine wrote that although his "history of creating tensions between blacks and Jews" lurked in the back of the minds of some Rutgers students, it was important to "take from him the more important aspect of his being [at Rutgers]—the national media attention he will bring to the cause, and in turn, help the larger issue, combating apartheid."[39] Whether it was tensions with African American students and their white counterparts or black and Jewish students, calls to set aside issues of discrimination in order to amplify their anti-apartheid efforts ultimately worked.

On April 23, 1985, more than five thousand Rutgers students and faculty, New Jersey residents, and out-of-state allies attended the Jackson rally. Ten student leaders spoke to the crowd that stretched from the Brower Commons steps to the College Avenue gymnasium. Zaid Shakir, a graduate student at Rutgers and president of the Islamic Society, first spoke to the crowd and disparaged President Bloustein. Shakir contended that Bloustein's protest against apartheid at the South African consulate in New York City and subsequent arrest that year meant nothing when he continued to economically support the South African regime.[40] The crowd erupted when Shakir forcefully stated, "It takes more than a great football team to make a great university. It takes people committed to a vision to make a great university."[41] Bloustein's

FIGURE 10.6 Jesse Jackson with members of Rutgers Committee for Total Divestment during a demonstration against apartheid and for Rutgers divestment, *Daily Targum*, April 24, 1985.

Courtesy of Special Collections & University Archives, Rutgers University

presidency had been characterized by the expansion of the university's foot-ball program and its entrance into "bigger-time athletics."[42] The primary goal of growing an athletic program would be to drive revenue into the univer-sity. Shakir's reference to the football team underscored his argument that the institution valued profits over people. Shakir was not the only speaker to pose a moral critique against Rutgers University and other businesses and organiza-tions that had not yet divested. Jesse Jackson noted that "what is really at stake is not South Africa's behavior nearly as much as the character of our nation, our universities and our religious institutions." He declared, "Don't just cry when they shoot people in the back. Divest so they can't afford the bullets to shoot somebody in the back."[43] Jackson's words summed up the aims of the divestment movement while enforcing the grave consequences of *not* divest-ing. Lives were at stake and the nation's universities had blood on their hands.

After the rousing demonstration, Jackson met with President Bloustein to urge total divestment. Although Jackson believed that Rutgers's partial divestment marked a positive start, he contended that "there [was] a very hot corner in hell reserved for those who can not [*sic*] make a decision in an hour of moral concern."[44] Jackson's statement, in part, referred to Bloustein, who believed that the focus on universities divesting was a "diversion from the problem of apartheid" and that more could be done on a federal level.[45] Bloust-ein resented what he felt was the undue attention and criticism being given to Rutgers University. He stated that "[Rutgers is] one of the most progressive universities in the country, and we are being tarred and feathered just like the others."[46] Bloustein's "tarred and feathered" comment was insensitive, espe-cially considering its connotations to racial terror in the United States. Addi-tionally, his opinion of the university as "progressive" did not match that of the minority students on campus who faced discrimination. His words did not resonate with those who wanted to see the university completely divest from its business interests in South Africa. Bloustein believed that partial divest-ment was sufficient, noting at a press conference that Rutgers only continued investments in corporations that were not complicit in furthering apartheid. He did not believe that Rutgers "should treat corporations that are responsible the same as those that don't give a damn."[47] Jackson, on the other hand, said, "Fundamentally, all the companies that are there . . . pay their taxes. And South Africa uses those taxes to oppress its people."[48] At the conclusion of their meeting, Bloustein announced that Rutgers's investment policy would remain unchanged.[49]

Conclusion

The RCTD ended their sit-in at the Mandela Center on May 13, three weeks after the highly publicized rally for divestment with Jesse Jackson. Although the coalition's campaign was not immediately successful, Rutgers eventually fully divested from companies that did business in South Africa. In October 1985, the Board of Trustees voted to sell all stocks by 1987. The full divestment totaled $6.4 million in ten companies, including IBM and Coca-Cola.[50] Student protesters and the sympathy they gained undoubtedly influenced the board's decision.

Despite the internal racial tensions that student groups such as the Rutgers Coalition for Total Divestment experienced, students were still able to come together and successfully petition the university to cut all ties to South African apartheid. Even with this positive outcome, multiracial collaboration did not continue to the same extent as it did during the decade of divestment protest. This raises an important question about the possibilities and limits of multiracial collaboration within social movements. Lisa Williamson said that there was "no way in hell" that black and white students could mirror this type of cooperation.[51] She believed that while black students were open to working with white students, "white students are not receptive and universities do not make an attempt to eradicate the situation."[52] Finally, Williamson stated that although "white students were involved with the movement for about 60 days—for blacks, it's a life-long struggle."[53]

The divestment movement was plagued with conflicts between black and white students as well as between black and Jewish students. There were internal calls to set aside these issues in order to focus the various groups' efforts on the goal of Rutgers completely divesting from their South African business interests. This was successful—publicly, the group appeared to be a cohesive and focused "rainbow coalition." They were able to garner attention on the issue for which they banded together in the first place—apartheid. Despite the success of the divestment struggle, the students' failures to seriously contend with racism and ethnic discrimination within the group led to hesitancy in cultivating multiracial movements on campus. However, it is important to look beyond the limitations of this movement. The anti-apartheid movement at Rutgers illustrated the power of students to hold institutions of higher education accountable and to force these institutions to evaluate their place in the world and reckon with their participation in broader systems of oppression.

11

"Hell No, Our Genes Aren't Slow!"

Racism and Antiracism at Rutgers during the 1995 Controversy

MEAGAN WIERDA AND ROBERTO C. OROZCO

At the start of the spring semester in 1995, chants of "Hey hey, ho ho, Francis Lawrence has got to go!" could be heard ringing out through the College Avenue campus in New Brunswick.[1] Though the weather was cold, the many students shouting this refrain were fired up. Just a few weeks earlier, Francis Lawrence, the president of Rutgers University, insinuated during a meeting with faculty that African Americans did not have the "genetic hereditary background" to perform well on standardized tests. Not surprisingly, these three words proved incendiary and caused many individuals to question whether the beleaguered president was fit to run the university.

Although the immediate context leading up to and including these infamous words will be amply explored, President Lawrence's remarks and the protracted question of whether he intended to utter them will not be the sole focus of this essay. Rather, it places Lawrence's statement within the larger context of the culture wars and institutional racism of the 1990s and traces the faculty and student activism that emerged in the wake of his remarks. The broader, more insidious culture of racism within society and the academy during the 1990s made Lawrence's words possible and, to many, believable. Indeed, the plausibility of Lawrence's inadvertent yoking of intellectual ability with genetic heredity would have likely been unthinkable without the long-standing imprimatur of science writ large. At the very moment that news outlets across the country picked up this story, *The Bell Curve*, a best-selling book arguing that cognitive ability and social mobility were linked to genetics, was also being widely discussed and reviewed in newspapers and journals as well as on the radio and television. *The Bell Curve*, like so many works of

FIGURE 11.1 President Francis Lawrence giving testimony.

Courtesy of Special Collections & University Archives, Rutgers University

"science" before it, seemed to give weight to Lawrence's words. In that respect, the incident at Rutgers highlights the persistence and tenacity of biological determinist thought within the academy and beyond.

That said, this essay aims to do more than simply recognize the pervasiveness of biological determinism on the banks of the old Raritan. As the title of this piece indicates, and in an effort to center the voices of those marginalized by institutional racism, the second portion of this essay explores the various ways students and faculty alike responded to this incident during a very polarized political moment. While several students pointed to Lawrence's stated commitment to diversity to show their support of the president, others resisted. A brief summary of the university's bias-prevention efforts during the 1992–1993 academic year, for example, noted that "racist acts" abounded on campus—in addition to those being sexist, homophobic, and anti-Semitic in nature—and that "most incidents reported occurred in residence halls," with the following highest number occurring "in the classroom on the part of the faculty." According to the Bias Prevention Steering Committee, the following two academic years included more racist "incidents" directed toward marginalized students on campus, indicating that prejudice was alive and well at Rutgers.[2]

Student activists from across all three campuses formed the United Students Coalition (USC) and members of the staff and faculty of color created the Coalition of Black and Latino Faculty and Staff (CBLFS). Each organization took a multifaceted approach to air their grievances, propose solutions, and begin healing from the damage caused by Lawrence's specific assertion and institutional racism more generally. For some, including the students of the USC, the path toward healing from and accountability for these racial injustices could only begin with the resignation of President Lawrence.

Although Francis Lawrence's arrival at the State University of New Jersey was heralded as a new era of multiculturalism and inclusion, with concerted efforts to boost minority enrollment and retention as well as to diversify the faculty, questions about parity—and the place of people of color within higher education more broadly—remained unsettled. It is this last point that the controversy involving Francis Lawrence calls attention to and that this essay attempts to resolve.

"RU Head Deserves Chance": Authority and Austerity in the Early 1990s

When Francis Leo Lawrence began his tenure as the eighteenth president of Rutgers University in the fall of 1990, it is likely that few envied the mantle he was expected to assume. The boom days of New Jersey's economy were coming to an end, and although higher education had been one of the principal beneficiaries during the 1980s, the latest state budget presaged trouble in the coming decade. Faced with a $600 million deficit—with an even greater short- fall projected for the following year—cuts to the budget were all but guar- anteed.[3] While many sectors found themselves vulnerable to corresponding shortfalls in funding, state financing for education writ large was meager. Indeed, following back-to-back years of significant reductions in state aid—to the tune of an astonishing 25 percent—Rutgers University decided to slash the upcoming year's fiscal budget. Support staff were laid off, a near moratorium was placed on the recruitment of new faculty, and various other expenditures were put on indefinite hold. Professors protested the university's failure to disburse agreed-upon research funds, and although a representative of the Faculty of Arts and Sciences denied it, students complained that fewer courses were being offered. More broadly, though, students were aggrieved about the declining quality and rising costs of undergraduate education at Rutgers Uni- versity. The newly elected Democrat, Governor James Florio, was threatening further cuts to the Department of Higher Education to the utter dismay of public colleges and universities; one newspaper described the scene as one of total "chaos." During this period, *retrenchment* was the watchword of the state government, and clearly, the students at public institutions like Rutgers were experiencing the brunt of it.[4]

In the face of this budget crisis, however, Francis Lawrence was touted as one of the most capable individuals to weather the ravages of austerity. Not only had he received a doctorate in French literature from Tulane University, but his subsequent tenure there as professor was quickly followed by a steady climb within the administrative ranks of the institution. Some of Lawrence's roles included acting dean of Tulane's women's college, assistant vice presi- dent for academic affairs, and the provost and dean of the university's gradu- ate school. By most accounts, Lawrence had become a seasoned and capable functionary over the course of more than two decades in New Orleans. More than that, though, Lawrence was depicted as an affable and approachable administrator, sensitive to the needs of the university community. Indeed, whereas his predecessor was described as having a "frequently adversarial style," Lawrence was, by contrast, characterized as a "mediator" who had made "significant steps in setting a new tone of reasonableness, compassion for stu- dents and openness."[5] And, at the outset of his tenure as university president, Lawrence worked hard to burnish this image.

Given how fraught the 1990–1991 academic year was slated to be in the wake of widespread austerity measures, perhaps the new president's attempts to ingratiate himself with the Rutgers community should not be surprising. Lawrence did not go so far as to join the protests of two student groups—Team Rutgers and the Campaign for an Affordable Rutgers Education (CARE)—who were protesting the budget cuts and tuition hikes outside the State House in

Trenton, but he nevertheless hoped to impress upon Governor James Florio and key state legislators the crucial role played by Rutgers within the state of New Jersey in an effort to safeguard its funding.[6] Indeed, Lawrence repeatedly emphasized the ways in which the university brought economic benefits to the state and its residents. This was a point that Lawrence stressed more broadly in the opening weeks of his presidency by turning his gaze to matters more local in scope. In his first major speech as university president before the University Senate, Lawrence recommended a number of measures to support students within the "urban school system" in the communities that played host to Rutgers, including guaranteeing admission to a number of "disadvantaged" eighth-graders if they maintained satisfactory high school grade point averages and met other academic requirements. Given that schooling in New Jersey was essentially segregated during this period—with African Americans and Latinx students living in underserved cities and whites living in their much wealthier suburbs—this proposal was perhaps not insignificant. Lawrence argued that "the university's public service efforts embrace[d] the entire state and the whole range of its citizens." In this same speech, he encouraged the faculty and administration to "recruit and to keep minority faculty in the higher proportions that we need to diversify our faculty composition" and enjoined university senators to "increase our efforts to employ, create a welcoming atmosphere and bring to tenure, more women faculty members."[7] Indeed, the promotion of multiculturalism and inclusion were at the very heart of many of his proposals. Expounding on Lawrence's opening gambits as president, one reporter argued that he was "building a reservoir of good will that [would] serve Rutgers very well in the future, and may even make the state's citizens love Rutgers."[8]

As it turns out, and perhaps predictably, this optimism proved short-lived. Indeed, some of the goodwill that Francis Lawrence fostered within the Rutgers community began to show signs of strain near the end of his first year in office. A series of articles published in 1991 reveal the extent to which the new president struggled to accommodate the needs of multiple and often competing constituencies within and without the university—the difficulty of which was no doubt compounded by the gravity of the state's budgetary crisis. Attempts to trim administrative bloat were met with targeted objections, the reprioritization of teaching inspired fears that the school was going to abandon its research mission, and a general wariness stemmed from the newfound branding of the university as the state's engine of economic growth.[9] Amid all of this tumult, Rutgers students made sure their voices were heard.

For example, in January and February of that year, several dozen students—many of them affiliated with CARE—staged sit-ins at Alexander Library on the College Avenue campus to protest the reduction in library hours. Indeed, in order to contend with budgetary shortfalls, the university withheld $1 million in library funding, delayed hiring new employees, and reduced library hours, which amounted to 126 hours each week across the university's seventeen libraries. Students—many of them black and Latinx—who were present at the peaceful protests understood full well the financial constraints imposed on the university but expressed frustration about the ways in which the administration chose to respond to them—notably those that impacted the quality of students' education. A spokeswoman for CARE, Mia Ji, lamented the fact that the university was "pumping much-needed funds into capital-improvement projects, financing and maintaining automobiles for 13 upper-level university officials, or throwing a $50,000 inaugural ceremony for Rutgers president Francis L. Lawrence." Many students, Ji among them, questioned the university's priorities.[10]

Tensions between the students and Francis Lawrence's administration showed no signs of abating over the next several years, and, indeed, intensified. Between 1991 and 1994, student groups staged sit-ins across all three campuses, organized rallies, disrupted meetings of the Board of Governors (BOG), and even orchestrated a short takeover of Bishop House—a large Italianate mansion in the middle of the College Avenue campus—in an effort to protest tuition increases, the lack of funding in higher education, the marginalization of poor students and students of color, and the corporatization of the university. Though Lawrence was prone to dismissing many of these actions as mere antics or theatrics, we would be remiss to overlook the very real concerns and critiques animating the measures taken by many of these students.[11]

In an article exploring barriers to educational access, reprinted in one of the university's student newspapers during this climactic period, student author-activist Robin Templeton argued that funding-starved universities were increasingly beholden to corporate interests seeking out "cheap research venues" instead of to the students they were mandated to serve. In an effort to attract much-needed investments, institutes of higher learning were effectively subsidizing the profit-making activities of corporations via budget cuts and tuition hikes. Templeton asserted that these measures only served to "legally segregate people of color and the poor from higher education." Students like Robert Alvarez echoed Templeton's arguments, noting that rising tuition costs disproportionately impacted students of color and working-class and poor students.[12] Various graphics showing the troubling disparities between the college completion rates of white versus black students between the 1960s and 1991 were printed and reprinted in student publications, lending further credence to Alvarez's and Templeton's claims. Another student and member of CARE, Staci Berger, challenged the curtailment of educational access in an article entitled "Education for All!" Not only did she argue that education was a right, but she maintained that it should be generously funded by the state. And to those "cynics" who wondered where the money to do so would come from, she reminded them that when "the state spends six times as much to incarcerate a prisoner as it does to educate its citizens, we have a misplaced sense of priorities."[13]

Clearly, the members of CARE were among the most engaged and radical student activists across all three of Rutgers's campuses. And though they were not representative of the entire student body, the general tenor of their activism appears to have resonated with students similarly discouraged by the state of higher education in New Jersey. Perhaps it is for this reason—among others, no doubt—that Francis Lawrence and the Rutgers administration were unrelenting in their response to the most outspoken and defiant students on campus. Though often described—and even self-styled—as a mediator, Lawrence was decidedly less conciliatory in his approach to dissent on campus. Not only did he publish a scathing op-ed piece in 1993 reasserting the right of the administration to set the terms of BOG meetings in the face of "fiercely partisan public demonstrations," but he also appears to have harbored minimal reservations about availing himself of the police to quash and quell demonstrations on campus.[14] The arrest and arraignment in municipal court of eleven individuals who participated in the takeover of Bishop House on the College Avenue campus in April 1992 was the source of particular resentment among students.[15] Though actions such as these moved students to call for his resignation in 1992 and again in 1993, the loudest and most insistent calls for his departure would not come until 1995.[16]

"Three Badly Articulated Words": The Enduring Nature of Scientific Racism in Higher Education

In his relatively short time at Rutgers, Francis Lawrence had managed to successfully alienate a number of constituencies within the university. Certainly, some of the antagonisms were long-standing, some were the product of the state and therefore the university's then current budgetary woes, and others still reflected the increasingly polarized historical moment that was the 1980s and 1990s. Everything—from abortion to affirmative action to multiculturalism to intelligence testing to sex education to school prayer—proved divisive, and in many ways these issues represented a referendum on the incredible social and political transformations of the 1960s. "The gulf that separated those who embraced the new America," writes historian Andrew Hartman, "from those who viewed it ominously—those who looked to nurture it versus those who sought to roll it back—drew the boundaries of the culture wars."[17]

In an effort to confront these issues, a number of students across the campuses in Camden, New Brunswick, and Newark formulated clear critiques of the state of higher education and their increasingly precarious place within it. Indeed, many of them felt betrayed by Rutgers and the Lawrence administration, which, in their opinion, was at best aloof and at worst verged on the autocratic.[18] Tensions had been long simmering at Rutgers. Thus, when an incendiary news story broke in Newark's *Star-Ledger* titled "Rutgers Chief Cites Genetics in Test Scores of Minorities," the university was a veritable powder keg ready to explode.

The article, which appeared on January 31, 1995, noted that during a meeting with approximately thirty faculty members in Camden in November of the previous year, Francis Lawrence discussed the increasing demands for accountability within higher education. For faculty members, accountability might take the form of periodic post-tenure review—a proposal actively pursued by the Lawrence administration during this period—but for students, this often meant relying on the conclusions drawn from test scores. "Whenever you try to kind of generalize across the board,'" Lawrence observed disapprovingly of standardized tests, "'you basically screw three-quarters of the population.'" What was frequently missing from these tests, he reasoned, was "'input assessment,'" or a consideration of the individual variables that shape different students' results. To underscore his point, Lawrence used the example of African American students, who typically scored below average on the Scholastic Assessment Test, or SAT. "'Do we set standards in the future so that we don't admit anybody with the national test,'" he mused, "'or do we deal with a disadvantaged population that doesn't have the genetic hereditary background to have a higher average?'"[19]

At first blush, it appeared as though Lawrence was rehashing old social Darwinist ideas, which argued that intellectual differences between people were the result of genetics and thus immutable. Placed within its proper context, it is clear that Rutgers's eighteenth president was attempting to disavow higher education's overreliance on hugely problematic standardized tests. His subsequent apology and interviews on the subject confirm as much. Still, institutions of higher learning throughout the United States have long been incubators of racial science—as well as white supremacy more broadly—and Lawrence's words invoked this troubled history.[20] Although nearly two months had elapsed between the pronouncement of these remarks and their widespread circulation via the *Star-Ledger,* the weight of Francis Lawrence's words— and three in particular—were in no way diminished by the passage of time nor his subsequent apology. Indeed, it did not take long for major news outlets throughout the country, such as the *New York Times* and the *Washington Post,* to pick up the story, and for individuals across a broad political spectrum to weigh in on Francis Lawrence's apparent yoking of African Americans' intellectual abilities with their "genetic hereditary background." Certain writers believed that though the president's phrasing was "ill-considered," his reputation as a "minority-sensitive administrator" with a track record of enrolling and retaining minority students had earned him a second chance; others were almost gleeful in their belief that the oversensitive president had been ensnared by the very trap of political correctness that he had helped to set; still others called for his resignation outright, either because they believed he had lost the support and confidence of the university community or because they believed him to be racist.[21]

The Bell Curve and the Repudiation of the Egalitarian Ideal

The question of whether Francis Lawrence was racist proved particularly enduring, in large measure because his remarks were concurrent with the publication of psychologist Richard J. Herrnstein and political scientist Charles Murray's controversial best-selling 1994 book, *The Bell Curve: Intelligence and Class Structure in American Life*. Although this mammoth text made a number of arguments, one of its central claims was that "cognitive ability," which could be expressed numerically and measured via IQ testing, differed between racial or ethnic groups, and that these differences stemmed from genetic transmission. According to the book's logic, then, African Americans—whose average IQs were lower than those of European Americans—were more likely to make up a permanent cognitive underclass within American society that sorted or partitioned according to intelligence. Indeed, although social class remained the "vehicle of social life," Herrnstein and Murray argued that "intelligence now pull[ed] the train." In their estimation, groups with high IQs were more likely to receive high SAT scores, attend elite colleges, be perceived as more proficient and productive, land more intellectually rigorous occupations, and earn higher wages; groups with high IQs were to become the "cognitive elite." The cognitive sorting in education, occupation, and income ultimately reified divisions within American society.[22]

These divisions were purportedly not welcomed by Herrnstein and Murray, but they nevertheless argued that the "problems of low cognitive ability" were not going to be solved by social welfare programs aimed at improving nutrition, early childhood education, and schools, for example. "To think that the available repertoire of social interventions can do the job if only the nation spends more money on them is illusory," they insisted. Firmly rejecting the foundations of the welfare state, Herrnstein and Murray maintained that "the government has no business getting in people's way," and proposed a series of thoroughly unsubstantiated policy prescriptions to allow every individual to have a "valued" place in society. And, though these recommendations were largely vague, there was no mistaking the authors' belief that "inequality of endowments, including intelligence, [was] a reality," and that "trying to eradicate inequality with artificially manufactured outcomes has led to disaster."[23] Indeed, there was nothing ambiguous about Herrnstein and Murray's belief that the alleged measurability of heritable racial differences essentially nullified the need for social welfare. Trenchant criticisms of *The Bell Curve* appeared almost immediately, though perhaps none have been as effective or as enduring as those of Stephen Jay Gould, a Harvard-appointed paleontologist and evolutionary biologist. Gould, who in 1981 published *The Mismeasure of Man*, which sought to demonstrate the "scientific weaknesses and political contexts" of biological determinist arguments about racial, sexual, and class distinctions between human groups, was especially well equipped to upbraid Herrnstein and Murray. Not only did Gould acknowledge that determinists had long relied on science—with all of its attendant pretenses to objectivity—to make seemingly dispassionate and authoritative claims about "inborn distinctions" between persons, but he underscored the ways in which these claims have always served a political purpose for society's most powerful.[24] In a November 1994 issue of the *New Yorker*, Gould brought all of this intellectual weight to bear on *The Bell Curve*. Indeed, Gould highlighted the ways in which Herrnstein and Murray's text obfuscated race, was riddled with errors, was suspect in its use of statistics, and had even failed to justify their key claim that the number known as *g*—or the "general factor" of intelligence—existed and could be measured. "It is," he argued, "a manifesto of conservative ideology; the book's inadequate and biased treatment of data display its primary purpose—advocacy." Continuing, he asserted that the text evoked "the dreary and scary drumbeat of claims associated with conservative think tanks: reduction or elimination of welfare, ending or sharply curtailing affirmative action in schools and workplaces, cutting back Head Start and other forms of preschool education, trimming programs for the slowest learners and applying those funds to the gifted." In his concluding paragraphs, Gould reaffirmed the unity of all people and urged his readers to "fight the doctrine of *The Bell Curve* both because it is wrong and because it will, if activated, cut off all possibility of proper nurturance for everyone's intelligence."[25]

"How Academic Racism Gets Its Start": The Normalization of Biological Determinism?

With this in mind, it is easy to see why Francis Lawrence's seeming tethering of the intellectual ability of African American students to their "genetic hereditary background" was so inflammatory, with its shades of Richard Herrnstein and Charles Murray on full display. Indeed, invocations of *The Bell Curve* in the wake of Lawrence's "three badly articulated words" abounded. "Lawrence's remark," noted one newspaper, "coming as it did in the wake of the furor over 'The Bell Curve,' a book that attempts to link intelligence and race, perhaps carried more resonance than it would have at another time." The article went on to note that according to Lawrence, "the verbal slip may have occurred because he had been reading reviews of the book, which he deeply disagrees with."[26] Chris Fitter, an English professor who had attended the November meeting that featured Lawrence's remarks, speculated that "because 'The Bell Curve' was out a few months ago and it was being talked about on the radio and TV, I think he had it in the back of his mind." Fitter also attempted to clarify Lawrence's meaning in that the president "was saying this was one more obstacle for the university to negotiate in maintaining a rapport with the community."[27]

The degree to which individuals believed that differences in intelligence were rooted in biology cannot be understated. While some commentators wondered if Lawrence had outright adopted the tenets of *The Bell Curve,* others went a step further and applauded the Rutgers president for his assumed candor regarding the supposed genetic underpinnings of racial difference.[28] In February 1995, the *Courier News* published a series of call-in responses they received to their "Hot Topic" question regarding Francis Lawrence's intimation that African Americans were genetically predisposed to score poorly on standardized tests. "Since skin color, hair color, muscle and bone structure are the products of genetic hereditary [*sic*]," mused John Kucek, from North Plainfield, New Jersey, "why not intelligence? Being disadvantaged in one area doesn't mean a person cannot excel in some other area. So, what's the big deal?" Another caller, Gilbert Finne from Edison, New Jersey, lamented that the "protestors do not even read or understand the many studies that have been made public." He argued, "President Lawrence apparently has read and understands that which has been published, and substantiated by statistic [*sic*] evidence. He must not be punished for his understanding and insight." Mary Ann Corley from Branchburg, New Jersey, chimed in, saying, "I just want to defend Francis Lawrence's statement of suggesting hereditary or genetic issues prevented disadvantages [*sic*] students from scoring better on standardized tests." Corley believed the question was a matter of opinion and could not understand "why everyone gets so up in arms when someone even mentions the suggestion that hereditary [*sic*] or genes have anything to do with it." "I happen agree with him [*sic*]," she finished. There were far fewer callers who seemed to reject the biologically deterministic implications of Lawrence's remarks. Perhaps it is for this reason the *Courier News* felt the need to remind their readers that, "contrary to some responses contained on this page—no conclusive, scientific link has been made between race and intelligence."[29]

Reexamining the incident years after the conclusion of his presidency, Lawrence wrote that it "stunned" and "mortified" him to have been so misunderstood. "I jumbled together several subjects in an awkward verbal stumble," he reflected, "that implied I believed the arguments of Charles Murray (author of *The Bell Curve*) that intelligence levels vary based on ethnicity and that minorities are genetically inferior." Rejecting this insinuation and taking comfort in the fact that many—including the Rutgers BOG—believed that his "misstatement" was a "clumsy mistake, not a racist manifesto," Lawrence reaffirmed his long-standing commitment to minority students.[30] Unfortunately, at the height of the controversy, the beleaguered president's attempts to shore up his reputation as an antiracist administrator and educator were somewhat hampered by his reliance on standout or singular African Americans. Lawrence trumpeted the support of Paul Robeson Jr., the son of Rutgers's most famous alumnus, Paul Robeson, a successful artist, athlete, actor, and political activist. By some accounts, he even trumpeted the achievements of Randal Pinkett, who, in 1994, became a Rhodes scholar. Appeals to individuals like Robeson and Pinkett are reminiscent of what historian Ibram X. Kendi refers to as "black exhibits," or the "strategy of exhibiting excelling Blacks to change racist minds"—or, in this case, to possibly deflect from charges of racism.[31] In doing so, Lawrence missed an opportunity to engage in a frank discussion about the real and persistent sources of racism and structural inequality at Rutgers. In the wake of the widespread retrenchment of funding in education and the indefatigability of biological determinism, his apologia appeared tone-deaf and self-serving. This latter point was something the students of Rutgers made sure he understood.

"We Can't Forgive, We Can't Forget": Student and Faculty Protest in the Spring of 1995[32]

Despite support from some New Jersey residents, Lawrence's comments polarized the university's various stakeholders, prompting an impassioned backlash from students, staff, faculty, and community organizations, including the Rutgers African American Alumni Association and the local chapter of the National Association for the Advancement of Colored People (NAACP).[33] The larger structural issues surrounding diversity at Rutgers undergirded arguments on both sides of the debate and prompted multiple constituencies and stakeholders to consider their relationship to the university. More than forty community members, staff, and faculty from all three Rutgers campuses gathered at the BOG meeting on February 10, 1995. Several individuals opposed Lawrence's continued role as president, while others were willing to forgive him for his comments. Among the latter was the BOG and the newly elected governor of New Jersey, Christine Todd Whitman.[34]

The Lawrence administration used demographic data to market Rutgers as a bastion of diversity. In his remarks at the February 10 meeting, the vice president for undergraduate academic affairs, Dr. Joseph J. Seneca, praised the leadership of Lawrence by stating that "we could not have attained these standings"—referring to student of color enrollment and faculty of color hiring numbers—"without an absolute commitment that starts with the President."[35] Yet, as the summary from the 1992–1993 bias-prevention report discussed earlier showed, racial tensions on campus were palpable, creating a climate that was often unwelcoming to students of color. Students and faculty pointed to this fact and to their own personal experiences to highlight the larger issues that impacted communities of color on and off campus. Although students engaged in the debate on whether Lawrence's statement was a mistake—many students of color believed that it was indeed intentional, making comments such as, "You slip and fall. . . . You don't slip and call someone genetically inferior"—activists held an expansive view.[36] What transpired during the spring semester in 1995 was a multifaceted response by communities of color that have historically demanded representation and resources at Rutgers University. For many, true justice could only be served with Lawrence's resignation.

Student-led protests across the three Rutgers campuses emerged to address the hurt and pain students of color felt because of President Lawrence's statement. Understandably, many students on campus rejected the notion of biological inferiority, connecting Lawrence's remarks to The Bell Curve and using the latter as fodder for the many demonstrations that opened the 1995 spring semester. Protesters cheered as the book was ripped up, the pages shredded into confetti, repeatedly chanting, "Hell no, our genes aren't slow!"—even brandishing signs advising Lawrence to "bell-curve his ass outta here."[37] In a letter to the Daily Targum praising student protesters, Garland E. Allen, a professor of biology at Washington University, observed that "the fact that Lawrence's remarks were closely related to 'The Bell Curve' is an ominous indicator of how academic racism gets its start and is transmitted through official channels eventually into educational policy."[38] In a similar letter of support addressed to protesters, Rodney D. Green, the director of Howard University's Department of Economics, echoed some of Stephen Jay Gould's criticisms in saying that "the trend towards more intense and vile forms of racism, marked by the publication of and publicity surrounding 'The Bell Curve,' goes hand-in-hand with increasingly regressive social practices and policies, from cutbacks in social services, to mass layoffs of workers, to reductions in student financial support as loans replace grants. . . . All of these changes," Green argued, "differently harm African Americans and thus have a racist character."[39] Both Allen and Green drew important links between the pervasive beliefs forwarded by Richard J. Herrnstein and Charles Murray and the rampant structural inequality within institutions of higher learning.

Other forms of student protest included sit-ins at BOG meetings, letters to the institution's administration, and commitments of solidarity from other student organizations. It is crucial to note, however, that student-led protests were not all sporadic. Both students and faculty seized this moment as an opportunity to organize and coalition-build. Two organizations developed out of the need to create a unified front among Black and Latinx students, staff, and faculty: the Coalition of Black and Latino Faculty and Staff (CBLFS) and the United Students Coalition (USC), an umbrella organization that brought together over forty organizations that supported the resignation of President

Lawrence, including the African Student Congress, President's Council, the Latino Student Council, the Paul Robeson Club, and the West Indian Student Association. Both united front groups convened in the spring of 1995.[40]

Lawrence's comments proved to be a point of division within the student body, and students on both sides of the debate opined about how the university should move forward. Newspaper articles and letters to the BOG demonstrate this fact. On February 9, 1995, the *Philadelphia Inquirer* published a photograph of an unidentified black woman looking at a white man holding a sign that read "He's Not a Racist—RU is #1 in Black Enrollment."[41] Another photograph shows a black man ripping that very sign in half.[42] One student demonstrated her support for Lawrence in a letter addressed to the Board of Governors. She stated, "United Students Coalition does not speak for all of the student body. There are many of us who do not support the demands of the USC. We are not as vocal (perhaps we will improve this) and we are not as dramatic, but we are here!"[43]

Despite opposition from the student body and administration, the USC forwarded a list of eight demands to the university administration and BOG. These included restructuring the BOG to reflect the diversity of the student population, increasing recruitment and retention efforts for Black and Latinx students, reestablishing support for campuses other than New Brunswick, and, among the most direct of the demands, the call for the resignation of President Lawrence.[44] The USC's demands and protests did not go unchallenged as the university took a rather hostile stance against events that it deemed disruptive to the governance of the institution. This stance was not unlike that taken by administrators in the face of the CARE protests a couple of years prior.

Administrators, including the BOG, the Board of Trustees, and President Lawrence's cabinet members, were the most resistant to listening to the needs and concerns of students of color. In January 1995, the BOG and the Board of Trustees released a joint statement reinforcing their support for President Lawrence:

> We call upon the members of the University community to recognize that these statements do not reflect the President's views and in the context of his enormous efforts for the University, his many superb public statements on these issues, and most importantly, his many accomplishments, that they are no basis upon which to judge this man.[45]

The statement cited Lawrence's commitment to diversity initiatives and the fact that "Rutgers University graduates more African American undergraduates than any other member of the Association of American Universities (aside from U of Maryland)."[46] Following the release of this statement, the university administration and BOG continued to support President Lawrence and defended his character. The BOG asserted that President Lawrence was not a racist; however, it gave little to no attention to addressing the ramifications of Lawrence's statements for students of color on campus. USC and CBLFS hoped to change that.

Student protesters and other members of the academic community saw the policies and procedures implemented by President Lawrence and the BOG as antithetical to supporting free speech on campus. They reflected upon President Mason W. Gross's administration, which spanned the years between 1959 to 1971, to critique Lawrence's handling of student concerns and treatment of students, particularly student protesters.[47] President Gross sought to address conflict that arose from students' concerns and the challenges they expressed regarding their experiences as students. Most notably, Gross's response was spotlighted during the 1969 protest and demands put forth by students at Rutgers–Newark when students commandeered Conklin Hall. Members of the Black Organization of Students staged a takeover to protest the lack of black students and faculty at the institution based in the largely black community of Newark. As a show of solidarity, students of the Black Student Unity Movement at Rutgers–Camden and the Black Student Protest Movement at Douglass College forwarded similar demands. President Gross engaged with student protesters by acknowledging their demands, welcoming differing perspectives, and introducing efforts to make Rutgers a more inclusive space. In managing all three institutions, he was not always able to meet the demands of students, staff, faculty, and community members, but he maintained a continuous level of transparency and communication of care for his constituents.[48]

In contrast, as discussed earlier in this essay, President Lawrence and his administration responded to student protests with police force and the implementation of institutional policies that limited the strategies and spaces in which students could resist the institutional leadership's decisions.[49] This, however, did not stop students from expressing their distrust and frustrations. To showcase the inequities faced by students of color, the USC organized three high-profile protests on the New Brunswick campus: the disruption of the university men's basketball team, a hunger strike by two students on Livingston College, and the "Day of Outrage" event, which led to the infamous shutdown of Route 18, the primary interstate that leads to the New Brunswick campus.[50]

"I Was Not Supposed to Be the Only One":
The Basketball Game Protest

The Rutgers versus University of Massachusetts men's basketball game was sold out. All alone, Jacqueline D. Williams, an African American student in her junior year, walked onto the basketball court and refused to move to allow the game to begin. Recounting the story of how she decided to commence the protest, Williams stated, "I was not supposed to the only [one]. . . . I was hoping

FIGURE 11.2 Student protest banner at Rutgers basketball game sit-in, *Daily Targum*, May 1, 1995.

Courtesy of Special Collections & University Archives, Rutgers University

I wouldn't be alone, without the student body. . . . I would not have been able to do it. It's not just me. It's everyone."[51] The *Asbury Park Press* described the scenario of the first few minutes of the protest, saying, "Sitting cross-legged, confident and alone at midcourt, the 20-year-old Livingston College junior brought the game to a halt, and the capacity crowd at the Louis Brown Athletic Center in Piscataway Township to its feet—some in anger, and others in solidarity."[52]

It took a few minutes for her peers to join her on the basketball court; however, one hundred and fifty protesters, most of whom were black, eventually joined Williams.[53] They were simultaneously met with a barrage of racial epithets, cheers of support for President Lawrence claiming that "he is not a racist" and calls to "Let's play ball." One protester shouted back, "You think this game is more important than this?" The vice president of student affairs cemented her support for Lawrence and aligned with the spectators who called for the game to continue, stating, "I think there were a lot of students who wanted to see the rest of the game. . . . These are students who understand what is going on."[54] Several local and national newspapers published a photo of Williams seated on the court while two police officers appeared to be speaking to her. This image represented the tactics used by the Rutgers administration to maintain their power over student protests and compounded the show of hostility toward the student activists. Still, students monopolized the national attention and continued to protest for the resignation of Lawrence and to forward their demands to the institution.[55]

While she was being lauded as a hero by her supporters, Williams alluded to overcoming several obstacles in her nonacademic life that compelled her to activism.[56] Lawrence's comments about race and test scores became personal for Williams, as she explained to the crowd at the basketball game: "I am a child who suffers from a blood disease due to genetics; I am a child who suffers from ulcers due to genetics. . . . I've suffered for seven years from a disease due to genetics. I'm [not] intellectually disadvantaged due to genetics."[57] Williams's declaration is part of a longer legacy of African American resistance to scientific racism and biological determinism.

"Until They Meet Our Demands": The Hunger Strike on Livingston College

In the midst of other protests during the spring 1995 semester, Rodney Jackson and Manny Figueroa, two students at Livingston College and Rutgers College, respectively, initiated a hunger strike. They sought to bring awareness to the issues faced by minority students at Rutgers.[58] Both students went on strike publicly at the Latino Cultural Center and received support from many of their peers for their act of resistance. Coupled with the earlier protests, like the halting of the basketball game and the multiple rallies outside of the president's office and sit-ins at BOG meetings, Jackson and Figueroa hoped that their demonstration would force the administration to concede to the list of eight demands put forth by the USC, including the resignation of President Lawrence.

When asked whether President Lawrence's comment cultivated a sense of unity among student organizations, Jackson responded, "I've been here three years and students before had been fighting for these same issues. These students did not just come together from Lawrence's statement, which only provided further proof that steps are needed to end sexism and racism."[59] As students continued to face resistance to their demands, they deployed more forceful methods of protest deemed disruptive by the institution and captured the attention of those who were making decisions at the institutional level.

A "Day of Outrage": The Takeover of Route 18

The basketball protest, hunger stike, and multiple rallies led to the USC's culminating protest. The April 10, 1995, "Day of Outrage" issue of *Black Voice/Carta Boricua* featured a quarter-page ad from the USC. The organization declared that the purpose of the protest was to hold the university administration accountable by acknowledging the hurt and pain inflicted on communities of color at the university. This publication was the final student declaration that demanded President Lawrence submit his resignation. As *Black Voice/Carta Boricua* writer Darryl Scipio described, "The students and faculty met inside the Voorhees Mall on College Avenue and marched via Route 18 to Lawrence's house."[60] Although the initial plan was to rally by President Lawrence's office and then march to the Latino Student Center to support Jackson and Figueroa, at some point in the beginning of the rally, USC leadership decided to march to Route 18. According to an interview with Scipio, Livingston junior Damon Morgan was the first person to cross the divider on Route 18. Other protesters soon followed Morgan's lead. Morgan was compelled to jump the divider because he wanted the protest to demonstrate a stronger show of force. He said that the rally "didn't seem like enough, it just seemed too contained to be a 'no holds barred' type thing. . . . There were cops 50 yards ahead of us and 10 yards behind us . . . it was hyped up to be a big thing and they [the USC leaders] just walked the highway. I wasn't content with just walking the highway."[61] With more than four hundred people participating in the protest, traffic was at a standstill. Police immediately confronted protesters and subjected them to excessive force and arrests.[62] Students of all genders were physically assaulted by police officers on the scene. They were beaten with clubs, sprayed with mace, tossed around, and "just treated like pieces of meat."[63]

Seven men of color were arrested—David Brinkley (Ayinde), Steven Guzmán, Jamal Phillips, Trevor Phillips, Otis Rolley, Damon Santiago, and Ebrahim Washington—and faced charges of "obstruction of administration justice with physical force, obstructing a highway with refusal to disperse when notified, and participating in a crowd of over 100 with refusal to disperse when given proper notice."[64] Otis Rolley, a senior at Rutgers College, was falsely accused of being on Route 18 at the time of the protest, although several other students corroborated that he was not present at the time. Steven Guzman, a senior at Livingston College, knew that those who were arrested were being used as examples to scare the rest of the student body, given how vocal these particular students were on campus. "So that's why they picked us seven. They didn't pick us because they identified us, they picked us for examples."[65] With the onslaught of negative press, the university issued a statement that the institution would not press charges, but the protesters remained vulnerable to charges from the township. Although seven young men were arrested and charged, the police continued to subpoena several students for information regarding the protest and maintained surveillance in an attempt to "identify as many of the protestors as possible so they can be charged."[66]

Throughout the beginning of the fall 1995 semester, several students reflected on the events of the previous semester and spoke about the ways the USC would continue to hold the administration accountable. On November 9, 1995, *Black Voice/Carta Latina* released a three-part story written by Scipio that illustrated the "Day of Outrage" events from the perspective of six of the seven male students of color who were arrested and charged. One issue that became clear in Scipio's interviews with these young men was that students were hesitant about the unity among the more than forty student organizations within

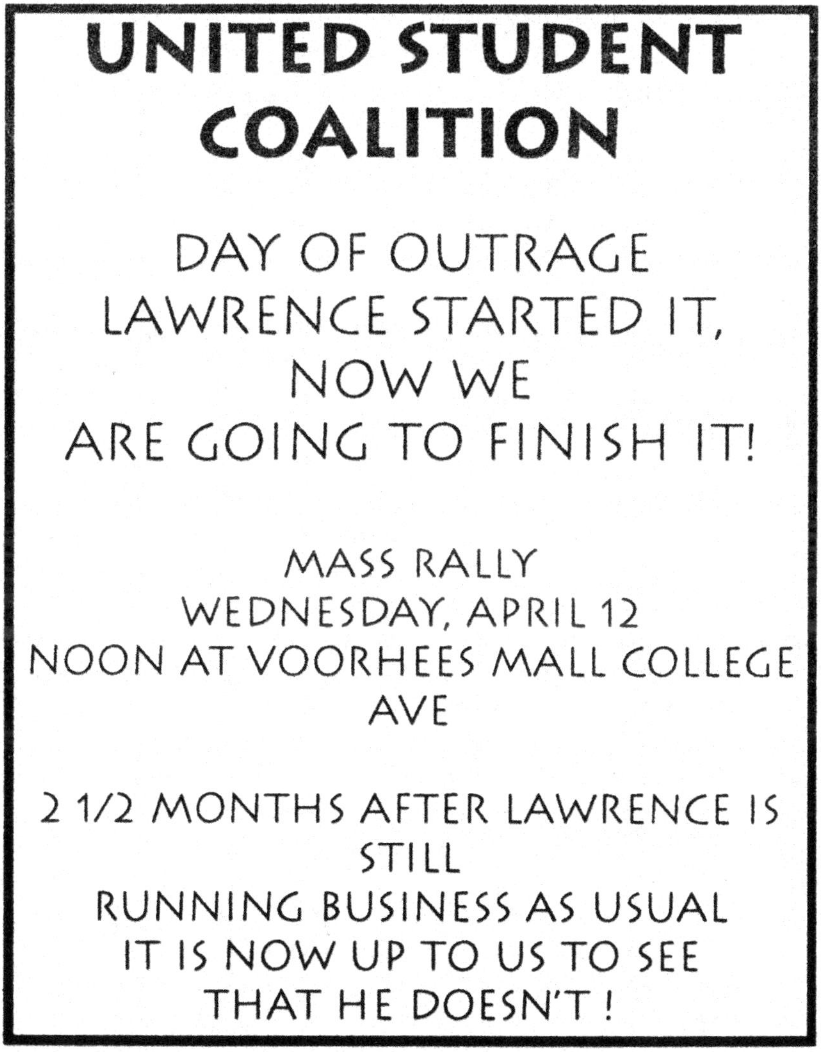

UNITED STUDENT COALITION

DAY OF OUTRAGE
LAWRENCE STARTED IT,
NOW WE
ARE GOING TO FINISH IT!

MASS RALLY
WEDNESDAY, APRIL 12
NOON AT VOORHEES MALL COLLEGE
AVE

2 1/2 MONTHS AFTER LAWRENCE IS STILL
RUNNING BUSINESS AS USUAL
IT IS NOW UP TO US TO SEE
THAT HE DOESN'T !

FIGURE 11.3 Student Coalition issued a call to campus community for the "Day of Outrage" protest, *Black Voice/Carta Boricua*, April 1995.

Courtesy of Special Collections & University Archives, Rutgers University

the USC, given that many did not show up to support those who were arrested. Both Morgan and Rolley had to appear in court because of their participation in the rally. Both students also severed ties with USC after their interactions with the legal system. Morgan's decision to leave the USC stemmed from the lack of support from his comrades during his hearing and disenchantment with the movement. He said, "Nobody showed up. . . . I ain't really get no calls from nobody. . . . I know now that I'm not trying to get involved in any more protests. That's the bottom line because after it all Lawrence is still president here. Ain't nothing changed."[67]

Students within the USC represented a variety of life experiences, interests, and opinions. Because of this, members had different viewpoints regarding strategy and method of protest. Otis Rolley argued that the USC was unsuccessful in getting Lawrence removed because the groups that made up the membership of the USC did not put forward all possible resources and energy into the movement. He said, "If we actually had all the resources of all those organizations that were on our list, and of their membership. I truly believe Lawrence would not be here." In Rolley's opinion, the USC did not live up to its potential, and for that reason, he ended his relationship with the organization after the "Day of Outrage."[68]

The impact of these student protests was widespread across campus. Although the emotional labor that it took for students like Jacqueline Williams to hold the administration accountable was immense, these protests prompted students to become activists and advocates for their own causes. Victor Carbonell from Passaic, New Jersey, recounted his experience as a student activist in the early to mid-'90s, speaking about his involvement with CARE and then later the USC. In his early years at Rutgers College, Carbonell remembered taking over buildings and demanding greater affordability, access, and support for students. "I don't know where we were, but I remember taking over some of those buildings. It was the housing building. I remember participating in those takeovers and chaining ourselves to those buildings."[69] He spent the latter half of his college career involved primarily in organizations like USC, Lambda Theta Phi Latin Fraternity, and multiple Latino student organizations under the Center for Latino Arts and Culture (CLAC). Carbonell was involved in every step of the Lawrence protests, from the initial rally at the president's office to the "Day of Outrage." Carbonell is one of the many students who participated in and contributed to challenging the campus climate for students of color during his tenure at Rutgers University. While students rallied, sat in, and marched, they were supported in large part by faculty and staff on campus who were developing their own response in alignment with the needs of the students and overall campus community of color.

Coalition of Black and Latino Faculty and Staff

Students were not the only group at Rutgers University to design and implement an action plan in response to Lawrence's remarks. In solidarity, several faculty and staff members brought concerns to the university administration. On February 10, 1995, faculty and staff across the three campuses developed the Coalition of Black and Latino Faculty and Staff.[70] Led by Dr. Walton R. Johnson, professor of social anthropology in the Department of Africana Studies at Rutgers University–New Brunswick; Janice L. Morrell, president of the Organization of Black Faculty and Staff at Rutgers University–Newark; and Dr. Miguel Estremera, Rutgers University registrar and cochair of the Latino Faculty and Staff Caucus, the coalition sought to support the interests of faculty and staff of color on campus to "be an active committee generating curricular and cocurricular activities that protect and enhance the academic growth and mental health of students of color at the university."[71] Furthermore, the coalition acknowledged the Lawrence incident as just one piece of the larger problem of systemic racism at Rutgers.[72] Faculty and staff developed an agenda to address this structural inequality and begin a healing process for communities of color to acknowledge and work through the hurt and pain inflicted by it.

The coalition's recommendations would influence part of the administration's response to the campus community. One faculty member, Dennis A. Mumble, listened to the recordings of Lawrence at the fateful 1994 faculty meeting and concluded that the president meant what he said regarding black students.[73] Although this statement was one of the most direct toward the president, other faculty and staff did not restrain their thoughts about how to move forward with accountability for a better racial climate. The initial letter to the administration included the following: "Over time people of color here at Rutgers have suffered from and struggled through institutional disenfranchisement. At best we have been tolerated."[74] These sentiments framed the recommendations drafted by the coalition.

Correspondences went back and forth between faculty and staff of the coalition and the institutional administration, including President Lawrence and the BOG. The coalition provided fourteen recommendations to the university, including the following:

I. All undergraduate students should be exposed, through the curriculum, to information that will assure the University's commitment to positive race relations from an academic perspective.

II. In order to assure continued recruitment and retention efforts for Black and Latino students, there should be increased funding and support for the following programs: Success in the Sciences Program; Solid GEMS Chemistry Program; the Carr and Minority Scholarship Programs; the EOF Program; and establish a high profiled [sic] Pre-College Preparation Program.

III. A stronger emphasis should be placed on "retention" in the admission process for Black and Latino students at the undergraduate, graduate, and professional levels.

IV. Inclusion of Black and Latino administrators at the decision-making level, specifically being chosen as members of the President's cabinet.

V. Due to the low number of Black and Latino faculty and administrators university-wide, there should be instituted support measures for increased recruitment as well as procedures that will insure job retention.

VI. Since Rutgers University is the State University of New Jersey, the Board of Governors should commit itself to the principle of proportional representation, so that the number of students, faculty, and administrators reflect the percentage of the Citizenry of the state of New Jersey.

VII. Increased funding support for college access, support, and retention programs such the Educational Opportunity Fund (EOF), the Carr and Minority Scholarship Programs, and Success in the Sciences Program.[75]

The coalition formed these recommendations based on their observations of how communities of color experienced oppression across Rutgers's campuses. The coalition specifically focused on academic and cocurricular initiatives. These recommendations also captured part of the demands that the USC submitted. For example, the coalition called for the diversification of the BOG to reflect the student body. Increased representation of blacks and Latinx in the student body, faculty, staff, and administration was of great importance to all organizations seeking racial change at Rutgers.[76]

Moving Forward . . .

During the spring 1995 semester, the administration responded to the demands of the USC and coalition with the creation of a task force composed of an external group of consultants. This task force was asked to create a Multicultural Student Life Recommendation blueprint. Five goals were outlined in this blueprint:

I. Fostering a sense of community by increasing communication, reducing bureaucracy, and improving civility, understanding, and sensitivity to cultural differences

II. Increase efforts to recruit and admit minority undergraduate and graduate students

III. Increase efforts to retain minority students by providing strong academic support

IV. Increase minority faculty recruitment

V. Improve the classroom climate for minority students through curriculum and dialogue[77]

The administration used the Multicultural Student Life Recommendation blueprint to reaffirm its commitment to diversity. It included details that aligned with the recommendations set out by the CBLFS and the demands made by the USC. These recommendations included an integrative process of bringing conversations about intercultural relations into the classroom through the help of faculty and the Teaching Excellence Center on campus, a commitment to have the vice president for undergraduate admissions submit plans for minority student recruitment along with allocating resources that focused on precollege programs for these students, and a stronger commitment from the university community to ongoing discussions via forums and conferences about race relations. And while the multicultural blueprint served as the next step for the university, many of these recommendations would be implemented at a slower pace than expected. Furthermore, although the document highlighted specific goals, the language was vague and did not outline a clear path to achieving the goals of supporting students of color and staff and faculty of color. Given the tensions that came to the fore on campus in the wake of Lawrence's comments, the administration may have hesitated to state specific initiatives for people of color for fear that it might have derailed into a conversation focused too much on identity politics, which for the most part was an argument made by supporters of Lawrence. The language used in the document reads as one that demonstrates a commitment to nonwhite students while maintaining the institution's responsibility to white people who may have shown support for Lawrence and a disregard for student protesters.[78]

After the "Day of Outrage," student protests quieted down, which allowed for an undisturbed university commencement. Many thought the work that both coalitions of students and faculty and staff did would be forgotten. However, the fight for resources and the ouster of President Lawrence was far from over. Undeterred by the administration's support of President Lawrence and the blueprint for a multicultural student life, students, staff, faculty, and community members continued to call for the resignation of the university's leader. That fall, the NAACP and some faculty members joined the call for resignation that students initiated.[79] While unsuccessful in their demand for his resignation, this brought greater attention to the need for Lawrence and his administration to be more intentional in their support for communities of color on campus.

". . . and the Struggle Continues"[80]

Among the many controversies to emerge during the 1980s and 1990s in the history of American higher education was the renewed focus on genetics as a marker of intellectual capacity, as prompted by the publication of *The Bell Curve*. Paralleling the release of this text was the hiring of Rutgers University's eighteenth president, Francis L. Lawrence. Of the many responsibilities he held, raising the academic profile of the university while maintaining its commitment to equitable access was of great priority. However, these efforts were overshadowed by deeper issues within the university that came to the forefront after Lawrence uttered those fateful words.

Given the legacy of student resistance, the response from students in the 1990s mirrored the work of student activists at Rutgers in previous decades. Twenty-five years later, the impact of racial inequities continued to permeate the campus community, which resulted in solidarity among students, staff, faculty, and community members.[81] The incidents that transpired in the spring of 1995 were part of a larger dialogue that was already taking place at Rutgers about race relations on campus but that was continuing to be ignored by the university administration.[82] As the university continued to contend with its past history and current reality, the voices of people of color became amplified through a united front of students, staff, faculty, and community members determined to hold the Rutgers administration accountable while developing people of color–led initiatives that could meet the needs of their community.

12

"Pure Grace"

The Scarlet Knights Basketball Team, Don Imus, and a Moment of Dignity

LYNDA DEXHEIMER

It was the Cinderella story of 2007. The Rutgers women's basketball team, a young squad with five freshmen and not a single senior on the roster, grew from the team that Hall of Fame coach C. Vivian Stringer called "a disaster" at the beginning of the season to reach the finals of the National Collegiate Athletic Association (NCAA) tournament.[1] The excitement on campus and throughout the region was palpable. The major broadcast networks dispatched reporters to the flagship New Brunswick campus. The Empire State Building glowed red for the Scarlet Knights. And, enthusiastic students signed an enormous good luck banner outside the College Avenue Student Center and planned viewing parties at which they hoped to watch their team take the title. Monica Morales, a reporter for WNBC-TV 4, deemed it "Scarlet Knight fever" caused by "a red-hot team and a crazed campus."[2] Hazel Sanchez of CBS-TV 2 noted, "Students here are really pumped up."[3] This was an event out of the ordinary at Rutgers University—and it seemed like it might turn out to be the rare occasion when a women's collegiate sporting event garnered as much enthusiasm and respect as a men's game.

The unlikely run of the Scarlet Knights ended in defeat by the Tennessee Lady Volunteers on April 3, 2007, with a score of 59–46. The "Championship Edition" of the *Daily Targum* on April 4 pictured despondent-looking team members on the cover, but disappointment was mixed with pride for Coach Stringer, the players, and the fans.[4] The team returned to New Brunswick to warm congratulations from Rutgers University president Richard L. McCormick, a bell-ringing ceremony at Old Queens, and a pep rally attended by more than 1,500 people, including the governor of New Jersey, Jon Corzine.[5]

One reporter called it "an absolute love fest."[6] But the news had not yet reached many of those celebrating inside the Rutgers Athletic Center that, just that morning, Don Imus and his producers had used racist and sexist language to describe the young players now being celebrated.[7] The controversy surrounding the remarks would generate thousands of news articles, hundreds of broadcast hours, and a chorus of national voices that included Senator John McCain, civil rights activists Al Sharpton and Jesse Jackson, political pundit James Carville, baseball legend Derek Jeter, Academy Award winner Spike Lee, and then presidential hopefuls Hillary Clinton and Barack Obama. The conversation would move from basketball to the First Amendment and on to rap and hip hop, illuminating societal splits along race and gender lines. Through it all, the players and Stringer kept their composure, earning accolades in the mainstream of media, culture, and politics for their dignity as individuals, while Imus was largely excoriated for his behavior as an individual. But this narrative of young innocents versus a "good person who said a bad thing" deflected the conversation away from structural racism and sexism by focusing on a single incident as if it had happened in a vacuum.

Media Matters for America, a nonprofit information center that monitors media for "conservative misinformation," was the first to highlight the remarks Imus and his producers made on CBS and also simulcast on MSNBC.[8] Their report noted that Imus had used the phrase "nappy-headed hos" to describe the players on the Rutgers team, a slur that would incite national outrage. A full rendition of the transcript, though painful, is necessary here to understand the scope of the discourse used by Don Imus and his producers Bernie McGuirk, Sid Rosenberg, Charles McCord, and Lou Ruffino.

IMUS: So, I watched the basketball game last night between—a little bit of Rutgers and Tennessee, the women's final.

ROSENBERG: Yeah, Tennessee won last night—seventh championship for [Tennessee coach] Pat Summit, I-Man. They beat Rutgers by 13 points.

IMUS: That's some rough girls from Rutgers. Man, they got tattoos and—

McGUIRK: Some hard-core hos.

IMUS: That's some nappy-headed hos there. I'm gonna tell you that now, man, that's some—woo. And the girls from Tennessee, they all look cute, you know, so like—kinda like—I don't know.

McGUIRK: A Spike Lee thing.

IMUS: Yeah.

McGUIRK: The Jigaboos vs. the Wannabes—that movie that he had.

IMUS: Yeah, it was a tough—

McCORD: *Do the Right Thing.*

McGUIRK: Yeah, yeah, yeah.

IMUS: I don't know if I'd have wanted to beat Rutgers or not, but they did, right?

ROSENBERG: It was a tough watch. The more I look at Rutgers, they look exactly like the Toronto Raptors.

IMUS: Well, I guess, yeah.

RUFFINO: Only tougher.

McGUIRK: The [Memphis] Grizzlies would be more appropriate.[9]

The entire exchange between Imus and McGuirk was sexist and racist, and tapped into deep and centuries-old prejudices in US society based on colorism and race and gender-based beauty standards. But it was the "nappy-headed hos" sound bite that garnered by far the most media attention. The media focus on a single phrase allowed white apologists to point the finger at black hip-hop and rap artists and claim a double standard, arguing that if African Americans could use such language to describe black women, then why not a white man? Further defense of Imus was laid on the grounds that the use of the phrase had been a mistake, an unfortunate slip of the tongue, and that he was an "equal opportunity offender" who had said worse about others. Lastly, there was the seemingly irrelevant argument that Imus and his wife raised a great deal of money for charity and deserved forgiveness.[10]

Framing the incident this way ignored several factors. First, at that time, many prominent voices in the black community, including the National Association for the Advancement of Colored People (NAACP), Calvin O. Butts III, and Jesse Jackson, were critical of the misogynistic language in some artists' music, so asserting that Imus was being held to a "double standard" was simply incorrect.[11] Second, the language employed in pitting the "cute" Tennessee team against the "rough" girls from Rutgers was a reflection of the long pattern in US society of denigrating women athletes on the basis of their failure to conform to socially constructed standards of femininity.[12] Third, the incorrect reference to Spike Lee's film *Do the Right Thing* (the speaker meant to reference Lee's satirical film *School Daze*) and the likening of the Rutgers women to a men's professional basketball team showed that the white men speaking on the airwaves were well aware of the societal stigmas associated with skin tone, hair texture, and body standards.[13] And finally, the comparison of the Rutgers players to animals and the insinuation that beating the Rutgers team might involve violent retaliation—"I don't know if I'd have wanted to beat Rutgers or not"—reinforced white racist beliefs that young black people are subhuman and dangerous.

While the national media twisted itself into pretzels to continue to message a condemnation of racism while accommodating a "double standard" argument that was of false equivalency, on the Rutgers campus, students, faculty, administrators, and alumni largely rejected the apologia. In her memoir, Stringer recalls that the first reaction of her team upon hearing of Imus's comments was "who?"—they had no idea who he was—followed closely by "why?"

Stringer felt the players were genuinely surprised by such an overt expression of sexism and racism, although she was not. As she put it, "There was a question mark at the end of their why and an exclamation point at the end of mine."[14] In the midst of celebrations for the team's accomplishments, Rutgers University president McCormick and NCAA president Myles Brand crafted a joint statement:

> The NCAA and Rutgers University are offended by the insults on MSN-BC's Don Imus program toward the 10 young women on the Rutgers basketball team. It is unconscionable that anyone would use the airways to utter such disregard for the dignity of human beings who have accomplished so much and deserve great credit. It is appropriate that Mr. Imus and MSNBC have apologized.[15]

Imus and his employers may have hoped the apology he had made—issued over the airwaves and not directly to anyone at Rutgers—was going to end the matter. But that would turn out not to be the case because the incident became a national story and the gravity of the slurs leveled at the players began to sink in among members of the university community. Rutgers University athletic director Robert Mulcahy III said it was never an option to ignore the comments, but that the initial low-key response from the university was out of a desire to not detract from the celebratory events taking place on April 5.[16]

Stringer recalled in her memoir that "it wasn't until I saw a printout of the full text that the magnitude of what he'd said really sank in" and noted not only the hurt caused by the "ho" insult, but also the "wannabes" one. She wrote that the "reference to dark- and light-skinned black complexions—an issue that continues to cause pain in our community"—was "more than a schoolyard taunt."[17] Team captain and Rutgers junior Essence Carson said that the players' first thought was "to let it slide," but that after reading the transcript, "it hit a little too close to home. . . . I've seen things happen to women and I've heard about things that happen to women. . . . We're glad to have the opportunity to stand up for what is right."[18] Stringer's and Carson's words conveyed a sense that the harm caused by the exchange on the radio was bigger than the Scarlet Knights basketball team or Rutgers, that in fact the harm was done to all women and particularly black women, a sentiment that would be echoed by many students and faculty on campus during the coming days. While the national conversation focused on the less important question of whether Don Imus was a racist, Stringer and Carson were calling for the incident to be situated within a larger context of structural sexism and racism, and to address it on those terms.

The snowball of outrage on campus was still small on April 6 when the *Daily Targum*, the student newspaper on the Rutgers–New Brunswick campus, issued a "dart" to Don Imus in its traditional "Laurels and Darts" weekly

FIGURE 12.1 Vivian Stringer coaching a Scarlet Knights basketball game in the 1990s.

Courtesy of Special Collections & University Archives, Rutgers University

opinion round-up. The paper called the Imus comments "snide" and noted his program was "known to shock the public, so it is no surprise Imus would make such negative remarks."[19] Criticism in the editorial focused on the gendered aspect of the offense, emphasizing that Imus had disparaged the femininity of the "rough" Rutgers team with respect to the "cute" Tennessee team, and did not mention race at all. In an individual statement issued on April 7, Coach Stringer linked gender and race together: "To serve as a joke of Mr. Imus in such an insensitive manner created a wedge and makes light of the efforts of these classy individuals, both as women and women of color."[20] President McCormick issued a second statement on April 8 condemning the "despicable" and "disgraceful, disgusting, and racist remarks" and expressing his pride in the team. The statement closed with a subtle acknowledgment of the growing national pressure on Imus, CBS, and MSNBC: "Ultimately, the decision about whether Mr. Imus remains in his position rests with his employers. We at Rutgers are taking this situation extremely seriously. We expect Mr. Imus' employers to do the same."[21] Stopping short of a direct call for Imus's suspension or firing, the statement was intended to definitively show that the university as an institution was taking the incident just as seriously as Stringer did, and the growing tide of public sentiment concurred.

A day later, the national media frenzy began in earnest. Imus had accepted an invitation to appear—and apologize again—on Al Sharpton's radio show. The fireworks emanating from that meeting set off a firestorm, and the story was the lead on every major television broadcast news program on April 9, 2007. Over Imus's expressions of remorse ("I'm a good person who said a bad thing") and acknowledgment that he had "ruined" the moment of pride for the Rutgers team, Sharpton pushed to keep the focus on the larger issue of structural discrimination, at one point bringing his own daughter into the booth to face Imus. "She is not a nappy-headed ho, she is my daughter," Sharpton told Imus. "It's about how my daughter and the daughters of a lot of people listening are going to be looked at in this world."[22] By this point, the National Association of Black Journalists had called for Imus's resignation, Jesse Jackson had led a protest outside the NBC studios in Chicago calling for consumers to boycott Imus's advertisers, the NAACP and National Organization for Women (NOW) had held an anti-Imus rally outside of NBC headquarters at 30 Rockefeller Plaza in New York City, and then presidential candidate Barack Obama had criticized Imus in a statement. By the end of the day, MSNBC announced it had suspended Imus for two weeks.[23]

Back in New Brunswick, the team felt the national scale of the controversy. Reporters had been barraging individual members with calls, texts, and emails throughout the weekend, including Easter Sunday, which was on April 8. Athletic director Robert Mulcahy issued a statement April 9 asking the media to stop directly contacting the student-athletes.[24] Team member Kia

Vaughn expressed her frustration at the unwanted attention. "During Easter, I have seven brothers, as everyone does know, instead of spending time with them and having fun, I had to cut off my phone. The media was trying to get through to talk to relatives and even people, being fans, were showing up in this moment of hurt. It was good to hear from some people, but to have to repeatedly express how I felt, I became really agitated."[25] Sophomore Heather Zurich noted that even if the team had wanted to ignore the controversy, "the media was calling our houses, our cell phones, following us around campus."[26] Essence Carson questioned where the national press was when the team made history for Rutgers as NCAA contenders. "We haven't done anything to deserve this controversy, but yet it has taken a toll on us mentally and physically. . . . We ask that you not recognize us in a light as dimly lit as this, but in a light that encompasses the great hurdles we've overcome and goals achieved this season," Carson asserted.[27] The players' statements illustrate the tension between the attention given to the team as individuals when they were asked to relate how they personally felt about being publicly attacked, the desire in the university community to continue to protect the students and emphasize the athletic achievements of the team, and the larger critical frames of sexism and racism that Stringer, Carson, and others were advocating be used to make sense of the controversy and advance progress on issues of gender and race.

Because the press largely continued to frame the issue as a referendum on Imus, that is the direction discourse took. Reporters asked students on the College Avenue campus if they thought Imus should be fired, and those whose comments made it on air—male and female, white students and students of color—told them he should be.[28] Mary S. Hartman, a Rutgers professor in the Department of Women's and Gender Studies and the director of the Institute for Women's Leadership, shared the email address of a CBS radio executive in a letter to the *Targum* and urged readers to write him and call for Imus's removal. "CBS Radio needs to make it clear that racist and sexist slurs will no longer be tolerated," Hartman wrote.[29] Rutgers history professor Deborah Gray White pointed out that allowing Imus to keep his position would be the true double standard: "If an administrator made that kind of comment, they would be fired. Anyone in corporate America who went into a board meeting and made that kind of remark, they would be fired."[30] These comments reflect the high level of disgust for Imus on campus, and the desire for him to be made an example of by drawing a clear line between acceptable and offensive speech. Even as Coach Stringer and President McCormick continued to avoid direct calls for his firing, momentum in that direction was building.

University leadership continued to resist that impulse. In an email to Rutgers faculty, staff, and students circulated on April 9 with the subject line "Denouncing Don Imus' Appalling Remarks," President McCormick framed the offense as both racist and sexist but indicated that the university's top priority was to support the athletes, their families, and the coaches.[31] The archival record indicates that responses from within the Rutgers community were largely positive. Adjunct professor Daria Torres from the School of Business in Camden wrote, "Thank you for your deliberate and swift reaction to this incident!"[32] First-year student Louise Pepe wrote of her pride in the basketball team and asked McCormick, "Please, when you speak with the team players next, mention how proud all of RU students are of them and how fortunate we are to have them as part of our University Family."[33] Professor George Pieczenik of the Department of Biochemistry and Microbiology wrote, "Very proud of you" to McCormick, and Professor Tod Marder of the Department of Art History wrote, "Great! Call me the unofficial Chair of the Faculty Committee to Honor Outstanding Athletics at Rutgers."[34] Emails poured into President McCormick's office from around the nation. The archive contains twenty-five folders of emails to McCormick, the large majority of which offered general support to the team and the university.[35] The president's office developed five standard email responses to cope with the volume, each tailored to the sender's message. The standard responses were titled "General Support"; "Support but Differing Viewpoints (e.g., should boycott, should have him fired, shouldn't have made a big deal of it, not happy how we handled)"; "Critical of Rutgers for Having Imus Fired"; "Raising Other Topics—especially rap music lyrics," and "Strongly Critical of the Team's Response."[36] The titles of these themed emails are an effective illustration of the range of public opinion.

A number of writers felt the university had not gone far enough in its criticism of Imus. A doctoral candidate in the Department of Political Science wrote that denouncing the comments was not enough and asked, "Will Rutgers join the chorus of voices demanding Imus' resignation or his termination?"[37] Student David Pennant wrote that it "is not enough saying that it was wrong. This is merely stating the obvious, as the person in power of this University and its main representative there should be a [sic] calling for this man's immediate resignation because this is not the first time he has violated." In another email to President McCormick, a writer expressed (in all capital letters) surprise that "THE UNIVERSITY IS NOT MAKING MORE NOISE OR DOING MORE IN RELATION TO THE CRUDE BUT HEARTFELT REMARKS MADE BY IMUS AND HIS PRODUCER. . . . WHY DON'T WE GET THE NAMES OF THE SPONSORS OF HIS PROGRAM AND BOYCOTT THEM? I DO BELIEVE THAT WILL GET THE RESULTS NECESSARY TO TAKE THIS RACIST IGNORAMUS OFF THE AIR."[38] But President McCormick and Coach Stringer held firm in their focus on the well-being of the students and their refusal to call for Imus to be fired. As Stringer recalled in her memoir, "Right from the beginning, I was clear on one point: I wasn't standing in judgment of Don Imus. . . . We wouldn't call for his job or for anything else. I was concerned with one thing only, and that was clarifying, in the world's eyes, who we were."[39] The day after McCormick's email to the Rutgers community, on April 10, Rutgers Athletics held a press conference to do just that, using the platform to introduce the players on the team as individuals and to call for social justice.

The press conference would turn out to be a turning point in the entire event. If up to that point the coach and players had the sympathy of people in the abstract, the poise and dignity the women exhibited at the press conference turned the abstraction into a reality. Coach Stringer introduced them as "ladies of class and distinction," "brilliant," "articulate," "bright, gifted, and hard-working." She noted that among them were valedictorians, musicians, and Girl Scouts. In short, Stringer projected an image of the young women that directly contradicted the image that Imus had presented—a group of young women who were intelligent, hardworking, and respectable. Stringer also recounted her own experiences with racism as a young woman. And then she called for change: "It's not about just these young women. I ask you, no matter who you are, who could have heard these comments and not been personally offended? It's not about the Rutgers women's basketball team, it's about women. Are women hos? Think about that. Would you want your daughter called a ho?"[40] Kia Vaughn passionately echoed this sentiment, when, during the question-and-answer session, she said, "He said the word 'ho.' Unless they have changed the meaning of that word and it stands for achievement, I am not a ho . . . I'm a woman, and I'm someone's child."[41] Heather Zurich offered an image of the team in stark contrast to the one inherent in the slur:

> I am proud when we walk through an airport on the way to or from a road trip dressed alike, in Rutgers gear with pressed pants and nice shoes. The ten of us love getting dressed up for banquets and I believe we present ourselves well—both on and off the court—even though Mr. Imus seems to think differently. But then again, he knows not one of us.[42]

Essence Carson dismissed defenders of Imus who argued that the pervasive use of offensive language in hip-hop and rap explained his use of it, and said no one, white or black, had the right to disparage women in that way. "As a society, we're trying to go to and surpass the point where we don't classify women as hoes. We don't classify African-American women as 'nappy-headed hos,'" she told the gathered reporters.[43]

The players were dignified, articulate, and witty, but beneath the disciplined way in which they presented themselves and their viewpoints, their youth and depth of emotion over the Imus comments were evident. Hearing directly from the student-athletes for the first time reminded the assembled reporters and the viewers of the CNN livestream that they were either still teenagers or barely out of their teen years. And while the team and Coach

FIGURE 12.2 2006–2007 Rutgers University Women's Basketball Team official photo.

Courtesy of Rutgers University Athletic Communications

Stringer tried to keep the focus on using the negative experience to open up a dialogue about sexism and racism, the players' words reminded the public that they were daughters and sisters who liked to get dressed up for parties, who laughed and had fun together, and who had just achieved what no other team in Rutgers history had—a place in a national championship. They felt that accomplishment was being overshadowed. As Essence Carson put it, Imus had "stolen a moment of pure grace from us."[44] The team also announced they had agreed to meet with Imus to hear him out, but would not say in advance where or when the meeting would take place or whether they would accept his apology. The players avoided an affirmative response to questions asking if they supported his firing, following the lead set by Coach Stringer and President McCormick.

Media coverage of that press conference was overwhelmingly positive and picked up Stringer's messaging about the larger societal issues at stake. A FOX news reporter called the Rutgers players "cool, calm, and classy."[45] In the following days, articles and op-ed pieces in regional and national newspapers ran with headlines such as "Stringer Directs Spotlight on 'Need for Social Change'" and "Rutgers Team Provides Role Model for Society."[46] Footage of Brian Williams interviewing Coach Stringer and Essence Carson on the *NBC Nightly News* featured them both reiterating the call for change they had made at the press conference.[47] Gwen Ifill, a prominent African American journalist who had herself been the subject of a racist insult by Don Imus, wrote an op-ed piece in the *New York Times* that placed the incident in a structural context: "This country will only flourish once we consistently learn to applaud and encourage young people who have to work harder just to achieve equal balance on the unequal playing field."[48] A few days later on NBC's *Meet the Press,* Ifill and Eugene Robinson of the *Washington Post* dismissed the notion that Imus's comments were forgivable either because they were made in the context of comedy or because the same kind of language was routinely used in rap and hip-hop music. Robinson further refuted the notion that the incident was distracting attention from the discussion of more important issues facing the black community. "I see a false choice there, basically . . . just because there are other issues—economic and other issues that face black Americans, the existence of those issues is not a reason to refrain from addressing the offense that Imus gave," said Robinson.[49] This kind of discourse reflected the more thoughtful narrative that was taking hold since the press conference. Although the media initially focused on whether Imus was a racist or a bad person or on whether he should be fired, Coach Stringer and the team successfully reframed it at the press conference as one incident in a society structured by sexism and racism. Notably, the reframe was led by black women and people of color and showed a marked contrast to earlier coverage.

The message of the press conference was articulated a day later at a Douglass College rally attended by hundreds of students, campus leaders, faculty, and state politicians. Attendants carried placards with messages such as "Racism and Sexism Are No Joke" and "Rutgers Women R Strong Women" and called for anger at Imus to be "channeled into combating racism and sexism."[50] Chidimma Acholonu, president of the university's NAACP chapter, said the protest was intended to show Imus that words have power: "Today we did not come to be angry, start fights or start any sort of up rest [*sic*]. We came to support our women's basketball team and to support a movement towards equality on all standpoints. . . . We ask not only for him to be removed from his position but to gracefully understand why he needs to resign."[51] The *Trenton Times* reported that black female faculty members at Rutgers had released a letter condemning Imus's slurs, arguing that his words "'must be understood within a long history of racial oppression' in which African American women have suffered from racism and sexism."[52] That evening, MSNBC announced it was dropping its simulcast of CBS's *Imus in the Morning.* The network attributed the decision to fleeing advertisers and the feelings of employees within NBC.[53] A day later, the same day Imus and his wife, Deirdre Imus, met with the team and their families, coaches, and advisors, CBS followed suit and fired Imus.[54]

The meeting on April 12 between the team and Imus was the culmination of the chain of events that had started on April 4. Those who were at the 2007 meeting have kept quiet about the specifics of the conversation for more than a decade. Coach Stringer wrote that "it was a genuine—sometimes very emotional—dialogue. . . . It was a truly cathartic experience for me and for the players, and I want to believe that it was for Imus and his wife, Deirdre, as well."[55] On WFAN radio the next day, Deirdre Imus told listeners, "These women are unbelievably courageous and beautiful women," and admonished those who had been harassing the players. "The hate mail that's being sent to them must stop. This is wrong. If you want to send hate mail, send it to my husband," she said.[56] Reverend DeForest "Buster" Soaries Jr., pastor of Coach Stringer's church, the First Baptist Church of Lincoln Gardens, who had advised the team throughout the ordeal, called it "the most intense experience of my life," characterizing the players and their families as "noble" and polite but "vocal."[57] Ultimately, the team decided to accept the Imus apology. In announcing that decision, Stringer said, "We hope that this will serve as a catalyst for change."[58] A few days later, she told the *Asbury Park Press*: "To win a national championship is one thing, but to somehow evolve the consciousness of the country is more important."[59] Measuring a national evolution of consciousness is difficult, to be sure, but the Imus firing indicated that the incident had touched a nerve with corporate America, the public, and the media in a way previous Imus insults had not. The presence of people of color in the corporate power structure may have contributed to the difference. NBC executives cited feedback from employees in explaining its decision to pull Imus from MSNBC. CBS board member Bruce Gordon, who is African American, called publicly for Imus to be fired. That Imus was ultimately fired showed that some within the power structure were willing to endorse the notion that racist and sexist words perpetuate racist and sexist structures even if the real motive for firing Imus may have been the exodus of advertising dollars. And, after all, the advertisers who pulled out of Imus programming were themselves powerful corporate entities such as Procter & Gamble, GlaxoSmithKline, General Motors, and Staples that had decided they no longer wanted to be linked with his kind of discourse.

To be sure, Imus also received plenty of support and Rutgers plenty of ire. Individuals as disparate as comedians Joan Rivers and Bill Maher, Republican Senator John McCain, and Democratic Party strategist James Carville walked the dubious line of defending him while agreeing that what he said was wrong.[60] Some letters to the editor from students published in the *Daily Targum* argued that the incident was either blown out of proportion, was a First Amendment issue, or was some kind of "reverse racism."[61] President McCormick received emails from the public asserting the players had somehow gotten what they deserved. "Respect has to be earned . . . if these ladies make a conscious effort to look and act respectable and like they respect themselves, everyone else will, too," read one email.[62] Another writer told McCormick, "Your women's basketball team does not meet standards for young women if they have tatoos [sic] and body piercings."[63] These writers were reiterating the same gender expectations, and the team's supposed failure to meet them, that the white men on the Imus show were playing on when they mocked the players on those terms. Clearly, the social justice message around gender and race that Coach Stringer and the team projected was falling on deaf ears within a segment of the population.

But it is also clear that the incident drew national attention on a wholly different scale from other racist, sexist incidents in Coach Stringer's history and in the history of women's sports more generally. What was largely underreported during the height of the anti-Imus outrage was that this was not the first time that Stringer and one of her teams had faced racial or gender discrimination. As she noted in her memoir, when coaching at Cheyney University of Pennsylvania, an HBCU, people pelted her players with food when they were eating in a host school's cafeteria.[64] And Justin Miller, a Livingston College 2002 alumni, noted that when he was a student covering the Rutgers women's basketball team for the *Daily Targum*, Stringer had asked players to cover their tattoos with white tape at the Big East tournament in Connecticut, a symbolic protest against a reporter who had mocked them as having playing skills inferior to their "tattoos and bravado." Miller wrote that the Imus incident made him realize "[Stringer] was fighting a bigger issue that had followed her players around much of their lives"—the problems of racism and gender bias.[65] The difference this time was that Imus's status as a prominent media figure catapulted the slurs into the national spotlight.

As much as the incident had been initially framed as one of race, and is largely remembered that way, students and faculty at Rutgers saw it equally as gendered and part of a larger pattern of discrimination in women's sports. *Targum* sports columnist Nic Martino emphasized the sexist nature of the slur by noting that the Imus crew had "reduced women's college athletics to a beauty pageant," demeaning the Scarlet Knights' athletic achievements and stealing what Essence Carson had called "a moment of pure grace."[66] Female students interviewed on the Rutgers campus concurred. "If you turn the tables, there's no way anybody would ever judge any male basketball players for not being attractive enough . . . it's not a modeling contest, they're incredible athletes," said one student in an interview. Women students noted that despite media coverage of the women's basketball team's success, and the higher-than-usual level of enthusiasm the team garnered relative to other women's sports at Rutgers, there was still much less attention given to Coach Stringer's team than was typically given to men's teams. "I don't think women's sports get enough respect at all, 'cause when I think about talking to my guy friends about women's sports, they just kind of laugh it off. Most of my friends didn't even know that our team was in the finals," commented one female student. Another said, "When the Rutgers football team was ranked, it was a really big deal, it was all over the news, versus when Rutgers women go to the Final Four and go into a national championship . . . it wasn't even that big a deal on campus."[67] The Scarlet Knights' experience with Imus was one episode in the larger story of gender equity in sports and in the larger society.[68] In no way was it an event that occurred in a vacuum, and multiple voices on campus used it as an opportunity to highlight the need for change.

In the end, this message of female empowerment took hold. Helen Wronski, the chairman of the Girl Scouts of Northern New Jersey Council, commended Coach Stringer "for the dignified manner in which she and the team have handled themselves. . . . The dignity and courage she and her young team have shown exemplify the mission of the Girl Scouts."[69] In a speech at Rutgers during her presidential primary campaign, Hillary Clinton recalled that when she was a student, girls were only allowed to play half-court basketball, and she urged the crowd to continue building a movement out of the recent events.[70] Essence Carson said in an interview with *Newsweek,* "It was an attack on women first. . . . He just made it race specific."[71] Player Matee Ajavon also emphasized gender when speaking at the press conference: "I think the message that needs to be conveyed starts with women. Black women, all colors. Women are equal."[72] This interpretation may explain why the team garnered so much support. Attacking a group of collegiate women athletes on the basis of their appearance as women was apparently too much for a society still polarized around racial issues, as the hip-hop/rap and "reverse racism" defenses of Imus indicated. Gender inequity apparently stirred support from the larger society in a way that racial inequity did not.

For Rutgers University and the state of New Jersey, the derogatory comments ended up producing an oddly positive effect. Rutgers communications executive Kim Manning wrote in a memo that "the result was unprecedented in the university's history—nearly 20,000 print, digital and broadcast stories about Rutgers, the vast majority of them positive."[73] The controversy attracted the attention of New Jersey–born baseball hero Derek Jeter, who wrote a sympathetic letter to the team.[74] Articles about Rutgers and New Jersey ran in the national press with headlines such as "There's Nothing Like a Little Jersey Pride," "The Rutgers Winning Team," and "Lady Knights' Grace Brings University National Acclaim."[75]

Don Imus's show was revived on cable/satellite radio less than a year after he was fired by the major networks. Given current realities, it is difficult to argue that the controversy marked a turning point in public tolerance for racist and sexist discourse, either in politics or in music. And certainly, sexism and racism are still structural problems in the United States. However, the willingness of Coach Stringer and the players to frame the harm done to them as not only individual hurt but also part of a larger, historic problem created a space for a critical national conversation around race and gender led primarily by black women.

While everyone's minds were clearly not changed, many people found the press conference to be important to their own ways of talking or thinking about race and gender. An African American woman in Ohio wrote to tell the team that she would use a tape of the press conference to motivate the young people with whom she worked. "It hurts my heart when my girls came to our meeting saying 'Why work as hard as we are when many white men see us as the "H" word!' [Imus's] statement makes it hard for people like me to tell young people hard work will get you ahead. But thanks for that positive press conference today that I can play for them at our next meeting," she wrote.[76] The *New York Times* published a letter from a self-described

> white, prudish suburban woman with all the requisite huffy indignation for all things racist and sexist. Yet I watched Don Imus most mornings. It often made me squirm, but I could justify the puerile banter as being just another part of urban culture that I just didn't get. So I was ready to defend Mr. Imus because of the platform he provided for in-depth, high-caliber interviews.
>
> When I saw the young women of Rutgers, I was shamed as I have never been shamed before. I suddenly saw my very real contribution to our racial divide. Indifference. I'd been willing to dismiss the denigration of African-Americans and women because it's become common and because it suited me.
>
> And I learned the true meaning of grace and courage from those young women.
>
> Thank you for showing me that I have much work to do.[77]

If the team had hoped to raise consciousness around larger issues of race and gender, these letters indicate that among some people, they had achieved their goal.

They may even have succeeded in raising the consciousness—or at least the conscience—of the individual by whom they had been directly wronged. Imus retired in 2018, and in interviews with the media, was asked if he had any regrets about his decades as an equal-opportunity offender. A few, he said. "The Rutgers thing I regret." Why? "I knew better," he replied. "It did change my feeling about making fun of some people who didn't deserve to be made fun of, and didn't have a mechanism to defend themselves," he said.[78] The Imus incident is a major part of Coach Stringer's story along with her success on the court, which includes reaching the 1,000-win mark as Rutgers coach and coaching the US women's basketball team to a gold medal in the 2004 Olympics. Writing for *Newsday* in 2018, sports columnist Barbara Barker observed that for all her basketball achievements, "for many, her greatest legacy remains the impact she had by refusing to allow her team to be defined by ugly rhetoric."[79] This impact opened up space for reflection and conversations around gender and race led by black women, defined on their terms and through the prism of their lived experiences. The impact was felt in corporate America, the news media, Rutgers University, and in households around the country, and is part of the foundation of current debates around the same issues of structural sexism and racism.

Epilogue

Scarlet and Black:
The Price of the Ticket

DEBORAH GRAY WHITE

The call to remember revolves around the very human need to tell stories
of our past in order to preserve our present and secure a future. . . . The
demand for acknowledgment is born of the circumstances that show us
that Black lives have always mattered but have been taken for granted.

–Jonathan Holloway, twenty-first president
of Rutgers University, June 19, 2020

It is only fitting that this final volume of *Scarlet and Black* should end where it
began, with the urgent student call for an investigation into Rutgers's odious
history with those who were dispossessed of the land on which Rutgers was
built, and those whose bodies were sold and exploited to finance its building.
On May 11, 2015, Chancellor Richard Edwards met with students who felt that
"improving the current racial and cultural climate at Rutgers was impossible
without answering questions about the university's early history." The book
Ebony and Ivy: Race, Slavery, and the Troubled History of America's Universities by
African American historian Craig Wilder had pointed to a "deeper, more painful narrative that had yet to be told."[1] Inasmuch as Rutgers was approaching its
250th anniversary, Chancellor Edwards agreed that the time was ripe for the
research and unveiling of this more unsettling history. In his words, "A true
telling of our early history was never more due—and never more necessary."[2]
Today, in the summer of 2020, an online petition is once again calling for
an accounting of Rutgers's racist past by renaming Hardenbergh, Frelinghuysen, and Milledoler Halls. According to the petitioners, respecting Rutgers's

history "means not forcing students to live and learn in spaces named after those who opposed their very existence, let alone their education."[3]

As we finish this third volume of *Scarlet and Black,* demonstrations across the country reveal how vital this kind of institutional history continues to be. In 2015 and 2016, young people across the nation demonstrated against the presence of Confederate flags and memorials, the killing of unarmed blacks by police and civilian whites, and the perceived rollback of the academy's commitment to diversity and inclusion. Today, young people, indeed citizens of all ages, are again walking not just campuses but city streets and rural drives to the chant of "Black Lives Matter." Like the Rutgers students who wanted a true depiction of African Americans in Rutgers history, Americans across the country are demanding a history of America that includes African Americans and other oppressed minorities. They want to know why the nation venerates traitors with monuments and dedicates streets, military bases, and government buildings to them; why slaveholders, perpetrators of Native American genocide, and supporters of segregation are revered as American heroes; why the names of sports teams are racial slurs—and how America got to the point that police can snuff out African American life in full view of cameras with no one immediately arrested for the crime. In 2015 and 2016, Rutgers students asked questions that the university is still answering: What is the role of American institutions, including universities, in making freedom a reality for all of America's citizens and for people across the world, what is the university's responsibility in imparting knowledge that is inclusive of everyone's experience, and what is the university's responsibility in preparing society to be inclusive and nurturing?

In 2015, Rutgers students sought answers to these questions by starting with the yet untold history of Rutgers University, a history that the three volumes of *Scarlet and Black* have begun to answer. Volume 1 shows how Native Americans, Africans, and African Americans were sacrificed so that Rutgers could be built; how the labor of an enslaved man named Will evidenced the building of the college by black hands; how, among so many others, the parents of the noted abolitionist and feminist Sojourner Truth were abused and left to wither away by insensitive owners who were subsequently revered as Rutgers's august founders; and how Rutgers's leaders and faculty defended slavery and white supremacy while they pressed for free black people to be sent back to Africa. This first volume also documents the presence of a vibrant black community in New Brunswick, one that resisted slavery in its organized activity that was both public and underground.

The second volume of *Scarlet and Black* chronicles Rutgers's disturbing history with African Americans from the end of the Civil War through World War II, first documenting how the administrators and faculty at Rutgers disseminated the ideological precepts of Anglo-Saxon supremacy on campus and throughout the world. Next, it illuminates the courageousness of Rutgers's first African American graduates, the way they braved campus racism—even when, as illustrated by Paul Robeson, it meant enduring physical and psychological assault. Finally, it shows that Douglass College—even though it was founded in 1918 in resistance to sexism and was rooted in a woman's movement aimed at upending entrenched ideas about female deficiency—also adhered to the same racism as its brother college. The first graduates, including Julia Baxter Bates, admitted by mistake, were just as courageous as the black men who composed Rutgers's African American forerunner generation.

This, the third and final written volume of *Scarlet and Black*,[4] has provided the explanation for the term *forerunner generation* used in the second volume.[5] These early black graduates made it possible for the baby boomers born after World War II to prevail. Although they put in massive amounts of work toward creating a university that now boasts of its diversity, and although they created the black campus political organizations that successfully demanded a cultural presence on campus and a multicultural curriculum, the faculty, staff, and black and brown baby boomers introduced in this volume's pages did not lay the foundation for change at Rutgers—the forerunner desegregation generation did. They got their foot in the door and made it possible for the late 1960s student activists to push that door wide open. In a very real way, the forerunners laid the foundation for this kind of history—the history described in *Scarlet and Black: Making Black Lives Matter, 1945–2020*—to be engaged and embraced by the Rutgers University community.

They also laid the foundation for the appointment of Rutgers's twenty-first president, a black scholar who is a specialist in African American history and an administrator of higher education. In an engaging lecture given in November 2016, historian Jonathan Holloway, then the Edmund S. Morgan Professor of African American Studies, History, and American Studies and the dean of Yale College, unknowingly addressed the students who had met with Chancellor Edwards in 2015. In a lecture titled "The Legacies of Jim Crow: Race, Recognition, and the Making of the Modern University," Holloway reflected on the benefits of history, and in doing so inadvertently endorsed the Scarlet and Black Project and the Rutgers students' demand to know the history of race at Rutgers University. Holloway opened his talk by musing about what happens when the unacknowledged become acknowledged. He asked: "What happens when things that were surrounding you all the time but that went unnoticed [are] finally noticed?"[6] He called this the "phenomenon of discovery," an occurrence that often gave way to "moments of convulsion" that were "potentially violent." In essence, Holloway, the black historian who was at one time also the chair of the interdisciplinary Yale Department of African American Studies, was validating Rutgers students' request to acknowledge the invisible history of Native and African Americans that heretofore had been unacknowledged but that with *Scarlet and Black* has begun to come into view. Indeed, *Scarlet and Black* has exposed men like Johannes Hardenbergh, Theodore Frelinghuysen, Philip and John Henry Livingston, Samuel B. How, James Neilson, and Henry Rutgers himself—men whose names grace the buildings and statues at Rutgers and the streets of New Brunswick—as white supremacists who profited from the labor and exploitation of black bodies.

As he did in his "Legacies of Jim Crow" lecture, Holloway argues that unveiling this more fully loaded history is, as James Baldwin said, "the price of the ticket."[7] It is the price that Rutgers and other universities must pay if they want to "pursue aspirations of supporting demographic complexity and inclusion." As Holloway reviewed the newly revealed histories of Georgetown and Brown Universities, institutions that had recently unveiled their own histories of the ways blacks had been sacrificed for the founding and survival of their respective universities, he argued that recognizing the history of all members of the university community—"learning their stories and valuing their contributions"—went a "long way toward meeting the price of the ticket." Acknowledging "the full and complex humanity that makes up our nation's campuses would be a down payment worth making," he said.[8]

President Holloway is not only fully appreciative of the history covered in *Scarlet and Black* but also of the path opened by the civil rights desegregation generation. The year that Vickie Donaldson spied Richard Roper and soon after met with a few other black students on Newark's campus to create the Black Organization of Students—1967—was the year Jonathan Holloway was born.[9] As he demonstrates in his book *Jim Crow Wisdom: Memory and Identity in Black America since 1940,* a personal memoir and intellectual history that spans the same period as this volume, Holloway knows that the desegregation generation made it possible for him to make a career and also thrive in the field of African American history.[10] He pays tribute to them for legitimating black studies, a field that was hardly on the margins in the year of his birth, but one that has since moved to the center of scholarly inquiry. His studies in black intellectual history, his passionate recounting of his parents' history, and his introspections about his race, class, gender, and color privilege have forced him to scrupulously think about "what happens when history is pushed aside in the faith that doing so would protect the future."[11]

Along with our new university president, we, the editors of *Scarlet and Black,* believe that we need to tell the stories of our past in order to preserve our present and secure a future. The students who met with Chancellor Edwards in 2015 asked for this research not as an end in itself but as a *precondition* to improving the racial and cultural climate at Rutgers. Today's petitioners are similarly insistent. As we complete this third volume, we are listening to citizens across America who understand that truth-telling about American and African American history is a foundation on which equality can be built. We see the volumes of *Scarlet and Black* and the digital archive that accompanies it[12] as a beginning, as the precondition for justice at Rutgers. We feel that these volumes have helped put Rutgers ahead of the curve in establishing a university that nurtures inclusiveness and practices fairness. We hope that Rutgers University uses this head start to complete what needs to be done to make this institution one that reconciles its past with present recuperative programs for African Americans. We expect that, in the courses and programs that it offers, the scholarships that it grants, the faculty that it hires, the admissions procedures that it endorses, and the environment that it fosters, Rutgers University can and will be a national example for making black lives matter.

ACKNOWLEDGMENTS

It is difficult to put into words the gratitude we have for all of the hard work that the members of the Rutgers community put into the Scarlet and Black Project. It has been more than successful—it has become a model for universities that study their relationship to slavery, to African Americans, and to other underrepresented minorities. We cannot overstate how important it is to have university faculty, administrators, and staff who "have our backs," so much so that when we are asked to share our knowledge about how to do this work, we never fail to stress the importance of foundational support.

We continue to thank former chancellor Richard Edwards for his foresight in initiating this project. He listened and responded positively to the disheartened students who visited him in 2015. Former vice president for academic affairs Karen Stubaus ensured that the initial funds were available to carry out Edwards's vision. Christopher Malloy, the current chancellor of Rutgers University–New Brunswick, and Felicia McGinty, the executive vice chancellor for administration and planning, have been unwavering in their support, even through the fiscal difficulties brought by the coronavirus pandemic. Our research about Douglass College was enabled by Jacquelyn Litt, the dean of Douglass Residential College, and Valerie Anderson, the executive director of the Associate Alumnae of Douglass College. Peter March, the executive dean of the School of Arts and Sciences, always supported our requests, as did Michelle Stephens, the former dean of Humanities at Rutgers University–New Brunswick.

We cannot say enough about the support we have received from the librarians of Rutgers University. Erika Gorder, the interim university archivist, has been our steadfast cheerleader and reliable support person throughout the writing of all three volumes of *Scarlet and Black*. Her genuine love of the project has been palpable. Always willing to go above and beyond our requests, she continues to be an indispensable member of the project's digital archive team.

We would also like to thank her student assistant, Stephen Dalina, whose work locating and scanning this volume's illustrations helped us to finish in a timely manner. We also thank Kate Rizzi, assistant director of the Rutgers Oral History Archive, who worked closely with our researchers and made the project's original oral histories available to the broader public.

We also extend our gratitude and thanks to Dr. Alexandria Russell, the project's postdoctoral associate. Alexandria joined our team as we were finishing up volume 2 and starting the writing of volume 3. One would never know that she came late to the project, so exceptional is her expertise and professionalism. Her work on the edited volumes and the digital archive has been magnificent. We really could not have finished this last volume without her.

The same goes for Dr. Jesse Bayker. A recent Rutgers alum and contributor to volume 1, Jesse joined our team as its digital archivist, and along with Alexandria is creating the Scarlet and Black web archive. His research and writing were critical to completing this volume, and his and Alexandria's ongoing work on the digital archive will continue to make this project relevant.

We also would like to thank the staff of the History Department. Rutgers's bureaucratic structure is, to say the least, challenging. And yet our staff handles the ever-changing procedures and the endless paperwork with aplomb. We are forever in debt to Tiffany Berg, the department's former business manager, who has been crucial in helping us manage the different parts of the project.

We would be remiss if we did not thank Anne Rogers, an independent editor who added consistency and polish to the manuscript, and Director Peter Mickulas and Executive Editor Micah Kleit of Rutgers University Press for their willingness to put this on the press's front burner. We, and Rutgers, are in their debt.

This book is dedicated to our late colleague Cheryl A. Wall, the Board of Governors Zora Neale Hurston Professor of English. A booster and unofficial advisor to the Scarlet and Black Project, she was personally committed to transforming Rutgers into the multicultural universe it boasts of today. Rutgers is forever in her debt for her willingness to say yes to all the calls for her service. In her research and writing, leadership and pedagogy she was a model of excellence. Elegance was her middle name.

NOTES

INTRODUCTION

1. "Conklin Hall Liberation 50th Anniversary Panel Discussion," March 13, 2019, Rutgers University–Newark, YouTube video, 48.14, https://www.youtube.com/watch?v=Vl-pCnl1EnI.

2. "Reflections on the Emergence of the Black Organization of Students (BOS)," *1969 Liberation of Conklin Hall: 40th Anniversary Commemorative Journal*, February 14, 2009, 14, https://web.archive.org/web/20160910161504/http://stream.newark.rutgers.edu/~danadml/conklin/documents/Conklin_Prog_Book09_FNL_R-1.pdf.

3. Katie Reilly, "Read President Obama's Commencement Address at Rutgers University," *Time*, June 2, 2016, https://time.com/4340310/barack-obama-commencement-address-transcript-rutgers/.

4. Rutgers–Newark Athletics, "Rutgers–Newark Tabbed 'Most Diverse' by Best Value Colleges," *News*, June 13, 2018, https://rutgersnewarkathletics.com/news/2018/6/13/baseball-rutgers-newark-tabbed-most-diverse-by-best-value-colleges.aspx; "Rutgers–Newark Ranked No. 1 in Ethnic Diversity by *U.S. News and World Report*," *Rutgers Today*, September 12, 2012, https://www.rutgers.edu/news/rutgers-newark-ranked-no-1-ethnic-diversity-us-news-and-world-report.

5. Martha Biondi, *The Black Revolution on Campus* (Berkeley: University of California Press, 2012); Ibram H. Rogers [Ibram X. Kendi], *The Black Campus Movement: Black Students and the Racial Reconstitution of Higher Education, 1965–1972* (New York: Palgrave Macmillan), 2012.

6. Although historians have recently accepted the idea of the "long civil rights movement," which dates the black freedom struggle from the early twentieth century through the 1970s, the use of the term *midcentury freedom struggle* here denotes the "classic civil rights movement" and the Black Power phases of the twentieth-century freedom movement that began shortly after the end of World War II. On the long civil rights movement, see Jacquelyn Dowd Hall, "The Long Civil Rights Movement and the Political Uses of the Past," *Journal of American History* 91, no. 4 (2005): 1233–1263.

7. Marisa J. Fuentes and Deborah Gray White, eds., *Scarlet and Black, Volume 1: Slavery and Dispossession in Rutgers History* (New Brunswick, NJ: Rutgers University Press, 2016); Kendra Boyd, Marisa J. Fuentes, and Deborah Gray White, eds., *Scarlet and Black, Volume 2: Constructing Race and Gender at Rutgers, 1865–1945* (New Brunswick, NJ: Rutgers University Press, 2020).

8. "Reflections on the Emergence of the Black Organization of Students (BOS)," 14.

9. Rogers [Kendi], *Black Campus Movement*, 11, 22.

10. Biondi, *Black Revolution on Campus*, 2–3.

11. Rogers [Kendi], *Black Campus Movement*, 2.

12. Biondi, *Black Revolution on Campus*, 3.

13. Rogers [Kendi], *Black Campus Movement*, 24.

14. Richard P. McCormick, *The Black Student Protest Movement at Rutgers* (New Brunswick, NJ: Rutgers University Press, 1990), 7, 93; Biondi, *Black Revolution on Campus*, 4.

15. Rogers [Kendi], *Black Campus Movement*, 84.

16. McCormick, *Black Student Protest Movement at Rutgers*, 17–18.

17. Ibid., 82.

18. Paul G.E. Clemens, *Rutgers since 1945: A History of the State University of New Jersey* (New Brunswick, NJ: Rutgers University Press, 2015), 175.

19. Ibid., 180.

20. Biondi, *Black Revolution on Campus*, 5; McCormick, *Black Student Protest Movement at Rutgers*, 20.

21. McCormick, *Black Student Protest Movement at Rutgers*, 20.

22. "Conklin Hall Liberation 50th Anniversary Panel Discussion," March 13, 2019.

23. Robert Curvin, *Inside Newark: Decline, Rebellion, and the Search for Transformation* (New Brunswick, NJ: Rutgers University Press, 2014), 100.

24. "Reflections on the Emergence of the Black Organization of Students (BOS)," 14.

25. McCormick, *Black Student Protest Movement at Rutgers*, 61; Howard Gillette Jr., *Camden after the Fall: Decline and Renewal in a Post-Industrial City* (Philadelphia: University of Pennsylvania Press, 2005), 77–79.

26. Other studies of Rutgers University that readers will benefit from include Clemens, *Rutgers since 1945*; Kayo Denda, Mary Hawkesworth, and Fernanda Perrone, *The Douglass Century: Transformation of the Women's College at Rutgers University* (New Brunswick, NJ: Rutgers University Press, 2018); McCormick, *Black Student Protest Movement at Rutgers*.

27. A digital archive has been created and will be continuously updated; see the Scarlet and Black Project Digital Archive, Rutgers University, http://www.scarletandblack project.com/archive/.

PART I: Prelude to Change

1. "African-American Students at Rutgers in the 1960s—Part 1: Black Student Life at Rutgers College and Douglass College, 1961–1965," presentation at Black on the Banks Conference, Rutgers University, November 6–7, 2015, YouTube video, 1:45.32, https://www.youtube.com/watch?v=Vi271ZZM6MQ; "Alone Together," *Rutgers Magazine: The Magazine for Alumni and Friends of The State University of New Jersey* (Winter 2016), https://ucmweb.rutgers.edu/magazine/1419archive/features/alone-together .html.

2. Ibid.

3. Ibid.; see also Richard P. McCormick, *The Black Student Protest Movement at Rutgers* (New Brunswick, NJ: Rutgers University Press, 1990), 18.

4. See this volume's introduction for more about Donaldson and Roper.

5. Kendra Boyd, Marisa Fuentes, and Deborah Gray White, eds., *Scarlet and Black, Volume 2: Constructing Race and Gender at Rutgers, 1865–1945* (New Brunswick, NJ: Rutgers University Press, 2020), ch. 3 and 4, 72–131.

CHAPTER 1: Twenty-Twenty Vision

1. Martha Biondi, *The Black Revolution on Campus* (Berkeley: University of California Press, 2012), 13.

2. Richard P. McCormick, *The Black Student Protest Movement at Rutgers* (New Brunswick, NJ: Rutgers University Press, 1990).

3. Olga Jiménez de Wagenheim, "From Aguada to Dover: Puerto Ricans Rebuild Their World in Morris County, New Jersey, 1948 to 2000," in Carmen Teresa Whalen and Víctor Vázquez-Hernández, eds., *The Puerto Rican Diaspora: Historical Perspectives* (Philadelphia: Temple University Press, 2005), 107.

4. Paul G.E. Clemens, *Rutgers since 1945: A History of the State University of New Jersey* (New Brunswick, NJ: Rutgers University Press, 2015), 172–173; Wagenheim, "From Aguada to Dover," 107.

5. Clemens, *Rutgers since 1945*, 172–173.

6. Olga Wagenheim, Thomas Mathews, and Kal Wagenheim, "Puerto Rico," *Encyclopedia Britannica*, 2019.

7. Juan Gonzalez, *Harvest of Empire: A History of Latinos in America*, rev. ed. (New York: Penguin Books, 2011), 81–96.

8. Howard Gillette Jr., *Camden after the Fall: Decline and Renewal in a Post-Industrial City* (Philadelphia: University of Pennsylvania Press, 2005), 56.

9. Wagenheim, "From Aguada to Dover," 108.

10. Ibid., 110.

11. Ibid., 114.

12. Ibid., 117.

13. David Listokin, Dorothea Berkhout, and James Hughes, *New Brunswick, New Jersey: The Decline and Revitalization of Urban America* (New Brunswick, NJ: Rutgers University Press), 2016), 54–55.

14. Gillette, *Camden after the Fall*, 53.

15. Thomas J. Sugrue, *Sweet Land of Liberty: The Forgotten Struggle for Civil Rights in the North* (New York: Random House, 2008), 265.

16. Ibid.

17. Alice Jennings Archibald Oral History Interview, March 14, 1997, by G. Kurt Piehler and Eve Snyder, 7, Rutgers Oral History Archives, https://oralhistory.rutgers.edu/interviewees/750-archibald-alice-jennings.

18. Ibid.

19. Sugrue, *Sweet Land of Liberty*, 161, 179.

20. Robert Curvin, *Inside Newark: Decline, Rebellion, and the Search for Transformation* (New Brunswick, NJ: Rutgers University Press, 2014), 61–62.

21. Karen Bodkin Sacks, "How Did Jews Become White Folks?," in Steven Gregory and Robert Sanjek, eds., *Race* (New Brunswick, NJ: Rutgers University Press, 1994), 89–99.

22. Ira Katznelson, *When Affirmative Action Was White: An Untold History of Racial Inequality in Twentieth-Century America* (New York: W.W. Norton, 2005), 129–132.

23. Ibid.

24. Ibid., 132.

25. Clemens, *Rutgers since 1945*, 6, 9–10, 103.

26. Ibid., 103–105.

27. *Scarlet Letter, Class of 1947*, Rutgers University–New Brunswick, NJ, 1947, Inventory to the Rutgers University Yearbook Collection, 1871–2005, Special Collections and University Archives, Rutgers University Libraries, Rutgers University (hereafter SCUA, RUL).

28. Brendan Lynch, "Affirmative Action for the Few, Not the Many: The History of the G.I. Bill and African American Veterans at Rutgers University," unpublished undergraduate research seminar paper, Rutgers University, Spring 2018, Professor Deborah Gray White.

29. McCormick, *Black Student Protest Movement at Rutgers*, 6–7.

30. Katznelson, *When Affirmative Action Was White*, 130.

31. McCormick, *Black Protest Movement at Rutgers*, 6–7.

32. Kendra Boyd, Marisa J. Fuentes, and Deborah Gray White, eds., *Scarlet and Black, Volume 2: Constructing Race and Gender at Rutgers, 1865–1945*, table 3.1, "African American Students at Rutgers, 1888–1943," 104–105.

33. McCormick, *Black Protest Movement at Rutgers*, 7, 47, 56.

34. Ibid., 34.

35. For information about black students who matriculated at Rutgers–New Brunswick and Douglass College, see Boyd et al., *Scarlet and Black, Volume 2*.

36. *Mneme*, 1954, "Bound Together," 1, 13, Rutgers University College of South Jersey, Camden, NJ, SCUA, RUL.

37. The demographic information of students of color from 1952 to 1975 was collected using a visual survey and biographical information.

38. *Mneme*, 1954, "Bound Together," 1, 13.

39. *Mneme*, 1953, "Graduating Class of 1953," Rutgers University College of South Jersey, Camden, NJ, SCUA, RUL.

40. *Mneme*, 1958, "Graduating Class of 1958," Rutgers University College of South Jersey, Camden, NJ, SCUA, RUL.

41. *Mneme*, 1953, "Esther Mae Gee," 14, Rutgers University College of South Jersey, Camden, NJ, SCUA, RUL.

42. Ibid., 33.

43. *Mneme*, 1952–1959, "Graduating Class of 195[–]," Rutgers University College of South Jersey, Camden, NJ, SCUA, RUL.

44. *Mneme*, 1954, "Graduating Class of 1954," 11–22, Rutgers University College of South Jersey, Camden, NJ, SCUA, RUL.

45. *Mneme*, 1958, "Graduating Class of 1958."

46. *Mneme*, 1960–1969, "Graduating Class of 196[–]," Rutgers University College of South Jersey, Camden, NJ, SCUA, RUL.

47. *Mneme*, 1960–1969, "Greeks," Rutgers University College of South Jersey, Camden, NJ, SCUA, RUL. Information on Sigma Epsilon Phi found on the chapter's Facebook page, where they note the original history of the chapter: https://www.facebook.com/pg/ructep/about/.

48. History of Omega Psi Phi at the Rutgers University College of South Jersey found on the graduate chapter's website: https://divinemedia.wixsite.com/chiupsilonques /chapter-officers.

49. History of Delta Sigma Theta, Theta Chi chapter: https://stockton.campuslabs.com /engage/organization/deltas.

50. *Mneme,* 1978, "LASO: Latin American Student Organization," Rutgers University College of South Jersey, Camden, NJ, SCUA, RUL.

51. *Mneme,* 1956, "William K.C. Chen," 6, Rutgers University College of South Jersey, Camden, NJ, SCUA, RUL.

52. See essays in part 2 of this volume.

53. *Mneme,* 1956–1970, "Administration and Faculty," Rutgers University College of South Jersey, Camden, NJ, SCUA, RUL.

54. Rick Rojas and Khorri Atkinson, "Five Days of Unrest That Shaped, and Haunted, Newark," *New York Times,* July 11, 2017, https://www.nytimes.com/2017/07/11/nyregion /newark-riots-50-years.html.

55. Ibid.

56. Thomas J. Sugrue and Andrew M. Goodman, "Plainfield Burning: Black Rebellion in the Suburban North," *Journal of Urban History* 33 (May 2007): 568–601.

57. Chris Rasmussen, "Recalling the 1967 New Brunswick Protests," *My Central Jersey,* July 14, 2017, https://www.mycentraljersey.com/story/news/history/new-jersey/2017 /07/14/recalling-1967-new-brunswick-protests/428509001/.

58. Ibid.

59. Gillette, *Camden after the Fall,* 43–44.

60. Lizabeth Cohen, *A Consumers' Republic: The Politics of Mass Consumption in Postwar America* (New York: Random House, 2003), 171.

61. Gillette, *Camden after the Fall,* 65–94.

62. Ibid, 17–61.

63. Ibid., 60.

64. Ibid.

65. Ibid., 61.

66. Ibid.

CHAPTER 2: Rutgers and New Brunswick

1. Alice Jennings Archibald, Oral History Interview, March 14, 1997, by G. Kurt Piehler and Eve Snyder, 26–27, Rutgers Oral History Archives, https://oralhistory.rutgers. edu/interviewees/750-archibald-alice-jennings.

2. Alice Jennings Archibald, "What the Negro Wants," Letter to the *Daily Home News* Editor, June 23, 1942, People file A, New Brunswick Free Public Library, New Brunswick, NJ.

3. As a result of the 1964 Civil Rights Act and the 1965 Voting Rights Act.

4. Patricia Sheehan, interview with author, Pamela Walker, August 17, 2018.

5. Ibid.

6. Chris Rasmussen, "'Web of Tension': The 1967 Protests in New Brunswick, New Jersey," *Journal of Urban History* 40, no. 1 (2014): 141.

7. Walter H. Waggoner, "A Woman Mayor Chosen in Jersey," *New York Times,* May 10, 1967, https://timesmachine.nytimes.com/timesmachine/1967/05/10/90586544.pdf.

8. Patricia Sheehan, interview.

9. Waggoner, "Woman Mayor Chosen in Jersey."

10. Patricia Sheehan, interview.

11. Reginald Kavanaugh, "Violence Hits New Brunswick," *Daily Home News* (New Brunswick, NJ), July 18, 1967.

12. "Trouble in New Brunswick," *New York Times,* July 18, 1967.

13. Kavanaugh, "Violence Hits New Brunswick."

14. Patricia Sheehan, interview.

15. Kavanaugh, "Violence Hits New Brunswick."

16. *Report of the National Advisory Commission on Civil Disorders,* March 1968, 3. The Kerner Commission was established by President Lyndon B. Johnson on July 28, 1967.

17. These two interviewees asked to remain anonymous.

18. "Annette Robinson" and "Cynthia Flowers," interview with author, Pamela Walker, November 28, 2018.

19. "July 18, 1967: 'The Night They Gave the City Away,'" *Daily Home News* (New Brunswick, NJ), May 18, 1969.

20. See the essays in part 2 of this volume.

21. Harvey Fisher, "Citizens' Group Presents Demands," *Daily Home News* (New Brunswick, NJ), March 14, 1969, 1.

22. "Chief Suspends Officer," *Daily Home News* (New Brunswick, NJ), March 14, 1969, 1; "8 Black Policemen Resign in Protest," *Daily Home News* (New Brunswick, NJ), March 15, 1967, 1.

23. "8 Black Policemen Resign in Protest," 1.

24. Richard J.H. Johnston, "Black Rampage in Jersey School," *New York Times,* March 19, 1969.

25. John Pribish, "Cops Tell Angry Youth: 'Cool It,'" *Daily Home News* (New Brunswick, NJ), March 19, 1969.

26. Richard J.H. Johnston, "New Brunswick Presses Search for a School Peace Formula," *New York Times,* March 20, 1969, 31.

27. Dick Rothschild, "City Adding Courses for Minority Pupils," *Daily Home News* (New Brunswick, NJ), June 21, 1972, 31.

28. Patricia Sheehan, interview; Rasmussen, "'Web of Tension,'" 149.

29. Patricia Sheehan, interview; Rasmussen, "'Web of Tension,'" 150.

30. Chris Rasmussen, "Creating Segregation in the Era of Integration: School Consolidation and Local Control in New Brunswick, New Jersey, 1965–1976," *History of Education Quarterly* 57, no. 4 (2017): 511. The Nyerere school was one effort in this regard. The Nyerere Education Institute was a short-lived, independent black school, the first of its kind in New Brunswick, that centered black experience and black cultural pride for children ages three through nine. Through the late 1970s and 1980s, it struggled financially before finally closing its doors in 1995.

31. Ibid.

32. Ibid., 511–512.

33. Rasmussen notes that with the transition of Aldrage Cooper out of public office into the private sector and the demise of the Community House, which had been the hub for black activism, there were fewer opportunities in local government and through mobilization for the realization of black community control of schools; ibid., 513.

34. David Listokin, Dorothea Berkhout, and James W. Hughes, *New Brunswick, New Jersey: The Decline and Revitalization of Urban America* (New Brunswick, NJ: Rutgers University Press, 2016), 88.

35. "Annette Robinson" and "Cynthia Flowers," interview with author, Pamela Walker, November 28, 2018.

36. Ibid.

37. Listokin et al., *New Brunswick, New Jersey*, 52.

38. "Women—Ogling the Oglers," *AYCE*, August 27, 1971.

39. *AYCE*, November 1970.

40. "Freebie," *AYCE*, November 1970.

41. Liberation News Service (LNS) was a national newswire deeply embedded in New Left media culture. Like services such as the Associated Press, LNS reporting was distributed around the country to be reprinted in journals, many of them alternative newspapers like *AYCE*.

42. For example, "The 3 R's: ROTC, Rutgers, Repression," a two-page spread in *AYCE*'s spring edition, 1972.

43. "J&J's the Name, and Profits the Game!," a two-page spread in *AYCE*'s spring edition, 1972.

44. "Asserting Independence," *AYCE*, Spring 1972.

45. "8 pg. High School Supplement," *AYCE*, November 1972.

46. "Going Through School Female," *AYCE*, November 1972.

47. See *AYCE*, May 1972.

48. "It Must Be Changed," *AYCE*, March 26, 1971.

CHAPTER 3: "Tell It Like It Is"

1. "University Notebook," *Rutgers Faculty Newsletter*, October 1963, 5, Special Collections and University Archives, Rutgers University–New Brunswick (hereafter SCUA, RUNB).

2. Ibid.

3. Ibid.

4. Ibid.

5. Richard P. McCormick, *The Black Student Protest Movement at Rutgers* (New Brunswick, NJ: Rutgers University Press, 1990), 13.

6. As recounted in "Introducing—A New Venture," *Rutgers Faculty Newsletter*, September 8, 1967, 1, SCUA, RUNB.

7. Gaynor Pearson and Willard Thompson, "Veterans and Professors," *Rutgers Faculty Newsletter*, November 1945, 50, SCUA, RUNB.

8. Ibid.

9. "Oath of Allegiance," *Rutgers Faculty Newsletter*, April 1949, 220, SCUA, RUNB; "Oath of Allegiance," *Rutgers Faculty Newsletter*, July 1949, SCUA, RUNB.

10. "Report of Committee on Academic Freedom," *Rutgers Faculty Newsletter,* March 1951, 357, SCUA, RUNB.

11. Ibid., 358.

12. Ibid., 358–359.

13. "President Clothier's Statement to the Board of Trustees January 19, 1951," *Rutgers Faculty Newsletter,* January–February 1951, 347–352, SCUA, RUNB.

14. Simeon Moss Oral History Interview, May 2, 1997, by G. Kurt Piehler, Sandra Stewart Holyoak, and Melanie Cooper, 45, Rutgers Oral History Archives, https://oralhistory .rutgers.edu/interviewees/1133-moss-simeon.

15. "President Clothier's Statement," 348.

16. Ibid.

17. Ibid., 349, 348.

18. Ibid., 349.

19. See Mary Dudziak, *Cold War Civil Rights: Race and the Image of American Democracy* (Princeton, NJ: Princeton University Press, 2011).

20. William Neal Brown Oral History Interview, February 25, 2005, by Shaun Illingworth, Allison Mueller, and Fernando Palma, 5, Rutgers Oral History Archives, https://oral history.rutgers.edu/interviewees/835-brown-william-neal.

21. Ibid., 23.

22. Ibid.; Ken Branson, "For William Neal Brown, the Full Circle of a Full Life," *Rutgers Today,* August 27, 2009, https://news.rutgers.edu/feature-focus/william-neal-brown-full-circle-full-life/20090827#.XQp_qOhKhPY.

23. William Neal Brown Oral History Interview, 23.

24. "University Notebook," *Rutgers Faculty Newsletter,* October 1960, 5, SCUA, RUNB.

25. Thomas Emerson and David Haber, "The Scopes Case in Modern Dress," *University of Chicago Law Review* 27, no. 3 (1960): 522–528.

26. Peter Simmons, "In Memoriam: David Haber," *Rutgers Law Media,* January 8, 2019, https://law.rutgers.edu/news/memoriam-professor-david-haber.

27. William Neal Brown Oral History Interview, 26.

28. Ibram H. Rogers [Ibram X. Kendi], "'People All Over the World Are Supporting You': Malcolm X, Ideological Formations, and Black Student Activism, 1960–1972," *Journal of African American History* 96, no. 1 (2011): 17–23.

29. Donald Harris Oral History Interview, February 28, 2013, by Shaun Illingworth, 23–25, Rutgers Oral History Archives, https://oralhistory.rutgers.edu/interviewees /1861-harris-donald; William Neal Brown Oral History Interview, 25–27.

30. William Neal Brown Oral History Interview, 25–27.

31. Rutgers School of Social Work, "2018 William Neal Brown Endowed Lecture Introduction," YouTube Video, 1:36, June 2018, https://www.youtube.com/watch?v=yML xaAofpRE.

32. Langston Hughes, "I, Too," in Arnold L. Rampersad and David Roessel, eds., *The Collected Poems of Langston Hughes* (New York: Vintage Classics, 1994), 46.

33. Quoted in Rogers [Kendi], "'People All Over the World Are Supporting You,'" 19.

34. "University Notebook," *Rutgers Faculty Newsletter,* December 1963, 5, SCUA, RUNB.

35. "University Notebook," *Rutgers Faculty Newsletter,* January 1964, 8, SCUA, RUNB.

36. "University Notebook," *Rutgers Faculty Newsletter,* February 1964, 4, SCUA, RUNB.

37. Jay Sigler, "Harry Hersh Schapiro," *PS: Political Science and Politics* 14, no. 1 (Winter 1981): 137.

38. "University Notebook," *Rutgers Faculty Newsletter,* March 1964, 7, SCUA, RUNB.

39. Stokely Carmichael and Charles V. Hamilton, *Black Power: The Politics of Liberation in America* (New York: Vintage Books, 1967), x, vii.

40. Ibid., x.

41. Ibid., viii.

42. Charles Hamilton, "A Conversation with Charles Hamilton," interview by Fredrick C. Harris, *Annual Review of Political Science,* May 2018, video, 40:42, https://www.annual-reviews.org/doi/full/10.1146/annurev-polisci-090117-120451.

43. The exact timeline for Hamilton's tenure at Rutgers is unclear. Sometime between his graduation from the University of Chicago in 1964 and employment at Lincoln University in 1966, Hamilton worked at Rutgers.

44. Hamilton, "Conversation with Charles Hamilton."

45. Carmichael and Hamilton, *Black Power,* xi–xii.

46. Hamilton, "Conversation with Charles Hamilton."

47. Ibid.

48. Ibid.

49. "University Notebook," *Rutgers Faculty Newsletter,* November–December 1966, 6, SCUA, RUNB.

50. Stanley Elkins, *Slavery: A Problem in American Institutional and Intellectual Life* (Chicago: University of Chicago Press, 1959).

51. Eugene Genovese, *Roll, Jordan, Roll: The World the Slaves Made* (New York: Pantheon, 1974), 5.

52. Ibid.

53. Ibid., 598.

54. Among other interventions, White debunked Genovese's ideas about the Mammy figure, a stereotype that restricted enslaved black women to the role of a jovial domestic "who identified more with her master than her fellow slaves"; see Deborah Gray White, *Ar'n't I a Woman: Female Slaves in the Plantation South* (New York: W.W. Norton, 1985), 54–56. In *They Were Her Property*, Jones-Rogers undermined Genovese's thesis that white women did not own enslaved blacks, and that they mediated, as opposed to endorsed, the violence African Americans suffered at the hands of male slaveholders; see Stephanie Jones-Rogers, *They Were Her Property: White Women as Slave Owners* (New Haven, CT: Yale University Press, 2019).

55. "Introducing—A New Venture," *Rutgers Newsletter,* September 8, 1967, 2, SCUA, RUNB.

56. Ibid.

57. George Sternlieb, "Suggests Home Ownership as Key to Riot Prevention," *Rutgers Newsletter,* September 22, 1967, 2, SCUA, RUNB.

58. Ibid.

59. Ibid.

60. Ibid.

61. Malcolm Talbott, "Universities Must Confront Challenge of Urban Ills," *Rutgers Newsletter,* March 8, 1968, SCUA, RUNB.

62. Ibid.

63. Ibid.

64. Ibid.

65. "TELL IT LIKE IT IS," *Rutgers Newsletter,* November 3, 1967, SCUA, RUNB.

66. "Chronology," n.d., box 33, folder 8 (RG 04/A16), Inventory to the Records of the Rutgers University Office of the President (Mason Welch Gross), 1936, 1945–1971, Special Collections and University Archives, Rutgers University Libraries (hereafter Records of the Office of President Mason Gross, SCUA, RUL); "Urban University Program," n.d., box 114, folder 8, Records of the Office of President Mason Gross, SCUA, RUL.

67. "Statement of the University Committee on Equal Opportunity," February 27, 1968, box 114, folder 8, Records of the Office of President Mason Gross, SCUA, RUL.

68. "Livingston Sets Minority Group Policy," *Rutgers Newsletter,* March 8, 1968, 1, SCUA, RUNB.

69. "Camden's SPEND Submits 'White Papers,'" *Rutgers Newsletter,* March 29, 1968, 6, SCUA, RUNB.

70. Jay Sigler, "To the Editor," *Rutgers Newsletter,* January 12, 1968, 2, SCUA, RUNB.

71. Ibid.

72. Ibid.

73. H.R. Kells, "Lack of Educational Chances for Disadvantaged Deplored," *Rutgers Newsletter,* April 12, 1968, 2, SCUA, RUNB.

74. "Chronology," n.d., box 33, folder 8, Records of the Office of President Mason Gross, SCUA, RUL; "List of Grievances and Demands from Black Organization of Students to Rutgers Board of Governors," April 19, 1968, box 21, folder 6, Records of the Office of President Mason Gross, SCUA, RUL.

75. "Letter from Charles H. Brower to Richard Schlatter," April 23, 1968, box 21, folder 6, Records of the Office of President Mason Gross, SCUA, RUL.

76. Rutgers University honored Robeson's legacy in 2019, the one-hundredth-year anniversary of his graduation, by dedicating a campus plaza in his name and calling him "one of the university's most distinguished alumni"; Rutgers University, "Paul Robeson Centennial Celebration," 2020, https://www.rutgers.edu/alumni/paul -robeson-100th-anniversary.

77. "Letter from Charles H. Brower to Richard Schlatter," April 23, 1968.

78. "Press Release from Rutgers News Service," May 21, 1968, box 21, folder 6, Records of the Office of President Mason Gross, SCUA, RUL.

79. Ibid.

80. "Draft Statement by Mason Gross on Martin Luther King, Jr. Assassination," April 5, 1968, box 21, folder 6, Records of the Office of President Mason Gross, SCUA, RUL.

81. "Statement from Rutgers College Student Council Executive Committee Signed by Student Body President Omer Brown," April 8, 1968, box 21, folder 6, Records of the Office of President Mason Gross, SCUA, RUL.

82. Ibid.

83. "The Rutgers College Student Council Minutes for Special Meeting," April 7, 1968, box 21, folder 6, Records of the Office of President Mason Gross, SCUA, RUL.

84. Martha Biondi, *The Black Revolution on Campus* (Berkeley: University of California Press, 2012); Paul G.E. Clemens, *Rutgers since 1945: A History of the State University of*

New Jersey (New Brunswick, NJ: Rutgers University Press, 2015); Gerard J. De Groot, *Student Protest: Sixties and After* (New York: Longman, 1998); David E. Lavin, Richard D. Alba, and Richard A. Silberstein, *Right versus Privilege: The Open-Admissions Experiment at the City University of New York* (New York: Free Press/Collier Macmillan, 1981); Ibram H. Rogers [Ibram X. Kendi], "The Black Campus Movement and the Institutionalization of Black Studies, 1965–1970," *Journal of African American Studies* 16, no. 1 (2012): 21–40; Ibram H. Rogers [Ibram X. Kendi], *The Black Campus Movement: Black Students and the Racial Reconstitution of Higher Education, 1965–1972* (New York: Palgrave Macmillan, 2012).

85. "Statement from White Students of Douglass College on Assassination of Martin Luther King, Jr.," n.d., box 21, folder 6, Records of the Office of President Mason Gross, SCUA, RUL.

86. Ibid.

87. "Summary of Progress for Rutgers Equal Opportunity Programs," April 1969, box 114, folder 8, Records of the Office of President Mason Gross, SCUA, RUL.

88. "Rutgers Seeks Ties with Negro Institution," *Rutgers Newsletter,* February 9, 1968, 1, SCUA, RUNB.

89. "University Plans Cooperative Program with North Carolina, Other Schools," *Rutgers Newsletter,* November 8, 1968, 1, SCUA, RUNB.

90. "Recruitment Drive for Negro Faculty Begins to Show Measurable Results," *Rutgers Newsletter,* March 8, 1968, 1, 3, SCUA, RUL.

91. "John R. Martin Named to Post," *Rutgers Newsletter,* May 24, 1968, 3, SCUA, RUNB.

92. "Graduate Education Sponsors Visits by King Scholars," *Rutgers Newsletter,* October 11, 1968, 1, 6, SCUA, RUNB; "Dr. Proctor Joins Education Faculty," *Rutgers Newsletter,* April 4, 1969, 3, SCUA, RUNB.

93. Rosemary Park, "When Rational Discourse Fails, Universities Fall," *Rutgers Newsletter,* April 26, 1968, 2, SCUA, RUNB.

94. Ibid.

95. Milton Schwebel, "Faculty Fears of Student Power Stem from Deep Roots," *Rutgers Newsletter,* November 8, 1968, 2, SCUA, RUNB.

96. Richard Poirier, "Constant Change Required to Meet Anguish of Young," *Rutgers Newsletter,* October 25, 1968, 2, SCUA, RUNB.

97. Ibid.

98. Ibid.

99. "'Black Caucus' Resolutions Startle Forum on Cause of Civil Disorders," *Rutgers Newsletter,* April 26, 1968, 2, 6, SCUA, RUNB.

100. Ibid., 6.

101. "Rutgers Opens Doors to 150 Disadvantaged Students," *Rutgers Newsletter,* May 24, 1968, 1, SCUA, RUNB.

102. "Rutgers College Begins to Study Suggestions in Susman Report," *Rutgers Newsletter,* November 22, 1968, 1, 4, SCUA, RUNB.

103. "A Report to the New Jersey Legislature Concerning the Recent Events and Disturbances at the Newark and Camden Campuses of Rutgers, the State University," prepared by Chancellor of the State Board of Higher Education Ralph A. Dungan, March 31, 1969, http://stream.newark.rutgers.edu/~danadml/conklin/documents/Report%20to%20the%20NJ%20Legislature_4a.pdf.

104. Harry C. Bredemeier, "Academic Values Face New, Unseen Dangers," *Rutgers Newsletter,* November 22, 1968, 2, SCUA, RUNB.

105. Ibid.

106. Ibid.

107. George Sternlieb, "Who Are the Disadvantaged? No Easy Answer," *Rutgers Newsletter,* December 20, 1968, 2, SCUA, RUNB.

108. Ibid.

109. Arnold Grobman, "Doubts Worth of Separate Black Studies," *Rutgers Newsletter,* December 20, 3, SCUA, RUNB.

110. Ibid.

111. Malcolm Talbott, "Urban Problems Can't Be Ignored," *Rutgers Newsletter,* February 14, 1969, 2, 4, SCUA, RUNB.

112. Ibid.

113. "Admission Demands of the Black Organization of Students at Rutgers–Newark," box 33, folder 9, Records of the Office of President Mason Gross, SCUA, RUL.

114. "Chronology," n.d., box 33, folder 8, Records of the Office of President Mason Gross, SCUA, RUL.

115. Ibid.

116. "The Liberation of Conklin Hall," Rutgers University Libraries, http://stream.newark .rutgers.edu/~danadml/conklin/Page400.html.

117. Richard P. McCormick, *The Black Student Protest Movement at Rutgers* (New Brunswick, NJ: Rutgers University Press, 1990).

118. "Chronology"; "The Liberation of Conklin Hall."

119. "Chronology."

120. Ibid.

121. "Rutgers University, the State University of New Jersey Urban University Program," n.d., box 114, folder 8, Records of the Office of President Mason Gross, SCUA, RUL.

122. Ibid.

123. "History of the Educational Opportunity Fund," n.d., State of New Jersey, Office of Higher Education, https://www.nj.gov/highereducation/EOF/EOF_History.shtml.

124. Mason Gross, interview by Frank McGee, *Frank McGee Sunday Report,* NBC, May 11, 1969; "Statement by Malcolm Talbott in response to Black Organization of Students Demands," n.d., *The Conklin Hall Project, Inside the 1969 Liberation of Conklin Hall,* Digital Documents, Rutgers University Libraries, http://stream.newark.rutgers.edu /~danadml/conklin/documents/Statement%20by%20Malcolm%20D.Talbott_1.pdf.

125. "Statement by the Members of the Newark College of Arts and Sciences Faculty," n.d., box 33, folder 9, Records of the Office of President Mason Gross, SCUA, RUL.

126. Ibid.

127. "Meeting of Douglass College Faculty," February 28, 1969, box 33, folder 7, Records of the Office of President Mason Gross, SCUA, RUL.

128. "Press Release," March 12, 1969, Rutgers News Service, box 33, folder 7, Records of the Office of President Mason Gross, SCUA, RUL.

129. "Press Release," March 17, 1969, Rutgers News Service, box 114, folder 8, Records of the Office of President Mason Gross, SCUA, RUL.

130. Rodney Carlisle, "Black Studies Seen as Valid Area of Academic Endeavor," *Rutgers Newsletter,* January 17, 1969, 2, 4, SCUA, RUNB.

131. Ibid.

132. Ibid.

133. Samuel DeWitt Proctor, "Education of Blacks Is a Shared Responsibility," *Rutgers Newsletter,* May 16, 1969, 2, 4, SCUA, RUNB.

134. Ibid.

135. Ibid.

136. Ibid.

137. Ibid.

138. "With Deliberate Speed: Rutgers Moving toward Expanded Program of Afro-American Studies," *Rutgers Newsletter,* December 5, 1969, 1, SCUA, RUNB.

139. Ibid.

140. Ibid.

141. "Letter from Lowell A. Douglas to Mason Gross," April 2, 1969, box 33, folder 7, Records of the Office of President Mason Gross, SCUA, RUL.

142. "Letter from Bernard Serin, Jean W. Day, Evelyn H. Wilson and Walter Bezanson to Colleagues," June 5, 1969, box 114, folder 9, Records of the Office of President Mason Gross, SCUA, RUL.

143. "Letter from Mason Gross to Rutgers College Faculty," June 25, 1969, box 33, folder 7, Records of the Office of President Mason Gross, SCUA, RUL.

144. "Report of Ad Hoc Committee Meeting on March 17, 1969," box 33, folder 7, Records of the Office of President Mason Gross, SCUA, RUL.

145. "Memo to Mason Gross and Charles Brower from Admissions Office Faculty and Work Study Students," February 28, 1969, box 33, folder 8, Records of the Office of President Mason Gross, SCUA, RUL.

146. "Report of Ad Hoc Committee Meeting on March 17, 1969."

147. "Letter from State Senator Alexander Matturri to Mason Gross," February 25, 1969, box 33, folder 7, Records of the Office of President Mason Gross, SCUA, RUL; "Letter from State Senator Edwin B. Forsythe to Robert C. Campbell," February 26, 1969, box 33, folder 7, Records of the Office of President Mason Gross, SCUA, RUL.

148. "Letter from State Senator Alexander Matturri to Mason Gross."

149. "Letter from State Senator Edwin B. Forsythe to Robert C. Campbell."

150. McCormick is the author of the seminal text on the era, *The Black Student Protest Movement at Rutgers,* cited earlier.

151. "Letter from Richard P. McCormick to Mason Gross," June 11, 1969, box 114, folder 9, Records of the Office of President Mason Gross, SCUA, RUL.

152. McCormick, *Black Student Protest Movement at Rutgers,* 85.

153. Clemens, *Rutgers since 1945.*

154. Thomas Frusciano and Benjamin Justice, "Rutgers History and Politics," in *Rutgers: A 250th Anniversary Portrait* (New Brunswick, NJ: Rutgers University Press, 2015), 61–62.

155. "Educational Opportunity Fund," Rutgers University–New Brunswick Admissions, https://admissions.rutgers.edu/eof.

156. "Educational Opportunity Fund Progress Report," State of New Jersey, Office of the Secretary of Higher Education, May 2015, 4–5, https://nj.gov/highereducation /documents/pdf/index/EOFPROGRESSREPORTFINALMay12015.pdf.

157. Cheryl Clarke Oral History Interview, September 21, 2018, by Kathryn Tracy Rizzi and Joseph Kaplan, 22–24, Rutgers Oral History Archives, https://oralhistory.rutgers. edu/images/PDFs/clarke_cheryl.pdf.

CHAPTER 4: Black and Puerto Rican Student Experiences and Their Movements at Douglass College, 1945–1974

1. Emily A. Langdon, "Women's Colleges Then and Now: Access Then, Equity Now," *Peabody Journal of Education* 76, no. 1, Access and Equity in Postsecondary Education (2001): 5–30.

2. Kayo Denda, Mary Hawkesworth, and Fernando Perrone, *The Douglass Century: Transformation of the Women's College at Rutgers University* (New Brunswick, NJ: Rutgers University Press, 2018), 65; Miya Carey and Pamela Walker, "Profiles in Courage: Breaking the Color Line at Douglass College," in Kendra Boyd, Marisa J. Fuentes, and Deborah Gray White, eds., *Scarlet and Black, Volume 2: Constructing Race and Gender at Rutgers, 1865–1945* (New Brunswick, NJ: Rutgers University Press, 2020).

3. Julane Miller-Armbrister, Audio of Unpublished Oral History Interview, January 14, 2019, by Shaun Illingworth and Kaisha Esty, Rutgers Oral History Archives.

4. Ibid.

5. Until 1969, Douglass women were required to wear long skirts when entering the Cooper Dining Hall. The association led to these skirts being called *Cooper skirts.* Many Douglass students pushed back against this institutional rule by carrying skirts in their book bags and throwing them over their jeans when entering Cooper Hall. As former Douglass student Susan Elizabeth Ryan explained about the changing culture of campus at the time, "Radical permissiveness existed cheek by jowl with sentimental rituals"; see Susan Elizabeth Ryan, "Piecing Art Together: Observations on Fluxus at Douglass, 1966–1970," in Geoffrey Hendricks, ed., *Critical Mass: Happenings, Fluxus, Performance, Intermedia, and Rutgers University, 1958–1972* (Amherst, MA: Mead Art Museum, 2003), 147.

6. New Jersey College for Women, "Student Life," *Red Book,* 1961–1962, 70, Special Collections and University Archives, Rutgers University Libraries (hereafter SCUA, RUL), SPCOL/UA, R-PUBS, LD 7071.5.A32.

7. The New Jersey College for Women was renamed Douglass College in 1955 in honor of its founder, Mabel Smith Douglass.

8. The term *confirmed black woman* is used because there may have been others preceding Baxter who passed as white; see Patti Verbanas, "Julia Baxter Bates: The Rutgers Alumna Who Proved the Scientific Case for Public School Desegregation," *Patch,* May 9, 2016, https://patch.com/new-jersey/newbrunswick/julia-baxter-bates-rutgers-alumna-who-proved-scientific-case-public-school-desegregation. See also Shaun Armstead and Jerrad P. Pacatte, "Race as Reality and Illusion: The Baxter Cousins, NJC, and Rutgers University," in Kendra Boyd et al., *Scarlet and Black, Volume 2,* 132–154. I guess we will keep the Vol 2?

9. Evelyn Sermons Field attended NJC as "Evelyn Sermons." For consistency, in this article she is referred to as Evelyn Sermons Field. For a discussion of early black women at NJC/Douglass, see Carey and Walker, "Profiles in Courage," 106–131.

10. See ibid.

11. As quoted in Denda et al., *Douglass Century*, 352–353.

12. M. Wilma Harris, "Black on the Banks: African-American Students at Rutgers in the 1960s," YouTube video, 1:49.56, November 6, 2015, https://www.youtube.com/watch ?v=bijAZqil9-g.

13. M. Wilma Harris Oral History Interview, December 11, 2018, by Kathryn Tracy Rizzi and Kaisha Esty, 8, Rutgers Oral History Archives, https://oralhistory.rutgers.edu /interviewees/1781-harris-m-wilma. Since its founding in 1766, Rutgers College was an all-male institution. Coeducation was voted on successfully by the Board of Governors in 1970, and the first coeducational class commenced in 1972; "Celebrating 40 Years of Coeducation at Rutgers," *Rutgers Today*, September 7, 2012, https://news .rutgers.edu/feature/celebrating-40-years-coeducation-rutgers/20120907#.XQa8d i3MzBI; "Rutgers College Goes Co-ed," *Douglass Alumnae Bulletin* (Fall 1971), SCUA, RUL; "The Impact of Coeducation at Rutgers College on Douglass College by Jacqueline Green, Douglass College '03," *Towards a New History of Douglass College: Essays by Students from Douglass*, https://www.libraries.rutgers.edu/scua/douglass_scholars /article8.

14. Under Dean Ruth Marie Adams, Douglass College introduced its first policy for students who needed financial support; see Douglass Residential College, "Douglass through the Decades," https://Douglass.rutgers.edu/our-history/Douglass-through -decades.

15. See Deborah Gray White, *Too Heavy a Load: Black Women in Defense of Themselves, 1894–1994* (New York: W.W. Norton, 1999).

16. M. Wilma Harris Oral History Interview, December 11, 2018.

17. Ibid., 9.

18. Evelyn Field (NJC '49), interview with Susan Schwirck (DC '71), December 28, 2007, Associate Alumnae of Douglass College Oral History Project, Douglass Library. Used by permission of the Associate Alumnae of Douglass College.

19. Ibid.

20. Warren was the younger sister of Constance Andrews (NJC '45); see Denda et al., *Douglass Century*, 84.

21. Ibid., 83.

22. Evelyn Field (NJC '49), interview with Susan Schwirck (DC '71).

23. Ibid.

24. Ibid.

25. For example, see Kevin J. Mumford, *Interzones: Black/White Sex Districts in Chicago and New York in the Early Twentieth Century* (New York: Columbia University Press, 1997); Siobhan B. Somerville, *Queering the Color Line: Race and the Invention of Homosexuality in American Culture* (Durham, NC: Duke University Press, 2000).

26. For example, see Linda Perkins, "The African American Female Elite: The Early History of African American Women in the Seven Sister Colleges, 1880–1960," *Harvard Educational Review* 67, no. 4 (1997): 718–757.

27. Denda et al., *Douglass Century*, 145.

28. Evelyn Field (NJC '49), interview with Susan Schwirck (DC '71).

29. Ibid.

30. Ibid.

31. Ibid.

32. "Celebrating the Life of Evelyn S. Field, August 19, 1927–December 3, 2015," Memorial Service Program, Evelyn Sermons Field (1949) folder, Associate Alumnae of Douglass College, Douglass Library.

33. Bernice Proctor Venable, "My Reflections and Insights, as a Douglass Student and Alumna," delivered at the book launch of *The Douglass Century: Transformation of the Women's College at Rutgers University,* Trayes Hall, Douglass Student Center, April 3, 2018. The Rutgers Oral History Archives interview with Bernice Proctor Venable, member emerita of the Rutgers University Board of Overseers, is sealed until 2021.

34. Ibid. As Denda et al. explain, as early as the 1930s, "traditionally, the only 'self-help,' or work study, jobs that the college offered were waitresses in the dining halls, assistants in departments, and babysitting"; see Denda et al., *Douglass Century,* 57.

35. Ibid.

36. Ibid.

37. Ibid.

38. Ibid.

39. Ibid.

40. The fall 2019 issue of *Rutgers Magazine* reprinted an article that first appeared in its winter 2016 issue, titled "Alone Together" by Leslie Garisto Pfaff. It covered the "Black on the Banks: African-American Students at Rutgers in the 1960s" conference held on November 6, 2015, an event that brought together black alumni who discussed their experiences at Rutgers and Douglass in the 1960s and early '70s. This section takes its inspiration from that piece, which details how black students weathered the mostly white Rutgers environment.

41. Denda et al., *Douglass Century,* 228.

42. Ibid.

43. Ibid.

44. Ibid.

45. Ibid. See also Wilson's comments presented at "Black on the Banks: African-American Students at Rutgers in the 1960s," YouTube video, 1:49.56, November 6, 2015, https://www.youtube.com/watch?v=bijAZqil9-g.

46. Ibid.

47. Betty Davis Oral History Interview, September 27, 2016, by Molly Graham, 11, Rutgers Oral History Archives, https://oralhistory.rutgers.edu/images/PDFs/davis_betty.pdf.

48. Ibid.

49. Ibid.

50. Barbara Morrison-Rodriguez Oral History Interview, October 18, 2015, by Molly Graham, 7, Rutgers Oral History Archives, https://oralhistory.rutgers.edu/images/PDFs/morrison_rodriguez_barbara.pdf.

51. Barbara Morrison-Rodriguez, "Black on the Banks: African-American Students at Rutgers in the 1960s," November 6, 2015, https://www.youtube.com/watch?v=VkDNmz-e04g.

52. Ibid.

53. Ibid.

54. M. Wilma Harris Oral History Interview, December 11, 2018.

55. Ibid., 13.

56. Ibid.

57. M. Wilma Harris, "Black on the Banks."

58. "Jamaican Finds U.S. Family Contrary to Native Customs," *Caellian,* November 8, 1963, 3.

59. Ibid.

60. Ibid.

61. M. Wilma Harris Oral History Interview, December 11, 2018.

62. Ibid.

63. Ibid, 3. Lena Horne was an attractive, light-skinned black singer and actress who was popular during World War II and the postwar years.

64. Rosalind Carmichael Oral History Interview, December 11, 2015, by Shaun Illingworth, Rob Alcantara, Vanessa Bodossian, and Sara Rolfsen-Kohn, 12, Rutgers Oral History Archives, https://oralhistory.rutgers.edu/images/PDFs/carmichael_rosalind.pdf.

65. M. Wilma Harris Oral History Interview, December 11, 2018.

66. Ibid.

67. M. Wilma Harris Oral History Interview, September 26, 2015, by Molly Graham, 18, Rutgers Oral History Archives, https://oralhistory.rutgers.edu/images/PDFs/harris_m_wilma.pdf.

68. Black women's hair care often involved hot irons and chemical relaxers that would straighten their naturally coily hair. Exposing the hair to water either reversed or diminished this effect. Black hair care has always been political in the United States, serving as a symbol of beauty, empowerment, respectability, assimilation, cultural pride, and/or radical politics. For a history of black women and hair care, see Noliwe M. Rooks, *Hair Raising: Beauty, Culture, and African American Women* (New Brunswick, NJ: Rutgers University Press, 1996); Ayana D. Byrd and Lori L. Tharps, *Hair Story: Untangling the Roots of Black Hair in America* (New York: St. Martin's Press, 2001).

69. Patricia Felton-Montgomery, "Black on the Banks: African-American Students at Rutgers in the 1960s," YouTube video, 1:49.56, November 6, 2015, https://www.youtube.com/watch?v=bijAZqil9-g.

70. Julane Miller-Armbrister, Audio of Unpublished Oral History Interview.

71. Ibid.

72. M. Wilma Harris, "Black on the Banks."

73. Ibid.

74. Patricia Felton-Montgomery, "Black on the Banks."

75. Julane Miller-Armbrister, Audio of Unpublished Oral History Interview.

76. Ibid.

77. Carey and Walker, "Profiles in Courage," 113. Please note it is most likely that Carmen Martinez also graduated in 1930 but the evidence does not say this for sure.

78. Paul G.E. Clemens, *Rutgers since 1945: A History of the State University of New Jersey* (New Brunswick, NJ: Rutgers University Press, 2015), 14.

79. Ibid.

80. Bernice Rozenweig, "Douglass Scholars—The Black Student Protest Movement at Douglass College," *Towards a New History of Douglass College: Essays by Students from*

the Douglass Scholars Program, SCUA, RUL, https://www.libraries.rutgers.edu/scua/douglass_scholars/article10.

81. Camille Zampetti, "Just Three of Us . . . ," *Caellian,* April 24, 1970. Two Puerto Rican students were admitted in 1967, Gloria Soto and Diane Maldonado. Two more were admitted in 1969, but one transferred after one semester, meaning that in 1970, when this article was written, there were three Puerto Rican students at Douglass.

82. Unpublished Gloria Soto Oral History Interview, March 8, 2019, by Carie Rael, Rutgers Oral History Archives.

83. Ibid.

84. Ibid.

85. Ibid.

86. Ibid. The Philip Carey Manufacturing Corporation lost several class-action lawsuits for exposing its workers to asbestos; Dave Foster, "Rapid-American Corporation/Philip Carey Manufacturing Corporation," Mesothemlioma.net, https://mesothelioma.net/rapid-american-corporationphilip-carey-manufacturing-corporation/.

87. Gloria Soto Oral History Interview, March 8, 2019.

88. Ibid.

89. Ibid.

90. Ibid.

91. Ibid.

92. Ibid.

93. Ibid.

94. Denda et al., *Douglass Century,* 144.

95. Gloria Soto Oral History Interview, March 8, 2019.

96. Ibid.

97. Ibid.

98. Efeginia Garcia, "The Puerto Rican Student: A Case of 'Mistaken Identity,'" *Caellian,* December 13, 1973.

99. Ibid.

100. Ibid.

101. "EOB: To Serve Minority Groups," *Caellian,* April 24, 1970. Such programs persisted into the twenty-first century in universities across the country. The University of California system adopted similar programs called "Summer Bridge" serving low-income and underrepresented incoming students.

102. Gloria Soto Oral History Interview.

103. Louis Economopoulos, "Livingston College Handbook," https://archive.org/stream/livingstoncollegoolivi/livingstoncollegoolivi_djvu.txt.

104. Gloria Soto Oral History Interview.

105. Ibid. Only five Puerto Rican students were admitted between 1967 and 1969; see Denda et al., *Douglass Century.*

106. The EOF or Educational Opportunity Fund was created in 1968 by the New Jersey Legislature to increase enrollment and financial support for underrepresented students in the state. It was established in response to the pressure of black and Puerto Rican student movements demanding increased enrollment, support, and diversity

in faculty; see Richard P. McCormick, *The Black Student Protest Movement at Rutgers* (New Brunswick, NJ: Rutgers University Press, 1990), 82.

107. Ibid.

108. Ibid.

109. Ivette Mendez, "Increased Admissions by Unified Effort," *Caellian,* December 13, 1973.

110. Efeginia Garcia, "The Puerto Rican Student: A Case of 'Mistaken Identity,'" *Caellian,* December 13, 1973.

111. Ibid.

112. "Racial Identity Dilemma: Introduction," *Caellian,* December 13, 1973.

113. Elizabeth Kelly, "Casa Boricua: Puerto Rican Students Get House," *Caellian,* September 22, 1972.

114. Department of Puerto Rican and Hispanic Caribbean Studies (RG16/B25/01), "Union Estudiantil Puertoriquenna, *Carta Boricua* Vol. II, No. 6, November 7, 1974," Rutgers Special Collection, accessed by Merylou Rodriguez.

115. The Youth March for Integrated Schools took place in 1958 and 1959 in Washington, DC. Organized by prominent civil rights leaders including the Reverend Doctor Martin Luther King Jr., Roy Wilkins, and A. Phillip Randolph, among others, the marches sought to bring attention to the issue of segregation in American public schools and to inspire young people to get involved in the movement. For more on youth organizing and desegregation, see Ibram H. Rogers [Ibram X. Kendi], *The Black Campus Movement: Black Students and the Racial Reconstitution of Higher Education, 1965–1972* (New York: Palgrave Macmillan, 2012).

116. Editorial, "Morals and Morale," *Caellian,* October 16, 1958, 2.

117. Letter to the Editor, "Two Answer Mr. Fel; One Views Segregation," *Caellian,* October 16, 1958, 2.

118. "Douglass Group Participate in Integration March Saturday," *Caellian,* October 30, 1958, 1.

119. The editorial reports that there was a total of 1,419 students at Douglass College.

120. Letters to the Editor, "Committee Airs Theme; Student Lauds Crusade," *Caellian,* October 20, 1958, 2.

121. Editorial, "On the March," *Caellian,* April 9, 1959, 2.

122. Douglass student and chairman of the GA Human Relations Committee Nancy Marrish (DC '62) planned the panel, and Adrienne Gostin (DC '60) led the discussion on May 12, 1960.

123. "Panel Report," *Caellian,* May 13, 1960, 4.

124. "NAACP Demands New Housing Rule Change," *Caellian,* March 17, 1961, 5.

125. Ibid.

126. "Moser-NAACP Join to End Dorm Bias," *Caellian,* November 17, 1961.

127. Ibid.

128. Ibid.

129. Betty Davis Oral History Interview, September 27, 2016.

130. Ibid., 12.

131. For further reading on student-led sit-in strikes, see Martha Biondi, *The Black Revolution on Campus* (Berkeley, CA: University of California Press, 2012), 3–4, 37–39, 44, 85–92, 127–128.

132. Marge Chary (DC '60), New Jersey regional chair of the United States National Student Association (USNSA), is credited with organizing this protest. The happenings of the USNSA were often reported, such as hosting several conferences and calling for support of the sit-ins. Ultimately, Marge Chary (DC'60) and Linda Fischer (DC '61), president of the Government Association, represented Douglass at the USNSA conference on the sit-in movement in Washington, DC, on April 22 and 23. "Fischer Attends NSA Meeting," *Caellian*, April 15, 1960, 4; "Report on the NSA Civil Rights Conference," *Caellian*, April 29, 1960, 4.

133. "Douglass Joins National Student Protest against Southern Lunchroom Segregation," *Caellian*, March 4, 1960, 1.

134. Thomas J. Sugrue, *Sweet Land of Liberty: The Forgotten Struggle for Civil Rights in the North* (New York: Random House, 2009).

135. Editorial, "With Liberty and . . . ," *Caellian*, March 11, 1960, 2.

136. Editorial, "A Need for Investigation," *Caellian*, April 8, 1960, 2.

137. Douglass College, *Red Book*, 1963–1964, 69, SCUA, RUL.

138. Ibid.

139. "NSA Urges Support for Negro Leader," *Caellian*, October 28, 1960, 1; "GA Officers' Motion to Urge SNCC Support," *Caellian*, November 4, 1960, 1. SNCC was an organization that formed out of the southern sit-in protests and was student led and driven. Encouraged by advisor and activist Ella Baker, SNCC drew an interracial coalition of college students into the civil rights movement and created space for student-driven actions and concerns. For further reading on SNCC, see Clayborne Carson, *In Struggle: SNCC and the Black Awakening of the 1960s* (Cambridge, MA: Harvard University Press, 1995); Barbara Ransby, *Ella Baker and the Black Freedom Movement: A Radical Democratic Vision* (Chapel Hill: University of North Carolina Press, 2003). For black students organizing on college campuses, see Rogers, *The Black Campus Movement*.

140. "Students Plan Election Protest: Rutgers to Support Pre-Election Day Demonstration; Protest Denial of Voting Rights in South," *Caellian*, November 4, 1960, 1.

141. Ibid.

142. L.M., "Malcolm X, Black Muslim to Speak at Blake Hall," *Caellian*, February 2, 1962, 3; "Malcolm X to Offer Views on Negro-White Separatism," *Caellian*, February 9, 1962.

143. L.M., "Separate Negro State; Malcolm X Stirs Controversy," *Caellian*, February 16, 1962. For more on this event, see chapter 3 in this volume, "'Tell It Like It Is': The Rise of a Race-Conscious Professoriate at Rutgers in the 1960s," by Joseph Williams.

144. "RU-Douglass NAACP Meets," *Caellian*, October 5, 1962, 8.

145. Letters to the Editor, "Easy Steps," *Caellian*, October 12, 1962, 3, 8.

146. Sue Hueman, "SNCC Announces Campaign," *Caellian*, December 7, 1962, 1, 4.

147. "Jail Term Continues for Civil Rights Champion; Violence and Demonstrations Continue in Georgia," *Caellian*, September 20, 1963, 1.

148. Donald Harris Oral History Interview, February 28, 2013, by Nancy Hewitt, Steven Lawson, and Shaun Illingworth, Rutgers Oral History Archives, https://oralhistory.rutgers.edu/64-interviewees/text-html/1860-harris-donald.

149. "Jail Term Continues for Rights Champion," 1, 8.

150. "Rights Rally," *Caellian*, September 20, 1963, 1, 8.

151. Editorial, "A Matter of Motives," *Caellian*, October 4, 1963, 4.

152. Letters to the Editor, "Rally," *Caellian,* October 4, 1963, 4.

153. Letters to the Editor, "Wrong Side," *Caellian,* October 4, 1963, 8.

154. Editorial, "The Persistence of Memory," *Caellian,* November 22, 1963.

155. Lucille Dukissette, "Smoldering Protest," *Caellian,* March 12, 1965.

156. "80 Picket to Protest Brutality," *Caellian,* March 19, 1965, 2.

157. "After Apathy, What?," *Caellian,* March 19, 1965, 2.

158. See the introduction by Deborah Gray White in this volume.

159. Gene Robinson, "Sounding Brass," *Caellian,* March 8, 1968, 4.

160. "SAS Changes to All Male Membership," *Caellian,* March 14, 1968, 4.

161. Gene Robinson, "Apology," *Caellian,* March 14, 1968, 4.

162. Quoted in Paula Giddings, *When and Where I Enter: The Impact of Black Women on Race and Sex in America* (New York: Bantam, 1984), 317–324.

163. Quoted in Biondi, *Black Revolution on Campus,* 27.

164. Rosalind Carmichael Oral History Interview, December 11, 2015.

165. McCormick, *Black Student Protest Movement at Rutgers,* 59.

166. Rosalind Carmichael Oral History Interview, December 11, 2015.

167. Bernice Rosenzweig, Douglass College '02, "Douglas Scholars—The Black Student Protest Movement at Rutgers," https://www.libraries.rutgers.edu/scua/douglass _scholars/article10.

168. Rosalind Carmichael Oral History Interview, December 11, 2015.

169. Ibid.

170. McCormick, *Black Student Protest Movement at Rutgers,* 58.

171. Denda et al., *Douglass Century,* 229; McCormick, *Black Student Protest Movement at Rutgers,* 56–60.

172. Julane Miller-Armbrister, Audio of Unpublished Oral History Interview.

173. Ibid.

174. Barbara Morrison-Rodriguez, "Black on the Banks."

175. See the introduction to this volume.

176. As noted earlier, Puerto Rican students at Douglass began building a community with students at Livingston College. The community that they built in the 1970s is covered in part 2 of this volume; see chapter 8, "We the People": Student Activism at Livingston and Rutgers College, 1960–1985," by Tracey Johnson, Carie Rael, and Brooke Thomas.

PART II: Student Protest and Forceful Change

1. For more comprehensive coverage of black student movements across the United States, see Martha Biondi, *The Black Revolution on Campus* (Berkeley: University of California Press, 2012); Ibram H. Rogers [Ibram X. Kendi], *The Black Campus Movement: Black Students and the Racial Reconstitution of Higher Education, 1965–1972* (New York: Palgrave MacMillan, 2012).

2. Richard P. McCormick, *The Black Student Protest Movement at Rutgers* (New Brunswick, NJ: Rutgers University Press, 1990), 82.

3. Paul G.E. Clemens, *Rutgers since 1945: A History of the State University of New Jersey* (New Brunswick, NJ: Rutgers University Press, 2015), 21.

CHAPTER 5: A Second Founding

1. "Black Law Students' Position on the Present Siege of Conklin Hall," box 3, folder 4, Records of the Black Organization of Students (BOS) at Rutgers–Newark, 1967–1973 (RG N2/02), Special Collections and University Archives, Rutgers University Libraries (hereafter SCUA, RUL).

2. Martha Biondi, *The Black Revolution on Campus* (Berkeley: University of California Press, 2012), 2.

3. Ibid.

4. Paul Tractenberg, *A Centennial History of Rutgers Law School in Newark: Opening a Thousand Doors* (Charleston, SC: History Press, 2010), 32–35.

5. In 1946, under the leadership of President Robert Clothier, Rutgers acquired the University of Newark, formerly the Dana Group—a group of postsecondary schools in the city of Newark including an undergraduate college of arts and sciences and schools of law, pharmacy, and business. In 1950, historian Paul Clemens explains, Rutgers also integrated "the two-year 'College of South Jersey' (later Rutgers–Camden), a much smaller institution than Newark, and incorporated its unaccredited law program under the umbrella of the Newark school"; Paul G.E. Clemens, *Rutgers since 1945: A History of the State University of New Jersey* (New Brunswick, NJ: Rutgers University Press, 2015), 5.

6. Tractenberg, *Centennial History of Rutgers Law School in Newark,* 35.

7. Ibid., 36.

8. Ibid., 39.

9. Ibid., 35.

10. Ibid.

11. Ethel Mae Moore, "2 Negro Girls Pass N.J. Bar," *Chicago Defender,* November 19, 1949, 1; "Jersey Gets Two Portias to Plead Your Case," *Baltimore Afro-American,* November 19, 1949, A17.

12. "Rites in Hampton for J. Bernard Johnson," *Baltimore Afro-American,* March 26, 1960, 18.

13. "Jaunting in Jersey," *Baltimore Afro-American,* November 26, 1949, A16. Little information could be found on Martha Belle Williams's life and career after she passed the New Jersey State Bar in 1949.

14. Ibid.

15. Samuel A. Haynes, "First Woman Lawyer Notable Trailblazer," *Baltimore Afro-American,* June 27, 1964, A12; "Richard's Marshall's Busy Life Earns Rutgers Alumni Award," *Baltimore Afro-American,* August 4, 1985, 15.

16. Data were taken from Rutgers University yearbooks and research was conducted using a visual survey and available biographical data.

17. *The Legacy,* 1963, Newark Law School, Rutgers University Yearbook Collection, SCUA, RUL.

18. Tractenberg, *Centennial History of Rutgers Law School,* 48.

19. Ibid., 49.

20. Ibid.

21. Robert Curvin, *Inside Newark: Decline, Rebellion, and the Search for Transformation* (New Brunswick, NJ: Rutgers University Press, 2014), 102.

22. Ibid., 4–6.

23. Ibid., 108–109.

24. Ibid., 114.

25. Junius Williams and Tom Hayden, *Unfinished Agenda: Urban Politics in the Era of Black Power* (Berkeley, CA: North Atlantic Books, 2014), 163–164.

26. Ibid., 194.

27. Willard Heckel to Mason Gross, April 17, 1970, box 59, folder 2, Records of the Rutgers University Office of the President (Mason Welch Gross), 1936, 1945–1971 (RG 04/A16), Special Collections and University Archives, Rutgers University Libraries (collection hereafter cited as Records of President Mason Gross, SCUA, RUL).

28. Ibid.

29. Ibid.

30. Fundraising brochure, April 17, 1970, box 59, folder 2, Records of President Mason Gross, SCUA, RUL.

31. Special Equal Opportunity Program for the Law School, May 24, 1968, box 59, folder 3, Records of President Mason Gross, SCUA, RUL.

32. This program was similar to the "Special Admissions" program at Douglass College in the late 1960s; see chapter 4 in this volume.

33. "Preliminary Evaluation of the First Year Performance of Specially Selected Group of Minority Students," Rutgers Law School, 1968–1969, box 59, folder 2, Records of President Mason Gross, SCUA, RUL.

34. Ibid.

35. Ibid. Twenty students were initially admitted into the Minority Student Program. One withdrew from the law school in the spring of 1969. Although this student was entitled to readmission in the second semester of the 1970–1971 school year, the data taken on the initial cohort was only nineteen students.

36. Ibid.

37. Council on Legal Education Opportunity, "What Is CLEO?," https://cleoinc.org /about/.

38. Michael Hunter Schwartz, "50 More Years of CLEO Scholars: The Past, the Present, and a Vision for the Future," *Valparaiso University Law Review* 2, no. 48 (Winter 2014): 626.

39. Educational Opportunity Program Description, box 59, folder 2, Records of President Mason Gross, SCUA, RUL.

40. "Preliminary Evaluation of the First Year Performance of Specially Selected Group of Minority Students."

41. Ibid., 9–10.

42. Ibid., 9–10.

43. Ibid.

44. Tractenberg, *Centennial History,* 56.

45. Ibid.

46. Funding brochure, March 1970, 1969–1970, box 59, folder 2, Records of President Mason Gross, SCUA, RUL. The Scholarship, Education, and Defense Fund for Racial Equality (SEDFRE) was formed in 1962 by the Congress of Racial Equality (CORE). SEDFRE had several functions, one of which was to offer scholarships to students

whose education had been interrupted by civil rights work. For more on SEDFRE, see Greta de Jong, "The Scholarship, Education, and Defense Fund for Racial Equality and the African American Organizing Tradition in the Era of Black Power," *Journal of Contemporary History* 48, no. 3 (July 2013): 597–616.

47. "Association of Black Law School Statement," box 59, folder 5, Records of President Mason Gross, SCUA. RUL.

48. Ibid.

49. Ibid., 11.

50. Ibid., 13.

51. Ibid.

52. "Black Law Student Union to Russell Fairbanks and O. Theodore Reid," November 17, 1970, box 81, folder 5, Records of President Mason Gross, SCUA, RUL.

53. "Proposal for Supportive Services [from Camden Law Students]," box 81, folder 5, Records of President Mason Gross, SCUA, RUL.

54. Vickie Donaldson interview, Rutgers–Newark in the 1960s and 1970s Oral History Collection (RMC-024), SCUA, RUL.

55. Robert Curvin interview, Rutgers–Newark in the 1960s and 1970s Oral History Collection (RMC-024), SCUA, RUL.

56. Rutgers University–Newark, "Conklin Hall Liberation 50th Anniversary Panel (Q&A)," YouTube video, 58.36, March 20, 2019, https://www.youtube.com/watch?v=VmsEgwCR5x8.

57. Newark College of Arts and Sciences, *Encore*, 1968, 180, Rutgers University Yearbook Collection, SCUA, RUL.

58. Joseph Browne interview, Rutgers–Newark in the 1960s and 1970s Oral History Collection (RMC-024), SCUA, RUL.

59. "Conklin Hall Project," http://stream.newark.rutgers.edu/~danadml/conklin/Page632.htm.

60. Vivian Sanks King interview, Rutgers–Newark in the 1960s and 1970s Oral History Collection (RMC-024), SCUA, RUL.

61. Richard P. McCormick, *The Black Student Protest Movement at Rutgers* (New Brunswick, NJ: Rutgers University Press, 1990), 34–38; Joseph Browne interview, Rutgers–Newark.

62. Vickie Donaldson interview, Rutgers–Newark; "Conklin Hall Liberation 50th Anniversary Panel (Discussion)," YouTube video, 48.14, March 13, 2019, https://www.youtube.com/watch?v=Vl-pCnl1EnI.

63. McCormick, *Black Student Protest Movement at Rutgers,* 39; Walter H. Waggoner, "Rutgers Negroes Seize Newark Hall," *New York Times,* February 25, 1969, 29.

64. McCormick, *Black Student Protest Movement at Rutgers,* 41.

65. David M. Halbfinger, "Anthony Imperiale, 68, Dies; Polarizing Force in Newark," *New York Times,* December 28, 1999, NY Region sec., https://www.nytimes.com/1999/12/28/nyregion/anthony-imperiale-68-dies-polarizing-force-in-newark.html.

66. Junius Williams, interviewed by Beatrice J. Adams, February 2019, Newark, NJ.

67. Ibid.

68. "Black Community Support BOS Seen in Spontaneous Gathering," *Rutgers Observer,* February 28, 1969.

69. Vickie Donaldson interview, Rutgers–Newark; "Conklin Hall Liberation 50th Anniversary Panel (Discussion)."

70. Joseph Browne interview, Rutgers–Newark.

71. Peter Jackson interview, Rutgers–Newark in the 1960s and 1970s Oral History Collection (RMC-024), SCUA, RUL.

72. William Doolittle, "Dr. Gross Signed Transcript of Talks," *Newark Evening News*, March 4, 1969.

73. William Doolittle, "Reject Rutgers Pact," *Newark Evening News*, March 7, 1969.

74. Ibid.

75. "Conklin Hall Liberation 50th Anniversary Panel (Discussion)"; Robert J. Braun, "Rutgers Profs Call Pact Too Soft on the Militants," *Star-Ledger* (Newark, NJ), February 28, 1969.

76. Robert J. Braun, "Rutgers Opens Its Doors to All Disadvantaged," *Star-Ledger* (Newark, NJ), March 15, 1969.

77. McCormick, *Black Student Protest Movement at Rutgers,* 73.

78. Vickie Donaldson interview, Rutgers–Newark, "Conklin Hall Liberation 50th Anniversary Panel (Discussion)."

79. McCormick, *Black Student Protest Movement at Rutgers,* 75.

80. Motivated by the Newark uprising of 1967, New Jersey's highest education administrators encouraged the state university's president and the legislature to create a program that would help underrepresented and economically vulnerable students obtain a college degree. The legislature passed the EOF initiative, making resources available to such students throughout New Jersey; see Middlesex County College, "EOF History," https://www.middlesexcc.edu/education-opportunity-fund/mcc-eof/eof-history/.

81. See the enrollment numbers in New Jersey Department of Higher Education, *A Report to the New Jersey Legislature Concerning the Recent Events and Disturbances at the Newark and Camden Campuses of Rutgers, the State University*, prepared by Ralph A. Dungan (Trenton, NJ, March 31, 1969), 1, http://hdl.handle.net/10929/49565.

82. *Mneme*, 1953, "Administration and Faculty," 8, Rutgers University College of South Jersey, Camden, NJ, SCUA, RUL.

83. "Report on Estimated Enrollment, 1954–1970," Rutgers University College of South Jersey, box 2, folder 2, Records of the Rutgers University Office of the President (Lewis Webster Jones), 1951–1958 (RG 04/A15/01), SCUA, RUL.

84. "Report on the Location of the South Jersey Campus of Rutgers, the State University," box 2, folder 2, Records of the Rutgers University Office of the President (Lewis Webster Jones), 1951–1958 (RG 04/A15/01), SCUA, RUL.

85. Howard Gillette, *Camden after the Fall: Decline and Renewal in a Post-Industrial City* (Philadelphia: University of Pennsylvania Press, 2005), 66.

86. Ibid. See also chapter 1 of this volume for a detailed demographic history of Camden's population and growth in the early to mid-twentieth century.

87. Ibid., 82.

88. Ibid., 66.

89. Ibid., 68.

90. Ibid.

91. Ibid., 11.

92. For more on BPUM and its politics, see Laurie Lahey, "'Justice Now! ¡Justicia Ahora!': African American–Puerto Rican Radicalism in Camden, New Jersey," in Brian D. Behnken, ed., *Civil Rights and Beyond: African American and Latino/a Activism in the Twentieth-Century United States* (Athens: University of Georgia Press, 2016), 152–171; Laurie Lahey, "The Black Peoples Unity Movement and Friends: The Brief Emergence of an Interracial Black Power Movement in Camden, New Jersey, 1968," *Journal of Civil and Human Rights* 3, no. 2 (2017): 30–61, https://doi.org/10.5406/jciv ihumarigh.3.2.0030.

93. "Camden Patrolman and Girl Are Slain in Hail of Bullets from Sniper's Gun," *Courier-Post* (Camden, NJ), September 3, 1969, 1–2; Carol Comegno, "'69 Riots: Tragic Turning Point for Camden," *Courier-Post* (Camden, NJ), September 10, 1989, 1; Carol Comegno, "Mother Recounts Daughter's Death," *Courier-Post* (Camden, NJ), September 10, 1989, 8.

94. Lahey, "Justice Now!," 152–153, 160, 164.

95. Gillette, *Camden after the Fall,* 72.

96. Ibid., 54–55.

97. "Memorandum of Agreement, Rutgers Camden Campus Expansion," Rutgers University–City of Camden, People of Cooper-Grant Community, box 52, Records of the Office of the President (Edward J. Bloustein Administration) (RG/04/A17), SCUA, RUL.

98. "Memo to Director William Wright on Physical and Capital Planning from Camden Regional Legal Services, Inc.," box 52, Records of the Office of the President (Edward J. Bloustein Administration) (RG/04/A17), SCUA, RUL; "Memo from Russell N. Fairbanks to Acting President Dr. Paul G. Pearson Regarding the Detailed Plan for Acquisition of Property in Camden," box 52, Records of the Office of the President (Edward J. Bloustein Administration) (RG/04/A17), SCUA, RUL.

99. "Cooper-Grant Community," box 52, Records of the Office of the President (Edward J. Bloustein Administration) (RG/04/A17), SCUA, RUL.

100. For a thoughtful and devastating account of Camden's struggle for housing rights and the destruction wrought by development that neglected people of color, see Mercy Romero, "Guidelines for Squatting: Concerned Citizens of North Camden, 1978–1990," *Biography* 42, no. 3 (2019): 586–609.

101. Lahey, "Black Peoples Unity Movement and Friends," 36.

102. Hoag Levins, "Reliving a 1969 Racial Clash: The Black Students Who Changed Rutgers," February 12, 2001, Historic Camden County, *News,* http://historiccamden county.com/ccnews03.shtml.

103. "Black Student Unity Movement List of Demands," February 10, 1969, box 35, folder 2, Records of President Mason Gross, SCUA, RUL.

104. Stephen Allen, "An End to Isolation?," *Courier-Post* (Camden, NJ), February 13, 1969, 13.

105. Ibid.

106. This particular demand was fully implemented, and the Paul Robeson Library maintains the Wiggins Collection today.

107. "Black Student Unity Movement List of Demands."

108. McCormick, *Black Student Protest Movement at Rutgers,* 62.

109. The building is now referred to as the Campus Center, but it was called the College Center in the documents from 1969.

110. "25 Blacks End Sit-In at Student Center on Camden Campus," *Courier-Post* (Camden, NJ), February 27, 1969, 1, 6. Ortiz had also led several confrontations with the police at the 1968 Democratic National Convention in Chicago; Chicago Department of Law (Raymond F. Simon, Corporation Counsel), *The Strategy of Confrontation: Chicago and the Democratic National Convention—1968*, September 6, 1968, 30, National Criminal Justice Reference Service, https://www.ncjrs.gov/pdffiles1/Digitization/88347NCJRS.pdf.

111. "Rutgers University–College of South Jersey Faculty Meeting Minutes," February 28, 1969, 2, box 35, folder 2, Records of President Mason Gross, SCUA, RUL.

112. "President Mason Gross to Thomas Warren and Roy Jones, Letter Regarding BSUM Demands," February 27, 1969, box 35, folder 2, Records of President Mason Gross, SCUA, RUL.

113. "Report to Faculty and Students Regarding BSUM Demands," Office of the Dean of the College of South Jersey, March 17, 1969, box 35, folder 2, Records of President Mason Gross, SCUA, RUL.

114. "Black Student Unity Movement List of Demands."

115. "President Mason Gross to Thomas Warren and Roy Jones, Letter Regarding BSUM Demands."

116. "Rutgers University–College of South Jersey Faculty Meeting Minutes," February 28, 1969.

117. "Report to Faculty and Students Regarding BSUM Demands."

118. "Black Student Unity Movement List of Demands."

119. "Report to Faculty and Students Regarding BSUM Demands." For an article voicing the opposition to honoring Paul Robeson, see Frank Galey, "Rutgers in Camden; Some Black Demands Seem Pretty Far Out," *Courier-Post* (Camden, NJ), February 21, 1969.

120. For more on Paul Robeson, see chapter 3 and the epilogue in Kendra Boyd, Marisa J. Fuentes, and Deborah Gray White, eds., *Scarlet and Black, Volume 2: Constructing Race and Gender at Rutgers, 1965–1945* (New Brunswick, NJ: Rutgers University Press, 2020); see also Rutgers University, Paul Robeson Centennial Celebration, https://robeson100.rutgers.edu/.

121. McCormick, *Black Student Protest Movement at Rutgers,* 64.

122. Will Bunch, "Locking Doors to Open Them," *Rutgers–Camden Magazine,* Fall 2017, 26–27.

123. Levins, "Reliving a 1969 Racial Clash: The Black Students Who Changed Rutgers."

124. Laurie Lahey, "'The Grassy Battleground': Race, Religion, and Activism in Camden's 'Wide' Civil Rights Movement" (PhD diss., George Washington University, 2013), 207; Lahey, "Justice Now!," 167.

125. "Puerto Rican Community, 1968–1971," box 87, folder 5, Records of President Mason Gross, SCUA, RUL.

126. "Puerto Rican Students-Representatives," box 48, folders 2–3, Rutgers University Dean of Student Affairs (Earle W. Clifford) Records, 1952–1973 (RG 15/F2), SCUA, RUL.

127. "Puerto Rican Community, 1968–1971."

128. It changed names once more, to *Black Voice/Carta Latina,* in 1995.

129. *Khuluma: Black Community Newsletter,* November 10, 1971, Campus Ephemera, folder 9, 1971, Special Collections, Paul Robeson Library, Rutgers University–Camden; *Khuluma: Black Community Newsletter,* March 8, 1972, Campus Ephemera, folder 10, 1972, Special Collections, Paul Robeson Library, Rutgers University–Camden; *Khuluma: Black Community Newsletter,* April 13, 1972, Campus Ephemera, folder 10, 1972, Special Collections, Paul Robeson Library, Rutgers University–Camden.

130. "The 50th Anniversary Celebration Gala of the Conklin Hall Liberation, Rutgers University–Newark," February 22, 2019, https://www.newark.rutgers.edu/events/50th-anniversary-celebration-gala-conklin-hall-liberation-0.

131. "Rutgers–Newark Tabbed 'Most Diverse' by Best Value Colleges," Rutgers–Newark Athletics, June 13, 2018, https://rutgersnewarkathletics.com/news/2018/6/13/baseball-rutgers-newark-tabbed-most-diverse-by-best-value-colleges.aspx.

132. "Minority Student Program Today," Rutgers University Law School, https://law.rutgers.edu/minority-student-program.

133. Ibid.

CHAPTER 6: Equality in Higher Education

1. "The Liberation of Conklin Hall Slide Show," John Cotton Dana Library, Rutgers University Libraries, Newark, NJ.

2. Morris Roth, Rutgers News Service, March 3, 1969, Rutgers University Libraries.

3. Richard P. McCormick, *The Black Student Protest Movement at Rutgers* (New Brunswick, NJ: Rutgers University Press, 1990), 41, 72; Paul G.E. Clemens, *Rutgers since 1945: A History of the State University of New Jersey* (New Brunswick, NJ: Rutgers University Press, 2015), 29–30.

4. Bernice Rosenzweig, Douglass College '02, "The Black Student Protest Movement at Douglass College," *Towards a New History of Douglass College: Essays by Students of the Douglass Scholars Program,* 2000, Special Collections and University Archives, Rutgers University Libraries (hereafter SCUA, RUL), https://www.libraries.rutgers.edu/scua/douglass_scholars/article10.

5. Historians of the Conklin Hall takeover agree that most white New Jerseyans opposed the BOS and President Mason Gross's response; see McCormick, *Black Student Protest Movement at Rutgers,* 40, 45; Clemens, *Rutgers since 1945,* 29.

6. "Betrayed," February 27, 1969, box 34, folder 3, Inventory to the Records of the Rutgers University Office of the President (Mason Welch Gross) 1936, 1945–1971 (hereafter Records of the Office of President Mason Gross, SCUA, RUL).

7. Erwin M. Perkins, March 4, 1969, box 33, folder 10, Records of the Office of President Mason Gross, SCUA, RUL.

8. Shirley Martin, February 27, 1969, box 34, folder 6, Records of the Office of President Mason Gross, SCUA, RUL.

9. Richard J. Hughes, February 25, 1969, box 33, folder 8, Records of the Office of President Mason Gross, SCUA, RUL; for more on the white protest, see "RU 250 Timeline—Conklin Hall," RU-TV Network, video, 3.21, https://videoplayer.telvue.com/player/qP-2KCQyrKocIA6sJgjxoKQ3ZzhhYbSe/media/356292.

10. McCormick, *Black Student Protest Movement at Rutgers,* 45.

11. Charles W. Rannells Jr., March 5, 1969, box 34, folder 3, Records of the Office of President Mason Gross, SCUA, RUL.

12. Mario Battista, March 8, 1969, box 34, folder 3, Records of the Office of President Mason Gross, SCUA, RUL.

13. "RU 250 Timeline—Conklin Hall."

14. "2 N.J. Candidates Want Ouster of Rutgers Head," *Philadelphia Inquirer*, March 2, 1969, 5.

15. Ibid.

16. Benjamin J. Macchia, n.d., box 34, folder 3, Records of the Office of President Mason Gross, SCUA, RUL.

17. "Club 35," February 26, 1969, box 34, folder 6, Records of the Office of President Mason Gross, SCUA, RUL.

18. E. Peterson, n.d., box 34, folder 6, Records of the Office of President Mason Gross, SCUA, RUL.

19. Benjamin J. Macchia, n.d.

20. See, for example, Howard Gillette Jr., *Camden after the Fall: Decline and Renewal in a Post-Industrial City* (Philadelphia: University of Pennsylvania Press, 2005), 39–122; Robert Curvin, *Inside Newark: Decline, Rebellion, and the Search for Transformation* (New Brunswick, NJ: Rutgers University Press, 2014), 35–127.

21. Seamus Smith, March 17, 1969, 3, box 34, folder 4, Records of the Office of President Mason Gross, SCUA, RUL.

22. G.A. Hale, March 5, 1969, 1, box 34, folder 4, Records of the Office of President Mason Gross, SCUA, RUL.

23. "Americanize or Leave," *Caellian*, February 28, 1969.

24. See, for example, Noel Ignatiev, *How the Irish Became White* (New York: Routledge, 1995); David R. Roediger, *Working toward Whiteness: How America's Immigrants Became White—The Strange Journey from Ellis Island to the Suburbs* (New York: Basic Books, 2005).

25. Stephen Pogust, "Rutgers Head Termed 'Lax,'" *Philadelphia Inquirer*, June 10, 1969, 6.

26. A.T. Gough, February 26, 1969, box 34, folder 6, Records of the Office of President Mason Gross, SCUA, RUL.

27. Clemens, *Rutgers since 1945*, 29.

28. Ibid., 28–30.

29. "Dealing with Campus Chaos—Notre Dame: 15 Minutes and Out," *U.S. News and World Report*, March 3, 1969, 34.

30. Francis R. McAlonan, February 28, 1969, box 34, folder 6, Records of the Office of President Mason Gross, SCUA, RUL.

31. "Firm State Role Asked in Rutgers Disorders," *Philadelphia Inquirer*, March 11, 1969, 5.

32. Anonymous, n.d., box 34, folder 1, Records of the Office of President Mason Gross, SCUA, RUL; emphasis in original document.

33. "Student Body," March 6, 1969, box 34, folder 2, Records of the Office of President Mason Gross, SCUA, RUL.

34. Susan Gahs Luthman, March 2, 1969, box 33, folder 11, Records of the Office of President Mason Gross, SCUA, RUL.

35. E. J. Palma, February 25, 1969, box 34, folder 2, Records of the Office of President Mason Gross, SCUA, RUL.

36. R. Santor, March 5, 1969, box 34, folder 5, Records of the Office of President Mason Gross, SCUA, RUL.

37. McCormick, *Black Student Protest Movement at Rutgers,* 116–117.

38. "Statement of Robert Swab and C. T. Miller," press release, March 4, 1969, 1, box 33, folder 9, Records of the Office of President Mason Gross, SCUA, RUL.

39. "2 Newark Aides Balk," *New York Times,* March 5, 1969, 17.

40. "Statement of Robert Swab and C. T. Miller," press release.

41. "12 Rutgers Secretaries Quit in Protest over Concession to Black Students," *New York Times,* March 2, 57.

42. Rutgers–Newark Faculty, box 33, folder 9, Records of the Office of President Mason Gross, SCUA, RUL

43. Kelly Heyboer, "Rutgers–Newark Marks 40th Anniversary of Conklin Hall Takeover," February 24, 2009, NJ.com, https://www.nj.com/news/2009/02/after_40_years _student_takeove.html.

44. "The 40th Anniversary of the 1969 Conklin Hall Takeover," 2009, John Cotton Dana Library Digital Preservation Initiative, Rutgers University Libraries, https:// web.archive.org/web/20180203191214/http://stream.newark.rutgers.edu/~danadml /conklin/index.html; "The Newark Experience—1969: The Conklin Hall Takeover," Research Guides, Rutgers University Libraries, https://libguides.rutgers.edu/newark /conklin; "Conklin Hall Liberation 50th Anniversary Panel (Discussion)," March 13, 2019, YouTube video, 48.14, https://www.youtube.com/watch?v=Vl-pCnlIEnI.

45. Heyboer, "Rutgers–Newark Marks 40th Anniversary of Conklin Hall Takeover."

CHAPTER 7: The Black Unity League

1. "Black Unity League Charter," February 1968, box 6, folder 1, Inventory to the Records of the Rutgers University Dean of Student Affairs (Earle W. Clifford Jr.), 1952–1973, Rutgers University Archives and Special Collections, Rutgers University Libraries (hereafter Records of Dean Earle Clifford, SCUA, RUL).

2. "Black Unity League List of Demands to the University," 1969, box 6, folder 1, 11, Records of Dean Earle Clifford, SCUA, RUL.

3. "Black Unity League Charter," February 1968.

4. "Jerome Harris to Earle Clifford," February 1969, box 6, folder 1, Records of Dean Earle Clifford, SCUA, RUL.

5. "Thomas Flynn to Howard Crosby," November 20, 1968, box 6, folder 1, Records of Dean Earle Clifford, SCUA, RUL.

6. Ibid.

7. "Black Unity League," February 11, 1969, box 6, folder 1, Records of Dean Earle Clifford, SCUA, RUL.

8. "Earle Clifford to Maurice Ayers," March 18, 1969, box 6, folder 1, Records of Dean Earle Clifford, SCUA, RUL.

9. "Minutes of the Meeting of the University Committee on Space Utilization," March 26, 1969, box 1, folder 2, Records of Dean Earle Clifford, SCUA, RUL.

10. Ibid.

11. "Jerome Harris to Earle Clifford," February 1969.

12. "Robert Ochs to Earle Clifford," July 7, 1969, box 6, folder 2, Records of Dean Earle Clifford, SCUA, RUL

13. "Black Unity League Ad Hoc Committee," 1969, box 6, folder 1, Records of Dean Earle Clifford, SCUA, RUL.

14. "Michael Borden to Robert Ochs," August 31, 1970, box 6, folder 2, Records of Dean Earle Clifford, SCUA, RUL.

15. Ibid.

16. Stuart Diamond, "Rutgers, City Consult to Halt Noisy Dancing," *Central New Jersey Home News*, September 29, 1970, box 6, folder 2, Records of Dean Earle Clifford, SCUA, RUL.

17. Ibid.

18. Ibid.

19. Campbell Allen for the *Newark Evening News*, September 30, 1970, box 6, folder 2, Records of Dean Earle Clifford, SCUA, RUL.

20. "Michael Borden to Earle Clifford," May 24, 1971, box 6, folder 3, Records of Dean Earle Clifford, SCUA, RUL.

21. "James M. Jeter Jr. to Earle Clifford," March 24, 1971, box 6, folder 2, Records of Dean Earle Clifford, SCUA, RUL.

22. "Earle Clifford to Black Unity League," June 11, 1971, box 6, folder 3, Records of Dean Earle Clifford, SCUA, RUL.

23. "Raymond Holmes to Earle Clifford," n.d. [sometime after June 11, 1971], box 6, folder 3, Records of Dean Earle Clifford, SCUA, RUL.

24. "Patrolman Day Campus Patrol Report," n.d. [Summer 1971], box 6, folder 3, Records of Dean Earle Clifford, SCUA, RUL; "Patrolman Fernandes Campus Patrol Report," August 24, 1971, box 6, folder 3, Records of Dean Earle Clifford, SCUA, RUL.

25. Ibid.

26. "Earle Clifford to Black Unity League," Summer 1971, box 6, folder 3, Records of Dean Earle Clifford, SCUA, RUL.

27. "Bill to Rutgers University," 1969, box 6, folder 1, Records of Dean Earle Clifford, SCUA, RUL.

28. "Ralph Taylor to Black Unity League," August 26, 1971, box 6, folder 3, Records of Dean Earle Clifford, SCUA, RUL.

29. "Thomas Flynn to Howard Crosby," November 20, 1968, box 6, folder 1, Records of Dean Earle Clifford, SCUA, RUL.

30. Huey P. Newton, "War against the Panthers: A Study of Repression in America" (Ph.D. diss., University of California–Santa Cruz, 1980), 14.

31. Simone Browne, *Dark Matters: On the Surveillance of Blackness* (Durham, NC: Duke University Press, 2015), 6.

32. Newton, "War against the Panthers," 77.

33. "Black Unity League," February 11, 1969.

34. Part of this legacy is the existing Africana Cultural Experience House at Douglass College and the African House at Rutgers University, which existed from the late 1990s into the early 2000s.

CHAPTER 8: "We the People"

1. "Livingston College: Annual Report of the Dean 1968–1969," Inventory to the Records of the Office of the Dean of Livingston College, Ernest A. Lynton (RG 21/A0/04), Special Collections and University Archives, Rutgers University Libraries (hereafter SCUA, RUL).

2. Linda Holmes, "Chisholm Attends Livingston Dedication," *Caellian*, April 24, 1970.

3. "Remembering the Rutgers Puerto Rican Student Movement of the 1970s," Department of Latino and Caribbean Studies Conference, panel 2, "Unsung Heroes," video, 1:39.40, October 10, 2016, https://livestream.com/accounts/4838057/events/6428319/videos/138824488.

4. Livingston College Catalog, 1969–1970 (RG 21 C-2), SCUA, RUL.

5. Ibid.

6. Ibid.

7. Ibid.

8. *Livingston in the Retrospect: 1969–1973* (Piscataway, NJ: Rutgers University–Livingston Campus, 1973), Livingston College Alumni, Rutgers University Libraries, https://archive.org/details/livingstoninretroonoah/page/n19.

9. Ibid. Camp Kilmer served as one of the largest deployment bases for the US Army in the 1940s. After the war it was a site of military administration and used for refugee resettlement. After September 11, FEMA used the site as a base of operations.

10. *Livingston in the Retrospect: 1969–1973*.

11. Paul G.E. Clemens, *Rutgers since 1945: A History of the State University of New Jersey* (New Brunswick, NJ: Rutgers University Press, 2015), 160.

12. *We the People* (Piscataway, NJ: Rutgers University–Livingston Campus, 1974), Livingston College Alumni, Rutgers University Libraries, https://archive.org/details/wepeopleoorutg/page/n5.

13. Ibid.

14. "Isolation of Livingston College Given as One Reason for the Student Unrest," *New York Times,* November 10, 1973, https://www.nytimes.com/1973/11/10/archives/isolation-of-livingston-college-given-as-one-reason-for-the-student.html.

15. Ibid.

16. *Livingston in the Retrospect: 1969–1973*.

17. *We the People.*

18. "Puerto Rican Demands," March 10, 1969, Department of Puerto Rican and Hispanic Caribbean Studies (RG 15/A2), box 34, folder 13, SCUA, RUL.

19. María Josefa Canino Arroyo, "The 40th Anniversary of the Department of Latino and Hispanic Caribbean Studies," Livingston College, Lucy Stone Hall, October 11, 2013.

20. "Remembering the Rutgers Puerto Rican Student Movement of the 1970s."

21. Ibid.

22. Ibid.

23. "Report to the Puerto Rican Community and Friends—Livingston College, May 1977," Department of Puerto Rican and Hispanic Caribbean Studies (RG16/B25/01), SCUA, RUL.

24. Ibid.

25. "Dr. María Canino's Remarks at LHCS's 40th Anniversary Celebration," Department of Latino and Hispanic Caribbean Studies, YouTube video, 30:35, November 14, 2014, https://www.youtube.com/watch?v=ePO2kp4RZME.

26. "Report to the Puerto Rican Community and Friends—Livingston College, May 1977."

27. Debbie Brookmeyer, "Puerto Rican Day a First for State," *Caellian,* April 10, 1970.

28. Canino Arroyo, "40th Anniversary of the Department of Latino and Hispanic Caribbean Studies."

29. Luis Nieves Falcón, *El Emigrante Puertorriqueño* (Rio Piedras, PR: Editorial Edil, 1975).

30. Luz Towns-Miranda, "Lin Manuel-Miranda's Mom on the Importance of Mothers' Mental Health," *Health and Science Wellness,* May 11, 2017, https://www.fatherly.com /health-science/dr-luz-towns-miranda-mental-health-care-mothers-postpartum/.

31. "Report to the Puerto Rican Community and Friends—Livingston College, May 1977."

32. Ibid.

33. Canino Arroyo, "40th Anniversary of the Department of Latino and Hispanic Caribbean Studies."

34. "Report to the Puerto Rican Community and Friends—Livingston College, May 1977."

35. Canino Arroyo, "40th Anniversary of the Department of Latino and Hispanic Caribbean Studies."

36. Ibid.

37. "Dr. María Canino's Remarks at LHCS's 40th Anniversary Celebration," Department of Latino and Hispanic Caribbean Studies, YouTube video, 30.35, November 14, 2014, https://www.youtube.com/watch?v=ePO2kp4RZME.

38. Ibid.

39. Ibid.

40. "Report to the Puerto Rican Community and Friends—Livingston College, May 1977."

41. Ibid.

42. Ibid.

43. Canino Arroyo, "40th Anniversary of the Department of Latino and Hispanic Caribbean Studies."

44. Department of Puerto Rican and Hispanic Caribbean Studies (RG16/B25/01), box 4, SCUA, RUL.

45. Department of Puerto Rican and Hispanic Caribbean Studies (RG16/B25/01), box 2, SCUA, RUL.

46. "Report to the Puerto Rican Community and Friends—Livingston College, May 1977."

47. Ibid.

48. Ibid.

49. *Livingston in the Retrospect: 1969–1973* (Piscataway, NJ: Rutgers University, Livingston Campus, 1973), Livingston College Alumni, SCUA, RUL.

50. Canino Arroyo, "40th Anniversary of the Department of Latino and Hispanic Caribbean Studies."

51. Department of Puerto Rican and Hispanic Caribbean Studies (RG16/B25/01), box 2, SCUA, RUL.

52. "Report to the Puerto Rican Community and Friends—Livingston College, May 1977."

53. Ibid.

54. "Isolation of Livingston College Given as One Reason for the Student Unrest."

55. "Report to the Puerto Rican Community and Friends—Livingston College, May 1977."

56. Ibid.

57. "Isolation of Livingston College Given as One Reason for the Student Unrest."

58. Ibid.

59. *We the People.*

60. Radical Student Movement, "University Repression: Same Fight, Same Enemy," *Daily Targum*, March 28, 1973.

61. Nicholas Iaroslavtsev, "Camden, New Jersey Riots (1969 and 1971)," *Black Past*, July 1, 2018, https://www.blackpast.org/african-american-history/camden-new-jersey-riots -1969-and-1971/.

62. Alfonso Narvaez, "1 Killed, 2 Shot in Camden Riots," *New York Times*, August 22, 1971, https://www.nytimes.com/1971/08/22/archives/1-killed-2-shot-in-camden-riots-mayor -declares-emergency-after-2d.html.

63. Radical Student Movement, "University Repression: Same Fight, Same Enemy."

64. Mike Hammer, "Hearing Group Set Today," *Daily Targum*, April 3, 1973.

65. Ibid.

66. "Report to the Puerto Rican Community and Friends—Livingston College, May 1977."

67. Ibid.

68. Dave Lipshutz, "Protests Continue for Third Day," *Daily Targum*, March 29, 1973.

69. Ibid.

70. Stanley Beiner, "52 Faculty Form Ad Hoc Committee for Justice," *Daily Targum*, April 5, 1973.

71. Ibid.

72. Matthew Knoblauch, "The Scarlet Beat: The Evolution of Law Enforcement at Rutgers," *Journal of the Rutgers University Libraries* 68, no. 2 (2016): 115–153, https://njh .libraries.rutgers.edu/index.php/jrul/article/viewFile/1988/3394.

73. Ibid.

74. Ibid.

75. Ibid.

76. Barry Carter, "Newark Archivist Revives Lost History of Puerto Rican Riots," *NJ.com True Jersey*, March 1, 2016, https://www.nj.com/essex/2016/03/newark_archivist _revives_lost_history_of_puerto_ri.html.

77. "Report to the Puerto Rican Community and Friends—Livingston College, May 1977."

78. Ibid.

79. Ibid.

80. Ibid.

81. Canino Arroyo, "40th Anniversary of the Department of Latino and Hispanic Caribbean Studies."

82. "Report to the Puerto Rican Community and Friends—Livingston College, May 1977."

83. "Puerto Rican Congress Charges Discrimination," *Daily Targum*, May 18, 1977.

84. Ibid.

85. "Congresso Boricua Letter to Bloustein, 1977," Department of Puerto Rican and Hispanic Caribbean Studies (RG16/B25/01), box 2, SCUA, RUL.

86. "El Boletin 10/16/78," Department of Puerto Rican and Hispanic Caribbean Studies (RG16/B25/01), box 2, SCUA, RUL.

87. Ibid.

88. Canino Arroyo, "40th Anniversary of the Department of Latino and Hispanic Caribbean Studies."

89. "Message to Black Students," *Black Voice,* September 24, 1974, SCUA, RUL.

90. Richard P. McCormick, *The Black Student Protest Movement at Rutgers* (New Brunswick, NJ: Rutgers University Press, 1990), 95.

91. Ibid., 95.

92. Ibid., 96.

93. McCormick, *Black Student Protest Movement,* 95.

94. "Ernest Lynton to Richard Schlatter," April 14, 1971, box 3, Records of the Office of the Provost and Vice President (Richard Schlatter), 1945–1972 (RG/MC15/A2) (hereafter Records of Provost and Vice President Richard Schlatter), SCUA, RUL.

95. 1971–1972 Livingston College Catalog (RG21/C2), SCUA, RUL.

96. Patricia Graham Oral History Interview by Molly Graham, April 27, 2015, 13, Rutgers Oral History Archives, https://oralhistory.rutgers.edu/interviewees/1957-graham-patricia.

97. Ibid., 12.

98. 1971–1972 Livingston College Catalog.

99. Vertamae Smart-Grosvenor was a chef, cookbook author, culinary anthropologist, writer, actress, and NPR contributor. In 1970, Smart-Grosvenor published an autobiographical cookbook titled *Vibration Cooking; or, The Travel Notes of a Geechee Girl* (New York: Doubleday, 1970). . For more on Vertamae Smart-Grosvenor, see Doris Witt, *Black Hunger: Soul Food and America* (Minneapolis: University of Minnesota Press, 2004).

100. Patricia Graham Oral History Interview, October 26, 2015, 11.

101. 1971–1972 Livingston College Catalog.

102. Patricia Graham Oral History Interview, October 26, 2015. Graham does not name the professor she spoke about in her oral history.

103. Ibid., 11.

104. Ibid., 11.

105. "Willie J. Smith Letter to Africa 1969," December 29, 1969, box 3, Records of Provost and Vice President Richard Schlatter, SCUA, RUL.

106. "AFRICA '70" promotional flyer, n.d., box 3, folder 8, Records of Provost and Vice President Richard Schlatter, SCUA, RUL.

107. "Melvin Drimmer to Mason Gross," July 17, 1970, box 3, folder 8, Records of Provost and Vice President Richard Schlatter, SCUA, RUL.

108. "AFRICA '70" promotional flyer, n.d.

109. *Livingston in the Retrospect, 1969–1973,* Livingston College Alumni Association, Livingston College, https://archive.org/details/livingstoninretroonoah/page/n15.

110. Ibid.

111. "At Livingston BWCG Awakens Women," *Black Voice,* October 15, 1974, SCUA, RUL.

112. Ibid. The term *double jeopardy,* as it relates to the black feminist movement, was coined by black feminist scholar and activist Frances M. Beal in a 1969 pamphlet

titled "Double Jeopardy: To Be Black and Female." The pamphlet was revised and published in *Sisterhood Is Powerful: An Anthology of Writings from the Women's Liberation Movement*, ed. Robin Morgan (New York: Penguin Random House LLC, 1970).

Beal's concept, now forty years old, of the double oppression black women face because of race and gender, is considered one of the foundational ideas of black feminist theory.

113. Ibid.

114. Ibid.

115. "Message to Black Students," *Black Voice*.

116. Mark Anthony Neal, *What the Music Said: Black Popular Music and Black Public Culture* (New York: Routledge Press, 1999), 109.

117. "Message to Black Students," *Black Voice*.

118. BGLOs emerged on college campuses across America between 1906 and 1963. The nine black Greek letter organizations are Alpha Phi Alpha fraternity, Alpha Kappa Alpha sorority, Omega Psi Phi fraternity, Kappa Alpha Psi fraternity, Delta Sigma Theta sorority, Phi Beta Sigma fraternity, Zeta Phi Beta sorority, Sigma Gamma Rho sorority, and Iota Phi Theta fraternity. For more on BGLOs, see Tamara Brown, *African American Fraternities and Sororities: The Legacy and the Vision* (Lexington: University of Kentucky Press, 2005); Lawrence C. Ross, *The Divine: The History of African American Fraternities and Sororities* (New York: Kensington, 2000).

119. The Delta Iota chapter of Alpha Phi Alpha was chartered in 1950. The Iota Psi chapter of Alpha Kappa Alpha was chartered on June 1, 1975. The Tau Zeta chapter of Omega Psi Phi was chartered on April, 24, 1974. The Eta Epsilon chapter of Kappa Alpha Psi was chartered on March 9, 1974. The Delta Zeta chapter of Delta Sigma Theta was charted on May 27, 1950, as a citywide chapter for Rutgers students within a fifty-mile radius of Rutgers–Newark; *The Rock, Volume II—1977*, 55–161, Livingston College Alumni Association, Livingston College, https://archive.org/details /rockvolumeiioorutg/page/154/mode/2up?q=kappa.

120. Gregory Burke, "Groovin'," *Black Voice*, February 1972, SCUA, RUL.

121. Cynthia Lynne Shelton, "Strategic Essentialism and Black Greek Identity in the Postmodern Era," in Gregory Parks, ed., *Black Greek Letter Organizations in the 21st Century: Our Fight Has Just Begun* (Lexington: University of Kentucky Press, 2005), 213–232.

122. "Second Chapter in State Kappas Get Chartered," *Black Voice*, March 12, 1974, SCUA, RUL.

123. Ibid.

124. Bro. Norm, "Groove Hold Voter Registration Drive," *Black Voice*, April 23, 1974, SCUA, RUL.

125. Norm Eping, "Omega Pearls Par-Tay with Day Care Center Children," *Black Voice*, February 19, 1974, SCUA, RUL.

126. Ibid.

127. Patricia Graham Oral History Interview, October 26, 2015, 8.

128. Gregory A. Burke, "Black Fraternities: A Socio-Political Perspective," *Black Voice*, September 25, 1973, SCUA, RUL.

129. Ibid.

130. Ibid.

131. Brother Henry C., "Response: Black Fraternities Strive for Unity," *Black Voice,* October 2, 1973, SCUA, RUL.

132. Ibid.

133. Ibid.

134. Annette Williams, "Black Sororities," *Black Voice,* October 23, 1973, SCUA, RUL.

135. *The Rock, Volume II—1977,* 172, Livingston College Alumni Association, Livingston College, https://archive.org/details/rockvolumeiioorutg.

136. Ibid.

137. Willie Webb and Soneni Bryant, "B.U.S.T. Mesthene Questioned at Meeting," *Black Voice,* October 8, 1974, SCUA, RUL.

138. Ibid.

139. "Emmanuel Mesthene, Rutgers Professor, 69," *New York Times,* June 14, 1990, https://www.nytimes.com/1990/06/14/obituaries/emmanuel-mesthene-rutgers-professor-69.html. Mesthene served as the dean of Livingston College from 1974 until 1977. He later joined the Philosophy Department and the Graduate School of Management for thirteen years.

140. 1969–1970 Livingston College Catalog (RG21 C2), SCUA, RUL.

141. Webb and Bryant, "B.U.S.T. Mesthene Questioned at Meeting."

142. Ibid.

143. Ibid.

144. *The Rock, Volume II—1977,* 111–122.

145. Webb and Bryant, "B.U.S.T. Mesthene Questioned at Meeting."

146. Ibid.

147. Patricia Graham Oral History Interview, October 26, 2015, 11.

148. From the Livingston College newspaper the *Medium,* September 24, 1974, 4. Quoted in Paul G.E. Clemens and Carla Yanni, "The Early Years of Livingston College, 1964–1973: Revisiting 'The College of Good Intentions,'" *Journal of the Rutgers University Libraries* 68, no. 2 (2016): 100, n.73.

149. William P. Barrett, "Livingston: Image a Problem," *New York Times,* May 5, 1974, https://www.nytimes.com/1974/05/05/archives/livingston-college-image-a-key-to-survival-suggestions-by-rutgers.html.

150. Ibid.

151. Knoblauch, "The Scarlet Beat," 115–153.

152. Clemens and Yanni, "Early Years of Livingston College," 101–105.

153. Ibid, 105.

154. Ibid.

PART III: Making Black Lives Matter beyond Rutgers, 1973–2007

1. On the black campus movement that swept across the United States, see Martha Biondi, *The Black Revolution on Campus* (Berkeley: University of California Press, 2012); Ibram H. Rogers [Ibram X. Kendi], *The Black Campus Movement: Black Students and the Racial Reconstitution of Higher Education, 1965–1972* (New York: Palgrave Macmillan, 2012).

2. See part 2 of this volume.

3. Barack Obama, "Remarks by the President at Commencement Address at Rutgers, the State University of New Jersey," May 15, 2016, Office of the Press Secretary, the White House, https://obamawhitehouse.archives.gov/the-press-office/2016/05/15 /remarks-president-commencement-address-rutgers-state-university-new.

CHAPTER 9: "It's Happening in Our Own Backyard"

1. Assata Shakur, *Assata: An Autobiography* (Chicago: Lawrence Hill Books, 1987), 3.

2. For historical scholarship on Assata Shakur, see Margo V. Perkins, *Autobiography as Activism: Three Black Women of the Sixties* (Jackson: University Press of Mississippi, 2000); Jasmin A. Young, "Strapped: A Historical Analysis of Black Women and Armed Resistance, 1959–1979" (PhD diss., Rutgers, the State University of New Jersey, 2018).

3. Alice Jennings Archibald, quoted in Ian Gavigan and Pamela Walker, "Rutgers and New Brunswick: A Consideration of Impact," chapter 2 in this volume; see also Alice Jennings Archibald Oral History Interview, March 14, 1997, by G. Kurt Piehler and Eve Snyder, 26–27, Rutgers Oral History Archives, https://oralhistory.rutgers.edu /interviewees/750-archibald-alice-jennings.

4. For a deeper discussion of the "New Five" and the shift from liberalism to increasing conservatism in the New Brunswick municipal government, see Gavigan and Walker, "Rutgers and New Brunswick," chapter 2 in this volume.

5. See Deborah Gray White, Mia Bay, and Waldo E. Martin Jr., "Racial Progress in an Era of Backlash and Change, 1967–2000," *Freedom on My Mind: A History of African Americans with Documents*, 2nd ed. (Boston: Bedford/St. Martin's, 2016). For more on the New Right and its link to the criminalization of African Americans and the war on crime, see Elizabeth Hinton, *From the War on Poverty to the War on Crime: The Making of Mass Incarceration in America* (Cambridge, MA: Harvard University Press, 2016).

6. During its tenure, the BLA became one of the most heavily surveilled radical groups in the country, and Shakur was wanted for her alleged involvement in a number of crimes attributed to its members.

7. Angus K. Gillespie Papers 1979–2002 (R-MC 086), box 5, Special Collections and University Archives, Rutgers University Libraries (hereafter SCUA, RUL).

8. Shakur, *Autobiography,* 52.

9. See Gavigan and Walker, "Rutgers and New Brunswick," chapter 2 in this volume.

10. Judith Cummings, "Angela Davis Asks Support for 'Political Prisoners,'" *New York Times,* October 8, 1973.

11. Cheryl Clarke Oral History Interview, September 21, 2018, by Kathryn Tracy Rizzi and Joseph Kaplan, 29, Rutgers Oral History Archives, https://oralhistory.rutgers.edu/ interviewees/2048-clarke-cheryl.

12. S.A. Riley, "Chesimard-Squire Trial Tops WCTC (Forum) Discussion," *Caellian* (Douglass College, New Brunswick, NJ), November 8, 1973.

13. Cheryl Clarke Oral History Interview, September 21, 2018, 29–30.

14. New Brunswick Defense Committee for Joanne Chesimard and Clark Squire, "Events of Chesimard Trial Cause Continuous Delays," *Caellian,* February 7, 1974.

15. See Rosa Mceary, "Acoli's Fate Placed in Hands of Jury," *Black Voice,* March 12, 1974; National Jericho Movement, "Acoli, Sundiata (Clark Squire)," https://www.the jerichomovement.com/profile/acoli-sundiata-clark-squire.

16. Assata Shakur, "Remembering a Revolutionary," http://www.thetalkingdrum.com /bla3.html.

17. Women Against Prison and assata shakur, "w.a.p. interviews assata," *Off Our Backs* 5, no. 11 (1976): 4.

18. Paul Gottlieb, "Kunstler Criticizes Law Enforcement," *Rutgers Daily Targum,* October 25, 1976.

19. Lou Saviano, "Kunstler Urges Jailhouse Protest," *Home News* (New Brunswick, NJ), October 22, 1976.

20. Pam Roberts, "Chesimard's Lawyer Wants Her Out of 'Dungeon' Cell," *Baltimore Afro-American*, July 10, 1976.

21. Liz Meny, "Feminists Publish Alternative Newspaper," *Caellian,* December 2, 1976.

22. Cheryl Clarke, "Assata Shakur: Strength behind Bars," *LABRYS,* December 1976.

23. Ibid.

24. Cheryl Clarke Oral History Interview, September 21, 2018, 32.

25. Cheryl Clarke, "'After Mecca': The Impact of Black Women on Black Poetry after 1968," unpublished dissertation (New Brunswick, NJ), May 2000, 275.

26. "Activists Going to New Brunswick for Chesimard Trial," *New York Times,* January 5, 1977.

27. Shakur, *Autobiography,* 249.

28. Ibid., 250.

29. Joseph F. Sullivan, "Courthouse Is Picketed as Chesimard Trial Starts," *New York Times,* January 18, 1977.

30. Annemarie Cooke, "Begin Jury Picks for Chesimard," *Home News* (New Brunswick, NJ), January 18, 1977.

31. On the Nazi presence at the trial, see Shakur, *Autobiography,* 120–121. Special to the *New York Times,* "Protests Mark Chesimard Trial," *New York Times,* January 12, 1974.

32. Ron Miskoff, "TASS Reporter to Cover Joanne's Trial," *Home News* (New Brunswick, NJ), February 19, 1977.

33. On the civil rights movement and racism in America as a Cold War issue, see Mary L. Dudziak, *Cold War Civil Rights: Race and the Image of American Democracy* (Princeton, NJ: Princeton University Press, 2011).

34. Vladimir Baydashin, "U.S. Authorities Persistently Persecute Nonconformists," TASS (Moscow, USSR), February 22, 1977, daily report, Soviet Union (FBIS-SOV-77-041), March 2, 1977.

35. Ibid.

36. Reginald Kavanaugh, "Judge Called Biased after Expelling Woman," *Home News* (New Brunswick, NJ), February 23, 1977.

37. Shakur, *Autobiography,* 246.

38. Kavanaugh, "Judge Called Biased after Expelling Woman."

39. Lorraine Stone, "Chesimard Supporter Attacks Critics," *Home News* (New Brunswick, NJ), March 1, 1977.

40. Shakur, *Autobiography,* 248.

41. Ibid., 246.

42. This exchange taken from Lawrence Nagy, "Chesimard Trial Erupts at the 'Doff' of a Hat," *Newark Star-Ledger,* March 3, 1977.

43. Ibid.

44. Lawrence Nagy, "Chesimard Defense Criticizes State's Tactics," *Newark Star-Ledger,* March 6, 1977.

45. Ibid.

46. Paul Brown, "Protest Signs Fail to Reach Jury," *Newark Star-Ledger,* March 16, 1977.

47. Joy James, ed., *The New Abolitionists: (Neo)Slave Narratives and Contemporary Prison Writings* (Albany: State University of New York Press, 2005), 91.

48. Lawrence Nagy, "Chesimard Guilty, Gets Life in Prison," *Newark Star-Ledger,* March 26, 1977.

49. All quotes ibid.

50. Shakur, *Autobiography,* 252.

51. Denyse Johnson, "Inquiring Photographer: Question—What Do You Think about the Conviction of Assata Shakur?," *Black Voice/Carta Boricua,* April 5, 1977.

52. Ibid.

53. Ibid.

54. Ibid.

55. S.A. Riley, "Chesimard-Squires Trial," *Caellian,* November 8, 1973.

56. Cheryl Clarke Oral History Interview, September 21, 2018, 30.

CHAPTER 10: Fight Racism, End Apartheid

1. Martha Biondi, *The Black Revolution on Campus* (Berkeley: University of California Press, 2012).

2. Paul G.E. Clemens, *Rutgers since 1945: A History of the State University of New Jersey* (New Brunswick, NJ: Rutgers University Press, 2015), 57.

3. Ibid.

4. *New Left* is an umbrella term for radical leftist activism and intellectual and cultural production in the 1960s and 1970s. On Rutgers and New Left organizing in the 1960s and 1970s, see chapter 2 in this volume; Matthew Countryman, "Lessons of the Divestment Drive," *Nation,* March 26, 1988, 408–409.

5. Countryman, "Lessons of the Divestment Drive," 408–409; see also Countryman, "Divestment, Then and Now," *Yale Daily News,* February 8, 2017, https://yaledaily news.com/blog/2017/02/08/countryman-divestment-then-and-now/.

6. "Activities against South African Apartheid," CISSAL pamphlet, Progressive Activist Files, 1921–1993, box 4, folder 27, Special Collections and University Archives, Rutgers University Libraries (hereafter SCUA, RUL).

7. Ibid.

8. "Anti-Apartheid Activities," Progressive Activist Files, 1921–1993, box 4, folder 27, SCUA, RUL.

9. For more on busing and antibusing protest, see Matthew F. Delmont, *Why Busing Failed: Race, Media, and the National Resistance to School Desegregation* (Berkeley: University of California Press, 2016); Matthew Delmont and Jeanne Theoharis, "Introduction: Rethinking the Boston 'Busing Crisis,'" *Journal of Urban History* 43, no. 2 (March 2017): 191–203.

10. "Anti-Apartheid Report #III," National Student Convention Records 1984–1992, box 4, folder 31, SCUA, RUL.

11. Afrikaans is a language that is rooted primarily in Dutch, and it also has influences from the indigenous languages of the region. It arose in the nineteenth century in South Africa, which was under Dutch colonial rule. The use of Afrikaans in black South African schools became a point of contention because it was deeply entrenched in the apartheid system as a whole and specifically in the ideology of the Afrikaner Nationalist Party (NP) that came into power in 1948. Apartheid as a policy came into being under this political regime. Scholar Hein Willemse writes, "Under apartheid, language was deployed as a tool of tribalism, in the service of this divide-and-rule policy"; Hein Willemse, "More Than an Oppressor's Language: Reclaiming the Hidden History of Afrikaans," *The Conversation,* April 27, 2017, https://theconversation.com/more-than-an-oppressors-language-reclaiming -the-hidden-history-of-afrikaans-71838. See also South African History Online, "A History of Apartheid in South Africa," https://www.sahistory.org.za/article/history -apartheid-south-africa. On the Soweto Uprising, see South African History Online, "The June 16 Soweto Uprising," https://www.sahistory.org.za/article/june-16-soweto -youth-uprising, and "The Soweto Uprising Leaves 174 Blacks and Two Whites Dead Following 10 Days of Rioting," https://www.sahistory.org.za/dated-event/soweto -uprising-leaves-174-blacks-and-two-whites-dead-following-10-days-rioting. For a complete list of youth casualties of the uprising, see South African History Online, "June 16 Soweto Youth Uprising Casualties," https://www.sahistory.org.za/article /june-16-soweto-youth-uprising-casualties.

12. Biondi, *Black Revolution on Campus*; Sekou M. Franklin, *After the Rebellion: Black Youth, Social Movement Activism, and the Post–Civil Rights Generation* (New York: New York University Press, 2014).

13. Statement of Rutgers Coalition for Total Divestment, National Student Convention Records 1984–1992, box 1, folder 5, SCUA, RUL.

14. On the nationwide scope of the anti-apartheid movement on college campuses, see Countryman, "Lessons of the Divestment Drive," 408–409.

15. Franklin, *After the Rebellion,* 89.

16. Kelly-Jane Cotter, "Internal Conflicts Plagued Divestment Coalition," *Daily Targum,* May 8, 1986, 1, National Student Convention Records 1984–1992, box 1, folder 6, SCUA, RUL.

17. Ibid., 1.

18. Ibid., 3.

19. Ibid.

20. Ibid., 1.

21. Ibid., 3.

22. See Biondi, *Black Revolution on Campus*; Franklin, *After the Rebellion*; Ibram H. Rogers [Ibram X. Kendi], *The Black Campus Movement: Black Students and the Racial Reconstitution of Higher Education, 1965–1972* (New York: Palgrave Macmillan, 2012).

23. On anti–affirmative action policies beginning with President Nixon, see Deborah Gray White, Mia Bay, and Waldo E. Martin Jr., "Racial Progress in an Era of Backlash and Change, 1965–2000," *Freedom on My Mind: A History of African Americans with Documents*, 3rd ed. (forthcoming).

24. "Proposal for Structural Change," National Student Convention Records 1984–1992, box 1, folder 5, SCUA, RUL.

25. Ibid. The use of the term *colorblind* here alludes to anti–affirmative action arguments that embraced a color-blind ideology as a tactic to dismantle and block critical civil rights legislation. Opponents of affirmative action often claimed that using race or gender in consideration for employment, education, or housing created "reverse racism" or "reverse discrimination"; see White et al., "Racial Progress in an Era of Backlash and Change."

26. "Proposal for Structural Change."

27. Address by Christine Kelly, "Movement Structure and the Dynamics of Racism in Rutgers Coalition for Total Divestment," I, National Student Convention Records 1984–1992, box I, folder 5, SCUA, RUL.

28. Ibid., 2.

29. Ibid.

30. "Proposal for Structural Change."

31. Cotter, "Internal Conflicts Plagued Divestment Coalition," I.

32. "Proposal for Structural Change."

33. Cotter, "Internal Conflicts Plagued Divestment Coalition," I.

34. Joyce Purnick and Michael Oreskes, "Jesse Jackson Aims for the Mainstream," *New York Times*, November 29, 1987.

35. "A Weekend of High, Low Moments," *Philadelphia Inquirer*, February 27, 1984.

36. Joseph Aronds, "Jackson Racist," *Daily Targum*, April 22, 1985, Progressive Activist Files, 1921–1993, box 5, folder 29, SCUA, RUL.

37. Eleanor Levine, "Diffusing the Jackson Controversy," *Daily Targum*, April 22, 1985, Progressive Activist Files, 1921–1993, box 5, folder 29, SCUA, RUL. For more on Kunstler, specifically his role in the Assata Shakur case, see chapter 9 in this volume.

38. Miriam Aronoff and Martin Goldman, "See the Cause," *Daily Targum*, April 22, 1985, Progressive Activist Files, 1921–1993, box 5, folder 29, SCUA, RUL.

39. Levine, "Diffusing the Jackson Controversy."

40. Global Nonviolent Action Database, "Rutgers University Students Win Divestment from Apartheid South Africa, 1985," https://nvdatabase.swarthmore.edu/content/rutgers-university-students-win-divestment-apartheid-south-africa-1985.

41. Kelly-Jane Cotter and Dave Pettit, "Jesse Jackson Addresses Crowd of 5,000," *Daily Targum*, April 24, 1985, I, Progressive Activist Files, 1921–1993, box 5, folder 29, SCUA, RUL. Shakir's speech to the crowd took on the form of a mock trial of President Ronald Reagan and Rutgers's president, Edward J. Bloustein. He indicted Reagan with "raising up a racist system" and Bloustein for using "our money"—student tuition—to support a "system of racism." At the end of the speech, the "jury" (the crowd of 5,000) found Reagan and Bloustein "guilty." Shakir's rousing address charged both the nation and the school of having priorities antithetical to the values that the nation and the university purported to hold, all the while using the money of the taxpayer or the tuition payer to prop up apartheid. His critique against the money spent on a football team mirrored his critique on divestment: He, and the crowd, felt that the university could spend its money on more productive initiatives to help the Rutgers students, the New Brunswick community, and the world.

42. Clemens, *Rutgers since 1945*, 324.

43. Ibid.

44. Kelly-Jane Cotter and Dave Pettit, "Jackson, Bloustein Meet to Discuss Divestment," *Daily Targum*, April 24, 1985, 1, Progressive Activist Files, 1921–1993, box 5, folder 29, SCUA, RUL.

45. Ibid.

46. Ibid.

47. Ibid.

48. Chris Conway, "Jackson Lashes Rutgers at Apartheid Protest," *Philadelphia Inquirer*, April 24, 1985.

49. Ibid.

50. "Rutgers Trustees Vote to Divest of South African Investments," Associated Press, October 18, 1985, https://nvdatabase.swarthmore.edu/content/rutgers-university -students-win-divestment-apartheid-south-africa-1985.

51. Cotter, "Internal Conflicts Plagued Divestment Coalition," 3.

52. Ibid.

53. Ibid.

CHAPTER 11: "Hell No, Our Genes Aren't Slow!"

1. "Protestors Want Him Out, but Lawrence Stands Firm," *Asbury Park Press*, February 9, 1995, box 2, folder 1, Walton R. Johnson Papers, 1949–2001 (R-MC 082), Special Collections and University Archives, Rutgers University Libraries (hereafter Walton Johnson Papers, SCUA, RUL).

2. "Brief Summary of 1992–'93 Bias Prevention Efforts," n.d.; "Cheryl Clarke to Bias Prevention Steering Committee Regarding 1993–'94 Incidents Reported," May 31, 1995; "Cheryl Clarke to Bias Prevention Steering Committee Regarding 1994–'95 Bias Statistics," June 7, 1995, box 4, folder 9, Walton Johnson Papers, SCUA, RUL.

3. Thomas Corcoran and Nathan Sovronick, "More Than Equal: New Jersey's Quality Education Act," in Marilyn J. Gittel, ed., *Strategies for School Equity: Creating Productive Schools in a Just Society* (New Haven, CT: Yale University Press, 1998), 57. See also Mary Crystal Cage, "Progress That New Jersey Colleges Made in the 80's Threatened by Financial Crisis, Higher-Education Leadership Vacuum," *Chronicle of Higher Education*, May 23, 1990.

4. "Rutgers '90–'91: New President, Tight Budget," August 23, 1990; "Rutgers President Looks for Balance," October 7, 1990; "RU Head Deserves Chance," November 7, 1990; various newspaper clippings, box 1, folder 5, Walton Johnson Papers, SCUA, RUL.

5. "Rutgers '90–91: New President, Tight Budget," August 23, 1990; "New RU Head Gets Top Marks," January 23, 1991, box 1, folder 5, Walton Johnson Papers, SCUA, RUL.

6. "RU Head Deserves Chance," November 7, 1990.

7. Corcoran and Scovronick, "More Than Equal," 54; "Rutgers President Stresses School-University Programs," October 20, 1990, box 1, folder 5, Walton Johnson Papers, SCUA, RUL.

8. "New RU Head Gets Top Marks," January 23, 1991.

9. "RU Bullish on Research," July 9, 1991; "Browder Is RU's Latest Ex-Official," July 10, 1991; "Resignation Starts Quake at Rutgers," July 10, 1991; "University President Francis L. Lawrence," n.d., box 1, folder 5, Walton Johnson Papers, SCUA, RUL.

10. "Sit-In 'Extends' Rutgers Library Hours," 1991, box 1, folder 10, Walton Johnson Papers, SCUA, RUL.

11. "Students Forced Out of BOG Meeting," November 16, 1992, box 1, folder 10, Walton Johnson Papers, SCUA, RUL; Francis L. Lawrence, ed., "Francis L. Lawrence," in *Leadership in Higher Education: Views from the Presidency* (Piscataway, NJ: Transaction, 2006), 365.

12. Adrienne Knox, "Students Are Arrested in Protest at Rutgers," *Star-Ledger,* May 1, 1993, box 1, folder 10, Walton Johnson Papers, SCUA, RUL.

13. "The Corporatization of the University," n.d.; "Education for All!," November 1992, box 1, folder 10, Walton Johnson Papers, SCUA, RUL. Assorted graphics illustrating disparities in education are scattered throughout this folder. See also Erica Simon, "Lawrence Resign NOW!," *In Our Time!* 2, no. 2 (January 1993), box 1, folder 10, Walton Johnson Papers, SCUA, RUL.

14. "Rutgers Won't Allow Censorship by Disruption," February 5, 1993, box 1, folder 10, Walton Johnson Papers, SCUA, RUL.

15. "RU Fascist?," January 1993, box 1, folder 10, Walton Johnson Papers, SCUA, RUL. See also Simon, "Lawrence Resign NOW!"

16. Simon, "Lawrence Resign Now!"

17. Andrew Hartman, *A War for the Soul of America: A History of the Culture Wars,* 2nd ed. (Chicago: University of Chicago Press, 2019 [2015]), 2.

18. On Francis Lawrence's aloof and autocratic style, see "Past Frictions Hurt Lawrence," February 11, 1995, box 3, folder 10, Walton Johnson Papers, SCUA, RUL; "Critics Say Aloofness Adds to Plight of Rutgers President," February 13, 1995, box 3, folder 4, Walton Johnson Papers, SCUA, RUL; "Style Change Needed for Rutgers' Lawrence," February 14, 1995, box 2, folder 6, Walton Johnson Papers, SCUA, RUL; "It's Time for Lawrence to Leave Rutgers University," February 24, 1995, box 2, folder 1, Walton Johnson Papers, SCUA, RUL; "Flash Point at Rutgers U," February 24, 1995, box 2, folder 4, Walton Johnson Papers, SCUA, RUL; "The Man behind the War of Words at Rutgers," n.d., box 3, folder 5, Walton Johnson Papers, SCUA, RUL.

19. "Rutgers Chief Cites Genetics in Test Scores of Minorities," January 31, 1995, box 3, folder 9, Walton Johnson Papers, SCUA, RUL.

20. For Lawrence's apology and subsequent clarifying remarks, see "President Lawrence's Apology," February 1, 1995, box 2, folder 8, Walton Johnson Papers, SCUA, RUL; "Rutgers President Disavows Remark about Heredity and Test Scores," January 31, 1995, box 2, folder 2, Walton Johnson Papers, SCUA, RUL; "Rutgers President Says Remark about Heredity Was an Error," February 1, 1995, box 2, folder 2, Walton Johnson Papers, SCUA, RUL; "Rutgers President Says He Didn't Mean Remarks on Heredity," February 1, 1995, box 2, folder 3, Walton Johnson Papers, SCUA, RUL. For more on the long history of institutions of higher learning within the United States fostering race-making, racial science, and white supremacy, see Craig Steven Wilder, *Ebony and Ivy: Race, Slavery, and the Troubled History of America's Universities* (New York: Bloomsbury Press, 2013); Louis Menand, "Morton, Agassiz, and the Origins of Scientific Racism in the United States," *Journal of Blacks in Higher Education,* no. 34 (Winter 2001–2002): 110–112; Peper Carroll, "Race Science and Columbia," The Columbia University and Slavery Project, https://columbiaandslavery.columbia.edu /content/race-science-and-columbia; Leslie M. Harris, "The Long, Ugly History of Racism at American Universities," *New Republic,* March 26, 2015, https://newrepublic .com/article/121382/forgotten-racist-past-american-universities; Adam S. Cohen, "Harvard's Eugenics Era," *Harvard Magazine,* March–April 2016, https://harvard magazine.com/2016/03/harvards-eugenics-era.

21. On a second chance being warranted, see "Beyond the Curve: Rutgers University President Can Recover," February 4, 1995, box 2, folder 1, Walton Johnson Papers, SCUA, RUL; "Strike One: Rutgers President Has Earned Second Chance," February 5, 1995, box 2, folder 1, Walton Johnson Papers, SCUA, RUL; "Ride Out the Storm: Rutgers President Is Owed a Second Chance," February 15, 1995, box 2, folder 1, Walton Johnson Papers, SCUA, RUL; "Lawrence Remarks Don't Match His Lifetime of Effort," n.d., box 2, folder 13, Walton Johnson Papers, SCUA, RUL. On the subject of Lawrence becoming a victim of PC culture, see "New Motto at Rutgers: No Mistakes Allowed," February 5, 1995, box 2, folder 5, Walton Johnson Papers, SCUA, RUL; "Race and Irony at Rutgers," February 10, 1995, box 2, folder 3, Walton Johnson Papers, SCUA, RUL; "Give Him a Break," February 17, 1995, box 2, folder 6, Walton Johnson Papers, SCUA, RUL; "On Being Genetically Correct," February 24, 1995, box 3, folder 2, Walton Johnson Papers, SCUA, RUL; "Unanswered Questions for Lawrence Detractors," February 28, 1995, box 2, folder 5, Walton Johnson Papers, SCUA, RUL. For articles calling for the president's resignation, see "Students Demand Lawrence Quit," February 2, 1995, box 2, folder 5, Walton Johnson Papers, SCUA, RUL; "National NAACP Joins Call for Resignation," February 2, 1995, box 2, folder 8, Walton Johnson Papers, SCUA, RUL; "It's Time for Lawrence to Leave Rutgers University," February 24, 1995, box 2, folder 1, Walton Johnson Papers, SCUA, RUL; "Black Clergy Call for Rutgers Chief's Resignation," February 28, 1995, box 3, folder 9, Walton Johnson Papers, SCUA, RUL.

22. Richard J. Herrnstein and Charles Murray, *The Bell Curve: Intelligence and Class Structure in American Life* (New York: The Free Press, 1994), 14, 292, 276, 25, 389, 416, 542, 536.

23. Ibid., 551. For other texts that exemplify the conservatism of the 1980s and 1990s, see, for example, Alan Bloom, *The Closing of the American Mind: How Higher Education Has Failed Democracy and Impoverished the Souls of Today's Students* (New York: Simon and Schuster, 1987); David Frum, *Dead Right* (New York: Basic Books, 1994); Lynne V. Cheney, *Telling the Truth: Why Our Culture and Our Country Have Stopped Making Sense and What We Can Do about It* (New York: Simon & Schuster, 1995); Dinesh D'Souza, *The End of Racism: Principles for a Multiracial Society* (New York: Free Press Paperbacks, 1995). For a broader look at conservative thought during this period, see Patrick Allit, *The Conservatives: Ideas and Personalities throughout American History* (New Haven, CT: Yale University Press, 2009), 255–276.

24. Stephen Jay Gould, *The Mismeasure of Man,* rev. and expanded ed. (New York: W.W. Norton, 1996 [1981]), 52–53. Critical works in feminist and postcolonial science and technology studies have long undermined the primacy of "objectivity" in science, have highlighted the ways in which scientific knowledge and authority cannot be extricated from human subjectivities or power structures, and have expanded the definition of both science and its practitioners. Some examples include Evelyn Fox Keller, *Reflections on Gender and Science* (New Haven, CT: Yale University Press, 1985); Donna Haraway, "Situated Knowledges: The Science Question in Feminism and the Privilege of Partial Perspective," *Feminist Studies* 14, no. 3 (1988): 575–599; Gyan Prakash, *Another Reason: Science and the Imagination of Modern India* (Princeton, NJ: Princeton University Press, 1999); Sandra Harding, *Science and Social Inequality: Feminist and Postcolonial Issues* (Urbana: University of Illinois Press, 2006); Kapil Raj, *Relocating Modern Science: Circulation and the Construction of Knowledge in South Asia and Europe, 1650–1900* (New York: Palgrave Macmillan, 2007).

25. Stephen Jay Gould, "Curveball," *New Yorker,* November 28, 1994. For additional assessments and critiques of *The Bell Curve,* see Michael E. Staub, *The Mismeasure*

of Minds: Debating Race and Intelligence between Brown and the Bell Curve (Chapel Hill: University of North Carolina Press, 2018); Dorothy Roberts, "Can Research on the Genetics of Intelligence Be 'Socially Neutral'?," in *The Genetics of Intelligence: Ethics and the Conduct of Trustworthy Research*, ed. Erik Parens and Paul S. Appelbaum, special report, *Hastings Center Report* 45, no. 5 (September–October 2015): s50–s53; Gould, *Mismeasure of Man*; Claude S. Fischer et al., *Inequality by Design: Cracking the Bell Curve Myth* (Princeton, NJ: Princeton University Press, 1996).

26. "Race and Irony at Rutgers," February 10, 1995, box 2, folder 3, Walton Johnson Papers, SCUA, RUL.

27. "Quote: Rutgers President Faces Firestorm over Seeming Bias," February 1, 1995, box 2, folder 13, Walton Johnson Papers, SCUA, RUL.

28. "Rutgers Chief Isn't the Enemy," March 10, 1995, box 2, folder 6, Walton Johnson Papers, SCUA, RUL; "National NAACP Joins Call for Resignation," February 2, 1995, box 2, folder 8, Walton Johnson Papers, SCUA, RUL.

29. "Callers Support Rutgers University President," February 6, 1995, box 2, folder 5, Walton Johnson Papers, SCUA, RUL.

30. Lawrence, "Francis L. Lawrence," 359.

31. "Minority Group Bolsters Rutgers President," February 7, 1995, box 2, folder 5, Walton Johnson Papers, SCUA, RUL; "Robeson Jr. Urges Lawrence Reprieve," February 7, 1995, box 2, folder 8, Walton Johnson Papers, SCUA, RUL; "Students Take Unrest to Streets, Demand Action," February 2, 1995, box 2, folder 10, Walton Johnson Papers, SCUA, RUL; Ibram H. Rogers [Ibram X. Kendi], *The Black Campus Movement: Black Students and the Racial Reconstitution of Higher Education, 1965–1972* (New York: Palgrave Macmillan, 2012).

32. This phrase appeared in Danielle Smith's published piece in *Black Voice/Carta Boricua* on February 15, 1995, where she states that the USC should continue to fight for their demands and work as a unified front.

33. M.E. Eversley, "State NAACP Slips in Effort to Oust Rutgers President," *Asbury Park Press,* July 11, 1995, box 2, folder 1, Walton Johnson Papers, SCUA, RUL; RAAA to Board of Governors, February 9, 1995, box 4, folder 15, Walton Johnson Papers, SCUA, RUL.

34. Speakers List, Board of Governors Meeting, Rutgers, the State University of New Jersey, February 10, 1995, box 4, folder 2, Walton Johnson Papers, SCUA, RUL; T. Zolper, "Managing to Offend Everybody," *Asbury Park Press,* February 12, 1995, box 2, folder 1, Walton Johnson Papers, SCUA, RUL.

35. Remarks by Joseph Seneca, Vice President for Undergraduate Academic Affairs, at the February 10, 1995, Board of Governors Meeting, box 4, folder 2, Walton Johnson Papers, SCUA, RUL.

36. Quoted in Jake Arnay, "Francis Lawrence on African American Genetics at Rutgers University," unpublished undergraduate research seminar paper, Rutgers University, Spring 2018, Professor Deborah Gray White.

37. "Students Demand Lawrence Quit," February 2, 1995, box 2, folder 5, Walton Johnson Papers, SCUA, RUL; "Legislators Vow to Back Students, Pledge Full Probe," February 2, 1995, box 2, folder 8, Walton Johnson Papers, SCUA, RUL; "Students Take Unrest to Streets, Demand Action," February 2, 1995, box 2, folder 10, Walton Johnson Papers, SCUA, RUL.

38. "Protestors Should Be Proud of Their Cause," February 14, 1995, box 2, folder 9, Walton Johnson Papers, SCUA, RUL.

39. "Howard U. Prof Sends Support to Protestors," February 16, 1995, box 2, folder 9, Walton Johnson Papers, SCUA, RUL.

40. United Students Coalition at Rutgers University, 1995, box 4, folder 19, Walton Johnson Papers, SCUA, RUL; B.J. Navarro, "Hunger Strikers Holding Out for Their Demands," *Asbury Park Press,* April 16, 1995, box 2, folder 1, Walton Johnson Papers, SCUA, RUL.

41. A. John-Hall, "From One Man's Casual Remark, a Movement Sprouts at Rutgers," *Philadelphia Inquirer,* February 9, 1995, box 3, folder 5, Walton Johnson Papers, SCUA, RUL.

42. Ibid.

43. Quoted in Arnay, "Francis Lawrence on African American Genetics at Rutgers University," 14.

44. United Students Coalition at Rutgers University, 1995.

45. Statement of Members of the Board of Governors and Executive Committee of the Board of Trustees, Rutgers, the State University of New Jersey, January 31, 1995, box 4, folder 2, Walton Johnson Papers, SCUA, RUL.

46. Quoted in Arnay, "Francis Lawrence on African American Genetics at Rutgers University," 13.

47. Simon, "Lawrence Resign NOW!" Mason Gross earned the reputation for being kind to protesters. Simon's article describes how Gross ordered pizza for student antiwar protesters as an example of this.

48. "Disruptions, South Jersey—Demand of Black Student Unity Movement and University's Response," 1969, box 35, folder 2, Inventory to the Records of the Rutgers University President (Mason Welch Gross), 1936, 1945–1971, SCUA, RUL.

49. "Student Protests—Rutgers (pre-1995)," box 1, folder 10, Walton Johnson Papers, SCUA, RUL. On February 5, 1993, President Lawrence published a response to activists: "To allow thoughtful, reasonable people to be heard, the board must [close down] the raucous circus of demonstrators, hecklers, and tantrum throwers (your phrases) who have made it [impossible] for people with legitimate concerns about the business actually on the board's meeting agenda to bring their concerns to the board." Days later, the administration implemented policies and procedures that required individuals wishing to speak with the BOG or other administrators to submit written testimony and warned that any disruption to the meeting would be met with legal consequences such as arrest. The enforcement of this policy highlights how the university created barriers to dialogue to uphold and reinforce its power; see "President Lawrence Letter to Newspaper," February 5, 1993, box 1, folder 10, Walton Johnson Papers, SCUA, RUL; J.C. Shearman, "Students Challenging Ban on Public Role at RU Board Sessions Delay Court Plans," February 12, 1993, box 1, folder 10, Walton Johnson Papers, SCUA, RUL.

50. Navarro, "Hunger Strikers Holding Out for Their Demands"; "Rutgers Battle Lines Harden," *Asbury Park Press,* February 9, 1995, box 2, folder 1, Walton Johnson Papers, SCUA, RUL; S.K. Livio, "I Was Not Supposed to Be the Only One," *Asbury Park Press,* February 9, 1995, box 2, folder 1, Walton Johnson Papers, SCUA, RUL; M.E. Eversley, "Protestors Want Him Out, but Lawrence Stands Firm," *Asbury Park Press,* February 9, 1995, box 2, folder 1, Walton Johnson Papers, SCUA, RUL. Although these three examples represent a more high-profile form of protest, this was not the only form that the USC engaged in. For example, on February 8, 1995, the USC penned a letter

to the State of New Jersey saying that Lawrence's comments the previous fall were not an isolated incident. Furthermore, they challenged the argument put forward by Lawrence's supporters that the president was committed to growing a diverse student body and faculty by noting that well-known authors Toni Morrison and Amiri Baraka departed from Rutgers after they were denied tenure. Morrison and Baraka are only two examples of professors of color who were reportedly denied tenure under the Lawrence administration. The letter also framed Lawrence's stated commitment to diversity as an act of paternalism. The writers claimed that although Lawrence placed people of color in high-ranking administrative roles, such as the dean of Livingston College and the vice president of student affairs, they were merely "syncophants [sic] of diverse hues" that reinforced Lawrence's "paternalistic" view; see Arnay, "Francis Lawrence on African American Genetics at Rutgers University," 11–12.

51. Livio, "I Was Not Supposed to Be the Only One"; D. McGrath-Kerr and C. Siemaszko, "One Student Tackles Prez of Rutgers," *New York Daily News*, February 9, 1995, box 2, folder 7, Walton Johnson Papers, SCUA, RUL.

52. Livio, "I Was Not Supposed to Be the Only One."

53. Doreen Carvajal, "Protest against President Halts Basketball Game," *New York Times*, February 8, 1995, https://www.nytimes.com/1995/02/08/nyregion/protest-against-president-halts-basketball-game-at-rutgers.html.

54. Ibid.

55. Ibid.

56. McGrath-Kerr and Siemaszko, "One Student Tackles Prez of Rutgers."

57. Eversley, "Protestors Want Him Out, but Lawrence Stands Firm."

58. Navarro, "Hunger Strikers Holding Out for Their Demands."

59. Ibid., A7.

60. Ibid., 1.

61. Quoted in Arnay, "Francis Lawrence on African American Genetics at Rutgers University," 7.

62. L. Reisberg and W. Gillette, "Police Want to Identify, Charge Student Protestors," *Asbury Park Press*, April 14, 1995, box 2, folder 1, Walton Johnson Papers, SCUA, RUL.

63. Quoted in Arnay, "Francis Lawrence on African American Genetics at Rutgers University," 8. See also D. Scipio, "Breaking the Silence: United Student Coalition Leaders Discuss the Day of Outrage Part One," *Black Voice/Carta Latina*, November 9, 1995, *Black Voice*, Spring 1993–Fall 1996, R-Newspapers, SCUA, RUL.

64. Scipio, "Breaking the Silence."

65. Ibid.

66. Reisberg and Gillette, "Police Want to Identify, Charge Student Protestors."

67. Quoted in Arnay, "Francis Lawrence on African American Genetics at Rutgers University," 8.

68. Ibid., 9.

69. Personal interview with Victor Carbonell, Rutgers alumnus of 1996, conducted on February 18, 2019, by Roberto C. Orozco.

70. "Coalition of Black and Latino Faculty and Staff," February 10, 1995, box 4, folder 4, Walton Johnson Papers, SCUA, RUL.

71. "Coalition of Black and Latino Faculty and Staff, Proposed Structure," February 1995, box 4, folder 4, Walton Johnson Papers, SCUA, RUL.

72. Other faculty entities outside of the Coalition of Black and Latino Faculty and Staff highlighted Lawrence's broader record on race during his administration and longer history of aggressive behavior toward student activists. For example, the Committee for Academic Freedom at Rutgers University released a flyer titled "Lawrence's Racial Slur Is Not an Isolated Incident." This document put a spotlight on Lawrence's handling of student protests, including that he "ordered or condoned the beating and jailing of students . . . is known to babble and digress in public addresses . . . and has made more than one such racial remark." See "Lawrence's Racial Slur Is Not an Isolated Incident," Committee for Academic Freedom at Rutgers University, February 1, 1995, box 4, folder 15, Walton Johnson Papers, SCUA, RUL; Arnay, "Francis Lawrence on African American Genetics at Rutgers University," 12.

73. "Letter from Dennis A. Mumble to University Administration," box 4, folder 3, Walton Johnson Papers, SCUA, RUL.

74. "Initial Memo by the Coalition of Black and Latino Faculty and Staff to Rutgers Administration and President Lawrence," box 4, folder 3, Walton Johnson Papers, SCUA, RUL.

75. "A List of Recommendations to Assure the Improvement of the 'Quality of Life' for Members of the Black and Latino Community (Students and Staff)," Coalition of Black and Latino Faculty and Staff, box 4, folder 4, Walton Johnson Papers, SCUA, RUL.

76. Ibid.

77. "Multicultural Student Life Recommendations," submitted by Francis L. Lawrence to the Board of Governors of Rutgers, the State University of New Jersey, box 4, folder 3, Walton Johnson Papers, SCUA, RUL.

78. Ibid.

79. Walton Johnson Papers, SCUA, RUL.

80. The title for the conclusion of this chapter is borrowed from Tariq Muhammad's published piece in *Black Voice/Carta Boricua* on April 13, 1994, where he speaks about the ongoing struggles of people of color at Rutgers University.

81. Martha Biondi, *The Black Revolution on Campus* (Berkeley: University of California Press, 2012); Robert Rhoads, *Freedom's Web: Student Activism in an Age of Cultural Diversity* (Baltimore: Johns Hopkins University Press, 1998); Ibram H. Rogers [Ibram X. Kendi], *The Black Campus Movement: Black Students and Racial Reconstitution of Higher Education, 1965–1972* (New York: Palgrave Macmillan, 2012).

82. T. Muhammad, " . . . and the Struggle Continues," *Black Voice/Carta Boricua*, April 13, 1994, in *Black Voice*, Spring 1993–Fall 1996, R-Newspapers, SCUA, RUL.

CHAPTER 12: "Pure Grace"

1. C. Vivian Stringer and Laura Tucker, *Standing Tall: A Memoir of Tragedy and Triumph* (New York: Crown, 2008), 246.

2. *News 4 New York*, WNBC-TV 4, March 27, 2007, disc 1, Records of the Don Imus Controversy, April 4–May 9, 2007 (RG 07/A1c), Special Collections and University Archives, Rutgers University Libraries (hereafter Records of the Don Imus Controversy, SCUA, RUL).

3. *Five O'Clock News,* WCBS-TV 2, April 3, 2007, disc 1, Records of the Don Imus Controversy, SCUA, RUL.

4. "One Step Short," *Daily Targum,* April 4, 2007, SCUA, RUL; Steve Williamson, "Fans Cheer Even in Loss," *Daily Targum,* April 4, 2007, SCUA, RUL.

5. *News 12 New Jersey,* April 5, 2007, disc 1, Records of the Don Imus Controversy, SCUA, RUL.

6. *Ten O'Clock News,* WWOR 9, April 5, 2007, disc 2, Records of the Don Imus Controversy, SCUA, RUL.

7. Media Matters for America, April 4, 2007, "Imus Called Women's Basketball Team 'Nappy-Headed Hos,'" Imus Transcript, Records of the Don Imus Controversy, SCUA, RUL.

8. "About Media Matters for America," n.d., https://www.mediamatters.org/about.

9. "Memo to Richard L. McCormick from Kim Manning," July 3, 2007, folder Imus Transcript, Records of the Don Imus Controversy, SCUA, RUL.

10. Faye Linda Wachs, Cheryl Cooky, Michael A. Messner, and Shari L. Dworkin, "Media Frames and Displacement of Blame in the Don Imus/Rutgers Women's Basketball Team Incident: Sincere Fictions and Frenetic Inactivity," *Critical Studies in Media and Communication* 29, no. 5 (2012): 421–438, doi:10.1080/15295036.2011.646282.

11. Clifford J. Levy, "Harlem Protest of Rap Lyrics Draws Debate and Steamroller," *New York Times,* June 6, 1993, https://www.nytimes.com/1993/06/06/nyregion/harlem -protest-of-rap-lyrics-draws-debate-and-steamroller.html; *FOX News at 5,* WNYW 5, April 10, 2007, disc 3, Records of the Don Imus Controversy, SCUA, RUL; Jesse Jackson, "In the End, Right Message on Imus Was Aired," *Chicago Sun-Times,* April 17, 2007, Media Relations folder, Press Coverage 10, Records of the Don Imus Controversy, SCUA, RUL; *Meet the Press,* NBC, April 17, 2007, Media Relations folder, Press Coverage 7, Records of the Don Imus Controversy, SCUA, RUL.

12. See Susan K. Cahn, *Coming On Strong: Gender and Sexuality in Twentieth-Century Women's Sport* (New York: Free Press, 1994); Rita Liberti, "Coming On [and Staying] Strong: Gender and Sexuality in Twentieth-Century Women's Sport," *Journal of Sport History* 40, no. 2 (2013): 297–307, http://muse.jhu.edu/journals/journal_of_sport _history/v040/40.2.liberti.html.

13. Spike Lee's 1988 film *School Daze* is a commentary on colorism and class and how they shape intraracial dynamics among African Americans. The film takes place at a fictional historically black college. In the film, the women students are divided into two groups: the "Wannabes"—which referred to primarily light-skinned women whose hair was either pressed straight or, if worn natural, had soft loose curls or wore weaves—and the "Jiggaboos"—women who were primarily brown or dark skinned with coarser, Afro-textured hair and who rejected weaves and chemical straightening. The rivalry between the two groups was meant to represent the issue of colorism within African American communities and the notion that light skin and "good hair" were more desirable. For works that discuss how American beauty standards are racialized and the impact that these beauty standards have had on African American women throughout history, see Noliwe M. Rooks, *Hair Raising: Beauty, Culture, and African American Women* (New Brunswick, NJ: Rutgers University Press, 1996); Maxine Leeds Craig, *Ain't I a Beauty Queen: Black Women, Beauty, and the Politics of Race* (Oxford: Oxford University Press, 2002); Kathy Peiss, *Hope in a Jar: The Making of America's Beauty Culture* (Philadelphia: University of

Pennsylvania Press, 2011); Blain Roberts, *Pageants, Parlors, and Pretty Women: Race and Beauty in the Twentieth-Century South* (Chapel Hill: University of North Carolina Press, 2016).

14. Stringer, *Standing Tall,* 266.

15. "Statement by NCAA President Myles Brand and Rutgers University President Richard L. McCormick Regarding Comments by MSNBC's Don Imus," April 6, 2007, Folder University Statements Don Imus, Records of the Don Imus Controversy, SCUA, RUL.

16. "Press Conference Transcript," Rutgers University Athletics, April 10, 2007, https://scarletknights.com/news/2007/4/10/April_10_2007_Press_Conference_Transcribe.

17. Stringer, *Standing Tall,* 267.

18. "Press Conference Transcript."

19. "Laurels and Darts," *Daily Targum,* April 6, 2007, SCUA, RUL.

20. "Statement from Rutgers Women's Basketball Head Coach C. Vivian Stringer," n.d., University Statements Don Imus folder, Records of the Don Imus Controversy, SCUA, RUL.

21. "Statement on Don Imus' Remarks by Rutgers President Richard L. McCormick," April 8, 2007, University Statements Don Imus folder, Records of the Don Imus Controversy, SCUA, RUL.

22. *Eyewitness News,* ABC 7, April 9, 2007, disc 2, Records of the Don Imus Controversy, SCUA, RUL; *The Situation Room,* CNN, April 9, 2007, disc 2, Records of the Don Imus Controversy, SCUA, RUL.

23. *FOX News at 5,* WNYW 5, April 9, 2007, disc 2, Records of the Don Imus Controversy, SCUA, RUL; *CBS Evening News,* WCBS 2, April 9, 2007, Records of the Don Imus Controversy, SCUA, RUL.

24. "Statement by Robert E. Mulcahy III," April 9, 2007, University Statements Don Imus folder, Records of the Don Imus Controversy, SCUA, RUL.

25. "Press Conference Transcript."

26. Ibid.

27. Ibid.

28. *FOX News at 5,* WNYW 5, April 9, 2007.

29. Mary S. Hartman, "A Call for Removal," *Daily Targum,* April 9, 2007, SCUA, RUL.

30. *NBC Nightly News,* WNBC 4, April 10, 2007, disc 2, Records of the Don Imus Controversy, SCUA, RUL.

31. "Email from Richard L. McCormick to Members of the Rutgers Community," April 9, 2007, folder 2, Records of the Don Imus Controversy, SCUA, RUL.

32. "Email from Daria Torres to Richard L. McCormick," April 9, 2007, folder 2, Records of the Don Imus Controversy, SCUA, RUL.

33. "Email from Louise Pepe to Richard L. McCormick," April 9, 2007, folder 2, Records of the Don Imus Controversy, SCUA, RUL.

34. "Email from George Pieczenik to Richard L. McCormick," April 9, 2007, folder 2, Records of the Don Imus Controversy, SCUA, RUL; "Email from Tod Marder to Richard L. McCormick," April 10, 2007, folder 2, Records of the Don Imus Controversy, SCUA, RUL.

35. "New Responses about Imus Remarks," n.d., Media Relations folder, Records of the Don Imus Controversy, SCUA, RUL; "Standard Responses," Records of the Don Imus Controversy, SCUA, RUL.

36. Ibid.

37. "Email from Elric Kline to Richard L. McCormick," April 9, 2007, folder 2, Records of the Don Imus Controversy, SCUA, RUL.

38. "Email from David Pennant to Richard L. McCormick," n.d., folder 2, Records of the Don Imus Controversy, SCUA, RUL; "Email from b.d. stewart to Richard L. McCormick," April 9, 2007, folder 2, Records of the Don Imus Controversy, SCUA, RUL.

39. Stringer, *Standing Tall,* 275.

40. "Press Conference Transcript," Rutgers University Athletics, April 10, 2007, https://scarletknights.com/news/2007/4/10/April_10_2007_Press_Conference_Transcribe.

41. Ibid.

42. Ibid.

43. Ibid.

44. Ibid.

45. *FOX News at 5,* WNYW 5, April 10, 2007, disc 3, Records of the Don Imus Controversy, SCUA, RUL.

46. Folders 1–12, Media Relations, Press Coverage, Records of the Don Imus Controversy, SCUA, RUL.

47. *NBC Nightly News,* NBC News Transcripts, April 10, 2007, Media Relations folder, Press Coverage 1, Records of the Don Imus Controversy, SCUA, RUL.

48. Gwen Ifill, "Trash Talk Radio," *New York Times,* April 10, 2007, Media Relations folder, Press Coverage 3, Records of the Don Imus Controversy, SCUA, RUL.

49. "Transcript of *Meet the Press,*" NBC, April 15, 2007, Media Relations folder, Press Coverage 7, Records of the Don Imus Controversy, SCUA, RUL.

50. Elisa Ung, "Rutgers Rally Cry: Fire Imus," *Philadelphia Inquirer,* April 12, 2007, Media Relations folder, Press Coverage 12, Records of the Don Imus Controversy, SCUA, RUL.

51. Elizabeth Olubodun, "Rally Calls for Boycott of Imus' Sponsors," *Daily Targum,* April 12, 2007, SCUA, RUL.

52. Bridget Wentworth and Mary Jo Patterson, "Players Hurt by Imus Remark," *Trenton Times,* April 11, 2007, Media Relations folder, Press Coverage 3, Records of the Don Imus Controversy, SCUA, RUL.

53. Patricia Alex, "Rutgers Rally Keeps Heat on Imus," *The Record,* April 12, 2007, Media Relations folder, Press Coverage 11, Records of the Don Imus Controversy, SCUA, RUL; *NBC Nightly News,* NBC, April 11, 2007, disc 3, Records of the Don Imus Controversy, SCUA, RUL.

54. Steven Williamson, "CBS Tells Imus to Take a Hike," *Daily Targum,* April 13, 2007, SCUA, RUL.

55. Stringer, *Standing Tall,* 280–281.

56. CNN, April 13, 2007, disc 5, Records of the Don Imus Controversy, SCUA, RUL.

57. *Larry King Live,* CNN, April 13, 2007, disc 5, Records of the Don Imus Controversy, SCUA, RUL.

58. Joseph Shure, "Team Accepts Imus Apology," *Daily Targum,* April 18, 2007, SCUA, RUL.

59. "Basketball Remains Top Priority for Stringer," *Asbury Park Press,* April 25, 2007, Media Relations folder, Press Coverage 3, Records of the Don Imus Controversy, SCUA, RUL.

60. *The Situation Room,* CNN, April 9, 2007, disc 2, Records of the Don Imus Controversy, SCUA, RUL; *FOX News at 5,* WNYW 5, April 11, 2007, disc 3, Records of the Don Imus Controversy, SCUA, RUL.

61. Dave Hamell, "Another Perspective on Imus," *Daily Targum,* April 12, 2007, SCUA, RUL; Alex Maro, "Give Imus a Break," *Daily Targum,* April 12, 2007, SCUA, RUL; Peter Anderson, "Criticism Lacks Credibility," *Daily Targum,* April 12, 2007, SCUA, RUL.

62. "Email from Patricia Webb to Richard L. McCormick," April 10, 2007, folder 4, Records of the Don Imus Controversy, SCUA, RUL.

63. "Email from Karen Emerson to Richard L. McCormick," April 10, 2007, folder 4, Records of the Don Imus Controversy, SCUA, RUL.

64. Stringer, *Standing Tall,* 272.

65. Justin Miller, "Talk Athletics Not Stereotypes," *Daily Targum,* April 13, 2007, SCUA, RUL.

66. Nic Martino, "RU Athletes Want to Put Imus' Words behind Them," *Daily Targum,* April 13, 2007, SCUA, RUL.

67. Blair, "College Candy," YouTube video, 3.40, April 11, 2007, https://www.youtube.com/watch?v=r_SY9vMNIpk.

68. Wayne Coffey, "Sex Games," *Daily News,* April 15, 2007, Media Relations folder, Press Coverage 9, Records of the Don Imus Controversy, SCUA, RUL.

69. "Letter to the Editor from Helen Wronski of Morris Plains," *Star-Ledger,* May 1, 2007, Media Relations folder, Press Coverage 6, Records of the Don Imus Controversy, SCUA, RUL.

70. Jessica Durando, "Presidential Candidate Pays Visit to Douglass," *Daily Targum,* April 23, 2007, SCUA, RUL; Erica Harbatkin, "Basketball Team Cited as Role Model," *Home News Tribune,* April 22, 2007, SCUA, RUL.

71. Raina Kelly, Mark Starr, and Eve Conant, "A Team Stands Tall," *Newsweek,* April 23, 2007, Media Relations folder, Press Coverage 1, Records of the Don Imus Controversy, SCUA, RUL.

72. "Press Conference Transcript," Rutgers University Athletics, April 10, 2007, https://scarletknights.com/news/2007/4/10/April_10_2007_Press_Conference_Transcribe.

73. "Memo to Richard L. McCormick from Kim Manning," July 3, 2007, Imus Transcript folder, Records of the Don Imus Controversy, SCUA, RUL.

74. "Angered by Imus, Jeter Writes RU," *The Record,* April 30, 2007, Media Relations folder, Press Coverage 1, Records of the Don Imus Controversy, SCUA, RUL.

75. Media Relations folder, Press Coverage 1, Records of the Don Imus Controversy, SCUA, RUL.

76. "Email from Alice Williams to Richard L. McCormick," April 10, 2007, folder 4, Records of the Don Imus Controversy, SCUA, RUL.

77. "Letter to the Editor from Lisa Wilson," *New York Times,* April 14, 2007, Media Relations folder, Press Coverage 1, Records of the Don Imus Controversy, SCUA, RUL.

78. Anthony Mason, "Don Imus: The Sun Sets on His Morning Radio Show," *CBS News,* March 25, 2018, https://www.cbsnews.com/news/don-imus-the-sun-sets-on-his-morning-radio-show/.

79. Barbara Barker, "Rutgers' C. Vivian Stringer Called Out Don Imus after Slur, and Won," *Newsday,* February 3, 2018, https://www.newsday.com/sports/columnists/barbara-barker/c-vivian-stringer-imus-rutgers-1.16505049.

EPILOGUE

1. Richard Edwards, "Foreword," in Marisa J. Fuentes and Deborah Gray White, eds., *Scarlet and Black, Volume 1: Slavery and Dispossession in Rutgers History* (New Brunswick, NJ: Rutgers University Press, 2016), vii.

2. Ibid., vii–viii.

3. Rutgers Alumni, "Demand Rutgers to Rename Buildings Honoring Slave Owners," Change.org, https://www.change.org/p/rutgers-alumni-demand-rutgers-to-rename-buildings-honoring-slave-owners.

4. The Scarlet and Black website and archive will continue to be updated; see the Scarlet and Black Project Digital Archive, Rutgers University, http://www.scarletand blackproject.com/archive/.

5. Kendra Boyd, Marisa J. Fuentes, and Deborah Gray White, eds., *Scarlet and Black, Volume 2: Constructing Race and Gender at Rutgers, 1865–1945* (New Brunswick, NJ: Rutgers University Press, 2020), 155–157.

6. "Dr. Jonathan Holloway: 'Legacies of Jim Crow,'" YouTube video, 1:38.34, November 14, 2016, https://www.youtube.com/watch?v=nGIQcKDO4DI.

7. James Baldwin, *The Price of the Ticket: Collected Nonfiction, 1948–1985* (New York: St. Martin's Press, 1985).

8. All quotes are from "Dr. Jonathan Holloway: 'Legacies of Jim Crow.'"

9. See this volume's introduction.

10. Jonathan Scott Holloway, *Jim Crow Wisdom: Memory and Identity in Black America since 1940* (Chapel Hill: University of North Carolina Press, 2013).

11. Ibid., 137.

12. See the Scarlet and Black Project Digital Archive, Rutgers University, http://www.scarletandblackproject.com/archive/.

LIST OF CONTRIBUTORS

BEATRICE J. ADAMS is a doctoral candidate in African American and African Diaspora history at Rutgers University. She received an MA in social sciences from the University of Chicago and a BA in history from Fisk University. Her dissertation examines African Americans' relationship to the American South, focusing on issues of identity, belonging, and migration. Centered on the experiences of African Americans who remained in or returned to the American South during the period referred to as the Second Great Migration (1941–1970), her project interrogates the role of migration in both the African Americans' quotidian realizations of freedom and in their conceptualizations of freedom. *Archives visited and acknowledgments*: Special Collections and University Archives, Rutgers University Libraries; Special Collections, Newark Public Library; Rutgers Oral History Archive. I would like to thank Erika Gorder, Vicki Donaldson, Angela Lawrence, Kathryn Rizzi, and Junius Williams and all the members of the Black Organization of Students Alumni Association (BOSAA).

JESSE BAYKER is the digital archivist for the Scarlet and Black Project and is responsible for creating the digital companion to the book series, www.ScarletandBlackProject.com. His research for volume 1 of *Scarlet and Black* brought to light the stories of two dozen enslaved individuals who helped build Rutgers and served its earliest officers and trustees. His archival discoveries enabled the dedication of "Will's Way," a walkway leading up to Old Queens in honor of a black man who toiled to lay the foundation for the college's oldest building. He holds a PhD in women's and gender history from Rutgers University. His scholarly interests include transgender lives in nineteenth-century America and the public histories of slavery in the mid-Atlantic region. *Archives visited:* Special Collections and University Archives, Rutgers University Libraries. *Acknowledgments:* Thank you to Erika Gorder.

LYNDA DEXHEIMER is a doctoral candidate in education, culture, and society at the Rutgers Graduate School of Education (GSE). She received an MSc in government and comparative politics (Latin America) from the London School of Economics and Political Science, and a BA in political science from Rutgers University. Her dissertation, "The Black Student Protest Movement at Rutgers University: A Case of Compromise and Qualified Success," centers the history of this pivotal social movement on the students who enacted it rather than on the institution that responded. Dexheimer is the executive director of the Rutgers Writing Program, Department of English. *Archives visited:* Special Collections and University Archives, Rutgers University Libraries. *Acknowledgments:* I thank my colleague, Joseph Williams, for the wonderful collaborative experience; my GSE adviser, Dr. Benjamin Justice, for the support and encouragement; and the women of the 2007 Scarlet Knights basketball team for the example they set of strength and dignity.

KAISHA ESTY is an assistant professor of African American studies and affiliated faculty in feminist, gender, and sexuality studies at Wesleyan University. She holds a PhD in African American history from Rutgers University–New Brunswick, and a BA and MRes in American studies from the University of Nottingham, UK. Her research interests include feminine virtue, African American women's history, and nineteenth-century US law and culture. She is working on her first book project, tentatively titled *Weaponizing Virtue: Black Women and the Struggle for Sexual Sovereignty,* which uncovers how ideals of chastity and virtue formed part of the resistive culture of enslaved and freedwomen from the antebellum era through the early twentieth century. *Archives visited:* Special Collections and University Archives, Rutgers University Libraries; Rutgers Oral History Archive, Associate Alumnae of Douglass College (AADC). *Acknowledgments:* Thank you to Shaun Illingworth and Kathryn Rizzi, director and assistant director, respectively, at the Rutgers Oral History Archive for the training, resources, and generous support in conducting oral history interviews. I would also like to extend special thanks to M. Wilma Harris, Julane Miller-Armbrister, and Jonathan Cobb for sharing their stories; to Miya Carey for being a resource and liaison with the AADC; and to coauthors Whitney Fields and Carie Rael.

WHITNEY FIELDS is a doctoral student in African American history at Rutgers University–New Brunswick. She received a BA in history and American studies from the College of William and Mary. Fields's dissertation explores the confinement and incarceration of black youth in urban cities from the early republic to Reconstruction, examining black children's experiences in the early penitentiary system and juvenile detention centers and investigating nineteenth-century prison and asylum reform. *Archives visited:* Special Collections and University Archives, Rutgers University Libraries. *Acknowledgments:*

I would like to thank the executive director of the Associate Alumnae of Douglass College, Valerie L. Anderson.

IAN GAVIGAN is a doctoral candidate in history at Rutgers University–New Brunswick. He is a historian of the modern United States who specializes in the history of politics, labor, and social movements. *Archives visited: All You Can Eat*, Special Collections and University Archives, Rutgers University Libraries. *Acknowledgments:* I would like to thank Pamela Walker in particular for her leadership, research, and writing, and thanks as well to the entire *Scarlet and Black* team.

TRACEY JOHNSON is a doctoral candidate in history at Rutgers University–New Brunswick. Her work investigates the visual dimension of the black arts movement in New York City. Her dissertation, "Carving Out a Space for Themselves: Black Artists in New York City," looks at visual artists' work as educators and institution builders in black communities, as well as at their struggle to gain access to mainstream museums. Her research has been funded by the New York Public Library, Emory University's Rose Library, and the Rutgers Center for Historical Analysis. Tracey graduated with a BA in history from the College of William and Mary in 2014. *Archives visited:* Special Collections and University Archives, Rutgers University Libraries.

JOSEPH KAPLAN is a doctoral candidate in African American history at Rutgers University–New Brunswick. He received his BA in history from the University of Puget Sound. His dissertation, "We at War: The Revolutionary Action Movement, Police Intelligence, and the Surveillance of New York's Black Left, 1960–1975," is a local study of the repression that black radical groups faced during the era of colonial liberation movements and urban rebellions. *Archives visited:* Special Collections and University Archives, Rutgers University Libraries. *Acknowledgments:* I would like to thank Kate Rizzi of the Rutgers Oral History Archive for allowing me to join her oral history interview with Dr. Cheryl Clarke, and a special thank you to Dr. Clarke and her partner, Dr. Barbara Balliet, for allowing us into their home.

KENNETH MORRISSEY is a master's student in the history program at Rutgers University–Newark. He previously earned a BA in history at Rutgers University–New Brunswick, and has received numerous awards and honors, including making dean's list every semester as an undergraduate at Rutgers, graduating summa cum laude, and receiving two awards from the mayor of Woodbridge Township for his work in the community. Morrissey is currently in the beginning stages of researching how environmental issues disproportionately affect people of color. *Archives visited:* Special Collections and University Archives, Rutgers University Libraries. *Acknowledgments:* I would like to thank Professor Deborah Gray White and all those in my seminar who helped me with my research and writing. I would also be remiss to not thank my mother, Joann Morrissey, whose loving support gave me the will to do my research.

ROBERTO C. OROZCO is a doctoral candidate in the higher education program at Rutgers University–New Brunswick. He received an MS in higher education from Florida State University, and a BS in marketing and international business and a BS in psychology from Iowa State University. His dissertation, "Aquí Entre Nos: Examining the Identity Development of Queer Latinx/a/o Student Activists in Higher Education," examines how queer Latinx/a/o student activists make meaning of their ethnicity and sexuality through their involvement in activism. Orozco situates his study using a theoretical perspective of Jotería studies and critical race theory while simultaneously asserting a Chicana feminist epistemology and the theoretical framework of *conocimiento*. *Archives visited:* Special Collections and University Archives, Rutgers University Libraries; Paul Robeson Library Archives, Rutgers University–Camden. *Acknowledgments:* I would like to thank the staff at Rutgers University's Special Collections and University Archives, especially Erika Gorder; Merylou Rodríguez, who initially invited me to be a part of this project; and my amazing coauthors, Beatrice Adams, Brooke Thomas, and Meagan Wierda, for their support through this process.

CARIE RAEL is a doctoral student in US history at Rutgers University–New Brunswick. Her dissertation focuses on immigration, Latinx community building, and the carceral state in Orange County, California. She received her BA and MA in history from California State University, Fullerton. *Archives visited:* Special Collections and University Archives, Rutgers University Libraries; Puerto Rican Community Archives, Newark Public Library. *Acknowledgments:* I would like to thank Erika Gorder and all the staff at Rutgers University's Special Collections and University Archives. Thank you to Dr. Kathy López and the Department of Latino and Caribbean Studies. A special thank you to Gloria Soto for sharing her story with me. Thank you to Yesenia López and Juber Ayala for providing materials from the amazing collections at the Puerto Rican Community Archives at the Newark Public Library. And because writing is collaborative, thank you to all the contributors and the editors of *Scarlet and Black* for their hard work in helping this volume come to fruition.

BROOKE A. THOMAS is a doctoral candidate in history at Rutgers University–New Brunswick specializing in African American history. Thomas's research explores continuity and change in the black clubwomen's movement during the twentieth century; her dissertation focuses on the political organizing and engagement of black women's organizations from the 1930s through the 1960s. Thomas received her BA in history from Spelman College and an MA in history from the University of South Alabama. *Archives visited:* Special Collections and University Archives, Rutgers University Libraries. *Acknowledgments:* I would like to thank Erika Gorder and the staff at Rutgers University's Special Collections and University Archives for all their assistance in the research process. I would also like to thank Yvette Bravo-Weber, assistant dean for the Minority Student Program at Rutgers University Law School in Newark, for insight into and sources related to the Minority Student Program at Rutgers.

PAMELA WALKER is a doctoral candidate at Rutgers University specializing in African American history and women's and gender history. She received a BA in history from the University of Tennessee at Knoxville and an MA in history from the University of New Orleans. She has coauthored articles in volumes 1 and 2 of *Scarlet and Black*. Walker's dissertation, "'Signed, Sealed, Delivered': How Black and White Women Used the Box Project and the Postal System to Fight Hunger and Feed the Mississippi Freedom Movement," examines the Mississippi Box Project, a grassroots antipoverty program founded by a Vermont pacifist, to gain a fuller picture of the participants in the civil rights movement. Her work has been funded by the Mellon Foundation, the American Philosophical Society, and the Mississippi Department of Archives and History. *Archives visited:* Rutgers Oral History Archive; Mt. Zion African Methodist Episcopal Church Archives, 1884–1949; and the New Brunswick Free Public Library. *Acknowledgments:* I would like to thank Barbara Saunders for her invaluable knowledge of New Brunswick history and for her generosity and patience during my time in Mt. Zion AME's archives. I would also like to thank Pastors Golden and Mattie Carmon for their enthusiasm regarding this research and for granting me access to Mt. Zion AME's private archive. I am also grateful to Kim Adams at the New Brunswick Free Public Library and for all of the resources available digitally at the Rutgers Oral History Archive.

EDWARD WHITE graduated from Rutgers University with a BA in history in May of 2019. He commissioned into the army the same year and served in Germany as an aviation officer. He chose to do research on "The Black House" because it was a great celebration of culture and diversity at Rutgers University and an important study of race issues that still resonate. Most of his research was derived from primary sources found in the Rutgers Archives, including original letters to and from faculty, as well as New Brunswick police reports. Delving into the Rutgers archives was a great experience and he would like to thank the entire Rutgers History Department for all he learned and experienced throughout his four years.

MEAGAN WIERDA is a doctoral candidate in the Department of History at Rutgers University–New Brunswick who specializes in nineteenth-century US history and the history of science and technology. Her dissertation, "To Count and Be Counted: Quantification in the Age of American Slavery," considers how the counting of people and the making of populations helped dictate the boundaries of freedom, slavery, and citizenship between the drafting of the US Constitution and the passage of the Fourteenth Amendment. Wierda earned a BA in history and lettres françaises from the University of Ottawa and an MA in history from Concordia University. *Archives visited:* Rutgers University's Special Collections and University Archives. *Acknowledgments:* I would like to extend a massive thank you to Erika Gorder.

JOSEPH WILLIAMS is a doctoral candidate in the Department of History at Rutgers University–New Brunswick. His research interests include black intellectual history, black women's history, and the history of American religious reform. His dissertation examines black women's production of religious thought in their creation of an intellectual community during the late nineteenth and early twentieth centuries. Williams earned an MA in history at DePaul University and an MTS in theological studies from Garrett Evangelical Theological Seminary. *Archives visited:* Special Collections and University Archives, Rutgers University Libraries; Rutgers Oral History Archives. *Acknowledgments:* A special thank you to the staff at Rutgers University's Special Collections and University Archives, and to Lynda Dexheimer for her contributions to the essay.

ABOUT THE EDITORS

MIYA CAREY is an assistant professor of history at Binghamton University. A recent Rutgers University alum, Carey served as the Scarlet and Black postdoctoral associate before becoming the Presidential Diversity Postdoctoral Fellow at Binghamton. Her forthcoming manuscript examines the role of social organizations for coming-of-age black girls in Washington, DC, in the twentieth century. Carey's publications include an article in *Washington History* that explores the relationship between Girl Scouting and the civil rights movement, and she has coauthored book chapters in volumes 1 and 2 of *Scarlet and Black*.

MARISA J. FUENTES is the Presidential Term Chair in African American history and associate professor of history and women's and gender studies at Rutgers University in New Brunswick, New Jersey. She is the author of *Dispossessed Lives: Enslaved Women, Violence, and the Archive* (University of Pennsylvania Press, 2016), which has won awards from the Association of Black Women Historians, the Berkshire Conference of Women Historians, and the Caribbean Studies Association. She is also the coeditor of the three volumes of *Scarlet and Black* (Rutgers University Press, 2016, 2020, 2021), and coeditor of the "Slavery and the Archive" special issue in *History of the Present* (November 2016). Fuentes's most recent publications are forthcoming from *Small Axe, English Language Notes,* and *Diacritics.* Her forthcoming manuscript explores the connections between capitalism, the transatlantic slave trade, and the disposability of black lives in the seventeenth and eighteenth centuries. She has received support from Oxford University, the McNeil Center for Early American Studies, and the Library Company of Philadelphia. She has served a number of professional organizations, including as council member for the Omohundro Institute of Early American History and Culture, as secretary for the Berkshire Conference of Women Historians, and as a distinguished lecturer for the Organization of American Historians.

DEBORAH GRAY WHITE is the Board of Governors Distinguished Professor of History at Rutgers University in New Brunswick, New Jersey. She is the author of *Ar'n't I a Woman? Female Slaves in the Plantation South* (1985); *Too Heavy a Load: Black Women in Defense of Themselves, 1894–1994* (1999); several K–12 textbooks on US history, and *Let My People Go: African Americans 1804–1860* (1996). In 2008, she published an edited work titled *Telling Histories: Black Women Historians in the Ivory Tower,* a collection of personal narratives written by African American women historians that chronicle the entry of black women into the historical profession and the development of the field of black women's history. *Freedom on My Mind: A History of African Americans,* a coauthored college text, is in its third edition. As a fellow at the Woodrow Wilson International Center for Scholars in Washington, DC, and as a John Simon Guggenheim Fellow, White conducted research on her newest book, *Lost in the USA: American Identity from the Promise Keepers to the Million Mom March* (2017). She holds the Carter G. Woodson Medallion and the Frederick Douglass Medal for Excellence in African American history, and was also awarded a Doctorate in Humane Letters from her undergraduate alma mater, Binghamton University. She currently codirects the Scarlet and Black Project, which investigates Native Americans and African Americans in the history of Rutgers University. With Marisa Fuentes, she is editor of the 2016 volume *Scarlet and Black, Volume 1: Slavery and Dispossession in Rutgers History,* and, with Marisa Fuentes and Kendra Boyd, editor of the recently published *Scarlet and Black, Volume 2: Constructing Race and Gender at Rutgers, 1865–1945.*